TWENTIETH-CENTURY BRITISH THEATRE

Claire Cochrane maps the experience of theatre across the British Isles during the twentieth century through the social and economic factors which shaped it. Three topographies for 1900, 1950 and 2000 survey the complex plurality of theatre within the nation state which, at the beginning of the century, was at the hub of world-wide imperial interests, and after 100 years had seen unprecedented demographic, economic and industrial change. Cochrane analyses the dominance of London theatre, but redresses the balance in favour of the hitherto marginalised majority experience in the English regions and the other component nations of the British political construct. Developments arising from demographic change are outlined, especially those relating to the rapid expansion of migrant communities representing multiple ethnicities. Presenting fresh historiographic perspectives on twentieth-century British theatre, the book breaks down the traditionally accepted binary oppositions between different sectors, showing a broader spectrum of theatre practice.

CLAIRE COCHRANE is Senior Lecturer in Drama and Performance at the University of Worcester, where she both teaches and directs medieval and English Renaissance drama in performance and new writing for the theatre. She is the author of *Shakespeare and the Birmingham Repertory Theatre 1913–1929* (1993) and *Birmingham Rep: A City's Theatre 1962–2002* (2003). Her other publications include essays on regional developments in contemporary Black British and British Asian theatre, and articles in journals such as *Theatre Research International* and *New Theatre Quarterly* on the historiography of amateur theatre.

TWENTIETH-CENTURY BRITISH THEATRE

Industry, Art and Empire

CLAIRE COCHRANE

CAMBRIDGE
UNIVERSITY PRESS

CAMBRIDGE UNIVERSITY PRESS
Cambridge, New York, Melbourne, Madrid, Cape Town,
Singapore, São Paulo, Delhi, Tokyo, Mexico City

Cambridge University Press
The Edinburgh Building, Cambridge CB2 8RU, UK

Published in the United States of America by Cambridge University Press, New York

www.cambridge.org
Information on this title: www.cambridge.org/9780521464888

First published 2011

Printed in the United Kingdom at the University Press, Cambridge

A catalogue record for this publication is available from the British Library

ISBN 978-0-521-46488-8 Hardback

For Henry, Jacob, Zephram, Lucas and Karuna
altogether with my love

Contents

Acknowledgements

It has taken a very long time to write this book and as a result some of the individuals who were involved in the preliminary stages of the project may well have forgotten about their contribution. However, I have to thank Russell Jackson, Brian Gibbons and Anne Watts of A&C Black, who passed a proposal for an anthology of documents to Sarah Stanton of Cambridge University Press, who then commissioned a history of twentieth-century British theatre. She subsequently passed me on to Victoria Cooper. That the book is now radically different to what was originally envisaged is largely due to my long-term participation in discussions held within the IFTR Historiography Working Group, and more recently in a similar group established under the auspices of TaPRA. As a result I owe an enormous debt of gratitude to my fellow historians for their good council over many meetings in cities all round the world. These include but are not confined to: Yael Zahry-Levo, Rosemarie Bank, Ken Cerniglia, Barbara Sušec Michieli, Pirkko Koski, Hanna Korsberg, Pentti Paavolainen, Henk Gras, Jan Lazardzig, Steve Wilmer, David Wiles, Joanna Robinson, Lucie Sutherland, Elizabeth Schafer, Gilli Bush-Bailey, Jim Davis, Tracy Davis, Kate Dorney, Ros Merkin and Fiona Mathers. Both Jacky Bratton and Tom Postlewait gave me valuable advice at crucial stages in the process of rethinking the project. David Ian Rabey helped me secure funding for project leave. Ian Brown, Richard Foulkes, John Bull and David Grant have all read and commented on chapters. Above all, Kate Newey has been a constant source of encouragement and practical advice throughout. I have had the opportunity to talk to a number of professional theatre-makers and I thank Liz Tomlin, Sian Redhead, Timothy West, David Buxton, Monica Stewart, David Forder and the late Joan Berly for their time and recollections. No theatre historian can function without archival resources and I am grateful to the staff of a range of theatre collections including those in Birmingham Central Library Department of Arts, Languages and Literature; the Special Collections and Archives,

Birmingham University; the Theatre Museum at Covent Garden, now the V&A Theatre Collections; the British Library; the Bodleian Library; the Shakespeare Centre; the Scottish Theatre Archive; the Manuscripts and Archives Collections, Aberdeen University; the National Library of Wales; the Flintshire Record Office; the South Wales Miners' Library; Tyne and Wear Archives Service; South Shields Local Studies Library; and the Linen Hall Library Theatre & Performing Arts Archive with particular thanks to Ophelia Byrne. Marisa O'Hara translated Welsh documents. I thank my colleagues at Worcester University where I have been permitted generous amounts of time to work on the book and where librarians Catherine Armitstead and Sue Fagg helped me with a steady stream of interlibrary loan requests. Natalie Wilcox has rendered vital assistance in assembling the typescript, and I am also grateful for the practical expertise of Allan Maund. The Society for Theatre Research awarded me the 2005 Anthony Denning Award which helped fund travel costs for interviews. The Arts and Humanities Research Council funded my work with a Research Leave Award.

Vicki Cooper has been infinitely patient and flexible over the time it has taken to produce this book and I owe her my heartfelt thanks. Rebecca Taylor has offered much excellent editorial support and reassurance. Lindeth Vasey has been an astute copy-editor. Philippa Tinsley kindly gave permission for the reproduction of Dame Laura Knight's *The Yellow Dress*, currently held in the collection of Worcester City Art Gallery, for use as the cover image.

My family have lived with this project and the huge piles of documents which I have generated with very little complaint and considerable amusement. I salute Jonathan, Benjamin, Thomas, Helen (1), Helen (2) and Ju-Fang Hsiao. A whole new generation has been born since I started and it is to them that I dedicate the book in the hope that they will grow up to enjoy the multiplicity of twenty-first century theatre. Finally I thank my husband John – for everything.

Introduction

This book explores the organisational and institutional structures, systems and modes of practice which shaped the experience of theatre in communities across the British Isles during the twentieth century. The selection of historical data for explication and analysis is not primarily driven by criteria of artistic innovation or value; rather the intention is to construct an overview which demonstrates the interdependence of social and economic factors in the creation and maintenance of theatre as cultural practice. It is my contention that these factors impose structures which might override other conceptual frameworks for historical analysis, such as those based on notions of discrete national identity or formed from binary oppositions of ideological and political allegiance or intellectual and aesthetic preference.

The key questions which the book seeks to ask are: How and where was theatre in the twentieth century organised, by whom and why? What different models of theatre were created, or indeed retained, and whose interests did those models serve? What different communities of interest and agency can be identified? What difference did it make to these diverse communities that theatre functioned within the political construct of the British nation state, and what difference does it make to the historical record if that diversity is more equitably represented? What happens to the historical record if the experience of the greater majority of the theatre-going or theatre-making population is examined, rather than the minority experience memorialised through the dominant historical discourse?

There are specifically British historical reasons derived from controlling monarchical/state strategies to restrict theatre outside London prior to 1843, which led to the concentration of professional activity in the capital.[1] However, any metropolis is inevitably associated with artistically high-status collective or individual achievement. Theatre historians have been traditionally drawn to the dynamic 'events' and 'heroes' of

their field of historical interest. London remains one of the most important international centres of great theatre, and of course this can happen
in a tiny, ramshackle venue in a London suburb, as well as in the prestigious endowed national institutions. Where, as in long historical surveys such as those provided in *The Revels History of Drama in English* or
in Simon Trussler's *Illustrated History of British Theatre*, selected attention was paid to regional or indeed other key component-nation developments, it tended to foreground significant initiatives which have been
associated with innovation or 'progress'. In *English Drama: A Cultural
History*, Simon Shepherd and Peter Womack acknowledge that 'English
drama' largely developed out of the London-centred theatrical system.[2]
In general, regional or 'provincial' theatre has been subordinate to the
metropolitan grand narrative and is thus effectively 'other'. The historical flaw in this approach is that despite the huge population of London,
the majority of the British people do not live there, although inevitably
every aspect of their lives, including the theatre they are able to access, is
affected by the power that emanates from the centre.

Until very recently the only substantive general history of regional theatre was George Rowell and Anthony Jackson's *The Repertory Movement: A
History of Regional Theatre in Britain*, which was published in 1984.[3] This
focused specifically on the development of a particular model of theatre
which had its origins in the modernist campaigns at the beginning of the
century. In 2010 Kate Dorney and Ros Merkin acknowledged the Rowell
and Jackson book as a starting point for a collection of essays on English
regional theatre[4] up until the end of the first decade of the twenty-first
century. The title *The Glory of the Garden* is taken from the controversial
Arts Council of Great Britain strategy document, also published in 1984,
which attempted to redress the metropolitan/regional imbalance through
adjustments to state funding provision.[5] These new essays represent
an important scholarly intervention which will hopefully pave the way
for more extensive studies. The collection, however, focuses on theatre
in England. Regional or *intra*national theatre in Britain is much more
complex.

AN UNSELFCONSCIOUS PROVINCIALISM

Until comparatively recently writers of British theatre history have displayed what Benedict Anderson, writing more broadly about nationalism, termed 'an unselfconscious provincialism'.[6] Anderson was targeting
European scholars 'accustomed to the conceit that everything important

in the modern world originated in Europe'. I would argue that a similar unexamined prejudice has driven much British theatre history to skew the record towards the assumption that everything important in British theatre happened in London. In the British context, however, the consequences of the metropolitan bias have to be examined within both a macro and micro frame, intranationally as well as regionally.

As a great metropolis London was at the centre of world-wide imperial power right up until the middle of the twentieth century, and post-empire the legacy still has global significance. London has remained, however, the metropolis of the formerly colonised nations, whose populations inhabit the large and small islands of the British archipelago, or what the Welsh historian Kenneth O. Morgan not quite accurately called 'two partitioned poly-cultural islands'.[7] The fact that by the end of the twentieth century, there had been a small but growing number of discrete historical studies of theatre in the British nations outside England was a sign both of the devolutionary forces at work in the wider political sphere, and also of indigenous theatre practice, which had developed greater confidence along with more autonomous means of development.[8]

When Baz Kershaw came to edit the third volume of *The Cambridge History of British Theatre*, separate invitations were issued to Scottish and Welsh historians to write parallel accounts of theatre in Scotland and Wales, which would complement the survey of the English/ metropolitan experience, which notwithstanding remained the dominant narrative.[9] There was, however, a significant omission in that the 'Province' of Northern Ireland, the remaining and much contested geo-political segment of the second largest island, which controversially remained British after the rest of Ireland shook off British colonial control in 1922, was not accorded a space to record its theatre. Such are the sensitivities around competing claims of national allegiance, this absence is not untypical,[10] but such occlusion of the record misses an opportunity to explore some of the more extreme effects of the legacy of colonial appropriation. Jen Harvie's *Staging the UK* is unusual in that it includes a Northern Irish case study alongside her other nations-wide examples of contemporary practice.[11]

Harvie applies Benedict Anderson's celebrated concept of nations as 'imagined communities' to the way British national identities are expressed through theatre. While she does not as she puts it 'wilfully' argue against the importance of politically engineered structures of national formation, her 'founding principle' is that national identities are neither biologically nor territorially given; rather they are 'creatively produced or staged' through a sense of shared cultural practice.[12] My focus on multiple communities of experience means that I am in complete agreement that national identity is not a biological or territorial given. But my analysis is far more grounded in the material conditions which are the product of the economic and legislative framework of the nation state. I argue that economic interests whether exploited, contested, disregarded or even willingly sacrificed have been key to the fluctuating fortunes of all models of theatre practice.

Furthermore, it is essential in my view to acknowledge the historical impact of the British nation state's imperial project and the shifting economic outcomes which for good or ill drove the working lives of the population. The empire looms large in this book. First, because the industrial prosperity, which had been one of the principle benefits of British global dominance, directly influenced the way theatre functioned as an industry at the beginning of the century and how and where its products were disseminated. Secondly, the decline of imperial power, and with it industrial decline and change, brought changing social formations and demographic patterns which could be seen in different patterns of theatre-making and theatre-going. Finally, by the end of the century, the human legacy of empire, what the historian Robert Winder dubbed 'colonisation in reverse',[13] could be seen in the rapidly expanding multi-cultural character of UK communities. The face of British theatre was literally changing, while any unified concept of what it means to be culturally British was coming under even greater challenge.

A CONTRAPUNTAL READING

My narrative attempts to weave together the theatres of four nations to demonstrate how theatre-makers in common with other communities of interest constantly cross national boundaries and respond to imperatives that may have little to do with allegiance to notions of national identity. Indeed, the cultural products of the imagined nation will always be the result of individual imaginations, often self-selected as representative of the collective and formed from many extra-national influences. In his discussion of the contradictions of the historic Anglo-Scottish Union after 1945, James Mitchell points to the confused nature of state nationalism as embodied in the United Kingdom. Arguing that the UK is a *union* rather than a *unitary* state (his emphasis), he points to the survival of some 'pre-union rights and institutional infrastructures which preserve some degree of regional autonomy'. Mitchell also quotes from James Kellas's study of

nationalism and the benefits of 'psychic income', 'those things which satisfy the mental and spiritual needs of human beings' and material interests: 'those things which are readily quantifiable in cash terms, such as
incomes and jobs'. Nationalisms may 'offer either or both'.[14] Throughout
the twentieth century the multiple negotiations among the native inhabitants of nations, nation state and empire within the United Kingdom
have provided both, but especially the incomes and jobs which in theatre
are also inextricably linked at a very basic level to the fulfilment of mental
and spiritual needs.

Writing elsewhere I have quoted Edward Said in *Culture and
Imperialism* where he suggests that we 'reread' the cultural archive 'not
univocally but *contrapuntally*, with a simultaneous awareness both of the
metropolitan history that is narrated and of those other histories against
which (and together with which) the dominating discourse acts'.[15] The
key point here is that not all 'other' histories are constructed in direct
opposition to the dominant discourse, some actually co-operate with it.
A rereading process which maintains that simultaneous awareness will
inevitably uncover contradictions. If a univocal reading predicated on
the dominating discourse is to be rejected, so it should be avoided in the
reading of others.[16]

As an English-born woman of British nationality from a family whose
genetic inheritance derives from all four of the UK nations, a theatre-
goer whose experience of life in Britain lies outside London, and who is,
moreover, the historian of a regional theatre, I seek to re-orientate the
reader's perspective in order to explore the dynamic relations between the
metropolis and the regions, and to present a more integrated narrative of
theatre. This book stresses the plural nature of British theatres and their
audiences.

THE LEGITIMATE THEATRE

First of all it is necessary to define the theatre which is to be explored in
the book. Very broadly the focus will be on the kind of theatre which
used to be known as 'legitimate'. This strategy may seem a little odd for a
history of twentieth-century practice but it opens up access to less ideologically constrained categories. For over a hundred years, and prior to
the 1843 Theatres Act, the term 'legitimate' was applied to theatre which
could present the strictly controlled drama of the spoken word, as it
was distinguished from the much more freely available 'popular' theatre of music, dance, circus, comic sketches, short melodramas, etc. Thus,

legitimate product included the plays of the British or European classical dramatic canon and new plays. Following the removal of the designation 'legitimate' in the strictly legal sense, the term still had (and continues to have) currency in the theatrical profession to differentiate the theatre of 'straight' plays from variety theatre. An actor could go 'legit' for example, and the term could carry connotations of intellectual or artistic aspiration however minimal.

The modernist intervention in theatre which began to gather momentum from the 1880s onwards, upped the ante on legitimate theatre by insisting on a drama that could be used as 'a weapon of social betterment' as Harley Granville Barker put it,[17] and that was intellectually and/or aesthetically avant-garde. Thus the 'new' drama and stagecraft emerged in the early 1900s, and by and large most historians of twentieth-century theatre have tended to track the subsequent development of performance practice predicated on modernist ideals. A by-product of this was the political campaign to urge the state to take responsibility for the financial support of the arts, including the 'exemplary' theatre. The result was that the principle of 'not-for-profit' professional practice, either in aspiration pre-1939 or in actuality, after the advent of state subsidy, dictated the data for historical enquiry. The problem about this approach is that it has led to the marginalisation or actual exclusion of the kind of 'for profit' theatre that had its roots in pre-modernist traditions and that a substantial proportion of the UK population had access to especially in the first half of the century. Not only does this skew the narrative away from the experience of community audiences, but it also fails to acknowledge the material circumstances that control the lives of the majority of jobbing theatre-workers and artists.

THE ECONOMIC IMPERATIVE

This book is not an economic history of British theatre as such. Its scope is wider. But it does discuss business structures and models of company organisation in both commercial and not-for-profit sectors and attempts to show how boundaries between the two have rarely been completely separate. My preoccupation with the economic has been much influenced by the seminal work of Tracy Davis, best known in her *The Economics of the British Stage 1800–1914*, published in 2000. As she trenchantly remarks:

Pretending that representation is not in league with markets, promoters, and technologies – the usual purview of business and economic history – and that capital is not behind them all, is to clash the cymbals, throw a handful of fairy dust, and expect Clio to clap like a child at its first pantomime. It is not so much that aesthetic concerns should be pushed away in favour of social science approaches to performance, for culture forms out of business activity, and vice versa. But just as managerial decisions are reactions to the environment as much as actions upon it, they take into account signals from the outside world.[18]

Her other potentially more inflammatory statement is that 'except in a few notable cases, theatre practitioners operated in their own self-interest, and not for the greater glory of dramatic literature, theatre aesthetics, or proletarian culture'.[19] They (we?) function as *homo economicus* – the rational being who will always act in his/her best interests.[20]

If this gauntlet is picked up and accepted then it becomes imperative to reach an understanding of the economic structures and market forces which underpin the success or failure of theatre as industrial practice. It also enables a re-examination of the circumstances out of which artistic innovation or celebrity arose, especially if that historical event has been disproportionately valorised by scholars from a variety of aesthetically-formed critical perspectives. If, as the Victorian neoclassical economist Alfred Marshall stated, economics is 'the study of mankind in the ordinary business of life',[21] then the study of the ordinary business of *theatre* life through its economic interests offers the possibility of entering more deeply into the *mentalité* of a cultural community. Furthermore, the area of enquiry naturally widens to encompass practice and practitioners who have been excluded from the dominant narrative.

The challenge for the historian of twentieth-century theatre, however, lies in the modernist intervention and in particular that aspect of modernism which was a conscious rejection of *modernity*, i.e. the innovations generated by industrial capitalism. As Tracy Davis implies, scholarly focus on theatre practice that satisfies critical criteria of literary or aesthetic excellence, or ideological orientation, has excluded extensive areas of historical enquiry. But no historian of pre-twentieth-century theatre would ignore practice *because* it functioned solely in the arena of free enterprise, which of course was the only option available. The same cannot be said for twentieth-century theatre where historians have been distinctly queasy about the profit motive. Also it has to be conceded that a not inconsiderable number of twentieth-century practitioners *were* primarily concerned with 'the greater glory of dramatic literature, theatre aesthetics', etc., etc. and at least in theory have consciously eschewed their own self-interest.

But artists have to live, and, as Davis insists, markets, promoters and technologies backed by capital (however it is accessed) remain essential to the performance project. The laissez-faire capitalism of 1900 which evolved into welfare capitalism after 1945 which was wrenched back to a more aggressive model of market capitalism after 1979 formed what Jim McGuigan dubbed the 'civilisational frame of capitalism'[22] within which all cultural practice was enacted during the twentieth century. To explore theatre as an industry is to uncover continuities of practice between the past and the present, indeed between nineteenth- and twentieth-century experience, which permits a different perspective on the modernist intervention. It demystifies and brings within the economic realm the working basis of even the most idealised of artistic experiment.

The economist Thomas G. Rawski argues that 'historians who neglect economics can lose sight of factors that affect every historical theory'. Economic theory he explains 'is built around the logical analysis of profit-seeking behaviour by large numbers of well-informed, independent individuals in competitive markets governed by legal systems that enforce contracts and ensure the rights of private owners'.[23] It is acknowledged that the behaviour of well-informed, independent individuals may, for a number of reasons, defy logical analysis. Profit-seeking may take unexpected forms. The notion of independence is endlessly contingent. A competitive market exists even in (especially in) the most heavily-subsidised of not-for-profit environments. All *professional* artists function within legal systems that enforce contracts. That almost talismanic organism in twentieth-century-theatre terms, 'the company' is not only an artistic ensemble, it is a financial and legal entity. The theatre/performance space as physical plant, no matter which sector it trades in, and of whatever size, capacity and fabric, is a mass of interrelated economic concerns. On the ground, whatever the rhetoric, it is difficult to maintain the orthodox binaries of profit and not-for-profit.

ENCOUNTERING THE POPULAR: PRIORITIES AND PREJUDICE

Blurring the boundaries between enlightened not-for-profit and the frankly commercial takes the enquiry into the territory of popular culture. A great deal of legitimate theatre was produced or promoted by business enterprises predicated on the profitability of a variety of entertainment genres. Conversely, in the exemplary sector in the age of public subsidy, controversy was caused by attempts to sustain financial viability by introducing more 'populist' product into the repertoire. Mass or even large audiences were a problem for the radical avant-garde at the beginning of the twentieth century, and the debate about what Richard

Schechner conceptualised as 'the efficacy-entertainment braid' has continued into the twenty-first.[24] Of course pursuit of modernist ideals has seen
the avant-garde embrace popular genres for both aesthetic and political
reasons and thus the 'illegitimate' has become legitimate as it were. Any
history of the material circumstances of theatre production and reception
in the twentieth century must take account of this in analysis of working
practices across the industry. However, it is important to recognise that
the highly selective appropriation of aspects of popular culture for ideological purposes has again led to the historical marginalisation of communal experience.

The historian of an art-form, it seems to me, has a responsibility to the
experience of the past which should override personal aesthetic or political preference. As I have argued elsewhere, a good deal of the theatre
enjoyed by large numbers of the British population throughout the twentieth century would be scarcely tolerable for the average theatre historian
nurtured in the taste judgements of the academy. Pierre Bourdieu has led
us to see that the hierarchy of cultural preference is a way of legitimating
social differences, marginalisation and exclusion.[25] To explore theatre via
the social as well as the economic is to become aware not just of other patterns of provision, participation and exploitation, but also other kinds of
cultural 'need'[26] and imperatives. Statistically more members of the population experienced theatre in the twentieth century either as audiences
for, or participants in, amateur theatre. My account of the amateur phenomenon in the interwar years especially outside England demonstrates
significant reasons why it was difficult to sustain professional theatre of
any kind, let alone the exemplary theatre of Barker et al. The fact is that
the legitimate products of professional theatre were also enjoyed by the
amateur and not so professionally competent.

Because of necessary limits on the length of this book I have been
unable to include further extended discussion of independent amateur
and community theatre in the latter part of the century. However, much
of the polemical writing critiquing public funding policy produced compelling statistical evidence of the continuing strength of the amateur
sector.[27] In 1985, John Pick, who became one of the fiercest critics of the
Arts Council, stated that 'In Britain there are (excluding schools, colleges
and universities) about 8,500 amateur drama societies, in contrast with
the 350 or so professional production companies that may be said to be
independently active in the course of any one year'.[28] In relation specifically to non-professional theatre outside England recent works by David
Grant on Northern Ireland, Greg Giesekam on Scotland and Ruth Shade

on Wales[29] have provided excellent accounts of a creatively important sector.

THE IMPACT OF THE MASS MEDIA

My intention to stay within the safe haven of legitimacy, even with blurred boundaries, cannot ignore radio, film and television. This is a history of live performance, but the importation of artistic product and human resources drawn from the theatre into the mass media had a profound effect on the working lives of practitioners and the social and economic systems within which they maintained their livelihoods. In the early years of broadcasting, radio not only employed professional actors but also (most notably in the nations outside England) was dependent on pools of local amateur actors. 'Live' television drama in the 1950s and early 60s required the skills of theatre-trained actors accustomed to the pressures of live performance. At the same time a number of future theatre directors cut their directorial teeth in television and/or benefited from training schemes financed by independent television providers. As I argue in my analysis of the changing demographic of performance, the representation, through television in particular, to mass audiences of other lives lived in other places and embodying different categories of social and cultural difference, assisted in a profound shift in the way the plural communities of the British Isles were experienced and understood.

The growing economic influence of television, in the last three decades of the twentieth century especially, tended to shift the balance of power between London and the regions still further towards the capital. Many actors were professionally compelled to locate themselves in or near the metropolitan sources and networks of employment and were reluctant to disadvantage themselves in the regions. Other actors were only able to indulge in the 'luxury' of theatre performance because their livelihoods were largely sustained by work in television.

THE PAST AND PERIODISATION

This account of British theatre invites the reader to encounter the twentieth century as the past and not as a still incomplete temporal sequence leading to a still unfolding present. In Simon Shepherd's recent introduction to *modern* theatre, the modern is defined as 'everything after 1900'. He continues: 'It is an introduction not a history, so it aims to explain the sorts of activity and thinking that seem characteristic of the modern period.'[30] His reading of the 'modern' plays freely with time and space, ranging over products, events, models of performance, ideologies and organisations, and identifying themes, parallels, contradictions and compromises, which add up to a discontinuous, but recognisable representation of how what is currently experienced as twenty-first-century theatre has been formed. My book, however, is a history and in treating the twentieth century as a 'period', I have set myself some quite deliberate historiographic challenges.

The historiographic practice of periodisation is the process of splitting up time into artificially neat divisions, which, labelled and loaded with significance, then becomes a way of mapping diachronically through a selected sequence of 'events' or perceived cultural changes.[31] The theatre historiographer Thomas Postlewait has written that 'we assume that the history of human events can be separated into specific epochs of temporal identities. Periods are thus discursive models for historical understanding, models based upon the structural idea of maintenance or stability and the temporal idea of divergence or difference.'[32] William A. Green in an essay published in 1992 on 'Periodisation in European and World History' makes the basic point that 'all periodization is founded on disciplined concepts of continuity and change. To be meaningful, historical periods must be distinguished by important long-term continuities. Times of transition between periods must be characterised by the dissolution of old continuities and the forging of new ones.'[33] As this introduction will have made clear what has interested me as a historian of theatre is the extent to which accounts of the twentieth century have tended to focus on tracing the evolution and continuities of the new rather than recognising the parallel continuities of the old. This tendency has also contributed to the further disparagement and thus marginalisation of the widely practised 'not new'.

Of course a great deal changed during the twentieth century. No sensible academic theatre historian can ignore the contribution of European modernism and the various models of the avant-garde which emerged from it. This is why a 'long' twentieth-century history may begin in 1880 with the event of the first productions in London of the plays of Henrik Ibsen, and the beginnings of the campaign waged by the arch modernists William Archer and Bernard Shaw to create a radical 'irresistible' theatre. But the 'new' theatre that had emerged by 1900 was not the theatre that the majority popular audience took pleasure in at the beginning of the twentieth century. To ignore that, or as more frequently happens in scholarly discourse, to acknowledge this mass experience only as a foil for the excellent products of the aspirational minority, is effectively to excise from the historical record a substantial aspect of twentieth-century cultural practice.

Historians of the range of formations out of which the national experience is constructed also uncover the structures which underpin identifiable trends, and this analytic objective very often determines another parallel division of time. Again the historian chooses a moment when the origins of cultural practices which appear to be characteristic of a specific century can be located in an earlier cluster of innovative events, or then locate some kind of watershed which represents an ending – a moment after which nothing will ever feel quite the same. Davis's *The Economics of the British Stage* focuses on the continuities of economic trends within a 'long' nineteenth century which sweeps her well into the twentieth century to halt at the year when the First World War broke out, an event in European history of such catastrophic impact that it has long been assumed to have rendered obsolete many fundamental ideological assumptions. Indeed, in twentieth-century British history the two 'world' wars probably supply the most accepted temporal markers.

For general histories the watershed of the Second World War brought about a profound shift in attitudes towards formal state intervention in the social, economic and cultural life of the nation. In theatre history the establishment of the Arts Council of Great Britain in 1945, after the principle of state funding for the arts for the good of the people had been tested throughout the war, has been seen to usher in a new era where the artistic objectives of theatre pursued on a not-for-profit basis assumed the ideological high ground. The problem with watersheds as with singular events is that undue emphasis underestimates the extent to which political attitudes and cultural practices do not change that easily or that quickly, or indeed can be reversed.

In order to try to achieve both a more inclusive and expansive account of how theatre was experienced across the British Isles in the comparatively recent past, I have chosen to treat the twentieth century as a one-hundred-year segment: that is as one of the most-commonly-accepted divisions of time and use that as my discursive model. While my analysis looks back to the preceding nineteenth century and, indeed, seeks to find more continuities rather than abrupt changes or divergences, nevertheless, I begin with a panoramic view of 1900: the temporal marker designated by the process of conventional notation to signal 'universally' the end of one era and the beginning of another. The visible shift in notation has a symbolic effect on public consciousness, which *feels* itself, however momentarily, to be on the threshold of something new. The history ends in 2000 on the cusp of not just a new century but a new millennium. Those of us who lived through that moment will recall the peculiar mixture of excitement laced with fear of what the new epoch would bring. Now into the second decade of the twenty-first century, we know what it brought, and my knowledge inevitably informs how I write. But if possible I would like this history to capture that moment when knowledge of how past processes had brought about the cultural products of that present might have informed reasonable expectations of the future. On a balance of probability, and taking into account significant pressure points, would the future bring continuity or radical change?

SPATIAL RELATIONS AND THE LANDSCAPE OF THEATRE

My methodology is spatial as well as temporal, and synchronic as well as diachronic. Writing elsewhere, I have quoted the geographer Edward Soja on the importance of spatialising the historical narrative; shaking up the normal flow of the linear text to allow more lateral connections to be made in order to reveal a map of 'simultaneous relations and meanings'.[34] In order to do that within my one-hundred-year segment, I have constructed three topographies of theatre for 1900, 1950 and 2000. This offered the opportunity to reify those simultaneous relations and meanings at historical moments not selected as a point of origin, or agent of change, or as part of an attempt to foreground a conceptually shaped sequence of activity. Each topography maps theatre onto the physical geography of the nationally divided landscape surveying changes to, and continuities of, the built provision and the political and economic reasons for this. Allied to this, the mapping of demographic change is essential to an understanding of the industrial and, indeed, the ideological rationale behind the development or cessation of theatrical activity. Shifting national and regional patterns of population growth influence the organisational basis of theatre.

This temporal strategy aligns with what the geographer Alan Townsend explains as the concept of fifty-year cycles in the dynamics of the world industrial economy. My years do not coincide with the years when leading industrial sectors peaked in levels of employment, but it will soon become clear that the regional consequences of the cycles of industrial ascendancy or decline, 'the marked impulses of growth and pauses',[35] have profound implications for the way theatre functions as an industry and, indeed, as a more informal, recreational cultural practice. In charting the changing dynamics of the relationship between the metropolis and the regions I have deployed the geographical concept of the 'core' and the 'periphery'.[36] The way in which resources are controlled by the centre of legislative and economic power impacts on the material conditions within which theatre, as with any other industry, is positioned in a specific regional context.

What the sociologist Henri Lefebvre defined as 'abstract space', and which I refer to in my mapping process as the space of power, produces other less tangible resources which nevertheless have material effects. Knowledge, influence, access to important and/or exclusive networks have tended to be located in the dominant centres of power and wealth, or their intellectual outposts, and thus create Lefebvre's 'dominant form of space',[37] which extends across national spaces, infiltrates the periphery and is capable of suppressing and limiting independent creativity. This it could be argued has been the long-term outcome of the historic concentration of theatre in London. But as a recent summary of the influential work on regionality by the geographer Nigel Thrift has pointed out 'local uniqueness' matters: 'The recovery of regions for social theory obligated the discipline to delve into the intricate dynamics of local actors who populated them' and 'made them work'.[38] In a more literal way this book 'delve[s] into the intricate dynamics of local actors'. In so doing I hope it paves the way for other much needed attempts to delve.

The book is divided into eight chapters each attempting to read contrapuntally across the plurality of theatre. This has necessitated quite a complex methodology as the foregoing will have indicated. I build very substantially on other theatre histories, both recent and much older, as well as auto/biographical accounts written by actors, managers and directors whose lives and work appear to exemplify the structural factors I explore. General histories of cinema, radio and television supply the background to the movement of theatre-makers across media in search of professional opportunity. I also draw on other disciplines, in particular political and industrial history, cultural and urban geography, social economics, and the history and sociology of mass migration and ethnicity, in order to understand broad industrial and demographic trends.

Chapter 1 'The topography of theatre in 1900' surveys the landscape of British theatre as it had been formed at the beginning of the century through a combination of geographical, political, industrial, economic and demographic factors. Chapter 2 'Structures of management' explains and explores models of management in both the dominant commercial and emergent not-for-profit sectors up until the Second World War. Chapter 3 'The profession of acting' explores the working lives of actors and increasing professionalisation. It discusses entry routes into the profession, including the extent of individual migration from the different nations of origin within the UK and the phenomenon of pro-am or pre-professional activity especially outside England. The chapter also examines the impact of the widening of opportunity represented by film and radio. Chapter 4 'The amateur phenomenon' explores the strength and diversity of amateur activity in the first half of the century with a particular focus on interwar activity in Wales. It also examines the different models of amateur theatre as they emerged in response to the shifts and differentials within the wider economic climate. Chapter 5 'The topography of theatre in 1950' surveys the landscape of theatre in 1950 and asks the same fundamental questions about the distribution, organisation and access to theatre as chapter 1. It considers the different patterns of theatre created by commercial interests and the early strategies developed through the introduction of state funding. Chapter 6 'The business of theatre' explains the business models of not-for-profit theatre and how the positioning of companies within the 'third sector' necessitated growing mobility between public subsidy and commercial sources of economic viability. Chapter 7 'The changing demographic of performance' looks at the way professional theatre became more socially and culturally representative. It is divided into three sections. The first reconsiders the emergence of the upwardly mobile 'new' actor in the 1950s and 60s both through theatre and television. The second section focuses on the widening of nationally distinctive opportunity for Scottish theatre-makers up until the end of the 1970s. The third is a detailed account going back to the 1950s of the ways in which Black British and British Asian theatre artists gained access to professional opportunity in theatre and television. Chapter 8 'The topography of theatre in 2000' maps both the built and demographic landscape of theatre across the four component parts of the UK between 1999 and 2000 and identifies the economic and social factors which contributed to continuity and change.

A word on websites: digital technology has unleashed a huge and ever-expanding mass of information. The historian has on the one hand the advantage of instant access to useful data, which has been generated by both 'lay' enthusiasts and academy-authorised scholarship, and on the other the challenge of having to navigate the truth claims of both. As a result the already unstable process of mapping and recording becomes ever more fluid and open to question even as previously unknown and unthought-of practices and personalities emerge to populate the historical landscape. Furthermore, unlike paper records or other products of old technology which can be pinned down and preserved, this virtual archive is constantly shifting and changing. A link is broken, the site decays and appears to vanish. Instability proliferates. At the time this book went to press all websites were actively available unless otherwise stated. Many produced by theatre organisations, promoters and funders had been designed and launched to a potentially infinite audience comparatively recently. In 2000 relatively few small-scale theatre-makers made their own websites. After more of a decade of the twenty-first century this has become the rule rather than the exception. It has become a means of writing individual histories 'about us' and, as I found in constructing my 2000 topography, these digital records have often revealed an unexpectedly lengthy existence especially in the companies first established in the 1980s. These records, however, also disappear. The company has endeavoured to change its 'brand' image or its policy or even its name, or sadly has ceased to exist leaving just digital fragments as testimony. Where I have drawn on sites which are no longer available I have signalled this in the notes, but I increasingly regard this 'documentary' evidence as an essential, if unstable, component in the historian's tool kit.

CHAPTER I

The topography of theatre in 1900

In order to delineate the principle features of theatre across the British Isles at the start of the twentieth century, it is important to be aware of the effects of stratification. Evidence of cultural practice in the case of buildings, for example, is literally embedded in different layers in the landscape. The form and structure of each building, its relationship spatially and conceptually to other built structures, is the product of human agency and a particular moment in time and, indeed, the convergence of other, past and often disruptive moments. That built landscape comes at the end of another more complex process where the elements of physical stratification in the natural environment become the source of social and economic formations.

This book explores theatre practice as a component in a whole matrix of social and economic activity, and thus this chapter focuses first on how theatre functioned in a wider industrial context in 1900 and the origins of that context. Because theatre is peculiarly dependent on performative interactions in space and the relationship of diverse groups of human agents in those spaces, it is also necessary to consider not only the materiality of spatial relations, but also the consequences of abstract notions of space. Thus the specificities of social space become part of the topography as well as larger abstract or imagined spatial frameworks. Nation and empire can be physically delineated and measured – flags are flown and borders agreed or imposed – and there are physical, especially, demographic, consequences. But the psychological impact of what Henri Lefebvre conceptualises as 'abstract space' or the 'dominant form of space', which I will call 'the space of power',[1] is of particular interest to the theatre historian as she records the way creative and expressive cultural 'need'[2] has been mediated or restrained within a political framework.

The other vital component of the topography is emptiness. If theatre appears to be absent from a landscape, why, and is that absence more apparent than real? The origins of emptiness can be simply geological – the presence of mountain ranges can be a major impediment – or they could be political, ideological and/or religious, and economic. Fear of theatre's capacity to persuade, dictate, subvert or undermine, and, moreover, the presence of large numbers of people packed together willingly in the same enclosed place, had led, since the sixteenth century, to a succession of legislative measures designed to control and limit its practice.

Dotted about the landscape in 1900 were a number of theatres surviving from the mid-eighteenth century which bore witness to locally won privileges granted by royal prerogative through parliament to erect a building and perform the 'legitimate' drama of the spoken word.[3] But even after the 1843 Theatres Regulation Act which officially removed what was in fact an industrial monopoly,[4] albeit widely ignored in practice, local licencing authorities in certain areas of Britain could still be heavily constrained by very deep-seated religious distrust mediated through influential members of the community. In any case in 1900, and indeed up until 1968, royal prerogative and ideological control were retained under the terms of the 1737 Stage Licensing Act which enforced the submission of all new plays to the Lord Chamberlain for scrutiny and effective censorship prior to performance. Add to that the anxieties about play piracy, which was still prevalent outside London until the signing of an International Copyright Convention in 1908 provided greater security,[5] then emptiness or absence can imply another causation. Theatres traded their heavily controlled artistic wares where business was likely to be good and where the buyers' tastes and predilections were well-known. Other attempts to fill emptiness were more complex and required other kinds of structural frameworks.

Key to the mapping process is the examination of the core–periphery relationship between metropolitan and provincial Britain. This book sets out to explore how theatre was practised and experienced outside London and thus redress the balance historiographically, but even the most dedicated regionalist has to acknowledge the dominance of metropolitan theatre not just in the historical record or contemporary perception, but in terms of ownership of actual resources. John Langton and R. J. Morris reinforce this in their introduction to the *Atlas of Industrializing Britain 1780–1914*, which sets out to illustrate in a series of different maps how the complexity of 'competing sets of spatial patterns' reveal the variations in lived experience in different parts of the country.[6] The editors nevertheless state unequivocally that: 'Britain was and remained a metropolitan economy. London was the largest city. Its citizens controlled the greatest accumulations of wealth. It dominated the major part of the banking, commercial and political systems.'

So this book, perforce, is also about how the core–periphery relationship has been accepted, rebalanced, negotiated or contested through a hundred-year period. I shall do my best not to use the term 'provincial' with its connotations of uncultured and unsophisticated narrowness of outlook and colonial subordination. But in 1900, as we shall see, the 'provinces' covered all the administrative units – including separate nations – which were subject to metropolitan control.

THE EXPANSION OF BUILDING-BASED THEATRE

To begin with buildings. In 1900 theatre was visibly contributing to the rapid expansion of the built landscape of Great Britain. *The Era Almanack* for 1894, the year the Theatrical Management Association (TMA) was formed as 'a protective body' for the industry, lists 319 theatres or public venues, excluding music halls, licensed for theatrical performance across the British Isles as a whole. By 1900, although some venues had closed and others opened, there were 343. There were 164 music halls.[7]

Given the extent to which licensed performances were given in various locations including town and village halls and assembly rooms, it is difficult to assess exactly how many 'theatres' were in existence or how many audience seats (or standing places) were available. The other difficulty, even with designated buildings, is that many theatres changed names with different managements. My attempts to count have relied on the annual *Era* listings which may have been dependent on managers' promotional efforts. The invaluable, more recent work of The Theatres Trust in identifying buildings that survived until the end of the twentieth century, together with the documented evidence of demolished theatres, has expanded numbers considerably.[8] However incomplete the figures might be, it is possible to get a sense of the exponential rate of growth in the English regions especially; the extent to which building provision clustered in different parts of the country, and in terms of the core–periphery relationship, how much more opportunity for theatre-making and theatre-going London could offer.

The most rapid building-based expansion in the final decade of the nineteenth century had been in London and its environs where there had been roughly a 60 per cent increase from 43 venues in 1894 to 69 in 1900. Thus at the beginning of the new century, the metropolis contained within its boundaries some 20 per cent of the total number of designated

British theatre venues. By this point while there was a continual process of reallocation and refurbishment of the building stock, London appears to have reached capacity. *The Era Annual* listing for 1907 shows London more or less static with 68 venues while outside the capital there had been a remarkable increase of 42 per cent to a listing of 389 venues.[9] The question then has to be asked whether, at this point in the first decade of the twentieth century, the balance of provision was becoming more equal. Or, given the extent to which the artistic product which was being circulated across Britain was manufactured by London-based companies, was metropolitan expansion being facilitated by other means?

A BUOYANT INDUSTRY

British theatre in 1900 was a bustling, optimistic industry. The pages of the weekly editions of *The Era* and *The Stage* read like a theatrical *Exchange & Mart* with pages of artistes advertising their availability, managers from all sectors of the industry looking for artistes, venues advertising their current programme, venues looking for product to fill empty weeks. Plays were the principal commercial product and they too were available for hire or purchase together with the acting ensembles formed to tour them or to showcase the talents of a particular actor. There were entries offering for sale plays owned by the recently deceased. In the case of particularly popular plays, distribution and thus profit was maximised with more than one company touring carbon copies to different circuits of theatres.

The old and the new were juxtaposed. The advertisements by managers of portable and fit-up companies for actors, ready and willing to take to the road and perform at a few days' notice, show just how much the popular practices of a much older Victorian theatre still survived. The postal addresses for portables ranging across Britain indicate a widespread network still existed of genuinely itinerant bands of players travelling with their theatres. 'Gent for Heavies, or Lead; Man and Wife for Responsibles; also Painter to act' was a not untypical situations-vacant advertisement.

On the same pages of *The Stage* there are advertisements for 'Scenorama Cinematograph' available for hire. Films lasting only a few minutes first arrived in British fairgrounds in February 1897, taken up by showmen eager to exploit a novelty attraction. Very rapidly film moved from the tents and penny gaffs to the music halls and new variety theatres and a wider societal spread of audience. In the spring of 1900 it was possible to see a film of Queen Victoria's visit to Dublin to receive the keys of the city from the Lord Lieutenant and an 'official' film of the war in South Africa. Assumptions about the imminent demise of the medium circulating in London in 1898 were obviously premature.[10]

There were clearly a large number of hopeful dramatists eager to strike it lucky in the market with a play which might achieve mass circulation. The chronological listing in the 1900 *Era Almanack* of new work first performed in the provinces from 1 December 1898 until 30 November 1899 gives a total of 158 productions.[11] Almost all were of full-length plays in a variety of genres or musical pieces. Thus to select at random: *The Master of Hope*, a domestic drama by Lanwarne Hawkins, premiered at the Grand Theatre, Stalybridge, on 3 December 1898. *The Guiding Star*, a melodrama by Carr Elkington, was staged at the Prince of Wales Theatre in Great Grimsby on 17 July 1899. Barbara White's farcical comedy *The Tourist* could be seen appropriately enough in the Aquarium Theatre in Brighton on 12 June 1899. On 26 June the Metropole Theatre in Glasgow staged a domestic Irish drama, *The Boys of Wexford* by E. C. Matthews. Two days later the same theatre enabled the copyright performance of a domestic drama by W. A. Brabner, *The Heiress of Daventry*.

The names of all the dramatists but Barbara White appear in the handlists of plays in Allardyce Nicoll's *English Drama 1900–1930*, which depended very heavily on the raw data supplied by *The Era*.[12] None survives to enter any kind of literary or historical canon. The lists are of value now as social documents of audience taste and commercial priorities and of the continuities of Victorian popular genres. However, included in the provincial premieres for that twelve months are names which do resonate in the academy-authorised canon. *Caesar and Cleopatra*, a chronicle play in five acts by G. Bernard Shaw, was given its copyright performance on 15 March 1899 at the Newcastle Theatre Royal. A few weeks later on 8 and 9 May in the Antient Concert Rooms in Dublin there were performances of *The Countess Cathleen*, a tragedy by W. B. Yeats, and *The Heather Field* by Edward Martyn.

Newcastle's opportunity to see *Caesar and Cleopatra* was a necessary copyright reading at 11 p.m. by Mrs Patrick Campbell's company. When the play was finally produced in London in 1907, it was part of an attempt to revolutionise opportunities for new dramatists.[13] The Dublin performances witnessed by audiences, which included leading English critics, launched the Irish Literary Theatre which ultimately became Ireland's National Theatre.[14] These are details in the larger narratives of epic figures in metropolitan-led theatre history. However, the fact that these first performances of plays by two Irish creative writers who were to have a major influence on twentieth-century theatre should be noted in a humdrum British 'provincial' listing is in itself an indicator of the topographical complexity of the end-of-century landscape.

Both Yeats and Shaw, both born in Dublin and both heirs of the Anglo-Irish Protestant Ascendancy, were implicated in, and benefited from, the colonial nexus which was the British nation state. In the last full year of Queen Victoria's reign, both men were able to position themselves to exploit intellectually and materially a theatre that was reaping the benefits of the entrepreneurial power of the world's first industrialised nation and indeed the nation state at the centre of the world's largest and most far-flung empire.

THE FORMATION OF EMPIRE

Since the 1800 Act of Union with Ireland, Great Britain was in theory a single economic unit governed by parliament in Westminster and composed of four nations bound together through a gradual process of English military conquest, annexation and legislation. Union with Wales dated back to the mid-sixteenth century, while the Act of Union with Scotland in 1707 was a parliamentary subjugation, which averted a possible invasion and enabled Scotland to achieve sufficient autonomy to engage vigorously in partnership with England in the pursuit of economic advantage.[15] Of course the individual histories of brutality, exploitation and cultural suppression, which are the *sine qua non* of colonial appropriation, continued to resonate powerfully in the creation of culturally distinctive 'imagined' nations within the United Kingdom. What did emerge, however, from this enforced yoking together, was a dynamically heterogeneous islands-nation state which launched the ships to take the imperial adventurers to trade and conquest overseas. In the first decade of the twentieth century the British Empire occupied one-fifth of the land surface of the globe and had a population of 400 million, 300 million of which were in India.

That this small group of islands should have developed into a dominant world power is in part due to the extraordinary variety of the physical landscape – more geologically varied arguably than any other area of similar size on the planet. Crucially Britain enjoys ample resources of water power combined with the close proximity of iron, coal and other minerals. In England these lie in the junction of the highland and lowland zones, running in a line from the estuaries of the Exe in the South-West of the country to the Tees in the North-East.[16] This naturally occurring set of circumstances replicated in Scotland and Wales resulted in a series of industrial developments which ultimately transformed the global economy.

The diversity of the coastline with great estuaries close to the coalfields and the main centres of the iron and steel industry enabled the growth of major ports and shipbuilding centres in each of the component nations. Cardiff's proximity to the coalfields of the South Wales valleys combined with a relatively flat terrain made it, before the First World War, the greatest coal port in the world.[17] Glasgow, in the Lower Clyde Basin, within reach of Scotland's largest coalfield in the Central Lowlands and near rich deposits of black-band iron ore, became the self-styled 'Second City of the Empire'. It has been argued that Belfast's 'Britishness' is in part based on its structure and role within the seaboard industrial region of Lancashire, Clydeside and eastern Ulster.[18] As Britain became the 'workshop of the world' so overseas trade became vital to the prosperity of the population which by 1880 stood at about 30 million. Economic historian R. S. Sayers made a rough calculation that 'around 1880 the British economy was geared to the ability to sell to the outside world the output of one worker in every five'.[19]

THE IMPACT OF INDUSTRIALISATION

The unprecedented growth of new theatre buildings and their distribution across the islands of late Victorian and Edwardian Britain clearly reflect the impact of industrialisation and urbanisation, which proceeded within the flexible framework of a free market economy largely unplanned by central government. By 1900 the British people (now about 37 million) were increasingly living in the continuously settled industrialised regions, where towns had effectively merged together, which the late-Victorian urban theorist Patrick Geddes named 'conurbations'.[20] Uniquely Great Britain had seven conurbations: six in England and Wales, and one in Scotland. Each, with the exception of London, had at its administrative core a regional-centre city, which had newly acquired city status. Indeed, an important aspect of the development of a strong civic consciousness could be seen in the ambitious schemes launched in the early to mid years of the nineteenth century to create architecturally impressive town centres complete with civic buildings, which usually included a theatre emblematic of civilised values.

In 1900 the regional conurbation populations were: South-East Lancashire (2,149,000, rcc [regional-centre city] Manchester); the West

Midlands (1,600,000, rcc Birmingham), West Yorkshire (1,527,000 rcc Leeds), Merseyside (1,022,000, rcc Liverpool), Tyneside (667,000 rcc Newcastle upon Tyne) and Central Clydeside (1,424,000 rcc Glasgow). London, however, effortlessly dominated the largest conurbation with a population of about 6,000,000.

To map theatres using a combination of the data sources available shows that out of the 274 'provincial' venues that include those in Scotland, Wales and Ireland, 171, more than 62 per cent, were located in England between the border with Scotland and the West Midlands conurbation. Populations in the old eighteenth-century market towns and villages with 'simple, rectangular, almost shed-like rooms',[21] which played host to the circuits of travelling theatre companies, had receded in the wake of wholesale migration from rural areas to the new industrial areas. There were still functioning theatres royal in the centres of the old agrarian economy in East Anglia and the South-West of England, including Norwich, Gloucester and Exeter. In 1900 Bath, which had been the first English regional town to acquire a royal patent theatre in 1768, still supported a completely rebuilt Theatre Royal together with a music hall. The Theatre Royal in the ancient city of York derived from a patent in 1769 and was by 1900 a palimpsest of different building styles. But the evidence of a theatre boom was to be found in significant clusters in the English industrial Midlands and North and, albeit in a very concentrated way, in the Central Scottish Lowlands.

There were theatres, most of which had been rebuilt or refurbished, in all the regional-centre cities that dated back to an earlier industrial period. Newcastle upon Tyne, granted city status in 1882, had been the home of an extraordinary group of engineering geniuses who between them almost literally powered the Industrial Revolution and then powered and armed the empire.[22] In 1900 the city was the administrative centre of some 90 square miles of mining towns, villages, shipyards, ports and possibly the largest armaments factory in the world. When the second Theatre Royal opened in 1838, it was part of a major scheme to rebuild the town centre. The theatre with its portico of Corinthian columns remains the city's most prominent theatrical landmark, built at the top of Grey Street which sweeps down to the River Tyne.[23] In 1900 six theatres were listed in Newcastle, although the Theatre Royal was temporarily dark having been badly damaged by fire the previous autumn. Two music halls are listed.

On either side of the River Tyne, South Shields and North Shields both boasted Theatre Royals, but South Shields also had a Grand Theatre and an Empire Theatre of Varieties. Gateshead, opposite Newcastle across the river, had the Métropôle Theatre, while there was yet another Royal in Jarrow together with the Peoples' Palace music hall. Wallsend had a Theatre Royal, Hebburn a Grand, while Ashington advertised the Miners' Theatre. Tynemouth enjoyed a Palace-by-the-Sea. Whitley Bay, which was a growing holiday resort, had a Pavilion Theatre and an Empire. Calculating on the basis of the Theatres Trust research into the 'live' or recently closed venues at the beginning of the century, there may have been as many as 43 theatres or music/concert halls serving the population as a whole.

THE ROYAL PRESENCE

The names given to the new theatres were emblematic of the prevailing expansive spirit and the totemic power of queen and empire. The 'Royal' title still carried the prestige of implied monarchical patronage, although the need for a royal patent bestowed by the monarch through parliament, and then renewed annually for a fee, was now effectively ignored. In analysing the practical consequences of the 1843 Theatres Regulation Act, Tracy Davis has demonstrated how 'overnight' the Lord Chamberlain changed 'from a defender of monopolistic rights to the instrument of free market competition'.[24] The reality by the end of the nineteenth century was that any small town or suburban theatre could be designated 'Royal' simply by whim of the proprietor and the agreement of the local licensing authorities. The blind eye turned by the Lord Chamberlain's office was indicative of the laissez-faire ideology which appeared happy to acquiesce in the use of royal affiliation as a commercial hook.

Just a cursory glance at the 1894–1900 TMA records shows that theatres royal in such arriviste urban areas as Rotheram (1894), Rochdale (1895), West Bromwich (1896), Smethwick (1897) and Barnsley (1899),[25] amongst many others, had been added to the select group of just 12 authentic patent-holders outside London which were honoured between 1768 (Edinburgh) and 1826 (Ramsgate).[26] There were other ways of signalling royal allegiance. Theatres could simply be the Queen's as in Gateshead, Farnworth and Leeds, or Victoria Theatres as in Salford and Burnley.

In the theatres of the other British component nations, the sovereign was a commanding bricks-and-mortar presence not only in the Theatres Royal of Cardiff, Glasgow and Inverness, but in Her Majesty's Theatres in Aberdeen and Glasgow. In Dublin, in 1897, a new Theatre Royal rose from the ashes of the 1821 building which had burned down in 1880. The Queen's Royal Theatre, opened in 1844 (in a grim irony coinciding with the first clear signs of the Irish potato famine in the west of the country), offered double-strength endorsement of the British crown's position in the local theatre economy.

The other increasingly visible epithet was 'Grand'. At least 28 Grand Theatres opened between 1878 and 1900 and there would be more to come in the new century. The first Grand Theatre may have been the Prince of Wales' Theatre in Glasgow, renamed in 1867. But the Grand trend seems to have gathered momentum, most noticeably in the manufacturing north of England after the opening of the Leeds Grand Theatre and Opera House in 1878. Leeds industrialists spent an unprecedented £62,000 on a theatre 'of metropolitan stature' with a seated audience capacity of 2,600, built over a three-quarter acre site which included a concert hall and six shops. The influence of monumental European (especially French) theatres and churches resulted in a magnificent Gothic façade (as a totality extending for 162 feet), complete with ecclesiastical spires which ornamented the roof.[27]

Comparing the façades of late-nineteenth-century opera houses to the propaganda function of the two-dimensional cathedral façade, Marvin Carlson has drawn attention to 'the ostentation of cultural rather than of religious iconography'.[28] As the leading citizens in the prosperous British manufacturing towns rapidly moving towards city status began to develop civic centres of sufficient grandeur to match their ambition, so it was essential to construct public buildings that instilled both pride and confidence.

The church-like impression of the Grand Theatre exterior was echoed in the tall Gothic arches and lancet windows incorporated into the design of Thornton's Arcade, the first in a series of eight spectacular shopping arcades built in Leeds between 1877 and 1900. Charles Thornton's development included the City Varieties Music Hall which he opened in 1865 as Thornton's New Music Hall and Fashionable Lounge. By 1900, four years after Leeds achieved city status, there were six theatres, with the addition of the Theatre Royal, the Coliseum, the Empire Palace and the Queen's Theatre. The architectural environment offered social and civic reassurance in the unashamed juxtaposition of recreation, culture and commerce.[29]

THE DISTRIBUTION OF INFLUENCE

The fact that in Scotland Glasgow, with its conurbation and larger population than the ancient national capital Edinburgh, was a quasi-capital was, Richard Rodger has argued, 'typical of British imperial urban systems generally', where as in Ireland, Wales, and further afield in India and Canada, no one city was allowed to become totally dominant.[30] Indeed, with Dundee and Aberdeen, there were four dominant Scottish cities that by the beginning of the twentieth century were reaching the point where they were home to some 30 per cent of the population. The lists in the 1900 *Era Almanack* suggest that Glasgow was better provided with, or was at least better promoting, more theatres and music halls than Edinburgh. The research by The Theatres Trust, however, identified approximately nine theatres capable of functioning in both cities, but as theatres had been built specifically for variety with additional music halls, the boundaries between legitimate and popular were more than usually blurred.

In Edinburgh, the Theatre Royal, which had been rebuilt several times by 1900, had been the first recipient in 1767 of a royal patent outside London. Against a background of ferocious Presbyterian opposition and some energetic evasion of the law, it had taken nearly thirty years to legitimise theatrical activity in the city. Tellingly, as Adrienne Scullion explains, the main reason why hostility to the patent finally abated was because the theatre was part of a much more ambitious architectural scheme to extend the boundary of the city to build the elegant neoclassical New Town area for Edinburgh's growing professional elite.[31]

By 1900, however, not only was there speedy rail communication between the two cities, but effectively the key theatre spaces had begun to merge. Edinburgh and Glasgow shared between them the four most important theatres: two Theatres Royal, the Royal Lyceum in Edinburgh opened in 1883 and the Royalty in Glasgow, rebuilt in 1879. All were under the management of Howard & Wyndham Ltd. which went on to open the brand new King's Theatre in Glasgow in 1904. In 1900, the company also managed the Tyne Theatre and Opera House in Newcastle. As a model of management, Howard & Wyndham, which was the first theatrical company to be registered on the Edinburgh Stock Exchange,[32] will be examined in greater detail in Chapter 2, but clearly topographically artists and audiences nominally divided by city boundaries and national borders were part of a nexus of theatrical taste and influence which in these No. 1[33] venues were also directly in touch with metropolitan theatre. The Edinburgh Royal Lyceum opened in 1883 with Henry Irving's London Lyceum production of *Much Ado about Nothing*.

Theatre proprietors and lessees could be criticised for attempting to spread audiences over too many venues in the same area. In South

Shields, for example, the Empire Palace was built next door to the Theatre Royal on the same main street, and this phenomenon of creating a modest 'entertainment quarter' was not unusual. There were advantages offered by 'localisation economies', which means in broad industrial terms, as geographer Alan Townsend explains, locating near other firms in the same industry to engage in 'complementary tasks and enjoy the benefits of a common pool of skilled labour and of specialised services'.[34] Theatres were built to capitalise on large, economically active populations in need of a range of service industries, including – nearly a quarter of a century before music and drama could be transmitted into the home via the first domestic radio receivers – arts-based entertainment.

In a sense as receiving houses or touring venues, the vast majority of theatres were effectively retail outlets, trading goods manufactured elsewhere. Many of the big theatres with dynamic managements developed an impressive reputation for home-produced, spectacular pantomimes which, often running from Boxing Day to Easter, were the nearest regional venues got to a long run. The occasional theatre lessee, like Robert Arthur, was a playwright and produced his own work. Otherwise, depending on a theatre's position in the circuit hierarchy, managements brought in a range of toured-in product which at the top end of the market could be the best the metropolis could offer.

The fact that in London, increasingly in the West End, there had developed a large number of play/musical comedy *producing* theatres in very close proximity is an example of what Max Weber called 'agglomeration'.[35] Manufacturing firms, i.e. theatres, could cluster together to achieve economies of scale by concentrating production at one point – again benefiting from the pool of skilled services including, in the case of theatre, a constantly available supply of actors. Once the product, often at enormous expense, had been created/manufactured, the manufacturers would then exploit the product to the maximum extent with long runs in their factory shops, so to speak, to customers, including the large numbers of visitors/tourists coming to the city.

The product of the actor-managers, such as Irving, Tree, Alexander, etc., was enhanced by their own charisma as star actors as well as the charisma of their favourite playwrights. Then in order to ensure nations-wide product dissemination and enable audiences from Belfast to Dublin, to Swansea, to Liverpool, to Edinburgh, to Aberdeen, etc., the play would be toured with the stars. Metropolitan glamour was available for all who could afford the price of a ticket. The prevailing metropolitan theatre aesthetic, imbricated with dominant societal values, could circulate nations-wide.

However, the sheer amount of touring product available was enormous, with, as already noted, existing commercial successes trekking round the regions as well as the large number of new plays. For the week beginning 18 October 1900, for example, *The Stage* lists 281 companies on the road. Companies going to the No. 2 or 3 venues could be very small and any connection with London could be minimal. What is difficult to track is to what extent artists travelling to conventional venues had local associations. Certainly the doyens of the regional/national circuits such as Frank Benson and Ben Greet, who toured several companies simultaneously, were usually booked in No. 1 venues, and built up loyal audiences everywhere they went.

THE RAILWAYS AND NATIONAL SPACE

All histories of turn-of-the-century British theatre cite the way the extensive rail network facilitated the movement of touring theatre companies across Britain. What perhaps is not sufficiently emphasised is the extent to which the railways were integral to industrial expansion as whole, and the density of individual rail networks is indicative of density of economic activity on which theatre entrepreneurs simply piggybacked.

Alan Townsend has stressed the fact that 'individual Victorian railway companies *competed* to reach and serve the coalfield areas', as well as other important cities and ports.[36] Large rural areas were treated as monopoly zones from which to construct lines, and private companies actively assisted in the promotion of other types of towns such as seaside resorts which developed on the coasts near the industrial areas. Blackpool, which became the great holiday resort for Lancashire workers who benefited from special excursions and cheap tickets, had in 1900 – if The Theatres Trust research is correct – potentially available no less than fifteen assorted playhouses, variety theatres and assembly rooms. Crewe, in Cheshire, which took on an almost mythical status in theatrical memoirs as the place of convergence and exchange for touring theatre companies, was 'conveniently placed' as one of the new railway engineering towns at the centre of company networks.

When we turn to look at the landscape of theatre in the other component nations of Britain, access to good, spatially inclusive transportation is very clearly one of the factors in distribution and density. While development in England seems wholly due to the operation of the free market,

albeit in complex ways within the constraints of the core–periphery relationship, in Scotland, Wales and Ireland the stratification of the landscape is more visible in terms of macro political and economic structural
interventions. Land, and rights of ownership of land, was a major political issue.

The first point to make, however, is that the net effect of vastly
improved transport is, as geographer Michael Freeman has shown in
maps demonstrating the impact of reduced travel times, the effective
shrinking of the size of the national space.[37] In the era of the train and
the electric telegraph, Aberdeen, 558 miles from London on the north-
east coast of Scotland and one of the four most important Scottish
towns, was perfectly accessible by the railway line which was constructed
all the way up the east coast linking Newcastle upon Tyne to Edinburgh,
Dundee and then Aberdeen. Robert Arthur who managed Her Majesty's
Theatre in Aberdeen also managed the Theatre Royals in both Dundee
and Newcastle. The 1900 *Era* lists Her Majesty's Theatre, which regularly
hosted London productions in Aberdeen, and a music hall, the Palace. In
1910 *The Stage Year Book*, which also mentions other suitable halls and
easily obtained portable sites in Aberdeen, described a mostly industrial
population employed in fishing, granite working, paper and textiles,
and 'comprises a class of people who are regular theatre and music hall
goers'.[38]

The railway line extended as far as Thurso near John o'Groats and could
also take companies to the Theatre Royal in Inverness, the gateway to the
Scottish Highlands. A music hall in Inverness opened in 1899. However,
although the Caledonian, the Northern British and the Highland rail
companies ran lines to the west coast of the Highlands, for industrial purposes the landscape appeared empty. The romantic, 'unspoilt' wilderness
measuring something in the order of 15,077 square miles of mountains,
lochs and islands had in fact suffered profoundly from human intervention. The brutal clearances of whole communities following the defeat of
the 1745–6 Jacobite rebellion, and the enclosure of large tracts of land for
sheep grazing by wealthy landlords had decimated the livelihoods of the
many original crofting and fishing villages.[39]

Trains, which had brought transport from the 1840s onwards to a
region where roads and even bridges had been scarce, could now take
native inhabitants away to seek better lives elsewhere and to service
Anglo-Scottish landowners and their guests, arriving to enjoy a cultural
ambience of 'invented' Highland tradition.[40] In 1900, as later, more ideologically motivated theatre companies were to find, it was possible to tour

round community halls in the Highlands, and as part of the Kailyard School of sentimental Scottish literature, a genre of plays had developed set in rural 'Scotch mist' locations. Gaelic, however, was still spoken in many of the islands, and partly as a means of cultural defence, a particularly conservative, puritan Presbyterianism had developed amongst leading members of some communities.

Queen Victoria had of course fallen in love with the Scottish Highlands, and Pitlochry, the picturesque holiday town which had built up after the purchase of her nearby Balmoral estate in 1852, was also on the railway line which linked Perth and Stirling to Falkirk and thence to Glasgow. Barbara Bell in her survey of nineteenth-century Scottish theatre has described the tour dates for a production in 1895 of Charles Hawtrey's London smash-hit farce *The Private Secretary*. Between the end of January and mid-March, W. J. Lancaster's company travelled to a total of twenty town venues from Greenock, due west of Glasgow, to Forfar, Brechin and Montrose in the east. All could be reached by rail. However, only five could be described as purpose-built theatres. The rest of the tour was to a range of mixed-use public or town halls, which were probably considered No. 2 or even No. 3 venues. Bell is at pains to point out with this example that not all touring productions were necessarily big, prestigious shows emanating directly from London's West End. Small companies possibly with local links could exploit an English/London product on a much smaller scale.[41]

In Wales and Ireland, communication systems very obviously favoured the efficacy of the imperial nexus. There were extensive rail links within the South Wales coalfields for industrial transportation. Holiday resorts, especially on the North Wales coast, developed at key points on the rail line which snaked round the coastline but effectively went from west to east towards England. The one or two theatres built in towns such as Llandudno, Rhyll – and Tenby on the south-west coast – entertained holidaymakers from big English cities such as Birmingham and Liverpool as much as they did Welsh workers. The same could be said for the mid-Wales line and the Cambrian line which took visitors to the spa town of Llandrindod Wells and to the coast to Aberystwyth. Theatres were constructed in both towns in the 1890s. But as Kenneth O. Morgan has noted the trains were primarily designed to link with English markets and urban areas.[42]

The natural topography of barren, mountain uplands created a human topography of tiny enclosed rural villages where Welsh was the language of everyday discourse. Travel from North to South Wales by road was difficult and there were marked cultural differences and even tensions between North Walians and South Walians. It was, claims Morgan, easier to arrange a rendezvous in Shewsbury which straddled the border, or even London.[43] There was no national capital in 1900 and Cardiff, despite its industrial sprawl and visible commitment to a grand civic-building programme, did not achieve city status until 1905. The city was declared the national capital fifty years later in 1955.

Writing about cultural renewal including theatre initiatives after the Second World War, Morgan claims that Wales had no strong dramatic tradition. There was 'no urban elite, no Abbey Theatre or audiences attuned to sophisticated dramatic expression'.[44] Certainly the fact that Cardiff, despite its size and conurbation character, did not sustain theatres to the same extent as comparable urban areas in England indicates a different kind of demographic and cultural history. *The Era* lists the Grand and the Theatre Royal, which had opened in 1878, a year after the old theatre burnt down. There seem to have been three music halls including Levine's Music Hall, which Oswald Stoll, a young music-hall agent, acquired to rename as the Cardiff Empire. Swansea, where the Grand opened in 1897, had an older, if erratic building-based tradition dating back to touring companies in the eighteenth century. An account by a disgruntled Drury Lane actor, published in 1887, but probably deriving from the 1840s, described 'an overgrown village run up for the convenience of the miners ... the atmosphere ... dense with coal and copper smoke'.[45]

Wales, for centuries treated as little more than a geographical extension of England and with an Anglophile Tory landed gentry, who, as in Scotland and in Ireland, concentrated land ownership in very few hands, developed late and then very quickly its main urban areas. Cardiff was no Edinburgh or indeed Newcastle. In 1801 it too was little more than a large village and its huge end-of-century population was, as we shall see, expanded by a very diverse influx of workers. Cecil Price, who published in 1955 an article on the way portable theatres operated in Wales from 1843 until 1914, built up a vivid picture of a popular dramatic tradition albeit one which originally crossed the border from England.[46]

Most of Price's evidence dates from the 1850s to the 1870s, but it is clear that unlicensed itinerant or semi-itinerant theatre was a familiar phenomenon right up until the First World War. He argues that portables arrived in Wales to take advantage of the new industrial villages and towns as a result of the 1843 Act, which excluded booth and tent theatres from the requirement that all stage plays and theatrical buildings should be licensed. They were in principle subject to local magistrates' control but in practice were deemed free to entertain while a fair or race meeting lasted.[47] Indeed, many local employers considered them a social benefit as the shows, especially suitably salutary melodramas, could be a powerful distraction from alcohol which in turn meant less absenteeism.

Some of the larger portables could accommodate an audience of two thousand and carried equipment to connect lighting to a town's gas mains. Some could stay in a town for as long as six months. One of most popular at the turn of the century was managed by Edward Ebley with a circuit which could include Dowlais, Pentre, Mountain Ash, Treorchy, Maesteg, Blaenavon and Pontypool. The huge repertoire of plays not only included well-known English melodramas together with abridged versions of Shakespeare, but in a custom which had continued since the 1870s, plays with Welsh topics and titles. A writer in a South Wales newspaper in 1936 remembered plays including *The Rocking Stone of Pontypridd*, *Llewelyn, the Last of the Welsh Princes*, *The Maid of Cefn Ydfa* and *Twm Shon Catti*.[48]

As Price, also records, however, 'Excommunication from membership of the chapels was both threatened and put into effect.'[49] In the 1851 religious census of all churchgoers, it was shown that half the Welsh population surveyed did not attend Christian worship at all. But D. Densil Morgan has put forward convincing evidence that by the end of the nineteenth century 'industrialism, far from being a harbinger of secularism, *strengthened* the hold which Christianity held on the mass of the people'.[50] The statistics are impressive. Nonconformity – comprised of four main denominations with Calvinist Methodists the strongest – shaped the religious beliefs of 1.5 million Welsh adults together with some 500,000 in Sunday Schools in a total population of 2.5 million.[51] These figures do not include adherents to Anglicanism or Roman Catholicism. Thus the impact of religiously motivated anti-theatrical prejudice should not be underestimated amongst community leaders of all classes including the urban elite.

Furthermore, Nonconformism, especially, was deeply implicated in the maintenance of a powerfully autonomous, grass-roots Welsh identity within which the Welsh language remained a vital component. While Price in his short survey of professional theatre in Wales states that Robert Redford who became the sole proprietor of the Cardiff Theatre

Royal in 1898 made 'Cardiff one of the best theatrical centres in Britain', this was largely based on the best of metropolitan touring product.[52] As we shall see in chapter 4 which focuses on amateur activity, community engagement in theatre found other outlets, especially when the church itself began to develop educational and recreational opportunities which encouraged creative expression.[53] There may not have been many theatres in Wales, but the landscape was littered with buildings for the performance of Christian worship and what was effectively a dramatic tradition of semonising. By the 1880s, as Kenneth Morgan himself points out, more and more new churches were 'imposing structures, with elaborate facades, and *theatrical* [my emphasis] almost Baroque interiors'.[54] While it is true to say that in Wales there was no tradition of the kind of brilliant literary drama which Irish playwrights had been exporting to London since the eighteenth century, there was certainly a popular performance tradition which was set in 1900 to grow stronger.

IRELAND AND CONSTRUCTIVE UNIONISM

Christopher Morash's map of how the English theatre touring system operated in Ireland describes a highly-efficient 'multi-national' circuit which linked up the four countries through a combination of sea and rail. As we shall see, Irish theatre was maintaining a vigorous cultural identity even when mediated through English managements, and Morash suggests that the quality of good touring companies had a ripple effect that in his view helped decentralise the Dublin-dominated Irish theatrical world.[55] When the Belfast Grand Opera House opened in 1895, in itself emblematic of burgeoning industrial success, a long-accepted Belfast–Dublin–Cork axis was reinforced. Morash describes how it worked to everyone's advantage: 'A company would arrive by steamship from Glasgow or Liverpool to play Belfast, travel south by train for a Dublin run, and then south-west by train (sometimes via Limerick or Waterford) to Cork, before taking another steamship to Bristol, Milford Haven or Liverpool.'[56]

The circuit had been established originally by Dublin companies in the 1730s, and by the 1780s evidence suggests that tours also extended to theatres much further west in towns such as Tralee, Galway, Castlebar and Sligo which supported a lively performance culture.[57] By the end of the nineteenth century, however, the west of Ireland had been ravaged by famine and mass emigration. In Scotland, the suppression of Jacobite rebellion had literally prepared the ground for the consolidation of broadly accepted political union, and for the most part comfortable economic co-existence. In Ireland, the combination of empty landscapes, poverty and wholly disproportionate land ownership by relatively small numbers of Protestant Ascendancy beneficiaries had created a state of chronic political unrest and violence, which could not be pacified, as in Scotland and Wales, by a share in imperial industrial success.[58]

As R. F. Foster explains in his history of modern Ireland, the industrial wealth concentrated into the Lagan Valley complex in the north-east around Belfast focused on the industries of textiles, shipbuilding, engineering and foundry work, which were identified with British imperialism. None of the entrepreneurs who founded the great Belfast shipbuilding firms was Irish and most were born or at least educated in England and Scotland.[59] There was quick passage across the Irish Sea to Glasgow and an interchangeable workforce between Clydeside and Belfast. Protestantism, in some instances taking a virulent 'Orange' extremist form, was inextricably linked to local power and a commitment to Great Britain. The rejection, in 1893, of the Liberal administration's Second Irish Home Rule Bill by the House of Lords, largely made up, of course, of landed aristocrats, was one of the factors which led to more than a decade of Liberal electoral eclipse and with it a time-honoured acknowledgement of Irish nationalist aspirations and the need for some sort of devolved parliament.[60]

One of the great ironies surrounding the central place that theatre came to occupy in the early-twentieth-century narrative of Ireland's cultural revival was that the idea of the Irish Literary Theatre was conceived over tea in the elegant drawing room of a great house on a landed estate in County Galway in 1897.[61] Neither Yeats, Lady Gregory, nor Edward Martyn had any experience of, or interest in, contemporary Irish theatre. In common with all the modernist interventions which were made in British theatre during this period, the Irish Literary Theatre was consciously constructed in opposition to theatre as popular industrial practice.

Furthermore, as Lionel Pilkington has cogently argued, Yeats's brand of mystical nationalism was better accommodated within a political system of 'constructive unionism', where British and Irish interests (as in Scotland) could mesh together but still give Ireland some autonomy.[62] Heavily influenced by European modernism and equally at home in metropolitan intellectual circles, Yeats's Celtic Theatre could have been established in London rather than Dublin. Lady Gregory envisaged touring the new company to the 'theatreless' areas of the rural west.[63] In the event Irish National Theatre touring in Britain did exert a widespread influence on future theatre radicals. But it is clear from accounts in Pilkington and Morash, that the new movement came into being in Dublin supported in principle by wealthy, titled Anglo-Irish patronage and the protection of the British Lord-Lieutenant.[64]

For Morash, the Irish Literary Theatre came into being 'by imagining an empty space where in fact there was a crowded room'.[65] Dublin, in 1900, with no meaningful industrial base, had appalling living conditions for the labouring poor. Indeed, the urban adult mortality rate was the fifth highest in the world. Foster points out tartly that Irish intellectuals went in search of pure Gaelic values at a time when there was an almost complete absence of decent water or sanitation in the tenements of the proposed capital of an independent Ireland.[66] And yet a strong nationalistic drama for popular audiences had been provided along with ready access to the best of English and, indeed, American touring theatre.

From 1884 until 1907, English entrepreneur J. W. Wilson ran the Queen's Royal Theatre as the 'Home of Irish Drama'. As both playwright and manager, Wilson capitalised on the benefits of the touring system by forming his Queen's Royal Company, which staged his own popular Irish-themed romantic melodramas to vociferously engaged audiences in Dublin, and then reversing the English company trajectory by touring the shows 'buoyed by reports of genuine Irish applause' to Belfast and Cork and on to Glasgow, Manchester, Bristol and London. With New York or even Sydney as tour dates, Morash has calculated that there may have been a total of more than 2,000 performances seen world-wide by 3 million people. The multitudinous Irish diaspora would welcome familiar Irish actors.[67]

DIVERSE AUDIENCES

Potentially every member of the population whatever the nation of origin or ethnicity was a shareholder to a greater or lesser extent in what Denis Judd has dubbed 'Great Britain Ltd.'[68] Economic migration across national borders within the United Kingdom meant each of the large cities had a variety of 'British' communities of discrete cultural and religious identity. The largest and earliest industrial migration was from Ireland. Bernard Shaw lived in genteel poverty in London after his arrival in 1876, but many of his compatriots, especially those who provided the much needed labouring muscle for urban development, were herded into slum conditions for which they, rather than generalised social inequalities, were blamed. By the 1901 census, the numbers of Irish-born members of the population had declined from the post-potato-famine peaks of the 1840s and 50s. However, the census counted 426,565 in England and Wales and 205,064 in Scotland, with large settlements in each of the conurbations as well as the minor 'Waleston' South Wales conurbation.[69]

The other major influx in the late nineteenth century, which would ultimately impact on whole areas of British cultural life including theatre and the entertainment industry as a whole, came from large numbers of Jews fleeing anti-Semitic brutality and state authorised pogroms in Eastern Europe. Initially many were herded into sweatshops in London's East End where they quickly transformed mass garment manufacture. Eventually other communities formed in Manchester, in particular, as part of the textiles' industry, but also in cities such as Glasgow, Hull, Liverpool and Birmingham. By the First World War there were 300,000 Jews living in Britain.[70] A strong community culture developed very quickly including a flourishing Yiddish theatre first founded in London in 1884.[71]

The purchase of black people in Africa, to enable British manufacturers to process and trade raw materials produced in the colonies, meant that there was a not insignificant black population in Britain from the eighteenth century onwards, especially in the main slave-trade ports of Liverpool and Bristol.[72] The post-slavery recruitment of over 30 million people from the Indian subcontinent to work for imperial interests in East Africa, the Caribbean and other countries brought a gradual drift of other ethnic groupings into Britain.

However, the sheer volume of trade and shipping, which passed through the major ports at the end of the nineteenth century, brought much larger numbers of non-Europeans caught up on the coat-tails of imperial enterprise. Cardiff became a veritable melting pot of different ethnicities particularly in the Tiger Bay area of the town. For example, Somalian seamen started to arrive in Cardiff to work in the docks shortly after the opening of the Suez canal in 1869 and many settled and married. By the end of the twentieth century, Cardiff had the largest British-born Somali population in the UK.[73] In Tyneside, the Tyne Dock handling more than 6 million tons of coal and coke a year made South Shields a boom town with a burgeoning population. These included large numbers of Arabs initially employed in the gruelling work of firemen and stokers on ships docked at the Port of Aden in South-West Arabia which had been a British colony since 1839. By 1916 the town was second only to Cardiff as the home of British Arabs.[74]

It is difficult to estimate how far immigrant communities might have availed themselves of leisure opportunities in theatre and music hall except as individuals. Also, as many would have been employed in very low paid jobs, or as in the case of some workers, like the Somalis for example, may have been saving to fund a return to their homeland, even the cheapest seats may have seemed an unnecessary luxury. More likely cultural differences, festivals, religious observance and prohibitions, etc. would have meant that communities turned inwards for what leisure and social interaction they enjoyed.[75] Both amateur and professional Yiddish theatre was obviously a way of maintaining a reassuring cultural identity.

As already indicated, there were very considerable tensions in towns and cities where Irish communities were settled, not least due to anti-Catholic prejudices in strongly Protestant urban areas such as could (and can still) be found in Glasgow. But at a time of political and popular turbulence over the Home Rule campaign, commercial playwrights and music-hall sketch writers were still able to exploit the comic and roman-tic possibilities of stage Irish stereotypes albeit much modified since the assault of Dion Boucicault on their more viciously racist manifesta-tions. E. C. Matthews's *The Wexford Boys* played at the Grand Theatre in Liverpool in September 1899 after the Glasgow premiere. *Rogue Riley or The Four-leaved Shamrock* was staged at Her Majesty's in Aberdeen in 1894. Matthews's *The Wearin' o' the Green*, originally premiered by J. Wilson at the Queens Royal Theatre in 1896, was in 1900 enthusiastic-ally billed as 'An Irish Operatic Play devoid of politics … the Best played, Dressed and staged Irish play on the road.'

How far black incomers to British cities enjoyed the representation of black faces on the British stage is difficult to judge. Michael Pickering has outlined the development of the phenomenon of 'nigger' minstrelsy from the original American blackface acts of the late 1830s to the home-grown professional minstrel troupes, who became incorporated into large-scale variety extravaganzas which could be seen throughout Britain by the end of the century.[76] He argues that late Victorian representation veered between a narrow focus on stereotypical 'nigger' proclivities and 'darkie' sentimentalism as exemplified by perennially popular dramatisations of *Uncle Tom's Cabin.*[77] But what is clear from trade-paper advertising is that by 1900 'real' black people were performing in these shows and man-agers were benefiting from authentic representation of these exotic others. Certainly there is evidence of black performers advertising their availabil-ity for employment *as black* people.

IMPERIAL THEATRES

Arguably the best place to experience and share in the visible glamour of metropolitan and imperial prestige was in the auditoria of late-Victorian and Edwardian theatres. In the boom period of theatre building and refurbishment which lasted from the 1860s until shortly before the First World War, the majority of the Royals, Her/His Majesties', Grands and then – in a conjunction of two vigorous entrepreneurial spirits, Edward Moss and Oswald Stoll – the chain of Empire variety houses, bore the hallmarks of the two most important theatre architects of the mid- to late-Victorian period, C. J. Phipps and Frank Matcham.

Both men, as leaders of their profession based in London, contributed substantially to the theatrical growth of the metropolitan landscape especially in numerous suburban theatres and variety houses. But the scale of their activities across the whole of the British Isles (Matcham's work included the 1888 Grand Theatre in Douglas, Isle of Man) and the powerful physical impact of their theatres stamped a particular visual aesthetic, inflected by the social semiotics of the period, on at least two generations of theatre-workers and theatre-goers of all classes. These were the buildings that announced 'theatre' in the urban landscape of 1900. For the historian, the surviving buildings, several of which have been recently 'rescued' and restored for twenty-first-century audiences, are visual documents of industry and empire, which signify more than late-nineteenth-century theatre convention and artistic trends.

Phipps's first original theatre was the 1865 Nottingham Theatre Royal, which he subsequently enlarged to increase audience capacity in 1884 and 1890. The building with its colonnade of giant Corinthian columns still commands a dominant position at the top of central Nottingham's steep Market Street. By 1880, in addition to rebuilt or altered buildings in Bath, Brighton and Dumfries, there were nineteen Phipps's originals including theatres in Bristol, Swansea, Dublin, Edinburgh, Aberdeen, Liverpool, Cork and Derry. As with the Leeds Grand, French theatres of the eighteenth and mid-nineteenth centuries were influential in the creation of what Victor Glasstone has described as 'a solemn, seemingly solid dignity quite different from the slender gimcrack feel of earlier English interiors'. Dignity and restraint in auditorium decoration, which, Glasstone explains, was always applied in low relief, were repeated in exteriors which confidently deployed classical architectural motifs. To quote Glasstone again, these were civic buildings 'of undeniable theatrical character' which 'made an important contribution to the Victorian street scene'. Phipps could be relied upon to create an ambience of appropriate cultural gravitas as the tensions of moral disapproval began to recede.[78]

The majority of Phipps's projects were 'straight' theatres undertaken prior to the 1890s when the construction of more socially and architecturally ambitious music halls and then variety theatres began. Frank

Matcham's working life spanned the whole of the boom period and moved effortlessly between legitimate and 'illegitimate', straight and variety. By 1912 he had begun to design cinemas and also pubs. An 'unacademic' architect who took over his father-in-law's practice the year of the 1878 Metropolis Management and Buildings Act Amendment, which provided a detailed regulatory framework for theatre architects, Matcham like so many Victorian creative engineers combined imaginative genius with a strongly practical understanding of the technical challenges of construction, acoustics and sightlines.

Victor Glasstone describes his 'remarkable grasp of the three-dimensional possibilities of auditorium design, using every trick to achieve maximum effect: dipping balconies, stage boxes stepping down and set forwards and backwards to better the sight line; the whole composition awash with a cornucopia of drapery and decoration, often architecturally "illiterate", but completely convincing and of a piece'.[79] In the collection of essays published about him in 1980 it is estimated that 80 of his original theatre designs were built; he was responsible for 30 major alterations of existing theatres and contributed significant work on some 30 more.

If the last three decades of the nineteenth century, which saw Queen Victoria declared Empress of India in 1876, can be considered the high noon of British imperialism, then Matcham's flamboyant, gilded palaces of recreation were arguably the most successful means by which audiences from all but the most underprivileged sector of society could come together in one place to celebrate, enjoy or simply gawp at the iconography of imperial opulence and exoticism. To be sure social segregation, as manifested in the physical compartmentalisation of stalls, pit, dress circle gallery, together with separate entrances and staged ticket barriers or segregated box offices, remained essential. It is well understood that the curved horseshoe circles of the typical Victorian theatre permitted display of the audience to each other. Marvin Carlson has pointed out that the development of the 'gods', as the uppermost gallery was dubbed, permitted access to the relatively poor, but also allowed them to view at a suitable distance the visible wealth and civic dignity on display below them.[80]

A Matcham or Matcham-influenced theatre played freely with a range of exotic influences, taking audiences on a virtual journey through European baroque and rococo and onwards to the eastern outposts of empire.[81] A frequent epithet applied to the decor is 'Moorish', and it seems no coincidence that the chain of variety theatres he built for Edward Moss and Oswald Stoll were 'Empires'. The Edinburgh Empire was decorated with any number of golden elephants and Nubian riders. As Christopher Morash acknowledges, the Grand Opera House in Belfast which Matcham built in 1895 remains (despite the best efforts of Republican bombers) Ireland's most opulent theatre. Described by the Theatres Trust as 'the best surviving example in the UK of the Oriental style applied to theatre architecture', the largely Indian-inspired features include, along with the large elephant heads, 'an elaborate composition of superimposed boxes surmounted by turban-domed canopies'. The exterior in brick and cast stone is a mixture of baroque, Flemish and oriental allusions.[82] When Annie Horniman, whose wealth financed the Abbey Theatre, turned away from Dublin to set up the first regional producing theatre company run on repertory lines in Manchester in 1907, she asked Matcham to refurbish the Gaiety Theatre.[83]

IMPERIAL DISJUNCTIONS

In October 1900, in the so-called Khaki general election, the Conservative and Unionist Party won a landslide victory largely on the back of the patriotic fervour generated by apparent military triumph in South Africa. In the Second Boer War, the last of Britain's directly imperial wars, the enemy was not a rabble of recalcitrant natives, but an alarmingly well-equipped (by Germany) and devastatingly effective Boer army.[84] At the beginning of the year, the news of a succession of humiliating defeats had created a crisis in business confidence. An editorial in *The Stage* on 8 February sought to allay fears raised by an alarmist report in the *Daily Mail* that more than 40 theatre companies were to forgo tours in the aftermath of the news of heavy casualties.

The *Mail*, founded in 1897 by Alfred Harmsworth (later Lord Northcliffe), was the first of a new kind of popular newspaper aimed at growing numbers of better educated and more self-confident members of the skilled working class and the new breed of service-industry workers, in retail, clerical and secretarial jobs that had also begun to include more women.[85] The *Mail*'s coverage of the Boer War, standing 'for the power, the supremacy and the greatness of the British Empire', sent sales rocketing in 1899 to over a million.[86]

Notwithstanding the need to address business-limiting reportage, theatre providers were anxious to ally themselves with patriotic enthusiasm. In the autumn of 1899 and early 1900, *The Era* devoted substantial column inches to emphasising the profession's contribution to the war effort. The extraordinary popularity of 'The Absent Minded Beggar', a poem urging succour for 'a gentleman in khaki ordered South' by Rudyard Kipling with music by Arthur Sullivan which Harmsworth commissioned, provided an excellent vehicle for performance at fund-raising events.[87] 'Pass the hat for your credit's sake, and pay-pay-pay', declaimed from the stages of theatres as far apart as Wigan and Southampton, swelled the coffers of the various funds set up to aid not just the British refugees in the Transvaal and the families of soldiers, but in the case of the *Daily Mail* fund, the fighting men themselves.

In the event an ignominious peace was negotiated in 1902 after which Afrikanerdom emerged relatively unscathed, and the British government, its imperial policy undermined, began the descent towards the electoral defeat in 1905 and 1906 which returned the Liberals to power. To a certain extent the Boer War demonstrated the collective strength of the empire in terms of troops sent by the other white colonies and black African soldiers who fought on the British side. But financially the war cost more than all the other nineteenth-century imperial wars put together.[88] Also as is well known, attempts to recruit for the war from the British working population had revealed shocking evidence of substandard physical fitness caused by poor living conditions and inadequate nutrition. The detailed demographic analyses contained in Charles Booth's *Life and Labour of the People in London*, published between 1889 and 1903, and Seebohm Rowntree's *Poverty: A Study of Town Life*, published in 1901 and based on research in York, showed that almost 30 per cent of the population were living in what Rowntree defined as primary or secondary poverty.[89]

These facts mean that there needs to be a careful consideration of the possible social composition of theatre audiences and what kind of theatres they attended. The 30 per cent of the population who lived in primary or secondary poverty and chronic employment uncertainty, would have struggled to pay even the 4d 'popular price' for a seat in the gallery. A wage quoted in 1901 for a York carter with a wife and two children, was given as twenty shillings a week with three shillings spent on rent.[90] Given the living conditions described in the reports, however, access to light, colour and warmth may have made the expenditure worthwhile. The 4d (four pennies) appears to have been the cheapest in the variety theatre venues, while the 'legit' theatres tended to charge 6d for the gallery and were generally slightly more expensive. The Tyne Theatre in Newcastle charged anything between £3 3s. and £1 1s. for a private box and 6s. for the dress circle, reserved orchestra stalls were 5s., Upper Circle 2s. and the Pit 1s.

Much more likely, the poor would have enjoyed the fit-ups and portables which, as we have seen, were still thick on the ground and did their
best to emulate the decor of the 'proper' theatres. The recollections of
George Hewins, who was born in 1879 and worked most of his life as an
agricultural and building labourer in Stratford-upon-Avon, included an
anecdote about travelling theatre about the time he was rejected as unfit
to fight the Boers. '"The threepenny gaff" we'd call it. We had all the
murders there was: *The Polish Jew, Maria Marten in the Red Barn*. It was
in a tent with steps up the sides.'[91]

The Austin Theatre travelled around Northumberland mining villages
between the 1890s and the First World War, piling scenery and hampers
onto open carts drawn by shire horses. Entertaining Durham miners with
carefully scheduled performances, including morning shows, to fit in with
work shifts, the theatre itself was constructed with a canvas roof held by
guy ropes and side panels of polished mahogany. There were red tip-up
best seats in the front and 'heavy red-plush curtains draped artistically
with tassels and baubles'.[92]

Records from the other end of the audience spectrum include the scrapbooks of performances attended between 1900 and 1950 and carefully
assembled by Dr Andrew Smith (*c*. 1885–1951), a comfortably-off Newcastle
general practitioner who appears to have gone to the theatre at least weekly.
The first volume of scrapbooks, dating from 24 October 1900 until the
end of the pantomime season (he saw several) in 1904–5, records 176 visits
to local theatres including the Theatre Royal, the Grand, the Tyne, the
Olympia and the Palace. Indeed, when Frank Benson's company came to
the Tyne Theatre with five Shakespearean plays for the week beginning
22 October 1900, Dr Smith appears to have seen them all.

He enjoyed the standard eclectic programme of straight drama and
musical comedy offered by an important No. 1 circuit which included
Irving in Arthur Conan Doyle's *Waterloo* and Charles Reade's *The Lyons
Mail*, the Kendals in *The Secret Orchard* by Egerton Castle, George
Edwardes's Company in *San Toy or, The Emperor's Own* (which he saw
several times) and *Kitty Grey*. He saw Lily Langtry and George Alexander
and a lot of Gilbert and Sullivan courtesy of the D'Oyly Carte Company.
It is also interesting to see that in the same time period he visited theatres
in Glasgow, Manchester, Douglas, Isle of Man and Llandudno. He also
saw fifteen shows in London.[93]

Increasingly late-Victorian and then Edwardian society was being
made aware of the huge disparity between rich and poor – the disjunction
between a slum dwelling in York which had no sink or running water and

shared pails and a midden privie between several families, and a household where a dinner with eight or ten courses was not unusual.[94] Not least
there were worries about the calibre of 'the imperial race'. The 1900 election returned Lord Salisbury to power, but it also saw the self-educated
Scottish miner, Keir Hardy of the Labour Representation Committee,
returned as the first socialist MP for the South Wales mining town of
Merthyr Tydfil: an augury of the first welfare reforms which would be
introduced later in the decade.[95]

Theatre in 1900, at the interface between two centuries, represented
the paradoxes and deep fault lines which ran through British society. At
one end it catered for a population which was still largely working class
and largely dependent on the continuing prosperity of heavy industry for
their livelihood.[96] This sector was now, as a result of a series of Education
Acts introduced since 1870, able to access free compulsory education at
a basic level. George Hewins could read. Working hours had improved,
although young women in solitary domestic service could still toil for
twelve hours a day.[97]

Trade union membership reached 2 million by 1900 after the decade
since the great dock strike of 1889 had shown that disciplined industrial action could achieve employer concessions towards better pay and
conditions.[98] However, this represented a little under 11 per cent of those
in employment. There was no automatic association of trade unionism
with socialism which tended to be rooted in Christian teaching rather
than Marx. But the older tradition of working-class self-education and
Nonconformist moral earnestness created the condition for new recreational and educational initiatives which would have implications for
theatre as cultural practice outside accepted industrial imperatives.[99]

But it should be emphasised, that for all the public displays of imperial enthusiasm in 1900, along with predictable pro-Boer activism in
Ireland and parts of Wales, the Khaki Election result was based on a
minority vote. A total of 3,262,696 votes were cast from a population
of 37 million. No women had the vote, and because of the complica-
tions of registration and franchise rights based on property ownership
or proof of one-year residence in rented accommodation, a significant
proportion of adult males were also disenfranchised.[100] Power was still
firmly in the hands of landed aristocracy and old vested interests. The
audiences glimpsed leaving theatres on the Strand in London's West
End in 1901 – 'My lady and her guest, in a splendour of diamonds and
low-necked dresses half-hidden under loose cloaks … my lord and his
guest, plainer, but no less immaculately garbed'[101] – embodied the other

end of the industrial continuum to which 'provincial' theatres could only aspire.

In *Industry and Empire*, Eric Hobsbawm ascribes the origins of Britain's industrial and imperial decline to a complacent adherence to patterns of industrialisation, which had once been revolutionary, but which by the beginning of the twentieth century were 'visibly archaic'.[102] 'Younger' industrial nations, in particular the USA and Germany, had caught up with the pioneers and were now racing ahead in scientific and technological innovation. Although British industries like shipbuilding and coal mining continued to expand up until the First World War – and may thus account for the continuing growth in regional building-based theatre speculation – the fault lines which would ultimately bring about collapse, and thus personal catastrophe for thousands of workers, were already apparent.

Furthermore, while in the mid-nineteenth century it may have appeared that the balance of economic power was beginning to shift northwards, by the new century as London's population continued to grow, it was becoming clear that metropolitan power had found new sources of energy. As Townsend explains, the industries which would start to expand – motor vehicles, electrical engineering, chemicals and pharmaceuticals – favoured not the old resource-based locations, but areas such as West London, Oxford or the West Midlands.[103] The service sector, which includes theatre, increased its share of national employment to almost 40 per cent by 1911, and this tended to concentrate in London and the South-East.[104] Over the first half of the twentieth century a completely new topography would emerge.

CHAPTER 2

Structures of management

Theatre at the beginning of the twentieth century flourished within a market economy predicated on a belief in the moral virtues of free enterprise and individuation. Theatre, especially building-based theatre, requires capital investment and sufficient working revenue in order to survive. If the primary function of theatre practitioners is to create and market a product of sufficient quality and/or popular appeal to make it financially self-sufficient, then clearly the law of the survival of the fittest seems entirely rational. The historian of the comparatively obscure Alexandra Theatre, opened in Birmingham in 1901 and run as an independent family business until 1968, dubbed the commercial imperative which shaped employees' lives the 'if-it' principle: 'what didn't come in to the box-office couldn't go out in the players' pockets'.[1] The overwhelming majority of professional theatre ventures operated on that basis until well into the 1950s.

If, however, a theatre is envisaged as a concrete embodiment of the cultural prestige of a nation which is expressed in terms of intellectual and artistic excellence and innovation, or if it functions as an *exemplary* instrument of social *betterment* and change, then achieving and maintaining a secure resource base, certainly in the prevailing political and economic climate of the early twentieth century, required a seismic shift in the national *mentalité*. Harley Granville Barker, who published *The Exemplary Theatre* in 1922 when he had pretty much given up active theatre practice, described his ideal theatre in evangelical terms. It would be like a chapel:

this new meeting house ... with its doctrines worked out in a human medium, its range from past to future, its analysis in method and synthesis in effect ... will be, by virtue of the unity in diversity for which it might strive, a microcosm, not only of the social world as it moves, laughs, weeps before our eyes, but as it has a sublimer being in the souls of men ... [2]

This passionate language, from a man who had earned his living in theatre since the age of fourteen, published with the critic William Archer a realistic costing of all the practical components of a national theatre project, and formed business partnerships with leading entrepreneurs such as J. E. Vedrenne[3] and Charles Frohman in order to establish his ideal theatre, was not untypical. For those who worked for a theatre that prioritised art over commerce and were convinced that an intelligent, challenging dialogue with audiences could effect social change, the campaign was akin to a crusade.

ECONOMIC CHANGE AND INDUSTRIAL PRACTICE

The practical implications of the concept of not-for-profit based as it is on altruism and the voluntary relinquishing of pecuniary advantage for the sake of the advancement of civil society, took the campaign for what William Archer termed 'an endowed theatre'[4] into the disputed territory of economic independence. The small group of metropolitan actor-managers, who achieved pre-eminent status amongst their contemporaries and in the subsequent annals of theatre history, did so because they projected the image of highly successful entrepreneurial artists and astute business men. Part of the glamour derived from the perception of their individuality and their ability to exercise independent managerial power. Furthermore in the emotionally charged, labour-intensive environment of the producing theatre, they effectively presided as patriarchs commanding great loyalty to what was analogous to a traditional Victorian family firm offering substantial employment opportunities. Alan Hughes has calculated that for Irving's 1899 production of Sardou's *Robespierre* there were probably 639 employees on the payroll, 284 of whom worked backstage or in administration and finance. The collapse of such a firm, which the formation of a limited liability company that same year unsuccessfully sought to stave off, was of no small consequence.[5]

Tracy Davis has sought to refute the myth that the final phase of Irving's career was destroyed by a grasping commercial syndicate which took over the lease of the Lyceum in 1899.[6] The Lyceum had been operating in deficit since 1896, bailed out only by Irving's relentless national and international touring. The 1898 fire which destroyed the bulk of his under-insured and irreplaceable scenery store was the final straw. Thus the decision, to surrender his independence to the overall control of a syndicate, registered as the Lyceum Theatre Company Ltd., prepared to invest in him and the theatre itself while not actually bankrupting themselves, was entirely rational. As a professional who had throughout his career supported the principle of the free market, Irving understood the nature of both commercial risk and economic necessity. By 1905 when he collapsed and died on tour in Bradford, it was clear that what he and the lavish resources of his independent management of the Lyceum represented were literally irrecoverable.

In the wider economy, the move from the dynamically led individual or family firm to the collective and finally the corporate enterprise, began with the series of Companies Acts put on the statute books between 1844 and 1867, which encouraged the establishment of first joint stock companies, and then limited liability companies. In charting the rise of the corporate economy, Leslie Hannah describes the benefits of 'a relatively cheap company form' for manufacturing industry that for my purposes can be extended to would-be theatre builders, investors and providers:

The facility of joint stock was more convenient than either a full partnership or the deposit of money with a firm, since the shares were readily transferable and rights to control which they carried strengthened the security of the investor. Finally with the granting of limited liability, the joint stock investor was also relieved of the responsibility for the whole of the debts of the firms in which he held shares.[7]

By the end of the nineteenth century, the growing confidence in limited liability as a practical business strategy meant that local investors could form into syndicates to take advantage of the theatre boom in the provision of new buildings and the maintenance of existing managements. It could be used as a way of salvaging the artistic product in the face of business failure, and, with a judicious balance of financial acumen, local networks of goodwill and artistic expertise, it could offer both new opportunity and greater security. However, as a mechanism to encourage more dynamic and profitable business practice, it could also be used to generate very large profits from centrally controlled, but widely distributed artistic product.

In the macro-economic sphere, the advance of industrial modernity was creating larger corporate structures that from a positive perspective offered more inclusive access to a wider range of high-quality resources to a greater proportion of the population. More controversially, however, the growth of the corporate economy from earlier joint stock origins thrived on opportunistic tendencies to centralise, homogenise and, above all, monopolise resources. In theatre on both sides of the for-profit/not-for-profit debate, the rise of dominant corporate theatre providers like Moss' Empires in the variety sector, and Howard & Wyndham in legitimate theatre, challenged entrepreneurial independence and innovation.

Furthermore, in the long term, this monopolistic model of theatre provision, proved vulnerable to newer, even more economically efficient and equally dominant kinds of provision based on technological innovation.

The other factor that is relevant to the study of theatre as industrial practice at the turn of the century is that the ethical basis of economic activity was coming under increasing pressure and was subject to a variety of ideological perspectives. Victorian Liberalism, resistant to emergent socialism and the doctrine of state intervention, legitimised competition in its allegiance to laissez-faire, but at the same time extolled the Christian virtues of individual philanthropy. 'New Liberalism' bolstered by a strategic alliance with the Parliamentary Labour Party founded in 1906 – the year of the landslide Liberal electoral victory – recognised the need for more interventionist policies to ensure the more equitable distribution of the nation's resources. The legislation which followed brought free school meals, old age pensions, labour exchanges and national insurance. However, as H. C. G. Matthew has pointed out, 'refurbished' Liberalism 'was an attempt to justify the free-market system by making it work "fairly"; it attempted a rationalization of capitalism, not its replacement'.[8] Early-twentieth-century British socialism was at a considerable distance from a Marxist ideology based on class conflict and collective revolution. There was no pressure within the British theatre, for example, to set up the 'People's Theatres', which were already operating in Europe, most notably in France and Germany.[9]

It is thus within the attempts to rationalise and humanise the harshest effects of capitalism that the structures that enabled theatre practice on a professional level need to be examined. It is also important to recognise that the rhetoric of not-for-profit obscured a more complex relationship with commerce and wider economic trends. The oft-quoted statement made by Barry Jackson, who was one of the most important of the private patrons of British theatre, that 'art has no possible relation to money',[10] is manifestly untrue – a fact borne out by his own management record. Historians, however, have continued to set up a binary opposition between moneymaking and art which ignores the reality of the way in which theatre practice in its different forms evolved and was sustained.

NEW MODELS OF MANAGEMENT

The 'if-it' principle operated at its most brutal in the grass-roots touring companies where bad management could result in desperate circumstances. There was the phenomenon of the 'bogus' manager, who typically would recruit a company of actors, demand an initial 'premium' from them, and then abscond with whatever profits had been made leaving the company stranded far from home. There were other simply-incompetent managers. In 1902/3, Ben Iden Payne, who was destined to become the first director of Miss Horniman's Manchester Repertory Theatre Company, was employed in Ian Maclaren's touring Shakespearean Company: weekly salaries were rarely paid in full and then not made up when coffers were replenished. If there were no bookings there were no salaries at all. Unsurprisingly the tour petered out.[11]

Psychologically the emotionally affective properties of theatre are likely to attract the entrepreneurial risk-taking spirit, and anecdotes of 'rogues and vagabonds' add raffish glamour and retrospective amusement to the popular historical record, but gloss over the social realities of haphazard and as yet unorganised working practices. In the case of colourful characters such as Frank Benson and Ben Greet, historians have been happy to accept constructed images of loveable eccentricity, derived from evidence of wilful insouciance of attitude to business imperatives, without considering what their surprisingly durable career trajectories might reveal about changing patterns of management.

Greet died intestate in 1936 with a total of £127 to his name,[12] but in his heyday, his companies were very familiar on the touring circuits and offered early career opportunities to numerous actors including Mrs Patrick Campbell, Lillah McCarthy and Janet Achurch. Indeed, in 1896 he set up the Ben Greet Academy of Acting in London where students such as Sybil and Russell Thorndike received training before going on to act with his company. His first company was formed in 1883, followed in 1886 by the touring Woodland Players, which launched the enduringly-popular professional outdoor 'pastoral' Shakespeare. Greet's biographer credits him as the first actor-manager to tour West End successes to small towns across Great Britain with as many as 25 fit-up companies travelling under his banner. With his brother William Greet, he profited from regional tours of *The Sign of the Cross*, and he also toured and played a range of English classical repertoire roles with the Ben Greet Comedy Company. Having, as the actor Allan Wilkie put it in a centenary memoir, 'no head for financial detail … when his affairs became hopelessly tangled in 1902 he transferred some of his activities to America'.[13]

The transfer of 'some' of Greet's 'activities' to America was in fact facilitated by Charles Frohman, then arguably one of the most powerful proprietor-entrepreneurs in New York and London and the producer in the modern sense of J. M. Barrie's *Peter Pan*. Greet's highly successful 'Elizabethan Stage Society of England' American tour of William Poel's production of *Everyman* followed the example of formerly more prestigious actor-managers including Charles Kean and Irving, who had bolstered shrinking home revenue in the lucrative market provided by appreciative international audiences. Thereafter Greet's companies regularly toured in North America appearing in Broadway theatres, and giving performances at Harvard University and the White House for Theodore Roosevelt. As Charlotte Canning has explained, simple staging of Shakespeare, classic English comedies including *She Stoops to Conquer* and the powerful religious impact of *Everyman* made Greet's repertoire and outdoor tradition ideal for the 'education and uplift' provided at the summer camps of the Circuit Chautauqua.[14]

The insistence that Greet did not care about money and had 'no head for financial detail' contributes to the biographical image of the genial artist unencumbered by gross material interests. It also belies the sheer operational complexity of his touring pattern, which would have required an extensive support network to sustain, and at the very least some measure of financial acumen. His brother William, who retired from the Royal Marine Artillery in 1877 as a lieutenant, went on to manage a number of London theatres including the Savoy where he was lessee from 1901 to 1903. He was one of the original members of the TMA in 1894.[15] His association from 1890 until 1914 with the Lyric Theatre, where Wilson Barrett first staged *The Sign of the Cross* in 1895, started with the role of business manager and treasurer until in 1896 he became lessee and manager. As the manager of Greet's Northern No. 1 company tour of *The Sign of the Cross*, his expertise would have contributed to the family interests.[16] Harriet Greet, sister to Ben and William, also toured with Greet's companies as business manager. Niece and nephew Daisy and Maurice Robinson were long-term company members. William Greet died in 1914, the same year Ben went to direct at the Old Vic under Lilian Baylis.

Obviously William Greet's managerial career could be regarded as part of a family enterprise, albeit one that developed without any previous theatrical tradition. Like so many new entrants to the profession in the mid to late nineteenth century including Beerbohm Tree, Alexander and Wyndham, the social origins of the Greets were solidly middle class. Greet *père* was a distinguished naval captain. However, while Ben Greet was very much the model of the old-style actor-manager, his brother's career trajectory represented a comparatively new departure. The role of the professional theatre

manager concentrating on business and administration emerges as part of a
new professional sector within industrial practice as a whole.

In Frank Benson's case, formal business structures secured his survival in the face of intractable debts exacerbated by the 1899 fire at the
Newcastle Theatre Royal, which destroyed most of his completely unin-
sured costumes and properties, and subsequently an ill-advised attempt
to mount a prestigious London season. Benson's scheme to attract
shareholders in his National Drama Company, set up to finance his
London venture, collapsed owing substantial sums to the investors. The
F. R. Benson Company Ltd., registered in 1901 and administered from
London, enabled his more prudent colleagues, including the actor Otho
Stuart who was a major creditor and co-director, to regulate his affairs.[17]

By 1910–11, however, Benson's commitment to deliver the annual
Shakespeare Festival at the Shakespeare Memorial Theatre was coming
under increasing strain as he got deeper and deeper into debt. The response
from the governors of the SMT was to form a syndicate to take over and
rename Benson's company The Stratford-upon-Avon Players Ltd. Benson
was thereafter employed as 'dramatic and artistic expert' on a weekly salary of £20 plus a percentage of the profits.[18] The syndicate and the company were wound up in 1914 on the outbreak of war, and by 1919 Benson's
association with Stratford was at an end. Benson, who continued touring
right up until 1932, was by no means the only old-style actor-manager
criss-crossing the British Isles throughout the interwar period. But at the
Shakespeare Memorial Theatre, the principle of the owners (who were the
members of the founding Flower family) and governors directly employing a resident company with an artistic director had emerged as a viable
managerial model.

THE OWNERSHIP OF THEATRE

Given the early-twentieth-century context of rapid building expansion,
the issue of how theatres were owned and/or controlled, and for what
reason, is important to an understanding of how industrial practice both
for-profit and not-for-profit developed and changed. There is, as Tracy
Davis has pointed out, confusion surrounding ownership, and the indiscriminate use of the term 'manager'[19] also tends to conflate a range of
operational roles. The listings in both *The Era* and *The Stage* persistently
blur the distinction between manager and proprietor and fail to make
clear where a separate individual or a group of shareholders had rights of
ownership over the primary capital asset.

In London, at the beginning of the century, the famous building-based actor-managements were generally maintained in theatres held on long-term leases. Much of the land on which theatres in central London were built was owned by the Crown or aristocratic families, and the lessee of the theatre, depending on the origins of the bricks and mortar, might not be the proprietor. A lessee was the 'actual and responsible manager' to whom the theatre licence was granted by the licensing authorities.[20] He/she was responsible for the ground rent, the conduct and condition of the building, and frequently spent large sums in refurbishment. Other would-be managers might then purchase a short-term lease or sub-lease as tenants, but would not be the licence holder, still less the proprietor. Irving handed over the remaining eighteen years of the Lyceum lease when the Lyceum Theatre Company Ltd. was set up. George Alexander leased the St James's Theatre from the proprietor the Earl of Kilmorey who owned the land.[21] Actor-managers such as Herbert Beerbohm Tree, and Charles Wyndham and Mary Moore who became proprietors and lessees of newly built theatres had to raise significant amounts of capital not only for the bricks and mortar but also to ensure the payment of annual ground rent. In 1897 Tree and his wife Maud were able to gather a number of wealthy investors, including the Anglo-German financier Ernest Cassel, Lord Rothschild and the banker Carl Meyer, to form The Playhouse Ltd. to finance Her Majesty's Theatre with capital composed of debentures. Tree's debentures amounted to £10,000 for a structure which cost just over £55,000.[22] Wyndham and Moore who built Wyndhams Theatre in 1899 and the New Theatre in 1903 on land owned by the Salisbury family also benefited from investment by a syndicate of wealthy friends who included at least two millionaires.[23]

What subsequently became important for the future of producing managements in London, which in turn, because of the nature of the core–periphery relationship across the UK had implications for regional theatre, was how theatre ownership was transferred. By the time Tree died in 1917, Oscar Asche, as the writer, producer and star of the legendary and immensely profitable *Chu Chin Chow*, was installed at His Majesty's as actor-manager for a run which lasted until 1921. His relationship to the building, however, was as a tenant-impresario renting the theatre, albeit with a production which, to their mutual benefit, had been partially financed by Tree.

In 1919 the theatre had passed into the hands of Grossmith & Laurillard Ltd., which became Grossmith & Malone Ltd. in 1921.[24] Between 1923 and 1926, Grossmith, a celebrated star and producer of musical comedy, was the licensed joint lessee with Malone. Eventually the named lessees became less recognisable while the long-term lease was owned by Associated Theatre Properties Ltd.[25] The next notably successful long run at His Majesty's was Noël Coward's 1929 musical *Bitter Sweet*, produced by the impresario C. B. Cochran, but again as a tenant of the theatre's more anonymous proprietors. Arguably a free-wheeling commercial buccaneer like Cochran benefited from this constantly shifting scene. His entire producing career blithely crossed every 'theatre' boundary from boxing matches and rodeo to intimate revue and musicals, and then on to introducing Eugene O'Neill to London audiences in 1923, and taking on Sean O'Casey's *The Silver Tassie* in 1929 after Yeats rejected it.[26]

Virtually every history of London theatre in the post-First World War period refers to the fact that as land values and theatre rents rose dramatically, building ownership or long-term lesseeship passed out of the hands of creative artists to business interests which profited from subleasing theatres to short-term producing managements. It became too difficult to survive within the narrow profit margins typically associated with individual actor building-management, and although war brought a boom in theatre attendance, in London especially, it also brought other economic constraints and pressures. On the whole managements did not seek to exploit audiences through raised ticket prices, and in any case the Entertainments Tax skimmed away additional profit. Introduced as an Amusements Tax in 1916, the original proposal was for a levy which ranged from 1d on tickets priced between 3d and 11d, to 6d on 10/6d tickets. The 1917 Finance Act increased the tax yielding the Exchequer some £5,000,000 and despite TMA lobbying, it remained in place after the war.[27]

While cinema, by then expanding even more rapidly, was also subject, at the point of delivery, to the tax, industrial reliance on human resources was minimal compared with theatre, and was less affected by the rising cost of raw materials including paper essential for publicity. Other wartime restrictions such as the ban on the sale of sweets after 8 p.m. – a total ban was imposed in 1918 – and the closure of bars after 9 p.m. also placed more pressure on sources of revenue for the less stable managements which lost heavily. In 1914 while some twenty theatres closed nations-wide, roughly the same number opened. Thereafter closures outnumbered new openings, which steadily declined.

Investment in the theatrical product in the hopes of a handsome return had always been essential to commercial survival. After the war what had been managed more discreetly within gentlemanly, and indeed gentlewomanly, circles, became more overtly speculative as rival sources of entertainment increased. The time-honoured, long-term expectations associated with settled artistic managements faded. New producing managements focused on the London market, operating with subleases, could come and go very quickly, and the artistic product lost the durability on which the regional touring system was based. By 1925, at the first TMA conference, concern was being expressed that the short plays, which then made up the bulk of the contemporary drama on offer in the London theatre, were simply not suitable for an evening in a regional theatre where the time frame for work-leisure balance differed from the metropolis.[28] The twice-nightly system of performance, which attempted some of the flexibility offered by cinema, had begun to be introduced before the First World War. By 1916 even some of the No. 1 touring theatres had taken this route to maintain profitability.[29]

There was some front-line independence in metropolitan theatre derived from building ownership. The Wyndham Theatres Ltd., which was registered in 1900 and also controlled the Criterion Theatre where Charles Wyndham had been a famous lessee, remained essentially a family firm and became the most important independent grouping in the London theatre. The actress Mary Moore, the widow of the dramatist James Albery, became Charles Wyndham's formidable second wife and managed his theatres after his death in 1919. These were then passed on to her son Bronson Albery and stepson Howard Wyndham. Out of this second generation emerged professional managers whose entrepreneurial skills had been honed through prolonged, active engagement in theatre practice at the highest level. Bronson Albery was a trained solicitor as well as a theatre owner prepared to engage with artistically ambitious work. In addition to his co-management at the three theatres, he helped set up the Arts Theatre Club in 1927. His entrepreneurial partnerships with actors including Lewis Casson and Sybil Thorndike, and later John Gielgud, contributed to the growth of a new metropolitan acting aristocracy.[30]

METROPOLITAN MANAGEMENT AND THE
EXEMPLARY THEATRE

Access to a suitable theatre in London was assumed to be crucial to attempts to launch an artistically innovative, fully-professional and, above all, autonomous management for theatre radicals, but within the complex economic context described above, this proved impossible to sustain long-term. Harley Granville Barker's experiments in repertory at the Court

(1904–7), the Savoy (1907–8) and the Duke of York's (1909–10) were either dependent on a successful partnership with a commercial impresario/ entrepreneur or, after finance for a short-term lease had been wheedled out of wealthy patrons, in management with his wife Lillah McCarthy. Both he and Shaw subsidised the work out of their own pockets as indeed did the actors who took part in productions for payment far below their usual professional rate. Shaw lost very heavily when he contributed to the short-lived Barker–Vedrenne management at the Savoy. At the Court where the long-term lessee was J. H. Leigh, the partnership, with Barker as artistic director and Vedrenne as business manager, anticipated the later model which became commonplace in producing theatre. As is well known the venture established Shaw as the most celebrated British playwright of his generation and set new standards of excellence in ensemble performance. The experiments foundered, however, in the disjunction in the perception of where value in the artistic product lay. Short runs of challenging plays or the more complicated operational model of true repertory – two or three plays rotating in any one week needed good storage and stage man-agement facilities, as well as an organised and receptive audience – ran counter to a business model which needed to exploit artistic success for economic survival.[31]

Personal subsidy and risk combined with wealthy individual patron-age form a recurrent pattern in early attempts to resist the profit-making imperative in metropolitan building-management. In her 1937 autobiography Gertrude Kingston describes the 'artistic London' of her youth as 'small navigable society' where it was possible to be 'com-muted' into 'a circle of people who *did* things'.[32] In her case, as with Lena Ashwell and Lillah McCarthy, all three professional actresses who worked with the top London managements were members of a social elite, which included members of the aristocracy and leading politi-cians. Leases or subleases seem to have circulated amongst individuals familiar with each others' interests. The Savoy Theatre had been built for Richard D'Oyly Carte, and his widow Helen, who was known to be a very astute business woman, was lessee 1903–4 and 1906–11.[33] During Lena Ashwell's brief period of Savoy management in 1906, however, J. E. Leigh was officially the lessee. Ashwell's opportunity to purchase the long lease and refurbish the Great Queen Street Theatre, which she renamed the Kingsway, came in 1907 via a gift from a wealthy, anonymous female patron, which ultimately embroiled her in an intractable personal indebtedness. This only exacerbated the strain caused by falling box office receipts.[34] The commitment to short runs of plays by new authors, which included the highly successful *Diana of Dobson's* by Cicely Hamilton, with advice and assistance by other sympathetic managers such as Alexander and then Frohman, who at one point engaged most of her company, still left her with the burden of the long lease which she sold in 1916.[35]

The history of her lesseeship is made more complex by the fact that in 1912 the Kingsway became the transfer venue for Shaw's *Fanny's First Play*, which under a Barker–Lillah McCarthy management sublease premiered at Gertrude Kingston's Little Theatre in 1911 and eventually (pace the bias against long runs) clocked up a total of 622 performances.[36] Kingston built the Little Theatre in 1910 inside the shell of Coutts's former banking hall in the Adelphi. The first to be built for the 'theatre of ideas',[37] the simply raked rectangular auditorium allowed uninterrupted focus on the stage. At first seating just 309, the Little was perfect for audience as 'congregation' prepared to see rarely performed classical drama, and new plays presented in runs of flexible length by dramatists (including Shaw) who were to remain theoretically anonymous. McCarthy's purchase of a sublease in 1911, by which point Kingston was experiencing financial difficulty, was enabled by a cash donation of £1,000 from Lord Howard de Walden. When Kingston proposed to raise the rent for the Little, McCarthy purchased another sublease for the Kingsway. Again de Walden provided finance.[38] Ultimately the war put paid to Barker's hopes that the Kingsway might prove a permanent solution to his managerial aspirations. The Little Theatre itself suffered bomb damage and Kingston relinquished the lease in 1915.

WEALTHY MEN AND WEALTHY WOMEN

While de Walden was only one of the wealthy theatre aficionados who gave assistance to needy artists, he may well have been the most spectacularly rich, owning substantial acres of real estate in London itself, the Dean Castle Estate in Kilmarnock, land in Wales, where he made a home at Chirk Castle in Denbighshire, and colonial interests in Kenya.[39] His name in association with both professional and, as we shall see, amateur theatre makes him an important patron, if still shadowy figure, in the interwar years. In general, if the rationalisation of capitalism was to be effective in the interests of the exemplary theatre, the beneficence of wealthy men and, indeed, wealthy women was considered essential in the absence of state patronage. Certainly this was the case in the plans put forward to construct a National Theatre.

A National Theatre: Schemes and Estimates, the Archer and Barker 'Blue
Book' privately printed and circulated in 1904 and finally published in
1907, was a detailed proposal covering all the major operational factors
involved in a large, building-based theatrical enterprise. The management
structure would be led by a director appointed by a board of trustees and
assisted by a reading committee, including a part-time literary manager
who would decide on the repertoire. The size (not less than 66), status,
working conditions, salaries and pension rights of the resident ensemble
were calculated. Ticket prices for a traditional proscenium-arched auditorium seating an audience of 1,350 were calculated as were the facilities
for refreshments. There would also be an acting school.

The proposal, which Barker makes clear in the introduction to the 1907
edition was largely William Archer's work, envisages certain financial
concessions from the state: a *rent-free* building on land provided by the
London County Council and tax exemptions, but states unequivocally
that it would be a 'waste of time' to go to Parliament for a direct grant
for the building. Instead 'we must look to private liberality to present a
Central Theatre to London and to the Empire. That is not only the most
profitable, but on the whole the most desirable event.' A private donation
of at least £100,000 from one wealthy individual (Donor A) would serve
as an example to inspire further munificence from others. The fund-raising
target was £500,000. Furthermore only in the event of proven managerial success would the theatre become "absolutely" – the property of the
nation.'[40]

The proposal was thus dependent on metropolitan finance and endorsement. Donor A was found thanks to the fund-raising efforts of Edith
Lyttleton, member of the Balfour family, wife of the Liberal MP Alfred
Lyttleton and a dramatist in her own right. Carl Meyer, who was subsequently awarded a baronetcy, was persuaded to donate £70,000. But by
the time Halford John Mackinder, the Unionist MP for Glasgow, put a
motion in favour of a state-assisted National Theatre in London to the
House of Commons in April 1913, only about £100,000 had been raised
and the time for state 'crowning' of the enterprise was deemed not to have
arrived.[41]

Ironically, the ramshackle Royal Victoria Hall, already nearly one
hundred years old, had a lessee whose efforts to bring coffee and edify-
ing amusement to the working classes of South London was supported
by a veritable army of benefactors, including the likes of the Duke of
Westminster and Lady Frederick Cavendish. With their help in 1887
Emma Cons raised the necessary £17,000 to buy the theatre's freehold

and secure an annual guaranteed endowment from the City Parochial Foundation.[42] More emergency aid, again overseen by the Duke of Westminster, was provided to get the Hall out of the over £3,000 deficit incurred when the building had to be improved in line with LCC safety requirements in 1904.[43] The music-hall licence, which permitted musical recitals and lectures as well as variety bills, enabled a programme that was a far cry from the theatre of ideas, as were the film shows introduced by Cons's niece Lilian Baylis. Average audiences per night in 1905–6 could range from 1,200 for variety to 2,000 for concerts and film.[44] What began as a philanthropic mission to the poor was bequeathed to Baylis along with a precarious, but resilient managerial independence. Baylis, already an experienced musician and dancer, became lessee on her aunt's death in 1912 and joined the ranks of professional managers. Her immediate and successful application for a dramatic licence[45] launched the Old Vic on a course towards legitimacy and Shakespeare production, facilitated by a series of directly employed actor-directors which by the early 1930s looked to give the theatre the status, if not the name, of a national theatre.

REGIONAL OWNERSHIP

Outside London, theatre proprietors/managers operated on a very different basis. Up until the 1920s, and despite the efforts of a small number of significant individuals, regional producing theatres or theatres with a resident acting ensemble were very rare, although the building expansion of commercial receiving or variety houses continued until 1914. *The Era Annual* for 1915 and 1916 lists a total of 483 regional venues across the UK not counting music halls. Out of these just three of the new-style producing 'repertory' theatres are given: the Abbey in Dublin, the Repertory Theatre in Liverpool and the Gaiety Theatre in Manchester. The Birmingham Repertory Theatre, which opened in 1913 and continued to produce right through the war, is not listed, neither is the Glasgow Repertory Theatre, which closed in 1914. It should be stressed, that the long-term dominance of these theatres in the historical record is not indicative of their immediate contemporary impact. In many respects what was to give them prominence was their relationship to the metropolitan campaign.

The dependence on a steady supply of toured-in product and the fact that companies travelled all over the British Isles made commercial theatre across all the UK nations effectively a unitary system. One striking feature of regional ownership/lesseeship is the extent to which the expansion of buildings provided business opportunities for theatre professionals – actors, writers, managers – to acquire, or attempt to acquire, sizeable personal fortunes by owning or leasing several theatres simultaneously. The practice of actor-managers leasing more than one theatre dated right back to the eighteenth century, but grew exponentially as more and more property became available for investment. Indeed, a major corporation like Moss' Empires, which controlled 29 theatres nations-wide by 1917, emerged on the back of what had become accepted industrial practice albeit at a lower level of financial capacity. Touring actor-managers or managers of regional touring product not only held the rights to plays, musical comedies and, perhaps most importantly, pantomimes, but also aimed to own or lease the touring houses.

Regional managers engaged in multiple theatre ownership have largely vanished from the historical record along with the commercial priorities of their enterprises. Indeed, in general histories of British theatre the names of Howard & Wyndham do not usually feature, let alone someone like Arthur Carlton, the managing director of Tours Ltd. and co-author of plays such as *A Sailor's Honour* and *The Prairie Flower*, who ran theatres in Devonport, Hereford, Ebbw Vale, Gainsborough, Saltley and Worcester.[46] Milton Bode's entry in the 1916 *Who's Who in the Theatre* defiantly states that he had 'never speculated in a London theatre or with a London production', although he became a well-known member of the TMA, and promoted and toured London successes. With an early background in circus and fit-up performance which led eventually to employment on George Alexander's provincial business interests, Bode was best known as a producer and manager of musical comedy and pantomime. By 1916 his tally of pantomimes had reached over 70.[47]

Bode formed business partnerships with the touring actor-manager Edward Compton and Robert Courtneidge. Courtneidge, the Edinburgh-born former actor whose musical comedy *The Arcadians* launched an eight-year lesseeship at London's Shaftesbury Theatre in 1909, had established himself as a successful manager, pantomime-creator and aspiring Shakespeare director at the Theatre Royal and the Prince's Theatre in Manchester between 1896 and 1903, and thereafter was a responsible for a string of musical comedy successes as well as his celebrated pantomimes. Robert Courtneidge Ltd., of which Bode became a director, would have brought the investment opportunities and further touring product associated with metropolitan popular theatre.[48] Compton set up his Compton Comedy Company in 1881, establishing a repertory of over 50 plays, including Shakespeare and eighteenth-century classics by Goldsmith and

Sheridan, which he toured relentlessly and with great regional popularity right round the UK until only two years before his death in 1918. Best known for the title role in Muskerry's *Davy Garrick* and meticulously careful in his touring management practice, Compton would have added some legitimate gravitas to Bode's free-wheeling speculative instincts.

Compton's first joint venture with Bode seems to have been the new build of a legitimate theatre in Dalston, Hackney, which they opened in 1898. Despite the financial failure of the venture, which dashed Compton's hopes of giving up his touring company, the partnership continued with Bode securing the long lease on the Theatre Royal, Huddersfield, in 1900. The Northampton Royal Theatre and Opera House was acquired in 1903, followed in 1906 by the Opera House and the Theatre Royal in Leicester. By 1907 Compton and Bode were joint proprietors of the New Royal County Theatre in Reading, where Bode established his base, the Royalty Theatre in Chester and the Theatre Royal in Leamington. All were ranked as either No. 2 or No. 3 venues.

Bode, with acting managers (that is, resident managers acting on behalf of the proprietor) installed in each theatre, would have approved overall seasonal policies including the engagement of his own touring companies and pantomimes as well as building maintenance. Compton's C.C.C. took an agreed proportion of box-office revenue when the company played in a Bode–Compton theatre. As co-proprietor/lessee Compton would have also shared in any year-end venue profits. Both men appear to have invested in Courtneidge's touring successes. For his part Courtneidge had a particular relationship with the Royal Lyceum in Edinburgh where his early career had been encouraged by J. B. Howard. During the war, his company appeared more regularly at the Lyceum than any other.[49]

Although Compton was not born in Scotland, as a member of the Mackenzie family his roots were in Scotland. He was always greeted as a favourite by Edinburgh audiences and regularly travelled to other Scottish theatres.[50] His additional business investment as a director of Robert Arthur Theatres Ltd. would have brought him within the orbit of the Arthur/Howard & Wyndham circuits of No. 1 houses in Scotland and England. Robert Arthur had rapidly expanded over the border from his management in Dundee and Aberdeen to become lessee of the Newcastle Theatre Royal and then on to the Royal Court in Liverpool and the Theatre Royal in Nottingham. He over-reached himself, however, in attempts to extend his theatre interests to the London suburbs, in particular his building of the Princess of Wales Theatre in Kennington in 1898.[51] Following a loss of over £4,000 in 1912, Howard & Wyndham took over the management of Arthur's company which nevertheless remained incorporated with F. W. P. Wyndham as managing director.[52] Bode and Compton acquired the Kennington Theatre, but Howard & Wyndham now controlled ten of the most prestigious No. 1 theatres outside London stretching from Aberdeen to Nottingham.

Inevitably ownership over such a wide geographical area meant proprietors were distanced from local concerns. Individual building acquisition within a comparatively limited area, however, had the potential to play a key role not just in the local entertainment industry, but as part of the fabric of the local economy as a whole. The Irish-American actor William Wallace Kelly owned the rights to W. G. Wills's hugely popular Napoleon and Josephine drama, *A Royal Divorce*, and made a fortune touring it with his wife Edith Cole. Play ownership was bolstered by building interests on Merseyside. In Birkenhead from 1897 Kelly was the proprietor of the old Theatre Royal and the lessee of the Metropole. In Liverpool in 1909 he bought the Queen's Theatre from Granville Theatres Ltd. which had financed the reconstruction of the 2,000 seat theatre in 1904 out of the shell of an older and much renamed and relaunched venue. The theatre was renamed Kelly's Theatre and programmed with popular dramas which attracted audiences from the dock areas.[53]

Kelly the prominent citizen served on Birkenhead Council, was made an alderman in 1929 and three times refused a mayoralty. Kelly the showman cultivated the image of the flamboyant actor-manager – frock coat, silk top hat and huge buttonhole – further enhanced by the anecdotes which collected around his famous touring show. But his management was also part of a wider spectrum of local theatre provision not overly concerned with cultural demarcation. In 1910 when the campaign to set up a new-style repertory theatre was gathering momentum, Kelly engaged the Leigh Lovel Company to stage Ibsen's *A Doll's House* and *The Master Builder* for a profitable week of performances. He entered into a negotiation with Alfred Wareing to host a short season by the Glasgow Repertory Company. When that fell through, in 1911 Kelly's Theatre provided the stage, on a profit-share basis, for the inaugural six-week run of the fledgling Liverpool Repertory Company.[54] Kelly also hosted performances by the Ulster Players. The subsequent fate of Kelly's Theatre – given over to variety after it failed to pay as a theatre for drama, then closed in 1916 and sold to a leading grocery firm as a warehouse – reflects the shifting fortunes of the building-based industry during the war. Kelly, however, continued with diversified theatre interests. In 1915 as Managing Director of the Shakespeare Theatre in Liverpool, he was congratulated by the TMA for facing down a pay strike by the National Association of Theatrical Employees.[55]

THE NEW GENERATION

Where long-term theatre ownership was associated with a particular the-atrical name or family, what had begun with a performer acquiring rights of ownership or residency in a showcase venue shifted to management as a career choice in itself. In Edinburgh, R. H. Wyndham, for example, had entered into managerial partnership with fellow actor J. B. Howard, pri-marily as an actor. His son F. W. P. Wyndham was well known as a tour-ing actor, but became far more successful as a manager joining Howard initially as joint lessee of the Theatre Royal in Newcastle at a propitious time in 1883.[56]

In Belfast, where the local environment was less favourable to theatre enterprise, a similar generational shift had the opposite effect. When the English actor-manager Joseph F. Warden died in 1898 his obituary praised his benign influence on the 'educative progress of the city, and his efforts on behalf of music and drama'. His management of the Belfast Theatre Royal dated back to 1864 and had seen not only the building of a new Theatre Royal in 1871 but ten years later, its rapid reconstruction after a fire. The opening of the new Opera House in 1895 provided the impetus for the formation of J. F. Warden Ltd. with Warden as managing dir-ector of both theatres. By 1904, his son Fred Warden, faced with the fact that attempts to make the Opera House a venue of choice for 'quality' audiences had failed, converted it to a twice-nightly Palace of Varieties. Managerial policy over the next decade lurched between the two theatres: refurbishment and higher prices at the Theatre Royal, which also failed, followed by seasons of 'new sensational drama'. At the Opera House the original name was restored along with higher prices. The final solution in 1915 was to raze the Theatre Royal to the ground and build the Royal Cinema, the profits from which enabled the survival of the Opera House as a live theatre.[57]

If independent ownership was hazardous, the relationship of the lessee to committees of local owners/shareholders brought other kinds of ten-sions. Where the early patent Theatres Royal had been built and financed by committees of local citizenry, they were leased out at an agreed annual rent to a succession of actor-managers. This was the managerial position which Howard & Wyndham bought into at the Newcastle Theatre Royal in 1883. Their reaction to the committee's refusal to commit to necessary refurbishment and technical upgrading was to relinquish the Theatre Royal lease, which went to Robert Arthur, while they took over the Tyne Theatre.[58] What followed was vigorous competition with the Royal to present the best of touring product and the most spectacular of home-grown pantomimes. In other cities what had begun a century before as an expression of civic pride and group aggrandisement became a site of struggle over the responsibilities of property ownership and the needs of industrial innovation.

In Bristol in 1925 a consortium, consisting of Bode, Courtneidge and Courtneidge's former London manager Douglas Millar, was able to buy the venerable Theatre Royal for £8,500, thus relieving the proprietorial committee of the burden of responsibility for a theatre which was by then in a deplorable state.[59] The long history of battles between the committee and the M'Cready family lessees in the nineteenth century had culminated finally in the building of the 'New' Theatre Royal as a wholly independent venture in 1867 by James Chute, who had married into the M'Creadys. The result in early-twentieth-century Bristol was a virtually impregnable class divide between the old Theatre Royal as primarily a melodrama and pantomime house, long abandoned to other lessees, and the Prince's Theatre as the 'New' had been renamed, functioning as a top-rank No. 1 venue managed by the Macready Chutes.[60]

THE MODEL BUSINESS MAN

It was of particular importance for a commercial management to nurture good relations with the community that supplied the paying audiences, and whoever had operational responsibility on a day-to-day basis had to maintain a strong public profile. Increasingly whether as owner-managers or acting-managers, the trend was to deliberately cultivate the appearance of respectable business professionals.

In Birmingham, neither of the two most prominent commercial managers – Polish-born Leon Salberg, who married into a family of local furniture manufacturers and bought the Alexandra Theatre in 1911, and Philip Rodway, originally a trainee solicitor who at twenty-two became the youngest acting-manager in England for the shareholders of the rebuilt Theatre Royal – had been trained in theatre. Salberg, 'a quiet, unemphatic little man', established his business knowledge and artistic priorities by a process of trial and error over nearly thirty years, retaining his independent ownership of a No. 2 venue in Birmingham and acquiring the Wolverhampton Grand in 1936.[61] For his part Rodway, acting throughout his career on behalf of shareholders (who included Compton and Bode), contracted, received, promoted and facilitated not so much with a singleness of artistic vision, but with a single-minded entrepreneurial vision predicated on the best-possible quality to ensure maximum productivity. Invited to join the Board he became Managing Director in 1913.[62] In 1918 he negotiated the purchase of all the shares of the neighbouring Prince of Wales Theatre bringing both it and the Theatre Royal as No. 1 houses under one management.[63] By 1928, however, facing the collapse of the old touring system, he was obliged to recommend to the shareholders that they accept an offer from Moss' Empires to take over the still profitable Theatre Royal while he continued to manage the Prince of Wales until his death in 1932.[64]

THE RISE OF THE CORPORATE ECONOMY

Tracy Davis castigates Leslie Hannah for failing to identify Moss' Empires as an outstanding example of the phenomenon of corporate merger.[65] The benefits of merger and centralisation of managerial responsibilities cut operating costs, increased profit margins and made share purchase more attractive. Most importantly, it was possible to mobilise corporate assets quickly to tackle competition or seize opportunities for takeover and assimilation. At the beginning of the century all advertisements for Moss' theatres trumpeted the joint capital of £1,650,000, which rose to £2,086,000 by 1906.

All three of the colonising, entrepreneurial individuals who created Moss' Empires started at the rock bottom of the entertainment industry. All took advantage of patterns of economic migration and areas of industrial prosperity. In 1899 the incorporation of Moss' Empires Ltd. merged ten separate companies and fourteen music halls, including Stoll's halls in Cardiff, Swansea and Newport.[66] The founders represented an unabashed commitment to the validity of wealth generation, which, moreover, derived its origins from a social class only just emerging to assert aspirational values in both the work place and the place of entertainment. All three were given knighthoods and it is unlikely that their audiences would have regarded their corporate strength as anything other than more confirmation of British industrial success.

Their presence in a history of legitimate theatre is necessary for two reasons. First, the building in the first instance of the ubiquitous Empires and latterly, even more opulent variety theatres, presented a challenge to every other provider of live entertainment in each town or

city the company entered. Secondly, the buying up of legitimate theatres like the Birmingham Theatre Royal also shifted the local dynamic
of provision still further, as did the very conscious challenge to the
legitimate/illegitimate binary. The dividing line between the two had
always been permeable throughout the nineteenth century in desperate managerial attempts to stave off bankruptcy, and the mixed genre
programmes offered by even the most established of No. 1 touring venues well into the twentieth century begged a lot of questions about the
nature of 'legitimacy'. The combined strength of the variety market
leaders lay in the fact that they had the resources to employ artistes as
distinguished in their own field as the doyens of legitimacy. Increasingly
they bought legitimate artists as well.

The 'sketch' controversy, which rumbled on for years while legitimate
theatre managers protested over the fact that their illegitimate colleagues
were not compelled to submit the scripts of sketches or one-act plays slot-
ted into the variety bills to the Lord Chamberlain, was symptomatic of
demarcation anxieties. Variety could do plays as well and pay for the priv-
ilege. In 1912 when the Lord Chamberlain finally extended his jurisdic-
tion to the drama presented in the halls, some three hundred 'sketches'
were presented as part of variety bills, and were performed by legitimate
actors.[67]

In Bristol, the battles against the variety giants waged by legitimate
managers included trying to block Walter de Frece's attempts to obtain
a drama licence for his Bedminster Hippodrome opened in 1911 and outrage at Stoll's vast new Hippodrome in 1912. As Kathleen Barker's survey of Bristol entertainment opportunities available just before the First
World War shows, audiences at the Hippodrome could not only see
leading music-hall personalities like George Formby and W. C. Fields,
but also one-act plays and scenes from Shakespeare. In October 1913, for
example, Sarah Bernhardt and her company gave a half-hour selection
from *La Dame aux Camélias* 'to a packed and hushed audience'.[68]

EVANGELISTS OF CHANGE

The rhetoric of the not-for-profit movement was positioned in direct
opposition to the values of the market economy. On paper and from the
speaker's podium the proponents of artistic modernism set out to demon-
ise the popular products of industrial modernity and in particular what
Harley Granville Barker condemned as 'mob appeal'.[69] The sociologist
Helmut K. Anheier identifies four primary functions of not-for-profit

organisations: the *service-provider role* where the organisation can deliver collective goods and services particularly for 'minority preferences ... that complement the service delivery of other sectors but *differ qualitatively from it*' (my emphasis); the *vanguard role* where organisations 'innovate by experimenting with and pioneering new approaches, processes or programmes' and are 'less beholden than business forms to the expectations of stakeholders'; the *value-guardian role* 'to promote and guard particularistic values and allow societal groups to express and promulgate religious, ideological, political, cultural, social and other views and preferences'; finally, there is the *advocacy role* which 'give[s] voice to the minority and particularistic interests and values they represent and [they] serve in turn as critics and watchdogs of government'.[70]

All four functions can be perceived in the models of not-for-profit theatre organisation which emerged, or tried to emerge before 1914. Yeats's original aim to create 'a theatre for ourselves and for our friends, and for a few simple people who understand from sheer simplicity what we understand from scholarship and thought',[71] was only at the most extreme, patrician end of a spectrum of coterie activity. The minority interest groups, led by a small number of dynamic individuals who launched the various play-producing societies in the 1890s and voluntarily contributed their resources of time, talent and cash, tried to build what William Archer envisaged as a 'compact majority' supportive of innovation.[72]

If the industrial strength of commercial theatre had created a system that effectively united British audiences in a common experience, so pockets of structural and artistic innovation, strategically positioned by a relatively small number of key individuals, created a network of avant-garde influence which stretched across the British Isles. While it would be wrong to say that the location of each venture was part of any kind of master plan, the sequence of events that followed on from the establishment of the Abbey Theatre in Dublin in 1904 saw the catalytic effect of evangelists of change literally travelling out from the metropolitan centre to encounter in Manchester, Liverpool, Glasgow and Birmingham a convergence of what appeared to be favourable local conditions. Each city was a regional centre at the heart of a conurbation. Each city, its industrial base apparently secure, looked to develop its cultural profile.

Annie Horniman's offer to give Yeats a theatre, which she built in 1904 at a cost of about £13,000, and an annual subsidy of £600 to the Irish Players until 1910, was made consciously as an outsider, albeit with no premonition of the likely consequences.[73] The two English men she worked with, Manchester-born Ben Iden Payne, and her fellow Londoner Alfred

Wareing, then business manager for Beerbohm Tree's tours, both organised the tours, which were an important source of company revenue for the Irish Players, and ensured a further circulation of artistic influence. The first arranged by Wareing included Cardiff, all the main Scottish cities plus Newcastle and Hull. The second booked by Payne began in Glasgow, went to all the principal English cities and finished in London. Wareing's professional theatre experience included advance agent for Benson and Actor-Manager [*sic*] for Mrs Bandman-Palmer's Company.[74] Both men were involved in the process of finding Horniman an alternative theatrical venture for her patronage. The idea of trying to found a Scottish national theatre in Glasgow or Edinburgh on the Irish model was rejected. As Payne advised 'she should be leery of any enterprise that bore a nationalistic tag'.[75] Wareing, however, who had developed contacts in Glasgow as early as 1900, instigated the formation of the Scottish Playgoers' Company in 1909, leasing from Howard & Wyndham the Royalty Theatre which became known as the Glasgow Repertory Theatre.[76]

The issue of ownership of an enterprise both in the sense of property ownership and *felt* ownership, was crucial to the long-term survival of the first 'repertory theatre' ventures. Both the companies in Manchester and Birmingham owed their existence to a wealthy patron, and in both cases patronage came through wealth inherited from Victorian trading success: Horniman from her grandfather's invention of packeted teas, and Barry Jackson as the youngest son of the founder of the Maypole chain of dairies. The main difference was that Jackson's Birmingham Repertory Company which emerged out of his locally-formed amateur Pilgrim Players in 1912 was entirely home-grown. While Horniman shared with Jackson an extensive knowledge of European culture and theatre, and Jackson had certainly been influenced by the Irish Players, Jackson absolutely owned his own theatrical home; he acted, directed and designed during the first decade, and continued to bankroll it until 1935. The playhouse which opened in Birmingham in 1913 was commissioned and built by Jackson as the first English purpose-built repertory theatre. Directly influenced by similar avant-garde theatres in Germany, and with a deliberately small audience capacity of only 464, the only other English building equivalent was Kingston's Little.[77]

The alternative company model of 'citizen' shareholders subscribing small amounts to launch the theatre as a viable business concern was adopted first in Glasgow in 1909, and then in Liverpool in 1911, and on the face of it was theoretically less vulnerable to individual vicissitude. In both cities enthusiastic members of the university community joined with other civic and industrial leaders in promoting the theatres. In the event, the Glasgow Repertory Theatre survived for five years, showing a profit only when Lewis Casson became artistic director briefly in 1914 after Wareing's fragile health provoked his departure. Glasgow's status as the 'Second City of the Empire' was probably the key factor in what was essentially an exercise in British cultural aggrandisement drawing its repertoire, many of the leading actors and, indeed, directors from Barker's Court ensemble. Jan McDonald considers that Wareing's theatre did try hard to encourage indigenous drama with three new, if not especially distinguished, Scottish plays produced each season, but the emphasis on European drama, including the first professional British production of Chekhov, *The Seagull* in 1909, may well have been the most enduring legacy.[78]

Donald Campbell is less sympathetic, accusing Wareing of only employing Scottish actors in minor roles and of 'feckless incompetence' on a business level. The rent paid on the Royalty was far too high, and Howard & Wyndham retained the profits on bar, cloakrooms and programmes. Campbell also points out that the departure in 1910 of the Glaswegian actor Graham Moffat, following a row over an audience complaint, not only lost to Scotland a popular performer genuinely interested in a Scottish theatre, but more importantly Moffat's comic satire on Sabbatarianism, *Causay Saints*. Some eighteen months later, retitled *Bunty Pulls the Strings*, Moffat's play was premiered in London at the Haymarket Theatre under Herbert Trench's management and ran for 617 performances, followed by another long run for Moffat's earlier Scots comedy *A Scrape o' the Pen* at the Comedy Theatre. *Bunty* subsequently toured extensively, but Moffat, like so many of his countrymen, did not return home in any meaningful way as an actor and dramatist.[79]

HONESTLY COMMERCIAL LINES

One useful way at looking at the evolving managerial structures of these early theatres is to consider the reasons for failure or the response to threatened failure. The 'Commonwealth', set up at the Liverpool Repertory Theatre to avert closure in 1914, brought together the 'company' as an artistic collective of actors and support staff, with the company as a legally incorporated concern of individual directors and shareholders. All united to contribute to a budget that would sustain the theatre's much-modified artistic policy and the living costs of the employees. The business, which stayed afloat, post-Commonwealth, until relative stability was reached in

1922, had to engage, as Grace Wyndham Goldie's history demonstrates, in significant compromises with the original vision.[80]

Annie Horniman, however, had laid great stress on 'a dramatic artistic venture on honestly commercial lines' when Manchester was 'chosen' as the location for the first English repertory theatre because it was deemed to be 'ready' for such an undertaking.[81] In the event when a large deficit forced her to sell the theatre in 1920, a public appeal to raise the purchase price of £52,500 by the sale of one shilling shares failed. The Gaiety was sold to a cinema company.[82] In Birmingham, Jackson closed down his theatre in 1924 following inadequate audience support for a production of Georg Kaiser's expressionist play *Gas*. It was only after a great deal of lobbying amongst civic support groups, etc. that he was persuaded to reopen. By that time his company was well established in London.[83]

One of the possible reasons for the Manchester failure, which Rex Pogson puts forward in the analytic conclusion to his history, was Horniman's determination to showcase her company in London. Her seasons at the Coronet Theatre began as early as 1909 and continued until 1914 and there were also tours to Canada and the USA in 1912 and 1913. The ensemble strength of the company, the ambitious range of plays and the major success of *Hindle Wakes* all contributed to a rapidly acquired and widely disseminated reputation for artistic excellence. What this also led to was the dilution of the core company presence in its home base and the departure of leading individual actors for more lucrative metropolitan pastures. When the war came, the company was as exposed as any other to economic and demographic turbulence. Indeed, the strong German Jewish community which had supported the Gaiety, along with other artistic organisations such as the Hallé Orchestra, inevitably retreated in the war years.[84]

In part because of the war, the growth in the national reputation of Birmingham Rep was much slower. The company survived until 1918, with the punishing schedule of a weekly change of bill typical of the short-run theatre. Protected by Jackson's wealth, the company maintained a defiantly austere artistic policy and almost wilfully rejected flamboyant publicity. The first Birmingham–London transfer of John Drinkwater's *Abraham Lincoln* to the Lyric Theatre, Hammersmith, was facilitated in 1919 on a profit-share basis by the Lyric's proprietor, the actor and director Nigel Playfair. The play ran for 466 performances. The second transfer in 1922 of Rutland Boughton's Celtic folk opera *The Immortal Hour* was to another Playfair-leased theatre, the Regent located near King's Cross. As J. C. Trewin put it, Jackson became a London manager because he now had 'a theatre close to three of the great rail termini, a useful position for any visitors from Scotland, the Midlands or the North'.[85]

What followed over the next thirteen years were fourteen productions presented with Jackson as impresario in a total of fourteen metropolitan theatres. These ranged from the Arts Theatre Club, where the first English translation of Pirandello's *Six Characters in Search of an Author* was staged in 1928, to the Court and the Kingsway which saw the revival of the Rep's British premiere of Shaw's *Back to Methuselah* in 1924 and the ground-breaking productions of Shakespeare in modern dress in 1925 and 1928. *Pace* all Jackson's protestations against the long run, his most popular success, Eden Phillpotts's *The Farmer's Wife*, ran for three years at the Court, and along with other popular productions toured extensively. The dynamic exchange that Jackson and his staff created between the regional city and the metropolitan core was grounded in secure physical resources in Birmingham, which had excellent workshop and wardrobe facilities, long-serving artistic support and administrative staff. In London itself he was able to turn the flexibility of sub-lesseeship to his advantage, and while not, as he always insisted, creating art to serve a commercial purpose,[86] he was able to use the economic staples of the long run and touring opportunities as part of his armoury, as well as the capacity to shrug away personal loss.[87]

INDUSTRIAL DECLINE AND CHANGE

By 1920 the industrial importance of live theatre to the wider economy across the UK had begun to decline considerably. Property investment shifted to cinema building, and year-on-year more and more theatres closed or were converted to cinemas. An economic boom which lasted roughly from mid-1919 until mid-1920 was followed by the fastest economic collapse in British history.[88] The old dominant export industries, which had brought such wealth and popular energy to the conurbations in Scotland, Wales and Northern England – especially the North-East – and Northern Ireland, never regained their pre-war strength, with devastating effects for the working population. The response from successive governments, including the short-lived 1924 Labour administration, was an essentially conservative economic policy, obsessed with maintaining a balanced budget, and wary of more state intervention than was deemed absolutely necessary to improve general health and living standards.[89]

That said, the war had brought a changed state-societal relationship. The principle of a guaranteed minimum payment to all unemployed workers and ex-servicemen and their families had been accepted, and rent controls were continued. A standard school-leaving age of 14 was introduced, and there was more provision for day-release teaching and scholarships.[90] The 1918 election brought voting rights to all the adult male population over 21, and for women over 30. Despite extreme poverty in the areas worst hit by the depression, this was a marginally more secure, better educated and more politically-aware society. Trade union power as manifested in a series of major strikes in the early 1920s grew stronger. But as far as theatre was concerned, the cheap warmth and light of the galleries were abandoned in favour of the even cheaper cinema. Amateur, participatory theatre became more important. Professional theatre providers turned their attention to cultivating an audience base amongst the more comfortably-off.

Even in the 'special areas' of mass unemployment, there were still jobs within the rising professional, clerical and junior managerial sectors. Statistically, however, these were most prevalent in 'inner Britain', i.e. Greater London and the East and West Midlands, where the newer consumer and service industries began to flourish.[91] The theatre industry of the 1920s and 30s reflects not so much evenly-experienced misery, but profound inequality, and the tendency, as Dudley Baines puts it, 'to *redistribute* income – from the unemployed to the employed'. Even as theatres closed, the unitary commercial touring system remained in place, but with control vested in fewer and more powerful hands operating from offices and boardrooms mainly located in London.

COMMERCE AND CO-OPERATION

In 1917, when *The Stage Year Book* published an article on joint stock companies, it had already become clear that in the boardroom legitimate/illegitimate rivalries had given way to common business interests. F. W. P. Wyndham is listed not only as managing director of Howard & Wyndham and Robert Arthur Theatres, but also a director of the United Theatres Company, controlling the Prince's Theatre and the Theatre Royal in Manchester, and, with Oswald Stoll, a director of the Coliseum Syndicate and the Opera House Syndicate.[92] By 1933, two years after Wyndham's death, the company's main office was in London and some very ambitious individuals had begun to work together. In 1928, A. S. Cruikshank, the son of the builder of the King's Theatre in Edinburgh, had taken over as managing director of Howard & Wyndham making the King's, and with it Cruikshank's formidable managerial skills, vital to the regeneration of the Howard & Wyndham empire.[93] C. B. Cochran had joined the Howard & Wyndham Board. H. M. (Harry) Tennent, formerly head of the Moss' Empires' booking department, and subsequently booking manager for Howard & Wyndham, formed a new company, Moss' Empires and Howard & Wyndham Tours Ltd., with his young protégé Hugh 'Binkie' Beaumont.[94]

Cochran had established fruitful relationships with selected No. 1 managements in cities such as Manchester or Glasgow by opening major shows, including *Bitter Sweet*, already destined for the West End, and running them for two weeks or sometimes as long as a month.[95] Beaumont, who began his theatrical career as a box-office assistant at the Playhouse Theatre in Cardiff, built on the same policy for straight plays 'ironing out' production problems in pre-West End regional tours. In 1936, Tennent and Beaumont founded the producing management H. M. Tennent Ltd. Beaumont, adept at forming mutually profitable relationships with the new elite amongst actors and directors, became the most powerful producer in metropolitan theatre for the best part of twenty years.

The ways in which leading commercial organisations, company directors and producers worked in each others' interests retained the unitary system at the top end of the touring market across the UK and began to create a very complex, but tightly integrated co-operative network. Not only were theatres directly owned or leased, but a company like Howard & Wyndham would also book productions for a range of other theatres.[96] In the early 1930s, the Littler family, Prince, Blanche and Emile, entered the frame with both pantomime and musical-comedy production companies and regional theatre acquisitions, which included initially the Opera House in Leicester and the New Theatre and Prince of Wales in Cardiff. While dominance in large-scale musicals, achieved largely by Emile Littler, accelerated after the Second World War, pantomime, which was essential to the regional theatre economy, made the Littlers the most celebrated of the 'Pantomime Kings' and financed the expanding portfolio of company and building interests.[97]

REPERTORY AND RESILIENCE

Lower down the food chain, and in response to the altered trends in metropolitan provision, 'straight' theatre began to return more strongly and on a locally managed and ensemble basis. 'Repertory' became something of a buzz word, although whether that meant a company with a rotating stock of plays or a resident company presenting short runs of plays remained fluid. In 1925, for example, the Lena Ashwell Players were invited to present the first of several summer seasons of plays at the York Theatre Royal as a fixed-term resident company.[98] Regional audiences were accustomed to the old-style touring companies such as Benson's and Compton's, which were in a very real sense repertory companies carrying a stock of plays, a selection of which would be part of a week's or a fortnight's visit. Charles Doran's Shakespearean Company and the Macdona Players, led by Esmé Percy, which held the touring rights to some thirteen of Shaw's plays, continued the tradition through the 1920s.

A clutch of commercial managers formed multiple 'repertory' companies that could be hired for a season to present a package of plays, again for the sake of industrial efficiency, staged twice nightly and changed every week. Thus Alfred Denville's stock companies came into this category, as did Frank F. Fortescue's repertory companies. Individual theatre owners also formed companies, resident for a season, which dovetailed with the panto, and employing a designated 'producer' to direct the plays. Sometimes, as with Leon Salberg in Birmingham in 1933, this was done successfully with attempts to achieve greater quality control after unevenly cast companies proved unsatisfactory.[99] In the same year the lessee of the York Theatre Royal, the frequently absent actor-manager, Percy Hutchinson, was found to be bankrupt after trying to stabilise the theatre with his own repertory company.[100]

More autonomous building-based repertory began to gain ground, albeit very fitfully and under great economic strain. In 1920 Virginia Bateman, the widow of Edward Compton, became lessee of the Grand Theatre in Nottingham in order to transform the C. C. C. into a resident repertory company. With her daughters Viola and Ellen managing the theatre as well as acting, a broad range of classic and new plays, which included new work by their brother Compton Mackenzie, and guest stars such as Sybil Thorndike and Henry Ainley, the Nottingham Repertory Theatre, began to attract praise from influential critics including J. T. Grein and St John Ervine. By early 1923, however, when recession was biting deeply across the country, Viola Compton was appealing for subscriptions to rescue the company which predictably failed to materialise.[101]

To make these proto not-for-profit repertory theatres viable professionally required considerable tenacity, a pragmatic approach to artistic policy and, ideally, the support of influential citizens in the local community who could form a powerful board. The Little Theatre in Bristol, founded in 1923, emerged out of such a group.[102] In 1927 the Northampton Royal Theatre and Opera House, now owned by the Northampton Theatre Syndicate which had constructed the neighbouring New Theatre, followed Liverpool in establishing the Northampton Repertory Players Ltd. on the same 'citizen' shareholder basis. As Richard Foulkes puts it, the Board of Directors was made up of the 'closely-interlocking "patriciate" ... which presided over Northampton between the wars'[103] and was thus very similar to the civic elite which governed the Liverpool Playhouse and enforced administrative prudence.

Northampton, a town most noted for shoe manufacture and just seventy miles from London, was no Liverpool either in terms of industrial and cultural heritage, critical mass of potential audience or capacity for economic collapse. But by the 1930s, the Liverpool Playhouse (renamed in 1917) had long abandoned any pretence of being an 'advanced' theatre. Under William Armstrong as the producer, i.e. artistic director, and the redoubtable Maud Carpenter as business manager and licensee, it was now 'an excellent theatre of the centre', pursuing a careful middle-of-the-road artistic policy, albeit with the advantage of flexible runs which were usually fortnightly, but could extend to several weeks.[104] Northampton, on the other hand, like Salberg's Alexandra, was compelled to retain weekly, twice-nightly rep giving the lie to the assumption that this system was automatically associated with industrial philistinism.[105] Indeed, in York at the Theatre Royal, where a limited company of citizen-shareholders was set up in 1934 chaired by Seebohm Rowntree, twice-nightly at popular prices was introduced in 1935 following the company's legal transition to non-profit status. Twice-nightly brought an immediate rise in audience attendance, while the right to claim exemption from Entertainments Tax for productions of an educational nature followed from the move to non-profit.[106]

AN ENGLISH SYSTEM

In 1934 Cecil Chisholm's survey of the repertory movement listed nineteen professional repertory theatres and fifteen professional repertory companies. The lists are not complete,[107] but they do show how Anglocentric the professional practice of independent-producing theatre was.[108] Only two companies are listed outside England, but both were of English origin. The Millicent Ward Players were based at the Palladium Theatre in Edinburgh, while the Brandon-Thomas Company played consecutive summer and autumn seasons at the Royal Lyceum and the Glasgow Theatre Royal. A. Stuart Cruikshank had experimented with a number of companies before finally settling for a long-term resident relationship with Jevan Brandon-Thomas in 1933, and then after 1937 with Wilson Barrett's Company. With the son of the author of *Charley's Aunt* and the grandson of the hero of *The Sign of the Cross*, Howard & Wyndham could be seen to be retaining its time-honoured associations with the doyens of Victorian theatre.[109]

English or English-by adoption actors with a mostly English repertoire were thus still colonising Scottish audiences, but more dogged attempts to bed into local communities were sowing seeds for a more independent future. In Perth in 1935 two former members of the Lena Ashwell Players, Marjorie Dence and David Steuart, journeyed north to embark on the onerous task of turning the 1900 Perth Theatre, which Dence's father had bought for them, into Scotland's first new producing theatre, albeit run on English repertory lines. When bankruptcy threatened in 1937, an appeal for a guarantee fund of £500 to be made up from small contributions by local people, the response was positive. In 1938 the Perth Repertory Theatre presented the first Scottish Theatre Festival, and in 1941, with its first grant from the newly established Council for the Encouragement of Music and the Arts, the company launched the first of a series of annual summer tours of the Scottish highlands.[110] In December 1939, the Dundee Repertory Theatre gave its first performance.

Where the economic circumstances were too difficult, independent professional producing companies could not survive. Ulster's political status, as British after the partition of Ireland in 1920, was made even more problematic by sectarian tensions and appalling levels of social deprivation which led to riots in Belfast by the starving unemployed in 1932.[111] Two attempts to set up semi-professional repertory companies in Belfast between 1932 and 1939 ended in bankruptcy.[112] The answer here as elsewhere across Great Britain – especially Wales – in the interwar period was amateur practice – the ultimate not-for-profit activity.

SHIFTING THE AXIS

The producing theatres that survived outside London in the interwar years developed management structures which, as Viv Gardner has suggested, resulted in 'a significant shift ... in the theatrical axis' away from the metropolis.[113] However, radical artistic innovation and challenge to societal mores were by and large incompatible with the 'if-it' principle. If the powerhouses of commercial theatre were concentrated in London, so too were the centres of the avant-garde found mainly in the network of small club theatres. Theatres including the Gate, the Everyman, the Mercury and the Barnes were run on shoestring budgets and could evade the censoring strictures of the Lord Chamberlain. Kingston's navigable society, to which I shall return in the next chapter, enabled creative exchange between artists and, indeed, sympathetic commercial managers like Bronson Albery. A virtual, if never actual, circuit also incorporated the two university 'repertory theatres': J. B. Fagan's Oxford Playhouse and Terence Grey's Cambridge Festival Theatre, both of which exerted long-term artistic influence, but were based on the coterie Oxbridge community.[114] A more substantive shift in the axis would require an entirely altered economic environment.

CHAPTER 3

The profession of acting

In his analysis of the developing importance of professional expertise and the emergence of a recognised professional class in twentieth-century British society, Harold Perkin states that 'the professional society is a logical continuation of industrial society'.[1] The rapid growth in the number of actors seeking employment in the expanding theatre industry raised important questions about professional status: how it was to be achieved, developed, protected and, indeed, classified socially. While these were the concerns that most obviously preoccupied actors at the beginning of the century, the gathering momentum of nationalist movements outside England, which, if anything, was intensified by economic and industrial turbulence, had implications for attempts to enable a more demographically equitable distribution of professional opportunity.

PROFESSIONAL ORGANISATION

The trend towards the concentration of corporate resources in the late Victorian industrial economy, which, as we have seen, fed directly into theatre organisation, stimulated a parallel growth in trade unions and professional associations. For actors collective organisation was both an acknowledgement of increased confidence in their status in society and a strategy to ensure reasonable working conditions and protection against exploitation. But at a time of increasing industrial unrest and the forging of new political formations, any one organisation tasked with representing the whole profession had to accommodate different political persuasions and new ideas about the function of theatre in society.

The formation of the British Actors' Equity Association in 1929 created the means by which salaries and terms of employment could be regulated and entry to the profession controlled. Equity, however, attempted to amalgamate two opposing factions: the Actors' Association, founded in 1891 with Irving as its first president, which in 1918 formally became a trade union and subsequently, more militantly socialist; and the Theatre Guild which had broken away from the AA in 1924, insisting on a non-political stance. The 1926 General Strike exposed the growing weakness and declining membership of the AA, which could not mobilise to support the strike. Guild members on the other hand collaborated with the TMA in permitting business to carry on as usual.[2]

The new organisation attempted to facilitate a compromise between hard-line labour militancy on one side and a reluctance to recognise the necessity for trade union status on the other. In the event, it was clear that the more conciliatory approach, based on traditional attitudes to the theatre's place in the social hierarchy had won the day, albeit after passionate debate. This brought together professionals from opposite ends of the political spectrum. The Labour 'Actors' MP', Robert Young, together with long-time socialist Lewis Casson, campaigned alongside such natural conservatives as Godfrey Tearle, the son of the Victorian actor-manager Osmund Tearle.[3] Tearle, along with Dame May Whitty and her husband Ben Webster, scion of the Webster theatre dynasty, were amongst the first provisional committee members. Michael Sanderson, noting the paradox of a trade union led by a professional elite, quotes the comments of Alfred Wall of the London Trades Council who advised the fledgling Equity: 'usually you know the demand for organisation comes from below. In this case the activities and enthusiasm have come from the leaders of the profession.'[4] These were the key figures who negotiated for a secure Standard Contract associated with a closed shop policy, which aimed to block employment in London theatres to non-Equity actors.

Sanderson's account of the development of actors' organisations highlights the contradictions and tensions within a profession still in need of societal acceptance, and where the function and status of an actor were rarely stable. Every actor who led a company, however ad hoc and impoverished, was a manager. That same actor might then revert to being an employee within someone else's company. A trade union representing both employers and employees was thus something of an anomaly. Furthermore, the hard-won establishment approval signalled by the creation of theatrical knights and dames led inevitably to the assumption that the metropolitan elite were the natural leaders of a professional association.

That said, it was the vulnerability of actors out in the regions that provoked the first major collective action. A campaign to make actors more corporately aware of the abuses inflicted on them through poor pay and working conditions – it was not uncommon for actors to contract

life-threatening illness in filthy theatres – largely orchestrated it seems
by the founder of *The Stage*, Charles L. Carson,[5] came to a head at a
meeting in Manchester in 1891. Robert Courtneidge and Frank Benson,
both of whom as touring actor-managers would have been all too familiar with most permutations of occupational hazard, were among the
principal architects of the original aims of the Actors' Association and
ensured that it would not impede harmonious relations between actors
and managers. Assured by Benson that an association of theatre artists
was not to be tainted by connotations of trade unionism, Irving agreed to
become the first president and in so doing launched and legitimised the
organisation.[6]

By 1907, however, two years after Irving's death, the tensions created
by conflicting professional priorities, further inflamed by the successful
strike action of the newly formed Variety Artistes' Federation, resulted
in dissident action both within and outside the AA. The rhetoric of
socialist activists, especially Harley Granville Barker, who was elected
an AA Council member in 1904, and the politically more radical actor
and playwright Cecil Raleigh, insisted that theatre was now a major,
wealth-creating industry which required robust workers' representation. The shift in power from the managers, who resigned en bloc, to
the reform group led by Barker, was taken much further in Manchester
where an alternative Actors' Union was formed with lower subscription
rates and strategic alliances with other trade unions. By the end of April
1907 the AU had some forty-two regional centres. But the departure of
the managers from the AA – including Barker who by 1907 was himself
a well-known manager – exposed structural vulnerability and financial
weakness. The eventual absorption of the AU into the AA and the rapprochement with managers, who returned to the fold in 1910–11, effectively put an end to attempts to locate actors within the wider trade-union
movement. Beerbohm Tree who gratified AA members with a commitment to rehearsal payments, became president, with George Alexander
as vice president. Actors it seemed needed their establishment and the
conservatism which came with it.

The fault line which ran through these attempts at industrial organisation was that actors, in work and scattered to every corner of the British
Isles, resisted any attempts at uniform social classification. Out of work
or eager to get a foothold in work, desperation could mean acceptance
of virtually any circumstances. Actors in the most basic fit-up or portable companies were effectively nomads. Violet Godfrey Carr's childhood
as a performing member of her mother's portable company would be

recognisable to any twenty-first-century traveller. Born in about 1908, by law she had to receive an elementary education and moved from school to school where as a 'theatrical', and thus different, she could be ostracised. The popular repertoire included many child roles, and from the age of 3 she was forced to observe a strict discipline in rehearsal and line-learning and taught to use make-up which was also a source of disparagement. 'Nice people didn't use make-up.'[7]

Touring companies were also dependent on local supernumaries. In 1911 an offer to employ George Hewins's wife as a dresser in Frank Benson's company for the Shakespeare Festival in the Memorial Theatre was a means of getting the Hewins family out of rent arrears. When George was recruited as a supernumerary carrying Ophelia's coffin in Benson's 'eternity' *Hamlet*, he was paid 3s. a show plus an extra 3s. if he stayed on into the early hours of the morning to rehearse the following night's play. Taken on as a regular by the super-master who was a local Stratford milkman, he was paid another 3s. to shave off his moustache to make him a more authentic monk. A matinee performance meant losing 18d wages as a bricklayer, which Benson duly made up.[8] This then was casual employment at the grass roots of the profession at a time when the AA was attempting to negotiate a standard minimum wage of £2 a week for the regular jobbing actor who spoke more than three lines.

In addition to the minimum wage, the aspirations of the AA remained the improvement of dirty and dangerous theatres, protection against bogus managers and universal payment for rehearsals and matinees. For actors who were members of the AA – and numbers dropped significantly when the managers departed – the organisation offered some modest benefits in addition to London club rooms and an employment agency service. There was free medical and legal advice and an arbitration service. Annually, *The Stage Year Book* carried details of court cases which offer some insight into the perils of day-to-day working hazards which the AA sought to remedy. In 1919 when AA membership was buoyant, an agreement was reached with West End managers for a Standard Contract of £3 for a week of eight performances and £2 for rehearsals. In 1920 a Standard Touring Contract was secured. Even so in 1922 when recession appeared to hit the theatre, the Touring Managers Association proposed to renege on the contract.[9]

Where collective organisation and radical politics did interface successfully in a single unifying issue was in the formation in 1908 of the Actresses' Franchise League. In 1907 the original constitution of the AA excluded women from its Council even though Gertrude Kingston had provided the first signature at the inaugural meeting.[10] In the case of the AFL, the endorsement of formidable women such as Mrs Kendal as the League's president, Violet Vanbrugh and Gertrude Elliott (Lady Forbes-Robinson) as vice presidents, and the support of luminaries including Ellen Terry added gravitas to the suffragette campaign. Also, as Sanderson points out, the declaration 'that women claim the franchise as a necessary protection for the workers under modern industrial conditions' had particular legitimacy coming from women whose work conditions were exactly the same as their male counterparts.[11] Their professional skills were deployed directly to service the cause with the League's Play Department responsible for a lively culture of suffragette plays produced during the years leading up to the First World War.

However, just as most of the more prominent AFL activity was associated with the metropolitan campaign for women's voting rights, so the majority of key negotiations and affiliations, which influenced the working lives of actors, took place in London. London was where the majority of the agents and touring managers had their offices. Ambitious actors might go on the road with touring companies, but they returned to London. Even those who had enjoyed extended contracts in the regional repertory theatres would gravitate back to London where metropolitan success was the primary career goal. In 1935, the year the London Theatre Council was set up, chaired by Lord Esher with evenly matched representation from actors and managers, and the Esher Standard Contract was negotiated for London theatres, it was estimated that 50 per cent of all actors worked and/or resided in London. Not until 1939 was a Standard Provincial Contract approved along with the establishment of a Provincial Theatre Council. There was to be a minimum salary of £2.10s., rehearsal payment and an acceptance of a closed shop policy.[12]

ENTERING THE PROFESSION

At the beginning of the century, entry and acceptance into the profession was a haphazard business. Success and subsequent celebrity more often than not depended on opportunities provided in particular circles of influence. Training was a matter of absorbing the example and advice of more established actors. For the majority, that was acquired on the road touring with companies of varying quality and reputation and playing to audiences who represented a complete cross section of the British population. Actors' memoirs recalling in their early years frequently shifting from company to company offer a valuable insight into working conditions. Maud Gill, by her own admission 'a comparatively unknown actress', joined the Birmingham Repertory Theatre for its second 1913–14 season and remained with the company as actor and – exceptionally for a woman – stage manager from 1920 to 1924, before being cast as Thirza Tapper for the three-year Court Theatre run of *The Farmer's Wife*. By the time her autobiography was published in 1938, she had also carved out a comfortable niche in the British film industry including reprising Thirza for Alfred Hitchcock's film of the play. Her recollections of her life prior to Birmingham Rep constitute a personal micro-history of available employment options in the years leading up to the First World War.[13]

Brought up in a London suburb and initially destined for a teaching career, the only semi-formal training Gill received was from a private dance tutor who arranged ballets for London productions and provided an opportunity to audition for Beerbohm Tree. Dancing, with her sister, as very junior members of the company, introduced her to the family environment cultivated at His Majesty's: supper in the Dome at the top of the theatre and subsidised taxis home after late-night dress rehearsals, matinee teas in Lady Tree's dressing room. She and her sister were also in the company which went with selected Tree productions to Berlin in 1907.

An advertisement in *The Stage* for a full company for 'First-Class Repertory Plays' appeared to offer the chance to engage with the new literary drama. Instead, Gill was precipitated, wholly unprepared, as a juvenile lead on a salary of 25s. a week, into a portable company. The theatre complete with second-hand, plush tip-up seats was a tent, the highest admission price 9d, and she had immediately to learn the art of 'gagging': that is, improvising a character's words based on an outline of the play's plot, which were more or less fixed in rehearsal. Unlike the main play *The Mariners of England*, which featured the Battle of Trafalgar with fire-crackers used to realistic effect, 'Gag Pantomimes' performed for children for the price of 1d were unrehearsed.[14]

What followed in the years up until mid-1913, when Gill joined her actor husband E. Stuart Vinden at Birmingham Rep, included a small part in a fourteen-week No. 1 tour of a West End success; a large Shakespearean Company which travelled with four tons of scenery and a repertoire of 28 plays; a melodrama company which was in its third year of continuous touring and paid her a generous weekly salary of £2. 10s.; a summer Pastoral Company where the usual seasonal request for 'absolutely lowest summer terms' was made even more exploitative by the 'no play, no pay' uncertainties of the weather. Gill does not name the companies, but it is clear that within the exigencies of basic survival, she is attempting to build up a body of relevant experience.

Security of a kind could be found in the 'blood and thunder' melodramas for which there were still ample audiences. The melodrama repertoire made money and thus companies were not constrained by the usual pattern of thirteen-week spring seasons, and sixteen-week autumn seasons which often meant summer unemployment: 'Hundreds of actors and actresses stayed with the same companies for years and hundreds who suit melodrama could not have got engagements in any other kind of stage work.'[15] Gill got 'back into Comedy' playing the juvenile lead in a fit-up tour of Richard Ganthorney's hugely successful satirical play *A Message From Mars* and the Gerald Du Maurier vehicle *Raffles*, which appear to have travelled literally the length and breadth of all four countries – to the Scottish Highlands, Welsh mining villages and Irish coastal towns. Length of stay in any one venue could occasionally be as long as a week or three days, but the norm was to move every day. The company carried its own collapsible stage, proscenium and full lighting equipment with interchangeable electrical and gas fittings. Every new venue meant the search for new lodgings and more of the obligatory 'theatrical digs' anecdotes for her memory bank.

What emerges from the narrative is a life of chronic economic insecurity and the importance of informal networks. The Shakespeare Company broke up during the 1911–12 period of violent industrial unrest amongst dock and railway workers for example. Only one engagement resulted from hours of trudging round agents' offices; the others came through word of mouth. The benefit, however, was a thorough grounding in theatre practice at its most quotidian. Gill also provides glimpses of the way companies engaged with local communities. The melodrama management staged Friday night competitions where local people were invited to perform a long speech from the play and their talents were judged by a panel of their neighbours. Alternatively, a draw was held of tickets with a lucky number which could win a suite of furniture. In an Irish town, there was an example of actors 'parading': that is, walking round the town dressed in costume to publicise the show, a practice considered humiliating by more fastidious actors, Gill included, which was dying out. Only in Wales, in Gill's recollections, were actors sometimes refused permission to perform.[16]

Gill is not the only actor whose published experiences contradict the commonly received view that touring practice at the grass roots automatically meant slipshod performance standards. She was at pains to stress the sincerity and conscious professionalism displayed by melodrama actors, which matched the response of audiences who could form strong attachments to favoured performers. She also describes the careful, personal economies practised by the portable actors in their attempts to ward off penury, and the rigid managerial rules about company behaviour enforced by the melodrama management determined to maintain a reputation for respectability. In contrast, the No. 1 company consisted of experienced, able actors but disappointingly 'normal'. 'They were all well bred and charming – one could have met them anywhere.'[17]

CHANGING SOCIAL ORIGINS

It is well known that good breeding – a prosperous or solidly professional middle-or even upper-middle-class background – increasingly characterised new entrants to the theatre. The popularity of amateur theatricals as a pastime in middle-class Victorian families and, subsequently, the proliferation of amateur societies was an obvious incentive. Much new drama produced in London was set in a middle-class or an aristocratic milieu which leading actors attempted to reproduce in their management style. Untrained amateurs could also pay to perform. There were numerous advertisements offering opportunities to stage-struck hopefuls in return for a financial contribution towards a new venture. This indeed was one of the main complaints behind closed shop proposals as the profession moved towards formal unionisation. It was also regular practice for untried would-be actors to pay a premium on entry into a company. In 1920 in Brighton, Ralph Richardson, who had no acting experience of any kind, invested part of a small legacy in offering payment of 10s. a week for the opportunity to join a locally based company.[18]

The priority placed on good education amongst the professional classes, which at its most enlightened benefited girls as well as boys, together with the relaxation of religious and moral scruples, also inculcated an intellectual seriousness amongst those entrants who would contribute to the exemplary theatre.[19] For every affluent 'silly ass' or debutante eager to go on the stage – and Gill met several on her travels – there was a Lewis Casson (whose father built church organs) or a Sybil Thorndike (the daughter of an Anglican minister) all too earnest about their calling. There was growing consensus that the new professionalism required a satisfactory level of professional expertise, and there was significant establishment support for the two most prominent schools: the Academy of Dramatic Art established by Tree in 1904 and initially based at His Majesty's Theatre, and

Elsie Fogerty's Central School of Speech and Drama founded in 1906 and based at first in the Albert Hall. Both schools could draw on eminent theatre practitioners who taught a range of technical skills from voice production to dance, general deportment and fencing.[20] Ben Greet's Academy of Acting, founded in 1896, also provided a professional grounding for a number of actors of future importance, including Mrs Patrick Campbell, Sybil and Russell Thorndike, H. B. Irving and Leon Quartermaine.[21] Professional training in music, which had been established in London under the auspices of the Academy of Music as far back as 1861 and eventually evolved into the London Academy of Music and Dramatic Art, brought together the two disciplines in the study of elocution and verse speaking.

Formal training was relatively expensive and inevitably narrowed the class base of those who could take it up. Although serious young actors received a serious training, a very substantial majority of students were young women from prosperous homes for whom the new establishments could also function as finishing schools en route to social success and a good marriage. Other aspiring actors had to resort to other sources of assistance. Maud Gill was not unusual in that she had received some private tuition. Many professional practitioners set up as tutors especially in elocution and voice production. At the top, metropolitan end of the market, there was Hermin Vezin, the American-born actor and manager who had a distinguished classical career in the English theatre. He trained individual actors who benefited from his physical techniques to improve voice production and diction. Rosina Filippi, who had trained with Vezin and acted with both Benson and Tree, held classes in different London venues and showcased her students in public performances at the Court Theatre.[22]

The other factor that was to impact on actor performance in classical theatre especially was the presence on the margins of London theatre of William Poel and Charles Fry as experimental practitioners. Poel, part visionary, part crank – albeit with considerable grass-roots theatre experience – was to exercise a long-term influence on future directorial and scenographic innovation in the production of medieval and early modern drama. But at a time when a well-trained voice was arguably privileged over all other skills, young actors benefited from his ideas.

Poel's insistence on his theories of verse speaking, his 'tuned tones' in which actors including Harley Granville Barker, Edith Evans, Esmé Percy were relentlessly drilled, left an important legacy. Basil Dean as a young actor in the Horniman Company cast as Claudio in Poel's 1908 production of *Measure for Measure*, described 'the long hours of solitary instruction ... in the end I found Poel had taught me the secret of rhythmic speech, the value of the operative word and the magic of Shakespeare when it was spoken both musically and intelligently'.[23]

Charles Fry, a self-taught 'Reciter' of Shakespeare and other poetic dramatists who also recited to music, was from 1885 Professor of Elocution and Dramatic Art at the Hampstead Conservatoire of Music. His 'costume recitals' of Shakespeare staged in unconventional venues, which ranged from swimming baths to workers' centres, were important for both social and artistic reasons. For actors, including Elsie Forgerty who went on to develop his methods, he provided an excellent vocal training and an introduction to little-known classical texts. Lewis Casson, for example, worked extensively for both Poel and Fry, playing for Fry major Shakespearean roles such as Polixenes, Cassius and Posthumous.[24]

THE ENGLISH IMPERATIVE

There was nothing comparable in the leading cities of the other nations to the high-profile London institutions, and the professional nexus associated with the metropolitan schools was missing. In general there was little organised training opportunity outside London at all apart from personal tuition. Sarah Thorne's school at the Theatre Royal in Margate, where Barker had a brief apprenticeship in 1891, ceased when she died in 1899. In 1901, Frank and Constance Benson set up a Dramatic School attached to the company where students paid fees for tuition in elocution, dancing, fencing, 'dramatic technique' and gesture. Travelling expenses for what was of necessity an itinerant school were paid by the company, and students had the opportunity to walk on and swell crowd scenes but no automatic right of entry to the company once the pupildom was completed.[25]

Inevitably, there were no institutional opportunities to develop a culturally distinctive actor 'voice' and style outside England. There was a proposal put to the St Andrew's Society in 1913 to found a 'School of National Drama' in Scotland on the lines of the Irish Players of the Abbey Theatre, but nothing came of it.[26] Ironically, the Abbey Theatre School of Acting had been established in 1911 by an Englishman, Nugent Monck. Monck had trained as a musician, acted in Poel's Elizabethan Stage Society and then formed his own amateur company specialising in medieval and Tudor drama. His production of Yeats's *The Countess Cathleen* led to Yeats's invitation to go to Dublin where he trained and directed a No. 2 Abbey company.[27] However, Monck's work followed on from the earlier consciously nationalist attempts of Frank and Willy Fay to develop a distinctively Irish acting style within their amateur companies out of which the first productions of the Irish National Theatre Society emerged.[28] Frank Fay's ability to transmit his own considerable vocal skills to inexperienced actors was coupled with an interest in verse speaking, which as early as 1899 had identified in Poel's 'upward tone'[29] the inflection best suited to the Irish voice. His training methods combined practical coaching with theatre trips to observe great performances, especially by visiting French classical actors, which were available to Dublin audiences at the turn of the century. Out of this was created an unsophisticated, but peculiarly still, musically elegant ensemble approach which suited the new Irish poetic drama and startled English critics accustomed to the burlesqued brogue of the traditional stage Irishman.[30]

For the average actor who wanted to forge a livelihood out of a passion, esoteric amateur experiment, however artistically instructive, was not a substantial basis for a career in theatre, and British actors born outside England had to face the fact that English companies were the principal means of entry to the profession. The Irish actor Whitford Kane, who was born in Larne in County Antrim, was told that the only way to get into theatre was to go to England. Both he and Cathleen Nesbitt, who was a few years younger, were brought up in Belfast and both came from middle-class families that had fallen on hard times. Kane was the son of a doctor who had some youthful theatre experience, but who died when Kane was two. Sufficient money was scraped together to pay for elocution training from a self-styled 'Professor of the Art of Elocution' in Belfast, who tailored his teaching materials to suit both the Catholic and Protestant communities. Kane with a Catholic nationalist uncle was perfectly happy to recite patriotic poems from both sides of the divide.[31]

His account of his classes, like his subsequent anecdotes about employers such as the actor-manager Mrs Bandmann-Palmer first encountered on a Yorkshire railway platform ('a plump *hausfrau* of fifty years feeding bits of biscuit to a little dog'), contribute to the rich store of Edwardian theatrical vignettes.[32] But Kane refused to denigrate the discipline and attention to individual actor development which he experienced despite managerial eccentricity. Of his elocution teacher, he wrote that there was no attempt to reduce his Irish accent to an imitation of standard English. The emphasis instead was on the value of sound and the cultivation of 'definite colour and vibrancy'.[33]

Cathleen Nesbitt's father was a failed businessman who owned an unsuccessful shipbuilding firm. Her elocution teacher, who encouraged a successful amateur performance on the stage of the Belfast Theatre Royal, combined with her mother's London contacts to enable a trial term with Rosina Filippi. Just as French lessons had been exchanged for elocution lessons in Belfast, so care of Filippi's children was bartered in exchange for further opportunities to train. A tiny, but perfectly executed comic role as a French wet nurse in the end-of-term showcase at the Court secured her an understudy and small-role contract with J. E. Vedrenne. Crucially, however, living in London, an opportunity to perform for charity in an aristocratic amateur company took her, via the navigable society, into the circle which included Lady Gregory. What followed was a reading for Yeats and a contract with the Irish Players for their 1911 American tour, and on her return the role of Perdita in *The Winter's Tale*, the first of Barker's experimental Shakespeare productions at the Savoy Theatre.[34]

Both Kane and Nesbitt entered Barker's managerial and directorial orbit and thus became part of the 'other' theatre establishment. Kane's career trajectory, however, was less meteoritic. His 'ten years in the provinces' as he put it, included two years with Bandmann-Palmer's repertoire of some 16 plays. His conscious decision to extend his 'apprenticeship' took him to Edinburgh to join the company of the Scottish actor William Mollison, whose portrayal of heroic national drama characters such as Rob Roy made him popular throughout Scotland.[35] Ironically, it was Mollison's attempt to appeal to English audiences by purchasing the provincial rights to John Galsworthy's topical play about industrial unrest, *Strife*, that gave Kane the opportunity to play the Labour leader David Roberts. Galsworthy's approval boosted his attempts to join the Barker/Frohman company at the Duke of York's where the first play was Galsworthy's *Justice*. What followed were invitations to join the Horniman company in Manchester and then participate in Basil Dean's opening season at the Liverpool Repertory Theatre.[36]

VARSITY MEN

The time-honoured, informal, person-to-person means by which employment was secured was also a way of introducing new kinds of artistic priorities. At a deep level, although it would not have been immediately obvious in the first two decades of the century, power relations were beginning to shift mediated through the influential networks created by the modernist campaigns. However, by the 1920s a potentially gifted actor, and, as we shall see, a gifted director, could achieve almost instant access to metropolitan theatre through the Oxbridge system. The importance of the two pre-eminent universities in the cultural as well as the political life of the nation remained a significant factor in the leadership of the industry.

The acceptance of student theatricals as an appropriate extra-curricular activity at Cambridge and Oxford was arguably as relevant for societal approval as the growing enthusiasm of members of the clergy. Indeed, the two were interlinked. In Cambridge the Amateur Dramatic Club (ADC) was founded in 1855 by F. C. Burnand, the future editor of *Punch* magazine and prolific writer of light plays. In 1907 the Marlowe Society was inaugurated by a production of *Dr Faustus* in part produced by William Bridges-Adams, who had just left Bedales School, and with Rupert Brooke as Mephistophilis.[37] In Oxford in 1880 the performance in Greek of the *Agamemnon* of Aeschylus, initiated by Frank Benson, had two direct consequences: the founding five years later of the Oxford University Dramatic Society (OUDS), and Benson's career as an actor-manager.[38]

The fact that Benson's company attracted a high proportion of actors from middle-class, professional backgrounds, some of whom like Benson were products of public school and university, created some animosity in the wider theatrical community. The importance of sport, especially team games, in the daily company routine, together with Benson's insistence on very lengthy rehearsals, provided more ammunition for those inclined to sneer at his provincial status. Notoriously, when Benson made a final, unsuccessful attempt to establish himself as a metropolitan star in 1900, Max Beerbohm's satirical review of *Henry the Fifth*, which he dubbed 'adequate meaning inadequate' and opened with 'Mr F. R. Benson is an Oxford man … the influence of university cricket has been seen in the cricket fields of many provincial towns visited by Mr Benson's company',[39] would have a devastating impact.

Unquestionably, Benson's companies over more than thirty years provided valuable experience and training to the generation of actors and directors who would go on to form the backbone of classical theatre in the interwar period. Later generations would not sneer at a preoccupation with the fit body of the actor or the way a collective *esprit de corps* was maintained. The historical record has tended to foreground personal idiosyncrasies through an undue emphasis on the comic anecdotes associated with Benson's performance career. But there was, albeit compromised, a considered idealism in his production style. The recruitment of university men, and indeed the daughters of professional families who could feel secure within the gentlemanly company ethos, was contributing to the new breed of socially and intellectually ambitious practitioners who would come to dominate the profession.

The university societies began to become more directly influential. The practice of employing professional directors and invitations to selected professional actresses to play female roles, allied with the elite status of the students, meant that ADC's and OUDS's productions could attract distinguished audiences which included theatre critics from national newspapers. Robert Speaight's recollections of Oxford in the early 1920s insist that there was an absence of class or other distinctions: 'People were taken at their real, not their social or monetary, value.'[40] However, his account of the daily civilities of intellectual intercourse, 'the ardent aesthetic curiosity', the way doors could open to the upper echelons of society and even when cash-strapped, the opportunities for European travel and the experience of European theatre, make it abundantly clear how privileged the Oxford milieu was. His contemporary, the Welsh actor Emlyn Williams, who unlike Speaight really was the archetypal scholarship boy from a working-class, Welsh-speaking home in Flintshire, paints a very similar picture. Although Williams's career at Oxford was not emotionally untroubled, his membership of the OUDS allowed him direct access to a career in London theatre.[41]

Speaight, who was to play the cowardly Lieutenant Hibbert in the first commercial production of R. C. Sheriff's *Journey's End* in 1929, is careful to stress that the OUDS's players were 'happy amateurs' who had a lot to learn once they attempted to enter theatre professionally. But unlike Whitford Kane, he did not have to serve a long apprenticeship, but went straight to the Liverpool Repertory Theatre largely as a result of meeting William Armstrong who was guest-directing the OUDS. Speaight's year at Liverpool was not a happy experience despite a range of good parts: 'I was quick to realise that star parts at Oxford, even under expert direction was no substitute for a systematic training at a drama school, or for a year or two finding my feet in a humbler repertory or on tour.'[42] The Oxford effect continued, however, as Speaight was invited to create the role of Becket in T. S. Eliot's *Murder in the Cathedral*, directed in 1935 in the Canterbury Cathedral Chapter House by another Oxford contemporary, E. Martin Browne.

The OUDS nexus between 1929 and 1932, described by Irving Wardle in his biography of George Devine, brought together key individuals who would contribute to transformative events in the metropolitan narrative. The undergraduate actors in the 1931 production of Flecker's *Hassan* staged at Oxford's New Theatre included Devine and Giles Playfair (the son of Nigel Playfair), William Devlin, Frith Banbury, Terence Rattigan and Hugh Hunt (who by 1935 was directing at the Abbey Theatre). Peggy Ashcroft was not only invited to play the role of Pervaneh, but found herself roped in to support Devine's successful bid to be president of the OUDS. John Gielgud, well on his way to becoming a major star, was invited the following year to direct his first production of *Romeo and Juliet*, bringing with him three young women artists later known collectively as Motley. Ashcroft played Juliet with Edith Evans as the Nurse. Devine, 'an ambitious amateur with influential friends', was cast as Mercutio, and began, as Wardle puts it, to draw 'the first of a series of magic circles' round the new generation of actors and artists who would go on to become the next theatre establishment.[43]

THE REPERTORY ACTOR

The repertory actor under contract to perform a number of roles within a resident building-based ensemble for a season of plays became an increasingly familiar figure after the First World War. The kind of roles played and the quality and ambition of the artistic challenge varied with the type of company, its managerial objectives and the expectations of the audiences. What was common to all was the enormous pressure of the short-run system, which could see a company producing between 30 and 35 plays in the course of a year. Even the top-of-the-range reps in Birmingham and Liverpool changed plays every two to three weeks, which could add up to 18 productions a year. Most theatres could only sustain one-week runs, many with the added burden of twice-nightly performances. The Old Vic itself was a short-run theatre with the annually assembled Shakespeare Company presenting 10 plays over eleven months with a three-week turnaround. Outside the old-style touring companies, 'true repertory' of a sort could only be seen at the Shakespeare Memorial Theatre in Stratford-upon-Avon, and that was confined to the two short spring and summer Festival seasons.

At the Memorial Theatre in the 1920s, William Bridges-Adams's New Shakespeare Company was given seven weeks to rehearse eight plays all scheduled to open over the course of the first week of the four-week spring season. Two more plays were added for the eight-week summer season. Unlike Benson who kept his stock productions for years and an equally familiar company of actors, Bridges-Adams had to start from scratch with productions each year, and despite a core of regularly contracted actors could not maintain a permanent ensemble. As Sally Beauman has pointed out, he came to depend very heavily on actors such as Baliol Holloway, Randle Ayrton and Dorothy Green for leading roles, who had all been trained in the traditions of late Victorian and Edwardian theatre and could respond quickly with their well-honed, traditional skills. While Holloway and Co. were robust, charismatic actors, they would have been accustomed to formulaic acting conventions, which assisted a speedy production process and which took a long time to fade from memory.[44] Formulaic casting even in the 1920s and 30s was still a convenient way of achieving an efficient production process especially in the commercial theatre.

The practice of employing actors to play 'lines of business', i.e. 'a number of roles within the bounds of his or her own speciality', dated as far back as the acting ensembles of the late sixteenth century, but became strongly entrenched during the popular ascendancy of melodrama. Even as melodrama in its purest form faded away to be replaced by more up-to-date domestic and costume dramas, 'crook plays' and light comedy after the First World War, a company resident for a season in a commercially run regional theatre could still be contracted on a similar basis.

Fraser describes the engagement of Leon Salberg's Alexandra Theatre Repertory Company in 1927: 'Leading Man, Leading Lady, Juvenile, Ingenue, Character, Grande Dame (or Dowager), Utility and other labels on them all'.[45] A typical company could have a core of between twelve and fifteen actors supplemented if necessary by local amateurs, and all expected to work within a twice-nightly, play-a-week system. This meant in any one week mentally juggling three plays; forgetting the previous week's play as soon as it came down on a Saturday night; performing the current play twice for six evenings of that week, while rehearsing the play for the following week during the day. Plays were cut to fit the time constraints of the twice-nightly schedule. Kate Dunn cites examples of actors given only the text of their own parts with the relevant cues inserted – a practice Shakespeare's company would have recognised.[46]

The evidence for how far actors achieved the DLP ('dead letter perfect') target for a new role in time for the first performance varies with individual recollections. Fraser records the occasional actor-collapse mid-performance which necessitated a substitute with a book.[47] But contributors to Richard Jerrams's account of weekly rep insist on high levels of professional competence underpinned by draconian contractual obligation especially from the managers of commercially run repertory companies. Jerrams quotes Janet Burnell employed as Leading Lady at the Coventry Theatre Royal for the 1935–6 season:

Prompts were very rarely needed. The occasional slip-ups were invariably coped with by the cast itself, leaving the audience unaware of any mishap or lapse of memory. To learn quickly and accurately soon became a habit. Different people had different pet methods, many writing out their cues and parts for final assurance. The one common denominator being to *forget quickly* … to wipe one's memory clear of the current play immediately after the last show on Saturday night.

Actors were employed to *work* and an important aspect of this was the DLP imperative. A new employee in one of Harry Hanson's companies was told there was no prompter: 'Mr Hanson pays you to learn your lines, he doesn't pay someone to do them for you. If you get yourself into a mess, you get yourself out of it.'[48]

This was theatre functioning as a service industry that privileged the convenience of the consumer and the demands of the business model that dictated its employment parameters. As Fraser emphasises, 'the wonder of it was that there was never any difficulty in recruiting a reasonably sound company for twice-nightly, weekly "rep," and that, with a few exceptions, those recruited seemed to enjoy the slavery and thrive on the drudgery'.[49] Weekly, if not twice-nightly weekly rep, functioned for – at a conservative estimate – something like fifty years, certainly into the early 1960s. For the jobbing actor it offered periods of security and if part of a resident company, the opportunity to bed into a local community where she or he could achieve a modest celebrity status.[50]

Richard Foulkes, supplying more detail about the financial basis of actor employment at the Royal Theatre in Northampton in the late 1920s and early 1930s, also pauses to wonder why actors put themselves through this treadmill. As a 'citizens' theatre, the commercial imperative was not predominant, but twice-nightly kept the company afloat. Between 4 August and 22 December 1930, 19 plays were produced. Just two, J. B. Fagan's *And So To Bed* and Frederick Lonsdale's *The Last of Mrs Cheney* which both made a profit, played for two weeks. Foulkes quotes Chisholm's assertion that a repertory management could not hope to provide a respectable service without spending £80 a week on actors. In Northampton the Board paid significantly less and there were also gender differentials.

In 1934 a company of eleven actors was employed for a weekly total of £54: the three principal male actors on £7, £6 and £5.10s.; the three main women £6, £3.10s. and £3. The last salary was for Freda Jackson, then

an early career actress who would go on to achieve a national reputation. Aged 25, a graduate of Nottingham University, and with two years,
teaching experience, she initially entered the company in mid-1933 as a
pupil. That is, her status was of an unpaid apprentice who, moreover, had
to supply her own personal wardrobe for modern plays. Not all theatres
operated this arrangement, and it only applied to women, as men who
were in shorter supply were a more valuable commodity. Jackson played
for five months unpaid before being put on the salary list. By the time she
left in late 1935, her salary had risen to £4.10s.[51]

Even when, as in Northampton, there were constraints on the intellectual and aesthetic demands of the plays selected for each season, there was
the adrenalin charge of live performance for audiences happy to recognise talent, and the promise, if successful, of moving on in the profession
and perhaps making it to the metropolitan theatre. The 'provinces' had
always been where actors served an apprenticeship, but the idea of the
on-the-job training supplied by the regional producing theatres becomes
firmly established at this period. Well-educated actors from professional
families, who might have sought out Benson in the early years of the century, could now embark on a career trajectory, which included a stint in a
well-regarded repertory theatre. Foulkes provides an analysis of the social
and educational background of the Northampton company members in
the late 1920s, ranging from public school, good girls' grammar school,
university and in several cases, RADA-training. Individual actors in the
early stages of durable careers such as Curigwen Lewis, Godfrey Kenton,
Max Adrian and James Hayter came to Northampton with previous
experience which included the Cambridge Festival Theatre, Bristol Little
Theatre, and the Lena Ashwell and Charles Macdona companies.[52]

Liverpool Playhouse and Birmingham Rep were the regional destina-
tions of choice, with Birmingham's greater financial security and multiple links to the metropolis making it an important breeding ground for
new actors in the interwar period. Both Ralph Richardson and Laurence
Olivier were contracted company members playing in Birmingham itself,
on tour with the money-spinning *Farmer's Wife*, and in selected London
productions. Olivier was with the company from 1926 until 1928, playing
over twenty roles which ranged from Uncle Vanya and Tony Lumpkin to
Parolles in *All's Well That End Well* and Malcolm in *Macbeth*. The short-
run regime could not allow the luxury of in-depth contemplation of character and innovative performance technique, but it developed the stamina,
flexibility and versatility required of actors seeking career advancement in
the mixed economy of pre-1939 theatre.[53]

Actors whose entire careers were to be based mainly in London also benefited from more discrete opportunities provided by the exemplary ethos and the focus on classical or modern literary drama. Gielgud's first major role was of Romeo in Barry Jackson's 1924 London revival of a production first staged on home ground in 1922. Edith Evans, already quite well-known in London in 1923, made the conscious choice to go to Birmingham to play in the British premiere of Shaw's *Back to Methusaleh*. A London agent secured Peggy Ashcroft's first professional engagement in Birmingham for a 1926 production of Barrie's *Dear Brutus*.[54] In Ashcroft's case what followed was constant, often indiscriminate movement between commercial West End contracts and more artistically challenging roles in the club theatres plus one more production in Birmingham where she was cast with Olivier in John Drinkwater's comedy *Bird in Hand* in 1929. The ultimate 'repertory' ensemble-based destination for all the individuals cited above, and Liverpool graduates such as Michael Redgrave in 1936, was the Old Vic. A year's contract from Lilian Baylis meant hard, unglamorous – in terms of the physical environment – and notoriously underpaid work. But it paid handsome dividends in artistic capital. For the 1932–3 season Ashcroft was contracted, at £20 a week, to play Imogen, Rosalind, Miranda, Portia, Perdita, Juliet, Shaw's Cleopatra, Kate Hardcastle, Lady Teazle and the title role in Drinkwater's *Mary Stuart*. 'It was like,' she later recalled, 'always running for a train.'[55]

NEW MEDIA, NEW OPPORTUNITIES

For actors, as for all theatre professionals, the relationship with the growing accessibility and technical sophistication of new electronic media was complicated. Not only was the urban entertainment landscape transformed by the expansion of cinema, but after 1920 and the advent of radio, the interior domestic space could hypothetically become the site of encounters with the voices and sounds of British culture on a hitherto unprecedented scale. The possibilities of television, which the BBC started to demonstrate with experimental broadcasts in 1929, were scarcely imaginable. As actors were forced to adapt to changing trends in theatre practice, they also had to work out how best to accommodate and exploit new and unfamiliar employment opportunities.

Leaving aside the threat to the survival of live theatre as a whole, the main challenge lay in the way the new media accelerated the centralisation of industrial practice. Film, radio and eventually TV could take the consumer on richly diverse imaginative journeys. The actual sites of production were far more restricted. Rachael Low's history of British film up until 1929 describes attempts to establish film studios in locations as varied as Paignton and Babbacombe in Devon, Kingsbury in Hertfordshire and St Anne's-on-Sea near Blackpool, but all were short-lived. By the mid-1920s virtually all the studios were concentrated in or around London.[56] The inevitable outcome was that film hopefuls in their hundreds had to gravitate towards London and its environs. As silent films became longer and more ambitious, more actors were employed. The opportunities for mass crowd work became plentiful, although as Low points out, British film crowd scenes could be woefully inept compared with the more sophisticated sequences created by European counterparts.[57] Indeed, for silent film without any literary or high art pretensions, theatre actors were not necessarily wanted and a separate pool of silent performers was developed along with strategies for training.

From as early as 1899, however, when Beerbohm Tree was filmed as Shakespeare's King John, established classical actors, generously remunerated, reproduced their stage performances for screen. In 1908 Godfrey Tearle laid the foundations for a film career that lasted into the 1950s in a film of *Romeo and Juliet* which used the Lyceum sets. Some Benson productions of Shakespeare including *Richard III* were filmed at the Shakespeare Memorial Theatre in 1911, the same year as Tree's *Henry VIII* was committed to film. Johnston Forbes-Robinson's *Hamlet* was filmed in 1913. Other plays from the actor-managerial romantic repertoire followed, including *David Garrick* with Charles Wyndham, *Caste* and *A Pair of Spectacles* with John Hare, and George Alexander's production of *The Second Mrs Tanqueray*.[58]

For most established actors film seems to have been about pecuniary advantage and for those who chose to become involved in production, investment opportunity. Charles Macdona and A. E. Matthews were, respectively, chairman and managing director of the British Actors Film Company, which Matthews set up in 1914 in Bushey building on work produced by Hubert von Herkomer. BAFC continued to produce a steady flow of what Low describes as 'unsensational and rather old-fashioned dramas' until 1920 when the company was taken over. Well-known actors such as Irene Vanbrugh, Godfrey Tearle, Gladys Cooper and Owen Nares appeared in their films, while Leslie Howard effectively launched his career with the company in the 1914 film *The Heroine of Mons*, directed by his uncle Wilfred Noy.[59] British silent film-makers also attempted to exploit well-known stage plays including *Hobson's Choice* (1920) and *Hindle Wakes* (1927). Ivor Novello featured in both Margaret

Kennedy and Basil Dean's *The Constant Nymph* (1928), which Dean produced, and Coward's *The Vortex* (1928).

The Jazz Singer, produced in America and shown in England in September 1928, ended years of tinkering with sound technology and confirmed the commercial viability of sound film despite some futile protestations to the contrary. It rendered many silent film performers unemployable and immediately upped the ante for the vocally trained stage actor. The American film industry continued to offer a realistic prospect of international stardom and high earnings, which by the early 1930s saw several actors including Laurence Olivier and Cedric Hardwicke literally criss-crossing the Atlantic between theatre and film.[60] However, the quota system first introduced by government legislation in 1927 ensured that a rising proportion of British films were seen on British screens. While the worst effect of this was the so-called 'quota quickie', by 1935 when the proportion had reached 20 per cent British producers theoretically had a somewhat better chance of combining financial with artistic credibility.

Actors employed in London theatres in the 1930s could appear on stage at night and line their pockets from work in film during the day. With the benefit of an easily dispersed presence on celluloid, a Gielgud or an Olivier had no need of the old-style touring system to maintain a star reputation outside the capital. An Equity report gives a clear picture of the demographic implications for the acting profession: 'London with its first-class theatres has its studios grouped within motoring distance and as a result it is from the London stage that the English film industry draws all but a very small percentage of its acting material.'[61] Pinewood Studios, built in 1934 and by 1936 controlled by J. Arthur Rank, and the colossal Denham Studios, built for Alexander Korda's London Film Productions in 1936 following the lucrative popular success of *The Private Life of Henry VIII*, were both sited on country estates in Buckinghamshire. When Tyrone Guthrie persuaded Lilian Baylis to contract Charles Laughton, who had played Korda's Henry, for a series of major Shakespearean roles at the Old Vic in 1933, audiences were agog to see the film star.[62]

The irony of this is that an industry with a nationwide distributive capacity, which could give some warmth and imaginative escape to the sector of society most vulnerable to the catastrophic effects of economic depression, manufactured films that for the most part, as Roy Armes has argued, organised 'the audience's experience in the sense of fostering social integration and the acceptance of social constraint'.[63] Moreover, in films other than the equally reassuring comedies with roots in the northern music-hall tradition, this was mediated through a distinctive idea of 'Englishness' represented by the leading actors, especially those employed by Korda, who included Leslie Howard (whose father was Hungarian), Robert Donat (whose father was Polish), John Clements, Flora Robson, Ralph Richardson and Charles Laughton. The film producer Michael Balcon remarked, albeit with hindsight, 'With the coming of sound there was a resistance to anyone who did not speak "stage English". Accents, dialect, regional or "class" intonations meant you were restricted to the character parts. The lamentable preference was for the English of the drama schools and South Kensington.'[64]

RADIO VOICES

While it has been estimated that for a variety of reasons, including pockets of extreme poverty and the technical difficulties of reception, about 13.5 million people did not have access to radio by 1939, it is safe to say that by the time the Second World War broke out listening to the 'wireless' had become firmly integrated into the domestic lives of the majority of the population. Once the problems of distortion and interference began to be resolved and the hours of broadcasting extended, this was a medium hungry for material which practitioners from across the whole spectrum of performing arts were eager to supply.

The main differences between radio and film were that radio remained live, the product was always 'fresh', it privileged the voice over all other physical attributes, and although the transmitted product became more deliberately centralised in London, the network of broadcast stations sited right across the British Isles permitted a degree of local autonomy. The dominant voice was inevitably English with clearly identifiable middle- to upper-class speech patterns and pronunciation. But other voices could be heard, and in the aftermath of the creation of the Irish Free State and the growth of nationalist movements in Scotland and Wales, there was a clamour for transmission in other indigenous languages. It would be 1933 before the first Gaelic radio play was broadcast, and produced by someone who did not speak or understand the language, but the first broadcast in Gaelic was as early as 1923.[65] In Wales initially both economic and technical factors prevented access to radio much beyond broadcast centres in Cardiff and Swansea, and even when Wales-wide across the whole country, comparatively little attention was paid to Welsh-language broadcasts until a separate Welsh home service came into existence in 1937.[66]

However, as technological requirements drove the relationship between the core and the periphery in the distribution of radio, so it also helped create a set of circumstances where a strand of actor development began to emerge alongside the metropolitan experience that laid the foundation for a new generation of professional actors working within culturally distinctive theatres. Paddy Scannell has explained how the period between 1922 and 1930 saw a buoyant local radio service, largely because in the beginning the reception range of broadcasting stations was very limited. In the earliest years, transmission across the British Isles was enabled by nine 'Main Stations' in major urban areas which included, in addition to London, Manchester, Birmingham, Belfast, Glasgow, Aberdeen and Cardiff. Their transmission capacity was augmented by ten extra relay stations with a similar geographical spread. All were linked directly to London through Post Office telephone lines, and once the technique of 'Simultaneous Broadcasts' was introduced, a programme transmitted from any one station could be shared by others, and all could receive a selection of London programmes.[67] The result was that copious amounts of broadcast material had to come from local providers, in particular available amateur performers.

Adrienne Scullion has stated in an argument, which can be extended to the other national and regional centres, that Scottish broadcasters working from the cluster of main and relay stations in Scotland 'tended to look to what was immediate and to use the cultural products and reference points of their own world view'.[68] For the provision of drama, where more ambitious amateur companies like the Scottish National Players were focused on nurturing an indigenous national dramatic repertoire, their enthusiasm and flexibility provided a resource which could thus be incorporated to local advantage. The actor-manager R. E. Jeffrey, who became producer for both Scottish main stations and Aberdeen's first Station Director, presented classics of the National Drama, such as *Rob Roy*, and new Scottish drama, especially the one-act chamber pieces which the Scottish National Players tended to prioritise. By the time Jeffrey moved to London to become the BBC's first Head of Drama in mid-1924, he had created what were core radio repertory companies accustomed to working quickly and efficiently with material that required not just a stock Scottish voice, but a range of accents and dialect.[69]

In general this very lively, genuinely local broadcasting service did not survive the centralisation policy implemented by the BBC's Director General, John Reith. The relay stations were not economic and there was an increasing desire to exercise more quality control and consciously spread metropolitan influence. By 1930 London was transmitting the National Programme while the Regional Programme was broadcast from programme-making centres serving the North, the Midlands, the South-West, Scotland and later Wales and Northern Ireland. The problem here was that technical priorities dictated a rather arbitrary construction of regional identity, which meant, for example, that dissimilar locales such as the Black Country and the Cotswolds were thrown together in one regional service. But what had been established was an acceptance of locally based individuals to voice the programmes, some of whom were either wholly amateur or aspiring professional actors. In Wales after the Second World War, radio employment became an important aspect of 'pre-professional' opportunity for young actors. In Scotland it helped, as Scullion has argued, to 're-create an atmosphere conducive to the creation of indigenous professional theatre', which could offer satisfying employment prospects for future professional actors.[70]

RADIO AND THE METROPOLITAN ACTOR

It took a long time before the full potential of what radio drama could achieve began even to be imagined, and initially there was a direct dependency on live theatre in London and readily available, classically trained actors. The first drama transmission on 14 November 1922 by the consortium then known as the British Broadcasting Company was of the Quarrel Scene in *Julius Caesar*, with Robert Atkins as Cassius and Robert Gill as Brutus, in a programme which also included scenes from *Henry VIII* and *Much Ado About Nothing*. During the early months of 1923 excerpts from current West End theatre productions were broadcast, but managements rapidly became alarmed about possible competition and withdrew co-operation. Cathleen Nesbitt and Lewis Casson were among the actors who helped fill the vacuum. Nesbitt cut and produced several Shakespearean plays, including *Twelfth Night*, *A Midsummer Night's Dream* and *Romeo and Juliet*.[71] Casson directed seven plays in 1924 which ranged from Maeterlinck's *The Death of Tintagiles* to Russell Thorndike's Grand Guignol *The Tragedy of Mr Punch*. He also directed an adaptation of *Medea* and the death of Queen Katharine from *Henry VIII* with Sybil Thorndike.[72]

Up until 1930 some theatre managements continued actively to discourage actors from radio performance. Val Gielgud, brother to John and a former actor who was Head of Radio Drama 1929–64, suggested that some young actors were nervous of adapting their voices to suit radio for fear of jeopardising employment opportunities in theatre. Older actors accustomed to filling large auditoria also had their vocal technique challenged. Val Gielgud described how Henry Ainley, playing Othello, had to be physically held away from the microphone to stop him treating the studio like Drury Lane.[73] However, over time such distinguished thespians as Lady Forbes Robertson, Lady Tree and Mrs Kendall were introduced to radio audiences. When R. E. Jeffrey transferred from Aberdeen in 1924, some 900 would-be radio actors were given microphone auditions. There was also the first, if short-lived, attempt to set up a core Radio Repertory company. Asa Briggs has stated that between August 1924 and September 1925 141 'plays' were broadcast although the category of 'play' was interpreted very broadly.[74] The introduction of the 'Mixing-and-controlling Unit', later known as the Dramatic-control panel, which had reached a stage of technical excellence by 1928 and enabled the mixing of music, voices, sound and crowd effects, began to indicate the potential for a whole new form of drama. The BBC Drama Repertory Company, reformed in 1939, began to create a new sector of specialist radio actors.[75]

NEW INFLUENCES

In 1934 the convergence of three individuals in the BBC North Region studios in Manchester brought together an eclectic combination of class origin, ideological orientation, educational and theatrical influences which would infiltrate new principles of training into a generation of actors radicalised by the economic inequalities of the 1930s. Manchester was an ideal breeding ground, in part because of the still vibrant cultural life, which had drawn Horniman and Co. thirty years earlier, but also because of the visible effects of the economic depression and industrial turmoil. The North Region's Director of Programmes, Archie Harding, 'an Oxford intellectual Marxist', engaged the voices of both Jimmie Miller (aka Ewan MacColl), then an unemployed socialist teenager who had founded an left-wing amateur theatre group, the Salford Red Megaphones; and Joan Littlewood, a disaffected ex-RADA student, who had literally walked part of the way from London to claim a job from Harding. Both became part of the group gathered around Harding working on innovative, dramatised radio documentaries, which set out to record and present the voices, sounds and environmental circumstances of ordinary working or *non-working* people across the huge and very diverse northern region.[76]

As joint leaders of Theatre of Action, which evolved into Theatre Union in 1936, MacColl and Littlewood shared a working-class family background, although as a South London scholarship girl, Littlewood had been educated in a rich literary heritage. Her love of Shakespeare had been nurtured in the gallery of the Old Vic, and for all her discontents at RADA, her medal-winning vocal excellence was what first attracted Harding. Her brief introduction to the dance and movement theories of Rudolf Laban while at RADA, however, signalled a new and subsequently important strand to the intensive actor training that she and MacColl set out to develop in the enthusiasts who gravitated towards their company. MacColl, self-educated and already aligned with the Workers' Theatre Movement spreading rapidly amongst politically radicalised communities, had sufficient knowledge of Russian and German agit-prop theatre, to recognise the need to access the flood of ideas about theatrical form and practical performance methodologies then circulating around Europe.[77]

Functioning precariously with mostly unpaid actors, what distinguishes Theatre Union was the emphasis on actor training. Unlike the majority of the interwar amateur groups, these were consciously pre-professional. Professionalism was not defined in terms of remuneration, but based on thoroughly honed craft skills. The rejection of the cash nexus in the other major left-wing groups such as Unity meant that amateur status was a matter of principle, which would eventually become problematic in later attempts to turn professional. Where the intention, as with Theatre Union, was to create a new, flexible theatrical language that could communicate political commitment clearly but through a range of theatrical forms, the most necessary commodity was time. Howard Goorney's account of the early Theatre Union training sessions quotes Anne Dyson who became an established character actress after the war. The Stanislavskian exercises were a 'revelation': 'the one luxury we had in those days was the amount of time … analysing everything in great detail, dissecting right down to the bone and then building up again'.[78]

By the mid-1930s, for the individuals who had opted out of the pressures imposed on the average jobbing actor, the influence of the Russian and European avant-garde was becoming better known, mediated as Derek Paget has shown, through publications such as Léon Moussinac's *The New Movement in the Theatre*, published in English in 1931.[79] However, MacColl and Littlewood were certainly not developing their ideas in a vacuum even within the British context. As a student at the Central School of Speech and Drama, Peggy Ashcroft read Stanislavsky's *My Life in Art* when an English translation appeared in 1924.[80] The presence in experimental London theatre since 1919 of the Russian émigré Theodore

Komisarjevsky (whom Ashcroft married in 1933) brought first-hand knowledge of Stanislavsky and Meyerhold. He had already transformed approaches to Chekhovian performance for actors such as Gielgud whom he directed in *Three Sisters* in 1926.[81] In 1927 Lord Howard de Walden sponsored a Komisarjevsky-directed, out-door production of Ibsen's *The Pretenders* performed in Welsh, by Welsh amateur actors in Holyhead.[82] *The Merchant of Venice*, given eight rehearsals at the Shakespeare Memorial Theatre in 1932, was the first of Komis's seven ground-breaking guest productions with the hard-pressed actors of the New Shakespeare Company.[83] In the same year, George Devine, as a result of his OUDS Mercutio, was cast in his reworking of Meyerhold's constructivist version of *Le Cocu Magnifique* for the Stage Society.[84]

There was no attempt, however, to translate the galvanising effect of sporadic experimentalism into any kind of systematic training until 1936, when the London Theatre Studio was established in a disused Methodist chapel in Islington under the tutelage of Michel Saint-Denis assisted by Devine. In complete contrast to the gadfly Komisarjevsky, Saint-Denis, the nephew of Jacques Copeau, was committed to Copeau's austere principles of forging an acting ensemble out of rigorous and extended physical and emotional exercises. Unlike Littlewood and MacColl working equally hard in northern isolation, Saint-Denis was part of the magic circle which included Gielgud, the Motleys, Olivier and Tyrone Guthrie. Bronson Albery who had originally introduced Saint-Denis's Compagnie des Quinze at the Arts Theatre in 1931 was another backer. The actor Marius Goring, who had first seen Saint-Denis on tour with Copeau at the Cambridge Festival Theatre in 1928, combined enthusiastic advocacy with strenuous fund-raising.

Even so, the structures of metropolitan theatre were not conducive to the emergence of the intended permanent company out of the LTS. For three years, until the outbreak of war, a very diverse range of students underwent training which included mask, clowning, improvisation and the psychology of acting. But as Irving Wardle points out, the training was focused on a theatre that did not yet exist. There were curious anomalies in the kinds of dramatic texts and skills tuition offered, and no one was prepared for the nuts and bolts of applying for, still less of holding down, a job. Yvonne Mitchell, whose recollections of the school contributed to the historical record, and Peter Ustinov, who was not temperamentally well-suited to the Saint-Denis ethos, became perhaps the best-known graduates.[85] As with so much of the experimental activity swirling around London in the interwar years, which permitted actors to dip in and out of opportunities for creative development, the value lay in the seeds sown for the future.

SPREADING THE WORD

It is important to emphasise, however, that influence did spread outside London. The opportunity to witness Komisarjevsky's Chekhov productions at the Barnes Theatre, or the expressionist drama and scenography presented by Terence Gray in Cambridge, and Peter Godfrey at the tiny Gate Theatre in Covent Garden, was not confined to a metropolitan coterie. In 1930, R. F. Pollock, a Glaswegian estate agent whose friends included many of the creative writers in the vanguard of the literary revival known as the Scottish Renaissance, founded the Tron Theatre Club based in the Keir Hardie Institute in Glasgow, then the home of a number of socialist amateur theatre groups. For Pollock who had engaged in amateur drama since boyhood, the Tron Club was a direct result not only of seeing the Barnes's productions in 1926, but also of experiencing first hand the theatre in Moscow.[86]

As an integrated, amateur, play-producing organisation, the Tron did not survive the emergence of splinter groups in 1933, but Pollock's focus on close reading and detailed extended rehearsals of European classics and new Scottish drama grew new, identifiably Scottish actors and spawned similar enterprises. From the Tron, then the Project Theatre, and, most importantly, the Curtain Theatre, which was founded in a terraced house in Glasgow in 1933 by Grace Ballantine, emerged future stalwarts of the professional Scottish theatre such as Eileen Herlie, Andrew Crawford and Paul Vincent Carroll. Duncan Macrae, who became arguably the most celebrated Scottish actor of his generation, acted and directed in all the groups, and in 1937 created the title role in Ballantine's production of Robert McLellan's *Jamie the Saxt* – the only Curtain play to be published and professionally revived.

McLellan's use of a synthetic, non-localised form of the Lowlands Scots dialect, which Macrae had to learn in order to play Jamie, was a deliberate attempt to assert the cultural importance of an idiosyncratic Scottish voice. While 'English' plays or European plays in English translation could still require the Scottish actor to 'appear' English for professional purposes, these amateur ventures combined artistic experiment with the linguistic challenge of Scots. Macrae's contemporary and fellow Curtain member, Molly Urquhart, working as a professional actress in the Cambridge Festival Theatre, was made to feel that even a carefully modulated Scottish voice disqualified her from playing major roles. Her semi-professional company, the MSU Players, established in a converted church in Rutherglen, near Glasgow in 1939, was her response to the need to give Scottish-born actors more opportunity. As with the new producing theatres in Perth and Dundee, any venture that attempted some kind of professional viability could not afford too much native experiment. But plays by well-known Scottish dramatists, including J. M. Barrie and James Bridie, or the Belfast-born St John Ervine, coupled with attempts to revive the popular success of the Scottish miner-dramatist Joe Corrie, contributed to the process of nurturing the post-war generation of indigenous actors.[87]

THE QUESTION OF COLOUR

If the maturing historiography associated with the work of Scottish, Irish and Welsh scholars is now enabling a far more equitable overview of professional development in the UK theatres outside England, research on how actors from communities of migrants from the farther reaches of empire emerged is only now beginning to gather momentum. The very limited data available suggests that the professional actor/performer of colour was mainly seen in variety or music theatre up until the Second World War. As Deidre Osborne pointed out, the more extreme racial segregation prevalent in the United States, led to more African American performers gravitating towards Great Britain, but 'racializing and judgemental codes' were still applied to companies touring the UK. The most notorious example was the campaign mounted by the English Variety Artists Federation in 1923 to block the popularity of a revue piece called *Plantation Days* by reducing the number of performances at the Empire Theatre, Leicester Square.[88]

The growing interest in avant-garde American drama, especially the plays of Eugene O'Neill which featured black characters, began to stimulate the employment of black actors in the interests of theatrical innovation. The arrival in London in 1928 of the major American musical *Showboat*, which featured black singers such as Paul Robeson who were also powerful actors, permitted a segue into experimental theatre. A 1929 Court Theatre revival of Peter Godfrey's production of O'Neill's *All God's Chillun Got Wings* replaced the original blacked-up actor with the African American Frank H. Wilson in the central role of the black lawyer Jim Harris and also included other black singers and actors. Wilson had both acted and sung the title role in *Porgy* (an early dramatisation of the novel which became George Gershwin's opera *Porgy and Bess*) and played a supporting role in the first New York production of O'Neill's play when Robeson played Harris.[89] Some reviews of *All God's Chillun* commented on the 'repellent' aspect of the theme of tragic miscegenation embodied by the black Harris married to the white Ella, who was played by Beatrix Lehmann. This was a play dealing, it was claimed, with 'very remote problems'.[90] When Paul Robeson played Othello opposite Peggy Ashcroft as Desdemona at the Savoy Theatre in 1930, the issue seems to have moved closer to home. Outside the uncertain critical response to Robeson's performance – the first by a professional black actor since the 1880s – there was racist hate mail and the suggestion that he was not welcome in the Savoy Hotel.[91]

Steve Nicholson's work on the plays submitted to the Lord Chamberlain for licensing during the 1920s and early 30s has drawn attention to the not inconsiderable number of plays set in various British colonies and focused on the power relations, including sexual relationships, between the colonised and their imperial masters. Where plays were refused a licence either by the Lord Chamberlain or local authorities, it was usually for fear of offence in diplomatic circles or distaste for the more lubricious representations of illicit sex between dusky maidens or lust-crazed 'coloured' men and misguided white men and women. Unless more evidence to the contrary becomes available, historians have to assume that the vast majority of the non-white roles were played by blacked-up and browned-up white actors, contributing to a discernible anxiety about the strains inherent in the maintenance of British imperial control, which was threaded through all levels of society.[92]

However, there were opportunities outside the constraints of the professional job market and through channels of political activism which enabled artistic co-operation across racial boundaries. In 1934 *At What a Price*, written and directed by the black Jamaican feminist Una Marson with members of the League of Coloured Peoples, was given a three-night run at the Scala Theatre following performances at the YMCA hostel Central Club. Deirdre Osborne has pointed to a 1936 Stage Society production of *Toussaint L'Ouverture* by the Trinidadian writer C. L. R. James, which featured black actors such as Robert Adams, Orlando Martins, R. E. Fennell, John Ahuma and Lawrence Brown.[93] As a member of the Independent Labour Party, James was naturally aligned to the metropolitan socialist nexus which also attracted Paul Robeson to Unity Theatre. Robeson's popularity as a singer, enhanced by regular radio broadcasts and appearances on the regional concert circuit, made his well-publicised,

voluntary involvement as a member of Unity's general council and performer in Unity's 1938 production of Ben Bengal's *A Plant in the Sun* a
high-profile vindication of working-class radicalism and emergent black
political consciousness.[94]

By 1939 there were definite signs that some members of the acting profession were taking advantage of new influences and opportunities that
would alter both the intra-national demographic of British theatre and
approaches to professional development and training. This was by no
means the case, however, for the majority of actors, many of whom continued to earn their living within the pressures of established industrial
structures. Although professional status was more clearly defined and
protected, there remained slippery boundaries between the amateur and
professional actor that, as limited state subsidy for the arts entered the
frame during the Second World War, created ideological and economic
tensions which were never fully resolved. But the cracks in the edifice
of empire which had become increasingly obvious during the 1930s did
have two clear, if still inchoate, effects which would impact on the acting
profession. Within the British nation state itself, there was a greater consciousness of separate cultural identities which could be mediated through
theatre. From outside Great Britain, other bona fide British citizens were
arriving in greater numbers with imperially legitimised claims to career
opportunity. For them access to the acting profession would prove more
difficult.

CHAPTER 4

The amateur phenomenon

While the combination of economic depression, catastrophic unemployment in once buoyant industrial areas, and the advent of cinema and radio meant that mass audiences for professional theatre greatly reduced in the period between the wars, non-industrial, amateur theatre-making in all kinds of communities and for a myriad of different purposes flourished. Thousands more British citizens *made* theatre for themselves than were prepared to attend externally provided professional theatre, which was either inaccessible or irrelevant to their lives. The phenomenon can be observed throughout all the nations, and it was particularly significant in areas where metropolitan dominance and economic constraints had made the growth of an autonomous, home-grown, professional theatre culture difficult to sustain. However, just as the effects of the depression were not all pervasive, so the provenance and development of different models of amateur theatre varied considerably.

The huge numbers involved and the diversity of the phenomenon have tended to exacerbate an historiographic tension about how amateur theatre is to be integrated into the historical record. On the whole professional theatre scholars have been reluctant to explore non-professional theatre, which conforms neither to favoured political nor aesthetic preferences. In the case of Wales, the fact that the overwhelming majority of theatre was conducted by a widespread network of small amateur groups led, until comparatively recently, to the assumption that there was no 'real' theatre in Wales before the more sustained growth of professional practice from the 1960s onwards.[1]

By far the best documented practice is of what Raphael Samuel felt to be the 'broken or lost ... moments' of left-wing or 'workers'' theatre[2] which functioned most vigorously during the 1920s and 30s and has been explored in some detail by, amongst others, Samuel himself, Ewan MacColl, Colin Chambers, Richard Stourac and Kathleen McCreery, and Linda Mackenny.[3] This, despite the undoubted importance of reconstructing the history of what was a widely disseminated, politically committed movement, has tended to skew the record on ideological lines. To the binary oppositions of commercial and not-for-profit, and amateur and professional, can also be added socialist workers' theatre versus ersatz bourgeois 'am dram'. The actual landscape of practice, as I argue throughout this book, is a good deal more complex than that. What is also important to recognise is that mapping a popular cultural practice largely unencumbered by economic constraints allows the historian to examine the ways in which theatrical trends circulating in comparatively exclusive circles at the beginning of the century were percolating down to the grass roots. Amateur theatre in the interwar period simultaneously raised consciousness about new possibilities *and* offered confirmation and even consolation about the worth of existing values.

Some of it, as already discussed, was deliberately *anti*-industrial, organised around models of the exemplary theatre for artistic or political purposes. Where it was linked to the gathering momentum of socialist consciousness across a wide spectrum of party-political allegiance, the economic context of unemployment and inequality was key to the formation of the workers' theatre groups and a very definite political agenda. Equally, if not more significant, the macro-context of growing nationalist consciousness in the UK's component nations was again, as discussed in previous chapters, a stimulus to *pre*-professional amateur ensembles. But, as I hope to show, amateur theatre also functioned autonomously within these communities as a means of sustaining cultural identity and social cohesion within extraordinarily difficult day-to-day circumstances.

The activity was certainly a by-product and expression of cultural democracy as it was developed through improved educational opportunity and enfranchisement. The gender equalisation of voting rights for all citizens which was finally achieved in 1928 when women, like men, could vote from the age of 21, inevitably inculcated, even in the bleakest conditions, a greater realisation of the legitimacy of better life expectations. Whether these looked to be achieved in areas of increasing affluence, or thwarted by economic deprivation, the space provided by collective performance endeavour could be a source of recreation and/or reassurance. Associated as it often was with educational initiatives, it was also one of the ways the institutional shapers or would-be shapers of public policy sought to maintain or contest existing social structures. At the same time, however, it gave agency to community groups within all levels of society which could float free of any over-riding ideological agenda.

BRITISH DRAMA LEAGUE

The British Drama League, set up in 1919, was emblematic of the dichotomies within the movement. The founder, Geoffrey Whitworth, then a young publisher, part-time adult education lecturer and passionate advocate of the National Theatre campaign, was inspired, he later claimed, by the 'peculiar dignity' of a play-reading conducted in a temporary YMCA hall by workers from the Vickers-Maxim munitions factory in the London borough of Crayford. Organised employee leisure opportunities, including drama groups, were a wide-spread feature of more civic-minded factory ownership. 'In a flash', Whitworth wrote:

I saw that a National Theatre, for all its costly elaboration, for all its perfection of professional technique, was no more and no less than a Community Theatre writ large. And for this a democratic background was the first essential, and the creation of a public consciously concerned with the practice of theatre art both for its own sake and as a major factor in the enjoyment of life.[4]

With Lord Howard de Walden as President, Harley Granville Barker as Chairman of the Council and Whitworth as Honorary Secretary and later Director, the BDL ensured the maintenance of the National Theatre debate through its annual conferences, discussion documents and articles in the journal *Drama*, which was first published in 1919.

Drama was much more than an organ for the NT campaign. Acting on Whitworth's conviction that 'True democracy implies the enrichment of the common life, therefore the theatre must come to the people, carrying rich gifts in its hands and at the same time receiving from the people in exchange all those treasures of art which life produces',[5] the primary aim was the dissemination of ideas and initiatives that would spread the word about the exemplary theatre and confirmation that at local level there was active engagement in dramatic art. Each edition carried reports from and about noteworthy organisations and events across the country. In addition to the lengthening lists of affiliated amateur societies and clubs – there were 5,000 by 1944 – there were contributions by luminaries such as Barker, Huntley Carter, the doyen of the 'new movement' in European theatre, Gordon Craig and Terence Gray. The number published in December 1921, for example, included an article on the Russian workers' theatre by Huntley Carter; an account of the advanced lighting system installed by Basil Dean at St Martin's Theatre and a description of Jacques Copeau's productions of Shakespeare at his Vieux Colombiers.[6] The organisation was simultaneously about creating a stronger, more innovative professional theatre and nurturing an energetically participating British population, who would also form a suitably educated audience base. The BDL became involved in the consultation towards the introduction of drama into the school curriculum and, in 1942, submitted a plan for a civic theatre scheme to the wartime government.[7]

With headquarters set up in London in 1921, this was, as a campaigning body, metropolitan-led and emphatically *British* in the aim to incorporate regional and other national groups into one all-embracing vision. Arguably, however, it was the purely amateur movement that gained the most from the BDL's efforts. What became the world's largest specialist drama lending library was established, using Annie Horniman's personal library as its nucleus. Play texts were available for individual reading and inspiration, and groups could borrow whole sets of plays for production purposes. In 1927, when the economic crisis which would lead to the depression was gathering momentum, a National Festival of Drama was inaugurated which facilitated groups competing in amateur play production. Respected professional practitioners taught in summer schools and adjudicated at competitions. Edy Craig taught and adjudicated extensively on behalf of the BDL. In 1932, for example, she travelled to competitive events in Edinburgh, Nottingham, Sheffield and Lincolnshire.[8]

Even when not under the auspices of the BDL, the competitive dimension to amateur performance was taken up with great enthusiasm across the British Isles. In Wales the eisteddfodau tradition was already well-established for poetry and music before a prize for drama was first awarded in 1915. The Scottish Community Drama Association, formed in 1926, set up its own competitions where local groups competed vigorously. In Ulster the competitive Northern Dramatic Feis was established by the Northern Drama League, which was founded in Belfast in 1923 by individuals associated with the Ulster Literary Theatre and Queen's University.[9] This competitive dimension to the promotion of participatory theatre remained controversial. For the umbrella organisations the growing numbers of groups eager to take part was the primary index of success and social efficacy. For observers more concerned with issues of performance quality and innovation, there were complaints that the art of the theatre had been reduced to a competitive sport.[10] Also, the sheer enjoyment afforded by amateur play-making, which often seemed to justify a cheerful disregard for the constraints and disciplines of professional practice, created significant tensions.

PROFESSIONAL/AMATEUR: BINARY AND OPPOSITION

The crux of the professional/amateur binary opposition lies in the shifting interpretation of the term 'amateur', which derives of course from the Latin verb meaning 'to love'. While professional mockery of amateur insouciance dates back at least as far as Shakespeare's depiction of 'rude mechanicals', the gathering importance of professional status in the theatre which I chart in chapter 3, and which was replicated across a range of specialist occupations in the twentieth century, intensified the pejorative connotations of the term. But early-twentieth-century radical suspicion of the profit motive, and the attempts to promote a viable not-for-profit theatre also, of necessity, subordinated the remunerative imperative to the compelling urge to make satisfying theatre for its own sake – for love in fact.

Because the European avant-garde infiltrated British theatre at the end of the nineteenth century largely through independent, unpaid initiatives conducted by groups united in opposition to popular commercial theatre, the 'amateur' acquired an intellectual kudos. The ultimate objective of the amateur in this context was to change the ideological and aesthetic basis of professional theatre and to reach a point where a new kind of professional status – in the sense that activists could earn a living from theatre – was viable.[11] The process by which the Fay brothers' Ormond Dramatic Society in Dublin entered the orbit of the Irish Literary Theatre and then gradually evolved towards the fully professional company established at the Abbey Theatre is an obvious example of how this was achieved.[12] The same could be said for the way the Birmingham Repertory Theatre grew out of Barry Jackson's home-grown Pilgrim Players.[13] In both cases, however, a very particular set of individual circumstances, including wealthy patronage, created the favourable environment for the professional trajectory.

Where conditions were less favourable, attempts to construct a durable cultural identity through a literary theatre established by volunteers were markedly less successful. Amateurs in the beginning remained amateurs to the end, unable, so David Kennedy claimed writing in 1951 about drama in Ulster, to 'make a permanent mark on the culture of a country'.[14] In Belfast, the Ulster Literary Theatre, originally conceived in 1902 as the Ulster branch of Irish Literary Theatre, never achieved professional status or a permanent home during the thirty-two years of its existence. Snubbed by Yeats in the beginning, the ULT (renamed the Ulster Theatre in 1908) almost by default in 1904 turned its attention to the production, mainly from within its own membership, of plays which focused on the Ulster experience often through satirical social realism. By 1934, it had premiered some 47 one-act and full-length plays, including work by Rutherford Mayne, Lewis Purcell, Gerald MacNamara and Thomas Carnduff – many of which were never published or simply disappeared.[15]

In his analysis of what he terms 'a lost heritage', Hagal Mengel suggests that Ulster's anomalous geo-political status – neither securely part of Britain nor of Ireland – was in part responsible for the tendency of the 'cultured class in the Province' to look either to Dublin or London for theatrical stimulus and neglect the possibilities on their own doorsteps. Moreover, the climate created by persistent sectarian strife, which in many ways contributed to the thematic energy of the best of the ULT plays, was not conducive to the settled economic conditions necessary for professional success.[16] Indeed, amateur theatre formed a bulwark against socio-economic strain. During the worst of the 1930s' industrial collapse, the Queen's University Dramatic Society formed a drama group called The Unemployed Workers of Belfast, who used the proceeds from performances of Marlowe's *Dr Faustus* and Sophocles' *Philoctetes* to buy textbooks for unemployed students following courses in the Extra-Mural Department.[17] In 1936, the Bangor Unemployed Men appeared at the Belfast Grand Opera House as part of the Feis. However, even without these particular circumstances, there were amateur groups all over Ulster 'from Omagh to Bangor and from Coleraine to Newry'.[18]

Even for professionals it is important to recognise the advantages of amateur status. For individual practitioners, especially at the beginning of the century, resisting rigid distinctions between amateur and professional permitted the development of artistic capital in the interests of career development. In London, the metropolitan nexus of play-producing societies focused on artistically challenging work meant that ambitious actors or directors could simultaneously earn a living in commercial theatre while involved in 'spare time' experiment. Radical outsiders such as William Poel and Edward Gordon Craig had the opportunity to mould and influence professional actors, but it was frequently easier to test controversial ideas with amateurs, who were less hidebound in their attitudes, more generous with their time and arguably more biddable.

Innovative directors like Edy Craig and Nugent Monck worked even more extensively with amateurs. Craig directed for the Leeds Civic Playhouse, lectured and wrote on amateur acting and advised on achieving striking scenographic effects by economical means.[19] For Monck's work on English Renaissance drama at his Elizabethan-style Maddermarket Theatre in Norwich, directing amateur actors gave a degree of creative independence impossible where livelihoods depended on financial viability. Even after his retirement in 1952, the Guild of Norwich Players remained an amateur company. Indeed, idealistic amateurs did not necessarily see professional status as a desirable goal. Willy Fay recorded the violent objections of some of the original amateur Abbey players to the proposal to turn the Society into a limited liability company as a precursor to professional status: 'They had come into the movement *con amore*, and resented its conversion into what in their view was a commercial undertaking. By going on to a professional basis, they argued, we had destroyed the special character of the movement, and they were no longer interested.'[20]

The same debates could be found in the Scottish initiatives, most notably in the Scottish National Players, which were launched in Glasgow in 1921 under the financial auspices of the St Andrew Society. As already discussed in chapter 3, amateur availability combined with the goal of staging new plays of 'Scottish character' made the Players enthusiastic recruits for early radio drama production and certainly laid the foundations for later professional development. During what were described as 'the golden years' between 1921 and 1931, 71 plays by some 36 writers were produced, usually by professional directors including Guthrie and Fay.[21] While there were several factors which prevented the consolidation of a fully professional organisation including the lack of a permanent building and the voluntary liquidation in 1936 of a limited liability company, there was also some active resistance to moving out of an amateur safe haven. In 1932 a split developed in the management committee between dramatists James Bridie and John Brandane, who wanted to move towards full professionalism, and other committee members reluctant to sacrifice the greater security offered by their more conventional professional livelihoods.[22] Bridie, who continued to practise as a doctor until 1938, was eventually instrumental in the founding of the Glasgow Citizens' Theatre in 1943, while the Players continued on an amateur basis before finally abandoning production in 1950. In some respects the Players' touring policy, which took performances to isolated towns and villages across Scotland in the 1920s, left the most enduring legacy. Provided in 1926 with a guarantee against loss for a tour by the Carnegie Trust because of the social and educational nature of the work, there was a prescience in the Players' recognition that a 'national theatre' could function most effectively by disseminating performance as widely as possible.[23] When the wholly amateur Scottish Community Drama Association was founded, the Players' example of what could be achieved and enjoyed without professional status and in the absence of other professional provision was a positive incentive. However, the enduring importance of the *pleasure* to be derived from amateur playmaking continues to raise questions about the relationship between amateur and professional and between theatre as work and theatre as play.

In Wales, between 1932 and 1935 a professional company touring as the Welsh National Theatre Players struggled to attract audiences and eventually collapsed with a substantial deficit. The writer and teacher J. Ellis Williams later claimed that the standard of performance was poor,[24] but the actress Evelyn Bowen, who led the company, complained that the refusniks were not really interested in plays as such. They regularly attended performances by hundreds of small local drama groups 'merely [my emphasis] to see their friends or their sisters or their sweethearts or brothers, performing in varying stages of perfection or imperfection'.[25] In 1947 in *The Other Theatre*, written at a time when the newly founded Arts Council was trying to establish professional theatre in so-called 'theatre-less' areas and encountering some resistance from amateur groups, Norman Marshall commented:

What puzzles me most about amateur actors is how seldom they go to the theatre. Even if they had no particular interest in the drama one would have thought they would be frequent playgoers if only to learn for their own sakes more about the craft of acting. But few amateurs believe they have much to learn from the professional.[26]

The reasons for the recreational strength of amateur theatre during this period are quite complex and, even in the evolving industrial landscape of the 1930s, were mostly about something other than challenging existing models of professional excellence. The fact that many communities made theatre by, with and for themselves was about other aspects of cultural priority, which called into question artistic criteria constructed on the basis of intellectual or aesthetic preference. Indeed, it could be argued that the very issues which so exercised modernists in their opposition to the industrial priorities of commercial theatre were integral to a continuum of distaste at the end of which lay amateur drama at its most stubbornly independent.

But the very different perspectives and ideological assumptions, which lay behind these independent efforts, reflect what was a deeply divided society in which residual and emergent cultural assumptions were quite overtly polarised in response to particular and quite different sets of economic circumstances. On the one hand, this was theatre culture as ordinary culture in which recreational labour assisted in the aggrandisement of social cohesion in secure communities or, where communities were under threat, provided a therapeutic focus for collective desperation. On the other hand, amateur theatre activity was also actively promoted across a wide spectrum of political and, indeed, religious affiliation. The sheer scale of the activity derived from parallel strands of educational initiatives linked to social change which dated back more than half a century.

ORIGINS

By the end of the nineteenth century, the social range of amateur theatre had widened considerably from the aristocratic divertimenti, which had featured in great households since the seventeenth century. Home theatricals in middle-class families became increasingly popular in the second half of the nineteenth century, and as Katherine Newey's research has demonstrated, gave women in particular ample opportunities to exercise their enjoyment of performance and play-writing skills for domestic entertainment. The leading play publishers Thomas Lacey and Samuel French created 'a market for the scripts, libretti, scores, instruction books, costume, make-up and scenery adapted for home theatricals'.[27] Quite strikingly elaborate scenic effects could be created by enthusiastic family teams – unencumbered by domestic chores in households well-provided with servants – and both play scripts and manuals specifically written for amateurs included detailed instructions for staging.

Amateur music and drama societies in the wider community had long been associated with regional commercial theatres. The large receiving houses in most towns and cities reserved at least one, if not more, regular slots in their season programmes for performances by local amateurs, and indeed maintaining good relations with enthusiastic and locally influential amateurs was a key responsibility of theatre managers. Many groups which staged productions in public theatres, including, of course, the university societies and Shakespeare reading societies, routinely brought in professional actresses, although this may have been more about honouring all-male social traditions than worries about exposing respectable women to disapprobation. As the biographies of actresses including Mrs Patrick Campbell, Cathleen Nesbitt and Edith Evans, who all came from middle-class families, demonstrate, by the end of the nineteenth century, amateur performance was an acceptable activity for young women.

Newey has also identified a number of instruction manuals for amateur performers published in the first decade of the new century, including *Amateur Theatricals: A Practical Guide* published in 1904. In 1907 Elsie Fogerty's adaptation of Tennyson's *Princess* 'adapted and arranged for amateur performance in girls' schools' was published together with copious practical advice on staging.[28]

The fact that practical drama was being advocated for schools – and girls' schools at that – is indicative of a burgeoning interest in the social, religious and educational efficacy of participatory arts. Nineteenth-century attempts to improve access to educational opportunities for adults as well as children had produced a succession of nationwide initiatives, including Mechanics' Institutes, Adult Schools, Working Men's Clubs and Institutes, branches of the Young Men's – and after 1877 Young Women's – Christian Association (YMCA/YWCA), and the University Extension Schemes and Settlements. Reading rooms and libraries helped support instruction that ranged from basic literacy and numeracy to lecture programmes which satisfied intellectual interests hitherto mainly the province of the older, urban-elite-led literary and philosophical societies. The growing emphasis on the liberal arts meant that drama, music and art groups were frequently set up as extra-curricular activities associated with a range of adult education organisations. The idea of purposeful recreation, allied to intellectual endeavour, practised in a time and place separated from the demands of the workplace, was conceived as integral to the generalised enrichment of participants' lives.[29]

The rapid growth of numerous different socialist organisations in the early twentieth century contributed to a veritable jungle of adult learning opportunities, competing to serve the interests of a generation of young people exposed to the twin stimuli of socialist ideology and industrial unrest. The Clarion movement launched through *The Clarion* newspaper, founded by Robert Blatchford and other sympathetic socialist journalists in 1891, was a major influence reaching a circulation of over 80,000 by 1908.[30] From its beginnings as a campaigning newspaper, Clarionism expanded into the famous Clarion cycling clubs, which were literally the vehicles for Clarion scouts tasked with carrying the socialist message all over Britain. While a member of Horniman's company in Manchester in 1908, Basil Dean attended the Clarion Easter 'meet' in Shrewsbury with Lewis Casson, and performed a scene from *Julius Caesar* as part of an opening concert.[31]

Collective recreation was as important as political propaganda with camera clubs, handicraft groups, brass bands, choirs and dramatic societies formed under the Clarion banner. As Dean put it, 'Fraternity was the password; Norfolk jackets and red ties for the boys, tweed skirts, white blouses and more red ties for the girls, were signals for recognition.'[32] In 1912 the National Association of Clarion Dramatic Clubs was established, and in the process – anticipating the later efforts of the BDL – an attempt was made to form a library of plays focused on Labour and Socialist subjects.[33]

While the movement began to decline after 1914, in part because of Blatchford's militarism, numerous clubs and societies continued. As an unemployed 15-year-old in Salford in 1929, Ewan MacColl was introduced to socialist theatre through his membership in the amateur Clarion Players. Nearly sixty years later he recalled the Sunday afternoon Clarion debates held in local restaurants which could attract 80 to 100 mostly male attendees, many of whom were also unemployed. Eventually as he moved towards Theatre of Action, he consciously determined there would be 'no coffee breaks, no larking about, no chit-chat' that he associated with the Clarion rehearsals.[34]

The Workers' Educational Association, founded in 1904, developed organisational strategies which ensured long-term survival. The educational base drew its strength from the relationship with the professional tuition available from existing university providers, but executive power was also placed in the hands of a strongly working-class membership.[35] In contrast to the secularism of the WEA, the revived Adult School movement, which had always tried to reach the grass roots of the working population, promoted a liberal, non-denominational Christian ethos of 'fellowship' together with a less sophisticated and, indeed, less professional approach to tuition. While there was rapid expansion before 1914, thereafter numbers declined as scepticism about Christianity as a pancea for social ills grew.

Educational Settlements, however, which were an offshoot of the Adult Schools, provided more professionally trained tuition in a range of arts including music and drama, which drew increasing numbers of working people. In 1922, E. Martin Browne, moving between his first involvement with professional theatre and a vocation for Christian ministry in the northern industrial areas, first encountered the former Anglican priest John A. Hughes, who was warden of the York Settlement. Under Hughes, who introduced handicrafts, orchestra and languages, the Settlement Community Players began to make a significant contribution to the cultural life of the city.[36] Just over a decade later in his *English Journey*, J. B. Priestley describes the Settlement drama groups in

Newcastle upon Tyne and East Durham, by then devastated shadows of their former prosperity.[37]

In the list of over 400 societies affiliated with the British Drama League published in *Drama* in 1924, it is clear to see that a significant number owed their origins to adult education initiatives. Societies ranged from the Kingston Adult School Dramatic Class, Gravesend WEA, Study Circle, Chesterfield Settlement to the Working Mens' College Dramatic Society and the Dramatic Art Centre based in the Mary Ward Settlement. A clutch of WEA groups are listed with home centres in Abergavenny, Lincoln, Manchester and Salford, and Wolsingham in Durham. There were numerous schools' groups affiliated to the BDL as well as societies based at universities and technical colleges.

But it is equally clear from the list that no one political or religious persuasion was represented by the numerous umbrella organisations. There were a number of groups linked to the Independent Labour Party (ILP). Several Jewish groups are listed alongside the College of the Resurrection Dramatic Society, the Lancashire Catholic Players and the Melton Congregational Church Amateur Dramatic Society. There were Women's Institute groups reflecting the growing strength of an organisation for women in rural areas, which had become independent in 1919 and thereafter spread rapidly across England, Wales and Scotland. Indeed, one important aspect of the amateur phenomenon was the way small communities, and women especially, in relatively isolated rural areas were able to encounter theatre as a recreational activity.

The Village Drama Society was founded in North Devon in 1918 by Mary Kelly. By 1926 there were 150 branches in touch with more than 2,000 villages. Branch members were tasked with taking plays to other villages so that in turn more branches would be created. 'We do not wish to make the villages imitate a more sophisticated form of drama than they can really understand, and we do not wish to force them to revive any form of art that is naturally dead; we wish to take them where they stand at the present moment, and to give this art room to grow.'[38] Yet again this is the exemplary theatre from below, educative, socialising and ultimately designed to raise the horizon of expectation of participants and audiences for a form of theatre which can contribute an extra dimension to their lives. The evangelical and, indeed, mildly patrician tone is unmistakable.

After 1918, adult educational participatory theatre became one component in a battery of strategies deployed by state institutions to capture the allegiance of the newly enfranchised working class. In his discussion of the convergence of significant events in 1926 which included the General Strike, Steve Nicholson has drawn attention to fears of Soviet-style revolution, which a rising tide of industrial action might have presaged. In the same year the publication of *The Drama in Adult Education* by the Adult Education Committee of the Great Britain Board of Education endorsed theatre as 'an unrivalled instrument for breaking down social barriers and establishing friendly relations'.[39] The Committee focused on a number of key initiatives including the work of the British Drama League, the Village Drama Society and churches of different denominations, which were now enthusiastically promoting drama. The Director of the Catholic Play Society reported on a venture in a church in Kentish Town where new specially written plays on the life of Christ had been performed:

The Players were drawn from members of the congregation, who were not necessarily all drawn from the parish. The part of the Madonna and the part of Christ were generally not taken by members of the congregation, but this was for a special reason. The players were in the main working-class lads who had grown up with the Church. Practically all the Players were still under 30 years of age. They numbered between 35 and 40. They were mostly of the working classes such as shop-boys, messenger boys, railwaymen, clerks in insurance offices etc.[40]

That time-honoured entrenched assumptions about class difference were still flourishing is made obvious by this last example – a shop-boy couldn't play Jesus – but conservative hegemony, as evidenced by parliamentary electoral voting patterns right up until 1939, remained an active factor in substantial areas of working-peoples' attitudes to individual self-esteem and the maintenance of living standards. To be sure there was a steady realignment of traditional working-class Liberal voters to the Labour Party, often encouraged by Nonconformist Christianity, but socialism was by no means automatically the ideology of choice. Perhaps what had changed most significantly were perceptions of obligatory deference to higher social status. Public performance in an amateur production made the previously invisible visible, and even in the Catholic church in Kentish Town, social classes mixed together in a common enterprise. Steve Nicholson quotes another example from the Education Committee report of the conscientiously egalitarian practices of the Bournville Dramatic Society run for all levels of the Cadbury family employees in their Birmingham chocolate factory – a product of Quaker Liberal rectitude.[41]

As the historian Martin Pugh has emphasised, the 1926 General Strike
was not about provoking bloody revolution despite a brief glimpse into
the abyss of violent class war. It was mainly a defensive action aimed at
warding off more wage cuts after the Conservative prime minister Stanley
Baldwin refused to restore subsidy to the beleaguered mining industry.
However, while the collapse of the strike after just nine days appeared to
represent a complete defeat for the unions – only the miners remained
obdurate for a few more miserable months – there was a strong level of
support amongst regional working-class trade unionists.[42] If it achieved
nothing else, it succeeded in undermining both the loyalty of working-
class Conservatives and governmental assumptions that it could exercise industrial control unchallenged. In 1929 the enlarged electorate gave
Ramsay MacDonald's Labour Party its strongest democratic endorsement
of the interwar period.

Analysing the aftermath of the collapse of the second Labour government in 1931 amidst economic disarray, Pugh offers an assessment of the
working-class electorate that seeks to account for the fact that they con-
spicuously did not continue to endorse the Labour Party in such large
numbers for the rest of the decade. In 1935, after four years of a power-
sharing National government under MacDonald, Baldwin's Conservative
Party won the General Election:

notwithstanding the grievance of unemployment, manual workers during the
1920s and 1930s displayed remarkably little predilection for a drastic soak-the-
rich policy, but tended rather to compare their own situation with that of other
workers. Their apparently limited aspirations were surely of a piece with their
politics; for their characteristic claim – faithfully reflected by the Labour Party –
was that the working man was entitled to work, and failing that, maintenance,
not that the distribution of wealth in society should be fundamentally altered.
Essentially the party appealed to the self-respect of the working class rather than
to any militant sense of class consciousness.[43]

When ambitious theatre-makers, who wanted much more to develop
from the amateur theatre movement than the 'apparently limited aspirations' displayed by many of the groups who enthusiastically competed for
BDL and SCDA competition trophies in the 1930s, fulminated against
poor copies of West End successes and unchallenging one-act plays,
they were arguably reacting to something which reflected the *mentalité* outlined above. Self-respect acquired through enjoyable co-operative
activity towards a goal which brought public recognition was sufficient.
Performing the products of a professional theatre out of reach both geographically and financially to the vast majority of the British population

was one way of accessing these privileges even in an ersatz version. Certainly adopting this view of how the phenomenon operated in the most extreme social circumstances in Wales goes some way to explaining why communal amateur theatre was for the best part of forty years *the* national theatre of the people.

THE WELSH EXPERIENCE

The particular strength of amateur theatre activity in Wales between the wars can be viewed within a set of social and economic circumstances which, although by no means unique, were none the less exceptional. Kenneth Morgan states that the collapse of its industrial, manufacturing and commercial life created:

> mass unemployment and poverty without parallel in the British Isles. After the seemingly limitless industrial progress of the half-century up to 1914, an advance that continued in its major features during the wartime years, south Wales plunged unprepared into a depression and despair which crushed its society for almost twenty years and left ineradicable scars upon its consciousness.[44]

The need for workers in mining, metal manufacture and quarrying, which had brought about the major demographic changes described in chapter 1, was reversed. Hopeless, long-term unemployed streamed out of Wales in the 1930s heading for the Midlands and South-East England. To make matters worse the depression in industry was also coupled by a depression in agriculture, especially in Welsh upland farming. As Morgan concedes there were areas of unemployment equally as severe in North-East England and in Clydeside, but in terms of sheer critical mass, the crisis was worst in Wales. The despair was exacerbated by the failure of the British government to put in place any effective ameliorative measures.

Clearly this was not an environment conducive to theatre as economic activity, but for society under stress, theatre as a communal, recreational activity was a way of preserving cultural identity.[45] While numbers of Welsh speakers were in decline after the First World War and relatively few were monoglot Welsh,[46] the Welsh language still had far greater currency as a medium of daily intercourse than native languages in Scotland and Ireland. Aside from the obvious fact that communities, especially in the rural north, could seal off their collective values and concerns behind a wall of incomprehensible language, if Welsh was vigorously maintained for literary and artistic purposes, it could form a linguistic bulwark against the forces of disintegration. This was brought sharply home to the metropolitan authorities in 1931 when a company based in Talysarn in North Wales was prosecuted for performing in a local school an unlicensed Welsh-language play *Y Grocbren* [The Gallows] by a journalist Gwilym R. Jones, opposing capital punishment. The subject matter became known when an application to stage the play on Christmas Day was rejected by the local magistracy. Up until that point requests for licenses made to the Lord Chamberlain's office had simply required a 700-word synopsis in English. The response from London was to appoint a Welsh-speaking examiner of plays.[47]

There were literally hundreds of drama groups. Surveying the scene in 1939 for an article published in the *Welsh Review*, J. Ellis Williams stated that there were 'at least five hundred drama societies and well over four hundred published Welsh plays'.[48] Samuel French, for example, carried a substantial list of plays in English/Welsh translation. Organisationally the key enabling factor lay in the parallel co-ordinating structures created by the extensive network of Nonconformist chapels, which operated in tandem, often led by the same dynamic personalities, with the labour organisations, friendly societies and trade unions.

While the dominance of Nonconformist Protestantism and with it the fabled anti-theatrical prejudice may have been exaggerated – in 1905 at a time of evangelical revival, some 60 per cent of the population had no religious affiliation – there is no doubt that in the rural, Welsh-speaking areas especially, the majority of the drama groups were linked to the chapels. As younger members of the clergy, trained in a more liberal, social-gospel-oriented outlook than that inculcated by old-style Calvinist Methodism, encouraged participatory arts amongst their congregations, they were building on a strong tradition for all-age educational provision which had developed separately from English initiatives in the nineteenth century. Indeed, Sunday School classes which catered for adults as well as children became an instrument of popular literacy in the Welsh language. The fact that the Nonconformist homiletic tradition had valued flamboyantly histrionic preaching skills – the art of the *hwyl*[49] which transfixed and swept congregations up in emotionally charged religious fervour – made it possible for ministers who often led and wrote for the drama groups, to claim that the Welsh were naturally theatrical.

Even when adherence to all Christian churches began to decline post-1918, undermined by wartime trauma and a more determinedly secular socialist, if not communist, ideology, the spirit of self-education and

creative leisure was also fostered by miners' halls and mechanics' institutes. Indeed, many of the halls that were built with funds raised from
workers' own earnings rivalled the churches in architectural splendour.
In South Wales, the Ferndale and Blaenllechau Workmen's Hall and
Institute, which opened in 1909, boasted two halls, the larger of which
seated fifteen hundred, reading and reference rooms, a swimming pool,
refreshment rooms and games rooms. In the extremely narrow coalfield
valleys the density of population was very high. In the Rhondda in 1911,
when elsewhere in England and Wales there was an average of 618 people
per square mile, the average was 23,680 per square mile.[50] In 1934, at the
height of the depression, the Anglo-Welsh dramatist Richard Hughes
described a packed audience of some two thousand made up of mostly
miners and school teachers:

It was hard for him to remind himself that outside these walls lay not a large
city but only one blob in that clotted string of dwellings which winds its length
up the Rhondda Valley – a town only one street thick where coal-grimed sheep
come down at night from the hills, and bleat among tramlines in search of
garbage.[51]

The historian Tim Williams has argued that what was distinctive in
Welsh cultural life was the importance of 'control from below'. In chapel
culture this meant the power that congregations or 'vestries' had over
their ministers and their ability to dictate and organise their own lives.[52]
The same applied to the resistance in workers' organisations to attempts to
impose educational opportunity from above, which led to the formation
of 'The Independent Working-Class Education Movement' in the early
1900s. Just as impressive library resources were developed in the workers'
institutes for the purposes of self-education, so recreational opportunity
was also self-generated.

An article in the *Observer* (15 May) published in 1932 praised amateur
play-making in Wales as 'the favourite pastime of an intelligent democracy'. Play-producing activities provided enjoyable communal recreation,
especially in the long, dark winter evenings, but the funds raised from
packed public performances also helped sustain the fabric of community
life. In 1934 a writer in the *Daily Herald* described the build-up to a week
of performances by competing drama societies held in the New Theatre
in Mountain Ash, the proceeds of which would benefit the local hospital.
To secure a 10s. seat for six performances in the thousand-seat theatre,
'Miners and their families subscribe small sums for many weeks ... the
position of the seats being chosen by lot.'[53]

Olive Ely Hart, who published in 1928 the single full-length English-language study of early-twentieth-century Welsh drama, described the audience for a play competition at the 1925 Pwllheli National Eisteddfod, held not in the main pavilion but in the town hall. There was a mixed group: old men and 'women who looked even older', boys and girls dressed in their best clothes, 'rowdy-looking boys' perched on window-sills, babies on mothers' laps. Lord Howard de Walden sat with the mayor at the front of the balcony. How far this audience was itself imagined in Hart's emotional engagement is a moot point. She felt, she wrote, 'very Celtic' just by walking in the crowds.[54] There is plenty of evidence, however, to confirm the seriousness with which audiences contemplated the event. Richard Hughes described the importance of the adjudication process and the effect on the audience. Very few left the theatre, but waited for some twenty minutes for the critic to collect his thoughts. Then they listened for nearly an hour while he discussed the whole range of a week's performances. 'They seemed to take as keen an interest in criticism as in acting, to savour it themselves as critically.'[55]

Even within the nations-wide context of popular enjoyment of competitive festivals, the commitment to the Welsh eisteddfodau was exceptional. At the foundational level of the eisteddfodau pyramid, there were probably thousands of local competitive festivals of music and poetry held in chapels and working men's halls. Then came more prestigious, but still numerous regional events, and finally, the National Eisteddfod, which moved annually between locations in North and South Wales. The value of performance appears to have been, and arguably remains, more deeply integral to quotidian community experience. The American anthropologist Carol Trosset has commented that 'Welsh people begin learning culturally approved styles of performance as small children, and what they learn influences their developing sense of self.'[56] The 'penny readings', for example, which were a regular feature of extended chapel life, gave the opportunity for children to compete for little silken bags which contained small coins. From her experience of the National Eisteddfodau in the 1980s, Trosset has argued that 'There is a prestige system … one in which people are honoured for the committed performance of ethnically relevant activities and for their demonstrated skill in these pursuits.'

Although as Prys Morgan has noted, some of the allegedly ancient symbols and rituals integral to the festival were in fact 'invented traditions' added in to bolster the concept of the 'imagined' land of poets and musicians, the National Eisteddfod was a powerful emblem of growing national self-confidence.[57] When the festival was reorganised to assume greater prominence in the 1880s, it was in the context of economic optimism linked of course to the industrial ties with England, and the nationalist demands of the Cymru Fydd movement associated with David Lloyd George and other leading Liberal radicals. Indeed, the emergence of a Welsh drama based on romantic representations of a heroic past was endorsed both by the charismatic popular educator O. M. Edwards at the Caernarfon National Eisteddfod in 1894 and by Lloyd George at the Bangor festival in 1902. A play that proclaimed 'lessons of the most exalted patriotism' was first performed as part of the National Eisteddfod in 1906.

The initiative to establish a Welsh National Theatre, which was launched in 1911 with Lord Howard de Walden's offer of a £100 prize, clearly attempted to exploit the competitive tradition. While his efforts to create something 'based a little on the history of the Abbey Theatre', which continued sporadically right into the late 1930s, failed, the kudos derived from winning a nationally recognised competition was a genuine incentive to aspiring writers.[58] *Change* by J. O. Francis, *Ar y Groesffordd* [On the Crossroad] by R. G. Berry, and D. T. Davies's *Ble Ma Fa?* [Where Is It?] and *Ephraim Harris*, which all won de Walden prizes, emerged from the distinctive, bilingual so-called 'Aberystwyth School' of new drama, much of which explored lives conflicted and disrupted by changing environmental pressures and patterns of belief.[59] Ironically, as Ioan Williams points out, even when plays specifically targeted Nonconformist hypocrisy and moral failure, chapel drama groups eagerly embraced them: 'criticism … actually sustained the establishment of liberal ministers and socialist teachers, who welcomed it enthusiastically as the raw material for a concerted cultural project'. Indisputable national legitimisation came with the first award of a prize for drama made at the 1915 Bangor National Eisteddfod.

The concerted cultural project as represented by the eisteddfod was structurally conservative with participants, performers and writers striving to achieve the approbation of the festival adjudicators. What was more socially radical, however, was that these events could temporarily blot out societal divisions based on class, economic or professional power, and, indeed, geographical position. The fact that the national festival moved its location annually across Wales, and there was thus no one culturally dominant centre also conveyed an ethos of democratic access. By the largely literary criteria set by the adjudicators, the standards were very high, and frequently the prize was not awarded. J. Ellis Williams, who formed a travelling theatre company from his WEA Welsh Drama Group in Blaenau Ffestiniog,[60] described winning the Flintshire Eisteddfod drama prize for his play *Twyllo he Lwynog* [To Trick an Old Fox], which was published in 1922.[61] In 1926, his Ibsen-influenced *Y ffon Dafl* [The Shepherd's Stick] won the first prize for the long play at the Swansea National Eisteddfod. His account of the critique which he received along with his prize from de Walden of £50 and a gold ring symbolising the marriage of the drama to the eisteddfod, shows how seriously the judges' views were taken and within an exclusively Welsh cultural context.[62]

Prizes were withheld from plays with controversial content despite obvious artistic merit. In 1934 the prize at the Neath National Eisteddfod was withheld from James Kitchener Davies's *Cwm Glo* [Coal Valley]. Davies, by profession a Rhondda schoolmaster and an advocate of Plaid Cymru, was also a lay preacher actively engaged in alleviating suffering in the mining communities.[63] *Cwm Glo*'s depiction of the impact of the depression on a shattered family where a daughter ultimately turns to prostitution was deemed too terrible to be shown to the Welsh public, although the play was staged in Swansea in 1935. By 1939 Ellis Williams, while highly critical of the poor quality of many of the plays circulating amongst the amateur groups, had come to regard the National Eisteddfod system as retrograde. Better, he argued, to put promising plays into performance by good amateur companies so that flaws could be identified and corrected, and a stronger writing culture developed.[64]

Although the amateur ethos made it difficult to nurture more formally skilled dramatists, there is evidence from accounts of censorship that community playwrights did attempt to confront social problems. The content of *Cwm Glo* was not unique. The obviously Ibsen-influenced *Yr Arch Olaf* [The Last Coffin] was written by J. D. Howells, a manager at the Nantgwyn Colliery, and staged at the Aberdare Little Theatre in 1934. The censor objected to an attempt at a realistic representation of a bandaged patient in the terminal stages of venereal disease. An English-language play *Men in Black* by Horace Morgan, performed in Dinas Powis in 1935, focused on the scourge of silicosis in mining communities. There were objections to a post mortem scene presented in half-light as if in a collier's kitchen – the usual setting for such procedures, which would have been very familiar to audiences. But viewed within the complexities of the wider socio-economic context where at its worst in the steam coal area of Merthyr Vale, for example, unemployment stood at over 51 per cent in 1935,[65] the niceties of innovation in dramatic writing were almost certainly not high on the popular agenda. That said, Wales, despite the extremes of particular circumstances, was no different from other areas of Great Britain in that, viewed as a whole, the economic terrain under-pinning political and cultural trends was not even. This too was clearly reflected in amateur theatre.

A DIVIDED SOCIETY

Although from the 1920s onwards the Labour Party had almost total con-trol of local authorities in industrial South Wales,[66] it was not a majority party across Great Britain as a whole or even within the working class. But while Raphael Samuel confirms this in his survey of different mod-els of socialist amateur theatre up until 1935, he insists that increasing class polarization of both culture and politics in the 1920s was 'the funda-mental condition' of these groups' existence.[67] The class base of economic inequality at the point when Ramsay MacDonald formed the National Government in 1931 is made clear by looking at the male unemployment figures extrapolated from the 1931 census. Out of a total British popula-tion of 44.5 million, the average male unemployment was 13.3 per cent. Of these over 30 per cent were classified as unskilled manual workers and over 14 per cent, skilled or semi-skilled manual workers. Over 74 per cent of the whole workforce came into these occupational categories. Conversely, unemployment amongst proprietors and higher order man-agers amounted to little more than 1 per cent. There was also a very obvi-ous north-south divide with the 'old' industrial areas in Scotland and the North-East experiencing twice the level of unemployment to that found in the 'new' industrial regions in the Midlands and the South.[68] It is thus easy to see how perceptions of gross inequality gained currency. The per-petual 'red haze' of anger felt by the teenaged Ewan MacColl in Salford, as he wore the cast-off clothes and ate the leftover food given by his mother's well-meaning employer, was on behalf of whole communities bewildered by what had happened to former prosperity.[69]

However, what the depression did not bring to the UK as in other countries, such as the United States, France and, of course, Germany, was financial collapse. British unemployment was high in 1929 at 1.5 million and had risen by 1932 to 3.4 million, but at that point in macro-economic terms the crisis began to bottom out. As Dudley Baines points out, the steep decline in international trade created the problem in the old exporting industries. In fact, the real income of most consumers rose in part because the price of imported food fell and released more dispos-able income for the purchase of more 'durable' goods such as new elec-trical domestic appliances and radios and gramophones.[70] Car ownership increased which in turn meant that workers in new industries could afford to take advantage of new suburban or greenfield housing developments outside the old urban complexes. There was a boom in house building with just under 4 million houses built between 1919 and 1939. In 1914 private rented housing accounted for 80 per cent of the housing stock. By 1939 this had been reduced to 46 per cent. By the outbreak of war, many more of the British people had become more accustomed to owning property, in particular bricks and mortar.[71]

The implications of this for a study of amateur theatre is that two parallel developments in the interwar years are directly reflective of the societal polarisation to which Samuel refers. The workers' theatre groups – the most radical of which, the Workers Theatre Movement was a self-declared 'propertyless theatre for the propertyless class', and the Little Theatre movement which saw groups of occupationally more secure amateur players moving into their own premises – grew pretty much simultaneously. The roots of both lay in the pre-First World War exemplary theatre campaign, but while one sector of revolutionary theatre-makers literally took to the streets, the other aspired to permanent homes, frequently reclaiming 'found' buildings made redundant from their original social or industrial use.

However, it is dangerous to assume a neat binary divide between bourgeois and workers' theatre based on class. The category 'worker' covers a very wide range of occupations from unskilled labourers to highly skilled craftspeople and indeed non-manual workers. The key factor is not objective occupational classification or, indeed, family heritage, but the subjective categorisation derived from self-identification. Membership of the Communist Party, out of which the Workers Theatre Movement emerged in 1926, was mainly led by middle- or, indeed, upper-class intellectuals and was relatively small. The ranks were swelled to about 10,000 by an influx of the unemployed – especially miners – after the shock of the General Strike failure, but by 1931 numbers had dropped back to 2,500.[72] Of the WTM membership in and around London where the majority of the groups were to be found, many were drawn mainly from the lower-status professions, teachers and clerical workers. Tom Thomas, who was the driving force behind the revitalised WTM, was a stockbroker's clerk although he, like other members, had periods of unemployment.[73]

That said, outside London and deeper into the depressed areas there were proletarian groups which conformed more readily to the worker stereotype. Most obviously Ewan MacColl's Salford 'Red Megaphones' was comprised of semi-skilled workers like himself or the unemployed.

In Scotland, one of the earliest and historically best-known groups, the Bowhill Village Players, formed quite independently in 1926 as a direct response to the social consequences of the General Strike. Extreme poverty and unemployment created the conditions that paradoxically enabled the miner playwright Joe Corrie to begin writing the sketches and short plays which he and his friends from an embattled locked-out mining community in Fife toured round local halls to raise morale and funds for the soup kitchens. The opportunity to tour as professionals under the name of the Fife Miner Players, following the success of Corrie's most celebrated play *In Time O' Strife*, took the amateurs out of the familiar environment shaped by their large, enthusiastic community audiences to territory dictated by the pressures of the marketplace. The novelty value of local, life-based one-act turns on the variety circuits paid dividends for a while, but commercial managers were much more resistant to full-length plays on serious political subjects, despite the undoubted authenticity of the actors.[74]

THE LITTLE THEATRE MOVEMENT

It would seem reasonable to assume that at the opposite end of the amateur spectrum, the majority of building-based 'Little Theatre' members came from the middle and lower middle class and were the products of affluence. Indeed, Linda Hornzee-Jones has argued this in her 'Performing Suburbia' examination of the social composition of groups established during this period.[75] Certainly several owner-occupier theatre groups emerged as a result of suburban expansion in the Midlands and South. These included the new towns that began to grow in the South-East such as Welwyn Garden City, first laid out in 1920, and Selsdon Garden Village, which began to expand in 1925. Both these new urban communities were built on the foundations of much older villages, and as populations grew and traditional rural industries declined, old farm buildings and schools became redundant and were subsequently taken over by the drama groups which quickly established themselves. In Welwyn Garden City in 1932, the conversion of part of the nineteenth-century Handside Barn into a 150-seater theatre was the work of several relatively new groups.[76]

C. B. Purdom, who later wrote the first biography of Harley Granville Barker, stimulated local enthusiasm by founding the Welwyn Garden City Theatre Society in 1921. Purdom was not only a drama critic and literary editor, but also an economist and author of two books on modern town development.[77] He and Dr L. T. M. Gray, who provided the initial finance to enable the conversion process, were both Directors of Welwyn Garden City Ltd. which built and ran the town. In 1934, an amalgamation of the drama groups formed the Welwyn Drama Club to take over the management of the theatre. What now, at the beginning of the twenty-first century, is the Barn Theatre Trust Ltd., a registered charity which wholly owns the still-amateur Barn Theatre at Handside, was originally the outcome of the highly idealised changes to the built landscape of Britain in post-First World War, which were clearly not predicated on economic pessimism. The new inhabitants of the Garden City were the beneficiaries of a utopian dream that imagined aspirational communities in a carefully planned semi-rural environment.

Even in Wales, the establishment of the first Little Theatre was linked to progress rather than decay. There was relative economic buoyancy in the tourist resorts of North Wales and in parts of Cardiff and Swansea where there was greater industrial diversity. Indeed, in Swansea, new nickel works met the expanding car industry's demand for nickel steel, and the port and nearby oil refinery received and then refined imports of oil from the Middle East. There were new public and domestic building programmes, including in 1920, the establishment of the fourth Welsh university college. Inevitably the local population incorporated the specialist professional and technical expertise represented by the scientists, engineers, lawyers, doctors, teachers, etc., who were vital to the maintenance of these developments. Indeed, there was considerable migration *into* the area from other parts of the UK.[78] It was out of this social strata that initiatives to establish a new amateur theatre company came.

The Swansea Amateur Players Society was set up in 1924, renamed the Swansea Stage Society in its second season and by 1933 had settled for the Swansea Little Theatre Players. At this point the Society was based in a Community Hall in Southend, near Mumbles Head on the part of the coast where there was rapid commercial and residential expansion and where the university college was located.[79] The poet Dylan Thomas was a member of the society in 1932 and 1933 while working as a journalist on the *South Wales Daily Post*. For all his passionate allegiance to Wales, he was nevertheless the English-speaking son of the senior master of English at Swansea Grammar School and happily made his mark in English classic plays like Farquhar's *The Beaux Stratagem*, Congreve's *The Way of the World* and even Noël Coward's *Hay Fever*. Although periodic attempts to amalgamate with the Swansea Welsh Drama Society failed, there were significant successes with Anglo-Welsh drama, especially the work of the former miner and political activist Jack Jones, which drew the attention of English audiences. The Society's 1938 production of Jones's *Land of My Fathers*, staged in their permanent home in St Gabriel's Hall in Swansea itself, was not only a success on home territory, but played at the Fortune Theatre in London and won a BDL national trophy.[80]

That Swansea Little Theatre was in close geographical proximity to areas of some of the worst social deprivation in the UK was not unusual. Some of the strongest Little Theatres were to be found in the northern depressed areas, often operating in buildings close to the once prosperous city or town centre and the central business districts where wealth had been created in the nineteenth century. In 1920, the Stockport Garrick Society, established since 1901, claimed to become the first Little Theatre by turning itself into a limited company to purchase a former mill in Exchange Street set against the backdrop of the grand Victorian viaduct. In 1929, in Newcastle upon Tyne, the organising committee of the People's Theatre, which had been founded as the Clarion Dramatic Society in 1911, raised a mortgage to purchase a former Nonconformist chapel for £3,000, and spent a further £1,500 on converting it to a 310-seater theatre. In 1931, the Halifax Thespians, formed in 1927, moved into the hall above the old Halifax Building Society where the society continued to play until the Second World War. In the same year, members of the Bolton Dramatic Society decided to set up the Bolton Little Theatre. After three years playing in the Co-operative Hall, the generosity of a local industrialist enabled them to open their own theatre in Hanover Street within walking distance of the Town Hall.[81] Located where they were, these theatres were not insulated from the impact of reduced trading and commerce, or the queues outside the Labour Exchanges. But equally, there was no immersion in the areas suffering the greatest deprivation.

In *English Journey*, Priestley describes the Bradford Civic Theatre, then based in rented accommodation in Jowett Hall, a former temperance hall and converted cinema on the edge of the city's 'Little Germany'. Post-First World War, the German immigrant community which had contributed to Bradford's industrial wealth was much reduced. The successful Jowett Motor Manufacturing Company had renamed itself Jowett Cars Ltd. and had relocated to the leafier suburbs in Idle. Priestley's journey produced a graphic, angry report on the sharp contrasts in living standards across England, and he is unequivocal about the social value represented by the Bradford Civic Theatre in the city of his birth. He describes it as part of 'a genuine spontaneous movement' in a city 'crowded with amateur actors':

The people who work for these theatres are not by any means people who want to kill time. They are generally hard-working men and women ... whose evenings are precious to them … these theatres are very small and have to fight for their very existence, but … I see them as little camp-fires twinkling in a great darkness … The point is that in communities that have suffered the most from industrial depression, among younger people who frequently cannot see what is to become of their jobs, and their lives, these theatres have opened little windows into a world of ideas, colour, fine movement, exquisite drama, have kept going a stir of thought and imagination for actors, helpers, audiences, have acted as outposts for the army of the citizens of tomorrow, demanding to live.[82]

This is again the passionate rhetoric of the exemplary theatre, and coming from Priestley it combined an advocacy of imaginative and literary drama with a popularising instinct, which was to make him a powerful propagandist for a more egalitarian society during the Second World War. He became President of the Bradford theatre in 1932, and when the Jowett Hall burnt down in 1935, gave the company the royalties for performances of his play *Cornelius*. After the company raised the capital to purchase the burnt-out shell and build a new theatre, the opening production in 1937 was the premiere of Priestley's *Bees On the Boat* with the gift of the royalties.[83]

In general, Little Theatre societies modelled themselves on the repertory movement ethos, and at their most ambitious attempted a comparable range of classic and modern drama. Priestley and Purdom were not the only influential patrons. The Stockport Garrick Society engaged with theatre radicals from the beginning of the century. Encouraged by Charles Charrington, the husband of the English Ibsen actress Janet Achurch, to produce Shaw and Ibsen, and subsequently visited by Horniman, Payne and Co., the Society's work was deemed to have prepared the ground for the new Manchester Repertory Company.[84] Shaw used the enthusiasm for his plays to teach the amateurs more about professional contractual obligations and performance rights. The custom of free or token admission charges or the use of public performance as a fund-raising exercise without regard to the pecuniary rights of the author, amounted, as Shaw informed the Garrick Society, to little more than piracy.[85]

By the 1920s when groups were beginning to own their own theatres, the volunteer membership had to cope with the rigours of maintaining a public venue while co-ordinating the practical challenges of play production. Norman Veitch's history of the People's Theatre in Newcastle details the struggle to stay afloat financially. Despite the amateur status, the group, frequently taking less than £5 a performance, were routinely faced with wholly unrealistic demands for the rights to stage the likes of Barrie and Galsworthy and, even in 1922, Wilde's *The Importance of Being*

Earnest. In 1921, the year the Society renamed itself the People's Theatre, Shaw first visited the group in its old Royal Arcade premises to see a production of *Man and Superman.* His proposal to accept a box-office percentage as royalty payment was a rational compromise which, in theory at least, became company policy.[86]

Veitch's description of the dual committee structure which evolved – one committee overseeing artistic policy including play selection and casting, and the other building and business administration – gives ample evidence of the organisational tenacity which was typical of the Little Theatre movement and contributed to its long-term survival into the twenty-first century.[87] Every one of the theatres cited above is still flourishing. In the 1930s the voluntary membership of each theatre represented a formidable range of financial, legal and technical skills. Sometimes the electricians, plumbers and builders ran their own small businesses. But how each would have been classified socially is much less clear. As Priestley put it, 'every second typist is an ingénue lead somewhere, every other cashier a heavy father or comedian'.[88]

THE SOCIALIST THEATRE

However structurally conservative the Little Theatre amateur groups became – and inevitably like their professional counterparts the primary objective by the 1930s was to maintain the viability of their organisations – their roots in the political milieu espoused by Shaw, Barker, Galsworthy and Co., places them, initially at least, in the wide spectrum of liberal socialism. Raphael Samuel's survey, which includes the dramatic clubs established by the Independent Labour Party and the widespread Co-operative Societies, shows how fluid and various the objectives of socialism were.[89] In the case of the more moderate ILP and Co-op groups, the main aim was to cultivate and educate the capacity for upward mobility.[90] The Auchterderran Dramatic Club, which Joe Corrie was in prior to the formation of the Bowhill Village Players, was within a Co-operative Drama section and gave the first performances of his one-act plays.[91]

The detailed historical documentation of the Workers Theatre Movement in part derives from the active co-operation of the key leaders of the organisation, most notably Tom Thomas himself, who, together with Ewan MacColl and other WTM actor-writers like Charles Mann, were interviewed and contributed their own written accounts of what had been achieved. As a determinedly revolutionary socialist theatre movement, it functioned most effectively from 1927 when Thomas rescued and revitalised a moribund first-phase WTM with a series of plays, which began with his own very successful adaptation of Robert Tressell's *The Ragged Trousered Philanthropists*.[92] It began to dwindle in 1935 when, in the altered political climate created by the rise of fascism, the policy of the People's Front was launched by the Communist International. While the WTM mobile tradition of taking vigorously non-stage-illusionist performance to rallies, political meetings, trade union socials, etc., continued when Unity Theatre Club was first set up in London in early 1936, the trend was to move theatre back indoors. The name Unity signalled a break with political sectarianism, and an open invitation to any participants or audiences who wished to join. Unity Theatres were established in locations such as Glasgow, Aberdeen, Leeds and Bristol where WTM groups had previously operated.[93]

Raphael Samuel singles out the remarkable openness of the WTM's 'workerist turn' to avant-garde experimentalism.[94] The commitment ideologically to the encouragement of audience participation, the adoption of revue-style sketches and songs and the near fanatical eschewal of all the trappings of conventional 'closed' theatre – the curtained stage, costume, props, make-up – were all learnt through encounters with the radical ideas circulating in Russia and Germany. At the peak of WTM activity, performances on lorries, at factory gates, on simple platforms erected on trestles, could attract hundreds, if not thousands, of spectators often in the thick of industrial dispute. The 1931 Red Pioneers tour of Scotland was particularly successful spawning at least six home-grown groups in strongly politicised areas of very high unemployment.[95] Also deploying traditional elements from British music hall and popular street performance, the WTM left an important legacy for succeeding generations of political theatre practitioners. But the fact that by the mid-1930s, the group members appeared trapped within a rigid, formulaic model of performance, which was artistically weak and politically simplistic, drew attention to the lack of craft skill and the negative perception of amateur status. Increasingly, professional directors and actors sought involvement with this new kind of exemplary theatre that created tensions about the primary political objective and 'worker' authenticity.[96]

Writing about the Glasgow Workers Theatre Group, which was set up by former members of Clarion and Co-operative groups in 1937, Linda Mackenney carefully details the 'working class' credentials of the membership. The skilled or semi-skilled occupations included bookbinder, clerical assistant, grocer, electrician, joiner, merchant seaman, etc. A few were unemployed and several were active members of the local branch of the Communist Party. But there was also support from within the left-wing intelligentsia who included, amongst others, the poet Hugh MacDiarmid and Helen Biggar, film-maker and sculptress who was the daughter of Hugh Biggar, a founding member of the ILP and former Lord Provost.[97] There was a significant step change in artistic innovation. GWTG's record of experimentation began with Clifford Odets's *Waiting for Lefty* and then included living newspaper, living cartoon, mass declamation, masques and pageants.[98] By 1941 when the establishment of Glasgow Unity brought together all the remnants of the key left-leaning groups not scattered by the war, the membership was socially and culturally very diverse.

The arrival of dancers and visual artists as refugees from Nazi-occupied Europe strengthened the international outlook already contributed by members from the Glasgow Jewish Institute Players.[99] While Glasgow Unity developed home-grown Scottish writing, there was in the early years within the context of the fight against fascism, a positive avoidance of an unduly nationalist bias. Robert McLeish's *The Gorbals Story*, premiered by Unity in 1946, was not only a hugely successful social-realist play grounded firmly in the awful living conditions of the urban industrial poor, it also characterised Glasgow as a cultural and racial melting pot. The play's slum location was populated by Irish Catholics, Scots Protestants, Highland migrants, Jewish workers and, even in a gesture towards the city's growing Asian community, an Indian pedlar.[100]

When the professional Unity limited company was set up in 1946, encouraged by the financial success of the extensively toured *Gorbals Story*, great care was taken not to signal any higher status for the 'fulltime' than for the 'part-time' company.[101] The modest grant of £500 [102] to professional Unity, awarded by the newly formed Scottish Committee of the Arts Council of Great Britain, was from a state-sponsored organisation already moving away from the wartime CEMA mission to encourage the participatory amateur arts.[103] In the event, however, as was the case with other professional Unity ventures, the company foundered, damaged in battles with the emerging Scottish theatre establishment – especially the increasingly powerful Bridie – and unable to maintain strong financial management.[104] Even the amateur Glasgow Unity folded in 1951.

Fundamentally what the 'Unity' concept was signalling was a much more ambitious move towards a collective performance endeavour, which for all the ideological reservations about the remunerative aspects of professionalism, aimed to achieve a socially and politically efficacious theatre at a distance from the purely recreational. While the nomenclature was different, and it was politically non-aligned, the Ulster Group Theatre, formed in the winter of 1939–40, was based on the same combining principle, but managed a successful mediation between amateur and professional. The semi-professional Northern Irish Players, which emerged from an amalgamation of three other locally-based amateur societies to introduce a 'standard of professionalism', came together with the Ulster Theatre and the Jewish Institute Dramatic Society. The actors in the Group Theatre, some of whom had professional experience, played in the Ulster Minor Hall in Belfast, surviving for the most part on little more than expenses. Alongside very competent productions of English classics and contemporary drama, there grew a body of work from Ulster dramatists – in particular George Shiels, Joseph Tomelty and St John Ervine. Over the next fifteen years nearly 50 plays were premiered by the company that, rather like comparable ventures in Glasgow, was to provide a launch pad for a new generation of Ulster actors.[105]

Across Great Britain, amateurs, with varying degrees of success, were evolving into professional practitioners with some support from state-funding initiatives. Simultaneously the autonomous amateur movement, valued during the war as a morale-booster, still appeared to be on an upward trajectory. In 1946 the Little Theatre Guild of Great Britain was founded to provide an umbrella organisation for all independent building-based societies, and a significant number of new groups moved into their own premises in the decade that followed. By 1956, however, the ACGB Secretary General W. E. Williams declared the strength of the amateur arts a threat to the stability of professional provision. Doing it for love was now not the same as doing it not-for-profit.[106]

CHAPTER 5

The topography of theatre in 1950

If the built landscape in 1900 was the product of nations-wide industrial prosperity and imperial confidence, in 1950 the scars inflicted by wartime bombing and the legacy of industrial decay from the 1930s were still all too visible. To be sure additional constructed layers to the environment bore witness to the industrial initiatives and housing developments of the interwar years, and there were some new theatres, but the spatial evidence provided by the topographical concentration of new build showed the geographical and demographic consequences of economic and social inequality. Lack of investment and maintenance in the worst-affected areas had resulted in the dereliction of physical infrastructure and the loss of population to more prosperous parts of the country.[1] Patterns of internal migration formed and reformed as circumstances changed, but the drift towards the Midlands and the South-East of England in search of new industries continued.

In Wales, for example, between 1939 and 1941, it appeared that the 1930s' haemorrhage of the population had reversed as at least 200,000 immigrants arrived seeking a safe haven from the war.[2] In the 1951 census, however, it was shown that 649,275 people born in Wales were then living in England and of those 190,722 were resident in the South-East.[3] The Irish were still coming to Britain at the rate of 60,000 a year after 1945.[4] While the creation of the Irish Free State in 1921 had meant that as a geo-political construct Great Britain had physically shrunk, Eire's economic dependence on British markets made, as R. F. Foster pointed out, 'nonsense of Irish "sovereignty"'.[5]

The need to service the war machine had revived heavy industry, accelerated the development of new industries such as plane manufacture and brought back full employment, but the six years of vigorously maintained 'British' unity in the face of unprecedented threat masked the underlying economic trends, which had been apparent even before the First World War. Pre-1939 much of the once bustling conurbations in the North-East,

Lancashire, Northern Ireland, South Wales and Central Scotland had been designated 'special areas' in need of palliative governmental intervention. Ironically, it was these same areas, including the major ports, that became crucial to the war effort – Glasgow, Liverpool, Cardiff, Belfast, Portsmouth, etc. – which suffered most from the Blitz. London was the worst hit, but in the regions whole city centres were destroyed – Swansea, Coventry and Belfast were rendered almost unrecognisable. Thus some theatre buildings literally exploded overnight. Six theatres were destroyed in Portsmouth and Plymouth; five in Liverpool, three in Hull, three in Southampton, four in Birmingham. In London, the Little Theatre and the Kingsway were among the nineteen or so theatres badly damaged or destroyed.[6] Only in November of 1950 did the Old Vic, bombed in May 1941, reopen as a fully-functioning theatre.[7]

Theatre building was not a priority in the context of the Labour government's struggle to meet its 1945 commitment to new and better housing to replace the pre-war slums and the innumerable homes destroyed or damaged in the war. Britain was bankrupt and in debt to the United States. The shortage of resources included building materials, labour and the investment necessary to boost an over-stretched economy. Indeed, rationing on food, clothes, petrol and other domestic goods was only gradually phased out. In 1950, the Labour Party was still just about in power following the February general election, but with an overall parliamentary majority of only five seats. By the end of August, British troops were fighting overseas yet again – this time in Korea in alliance with the USA – and within a few months the prime minister, Clement Atlee, would commit over 10 per cent of the gross national product to a three-year defence programme.[8]

In his analysis of the political choices made by central government in the years immediately following Labour's landslide electoral victory in 1945, the historian Peter Clarke refers to a Churchillian image of 'Britain standing at the intersection of three overlapping circles: Europe, the Empire, and a transatlantic partnership'. The result Clarke suggests 'was an over-extension of Britain's role in all directions simultaneously'. Britain had proved itself to be a great nation on the battlefield, but as the chief scientific adviser to the cabinet, Sir Henry Tizard, warned, 'if we continue to behave like a Great Power we shall soon cease to be a great nation'.[9]

Increasingly overshadowed by America's growing global influence, the tensions caused by the transatlantic partnership were not just economic and military, but also more broadly destabilising as the exhausted British population could only admire and envy the access to consumer goods enjoyed by their American counterparts. American popular music, dance and, above all, film were a pervasive influence. In the theatre London productions of dynamic new American musicals and the British premieres of challenging new plays by American dramatists, such as Arthur Miller and Tennessee Williams, added to the impression that both literally and in the ideological abstract the space of power was emanating from across the Atlantic ocean. A scarcely acknowledged consequence of this was the impact on British artists whose colonial heritage functioned 'naturally' to impose a position of inferiority and subordination.

EQUAL RELATIONS

The imperial circle was shrinking to be replaced by a federation of equals, the theoretically more equitable construct of the Commonwealth. The most radical step in the dismantling of empire, the granting of independence to the Indian subcontinent in 1947, was achieved at the cost of separating India as a non-sectarian, but predominantly Hindu state from the Muslim state of Pakistan. The loss of at least half a million lives through internecine violence was just one of the demographic consequences. Loss of land and the disruption of traditional career expectations caused by the displacement of whole communities, especially in North India, meant that migration to the 'mother country' appeared to offer better prospects.[10] In London, the desire to retain the once-colonised peoples within a benign, but nevertheless metropolitan sphere of influence was signalled in the continuing right to British nationality, confirmed under the terms of the 1948 Nationality Act. For those coming to Britain to make a better life, the terms of the Act were unequivocal. Any citizen of a British colony or Commonwealth citizen had the status of a British subject. To anyone, anywhere, living in the parts of the globe still directly ruled from Britain or who acknowledged the British sovereign as the head of *their* commonwealth, it would have appeared axiomatic that they had rights of domicile in Great Britain.

The result was the beginning of what Robert Winder has called 'colonisation in reverse'.[11] The demographic phenomenon that had evolved spasmodically in a series of economically contingent fits and starts to form the non-white communities already settled across the UK began to gather momentum after 1945. The symbolic starting point is usually seen as the disembarkation in London of the passengers on the SS *Empire Windrush*, which had sailed from Kingston, the capital of Jamaica, the largest of the British island colonies in the Caribbean in May 1948. Two days after the ship docked at Tilbury on 21 June, a letter was sent by eleven Labour MPs to the prime minister, Clement Atlee, expressing concern that Britain would become an 'open reception centre for immigrants not selected in respect to health, education, training, character, customs and above all whether assimilation was possible or not'.[12]

Of course, as Winder points out, compared with levels of Irish immigration, the arrival of hundreds – rather than thousands – of Black British migrants was a mere trickle. Also the accumulated weight of symbolic significance attached to the *Windrush* 'event' has led to a distortion of documentary evidence that shows how diverse the passengers were even amongst the Black Caribbean component. Instead of the mythologised 492 Jamaican males arriving en masse, passengers' recorded 'Countries of last Permanent Residence' included, as Matthew Mead has sought to show, Trinidad, British Guiana, St Lucia, Uganda, Kenya, Barbados, Italy and even Scotland.[13] While many of the passengers were indeed men and of these there were a large number who were born in Jamaica, there were significant numbers of women and whole families including children. There were also some sixty-six migrants from Poland destined to swell the large numbers of Poles who arrived in the post-war years. Mead cites the 1951 census details of place of birth for an increasingly heterogeneous population: '2,024 residents were born in British Guiana; 6,447 in Jamaica; 1,569 in Trinidad; 110,767 in India; and 11,117 in Pakistan, while the numbers for those born in Poland were 151,736; for Germany 96,379; and Italy 33,159'.[14]

The effect of homogenising former colonial subjects into an undifferentiated mass of 'black', and thus threatening, aliens, who were nonetheless essential as a source of much-needed industrial labour, was to ignore and undervalue individual and very specific cultural heritages. The natural tendency of migrants with shared backgrounds to group together for protection was exacerbated by housing policies in cities such as Birmingham, Leeds, Manchester and Glasgow, which effectively ghettoised new arrivals, eventually completely transforming the physical appearance and cultural identity of selected urban areas. London as a centuries-old, international melting pot absorbed the largest numbers, but employment opportunities in the factories and foundries of the English Midlands and the North had begun to create growing communities of visible difference.

Within a national context of grudging acceptance and generalised assumptions that the vast majority of Black British – even those who were highly qualified – would be employed in low-grade unskilled or semi-skilled work, there were very few opportunities for aspiring actors. Robert Adams writing in *New Theatre* in November 1947 pointed out that 'in variety and on the music halls, the Negro is expected to roll the eyes, have flying feet for tap-dancing, be a buffoon generally or sing Negro spirituals or sentimental mush'.[15] The article was published not long after the demise of London Unity's professional company where Adams had been well-reviewed for his performance as Jim Harris in *All God's Chillun' Got Wings*,[16] but even that success contributed to his perception that 'The Negro artist is still considered not as an artist in his own right but as something contributory to the support of the white artists.'[17] The focus on the black experience in American drama had created a situation where professionally, African American actors were considered of a higher calibre than Black British artists. A particular source of irritation had been the importation into London of the entire American Negro Theatre production of *Anna Lucasta*, a play by Philip Yordan about a reformed prostitute and her avaricious family, which ran for two years in 1947–8 at His Majesty's Theatre. Black British artists like LAMDA-trained Pauline Henriques were encouraged to think themselves lucky to be employed as understudies.[18] As the success of *Anna Lucasta* and another American play *Deep are the Roots*, by Arnaud d' Usseau and James Gow presented at Wyndhams Theatre in 1947, demonstrated, there was an audience in London for plays about the black experience, but as something which happened at a safe distance, somewhere else and certainly not to be mediated by Black British actors.[19]

The challenge that Adams threw down to *New Theatre* readers was the reminder of intertwined histories, 'We Negroes are perhaps more closely related to you English than any portion of the Commonwealth. Recognise us as equals, give us the opportunities to contribute as equals.'[20] The point was that in terms of education and training the individual Black and Asian artists who were beginning to emerge were in every way the equal of their white peers. Jamaican-born Henriques had been brought to settle in London in 1919 by her father, determined to educate his children in the English system, a by-product of which created a passion for theatre-going. Adams himself had competed as a wrestler, but trained for the bar and ultimately returned to his native Guiana as a head teacher. Henriques later described how she and other *Anna Lucasta* understudies, including Earl Cameron and Errol John, joined together to perform Thornton Wilder's one-act play *The Happy Journey* in a small Hampstead theatre forming, she claimed, 'the nucleus of what we were beginning to think of as the Black British Theatre Movement'.[21]

In 1950 there was still little evidence of a movement gathering momentum, and apart from variety shows virtually no serious engagement with audiences outside London. Kenneth Tynan's bold idea to cast Henriques as Emilia in his production of *Othello*, which featured the African American Gordon Heath in the title role, offered a glimpse of future possibilities while simultaneously confirming the pro-American bias which had so infuriated Adams.[22] As a six-month tour to the mostly school and church halls of 'theatreless' towns sent out under the auspices of the Arts Council of Great Britain, however, the project was an example of a strategic intervention in the provision of theatre, which attempted literally to circumvent the obstacles created by commercial priorities. As an exercise in promoting the interests of black artists it did little more than whet appetites which could not be satisfied.

The result of the 1950 general election was a portent of what would happen in 1951 when the Conservative Party still led by Winston Churchill was returned to power.[23] The mid-century British population, already enlarged by the so-called 'baby boom' of 1946–8, had been encouraged to expect, within the broadly agreed ideology of 'welfare-capitalism', significantly improved prospects. The 1944 Education Act, the 1945 Family Allowance Act, and in 1946, the National Insurance Act, the National Health Service Act and the National Assistance Act legislated for better educational opportunity and the 'cradle to the grave' welfare state. What Alan Sinfield has attributed to basic timidity in the Labour Party leaders and piecemeal planning allied to 'paternalistic Victorian assumptions' led to the compromises exacerbated by economic constraints which inevitably generated disappointment and resentment.[24] Nationalisation of the industries producing basic utilities – coal (1947), railways and electricity (1948), gas (1949), and in 1951 iron and steel – was controversial not least because of arguments about centralised inefficiency. But at this juncture, when it was important to bolster confidence in a Labour-led new society, the move to public ownership of the very resources that had underpinned Britain's industrial wealth in the past had tremendous symbolic impact.

Positive symbols were important. In 1950 plans were well under way for 'a great symbol of national regeneration',[25] which was a reminder of past greatness and a promise for an equally dynamic future. The 1951 Festival of Britain marked the centenary of the 1851 Great Exhibition, which had proclaimed the extent of Britain's industrial prestige at the peak of its power. The vision in 1950 was for a celebration that would take place across Britain in numerous events and local festivals, but which would primarily focus on a project of site clearance and physical regeneration on London's semi-derelict South Bank. The building projects, including the new Festival Hall and a range of modernist architectural constructions such as the Dome of Discovery and the Skylon,[26] also made use of strategically useful repair jobs like the Old Vic. Between the Festival Hall and the celebrated, but distinctly shabby old theatre was a portentous empty space envisaged as the site of the National Theatre. The National Theatre bill had passed without division through parliament in January 1949 based on a plan that the Treasury would give £1,000,000 to build the theatre on land donated by the London County Council.[27] The foundation stone laid in 1951 by Queen Elizabeth was later quietly moved, and it would have been obvious to all that the £1,000,000 was not enough to build and equip the theatre. Indeed, even the Arts Council's promised grant of £50,000 towards the Old Vic repair was withdrawn. The Governors were forced to borrow to supplement other smaller grants.[28] When it did reopen in November 1950, there were still hopes of its 'coronation' as the National Theatre.[29]

The nations-wide dimension to the Festival, which would include the already established Edinburgh International Festival and the Aldeburgh Festival, was to be given moral support and encouragement but little in the shape of cash. In his commentary on what the Festival's theme of 'the Land and the People' represented for the national cultural *mentalité*, Robert Hewison notes the 'comfortably democratic words from the lexicon of wartime propaganda that created a space within which to explore the way a nation had shaped its environment'.[30] For all the aggressive modernism of the planned exhibition architecture on the South Bank (much of which was later swept away by the Conservatives), the prevailing ethos was neo-romantic and preoccupied with a view of Britishness exemplified (with yet another symbol) in the Lion and the Unicorn Pavilion. Like the heraldic beasts, the British people's 'native genius' had two dimensions: 'realism and strength' and 'fantasy, independence and imagination'.[31] As the state through its central agencies sought to disseminate 'the arts of peace' and thus shape the cultural environment, there were real questions about how those imagined and potentially contradictory attributes were to be brought into a productive reconciliation.

A BRITISH PROJECT

The paradox at the heart of state control for the public good was that creating the means of equitable distribution of resources made the recipients simultaneously more capable of autonomy and independence and at the same time bound them ever more closely to the central benefactor. On the macro level, of course, this had implications for interdependence within the component parts of the British state and, in particular, for nationalist aspirations in Wales and Scotland. For Labour politicians like former Welsh miner Aneurin Bevan, who was the architect of the NHS, devolution would damage the Welsh interests that had benefited from social reforms.[32] For Scotland, Labour Secretary of State, Tom Johnston, used the threat of Scottish nationalism to develop substantial administrative devolution to the Scottish Office. He was clear, given the extent of Scottish social and economic problems, that political devolution to an Edinburgh parliament would do little more than 'administer an emigration system, a glorified poor law and a graveyard'.[33]

At the micro level of state-resourced access to the arts, the establishment in 1940 of the Council for the Encouragement of Music and the Arts (CEMA), which evolved in 1945 into the Arts Council of Great Britain chaired by John Maynard Keynes, created similar tensions between enablement and control. Some well-established arts institutions – in the theatre these included the Shakespeare Memorial Theatre, the Birmingham Repertory Theatre, the Liverpool Playhouse – were wary of subsidy dependency and the constraints that might bring. In truth, only semi-independent itself and functioning from 1945 onwards under the auspices of the Treasury, ACGB was chronically cash-restricted. The initial goal of the small salaried staff was to build on CEMA's wartime planning that literally mapped out a nations-wide arts provision based not on the economic imperative to locate the largest potential paying audiences, but rather where absence of access to the arts was diagnosed. Hence the focus on 'theatreless areas', which even in 1950 were still being supplied with Arts Council-managed tours.[34] 'Theatre', however, in the post-war definition meant professional provision. Amateur activity, as part of the spectrum of participatory arts which had been central to CEMA's founding principles did not feature on the map.

After 1942 when Keynes became chairman of CEMA, various ideological binaries – amateur/professional, for profit/not-for-profit, independence/control – came under considerable pressure. Keynesian theory of economic pump-priming and demand management, which would

dominate Western economic policy until the 1970s, compelled governments to accept the legitimacy of active intervention to control the societal effects of the unfettered marketplace. As a liberal technocrat with a
genuine passion for the arts, Keynes effectively embodied the enablement/
control tensions within the Arts Council. CEMA had established Regional
Offices in ten English towns, a Scottish Committee in 1943 and a Welsh
Committee in 1944. Northern Ireland also acquired a CEMA in 1943, but
it appears to have functioned separately and is not mentioned in any of
the published ACGB documentation.[35] Specialist advisory art-form panels
were built into the structure of the new Arts Council and offered the
potential for autonomous policy-making. But final authority lay with the
Chair, sixteen Council members and their executive officers. Despite the
devolutionary promise of his rhetoric, ultimately it was Keynes's essentially
metropolitan tastes and preference for circulating metropolitan excellence
using commercial expertise operating on a not-for-profit basis that established the dominant funding agenda in the immediate post-war period.
His commitment to the financial needs of the Royal Opera House, Covent
Garden, which reopened in April 1946 just before his death, was integral
to a dream to make London 'a place to visit and to wonder at'.[36] In 1950,
£170,000 out of a total Treasury grant of £600,000 (£100,000 of which
was an advance for the 1951 Festival) was spent on the Opera House. The
argument put forward to justify the obvious imbalance in funding priorities, demonstrated by the pie chart published in the 1950–1 ACGB Annual
Report, was that key London venues (Covent Garden, Sadler's Wells, the
Old Vic), together with orchestras that played in London, were *national*
assets and thus should be valued by all irrespective of whether the bulk of
the population would ever have the opportunity to enjoy them.[37]

The relationship of the Scottish and Welsh Committees to the central body differed in that since 1946 the Scottish Committee had been
permitted autonomy in the administration of its block grant, which in
the 1950–1 financial year amounted to £52,500 and included funding for
the Edinburgh Festival.[38] In 1950 the Welsh Committee still had advisory status, although since the inception of CEMA, Welsh sensibility as
embodied in the individuals who directed policy had been at the core of
the organisation.[39] Up to a point, then, separate national interests were
considered but were also firmly incorporated into the *British* and indeed
metropolitan project. Dr H. O. Mavor, aka James Bridie, who had served
on the main Council and had a continuing membership of the Scottish
Committee and the Edinburgh Festival Committee, was very insistent
on devolved powers.[40] But the Anglo-Scottish character of the Glasgow

Citizens' Theatre, which he battled to found in 1943, derived from Bridie's own professional engagement with the English theatre establishment and concomitant lack of confidence in home-grown performance and directorial skills.[41] Similarly, there appears to have been little Scottish Committee questioning of the largely Anglo-centric seasons of the associated Perth and Dundee repertory companies. The essentially metropolitan Edinburgh Festival Committee's emphasis was on international performance of the highest quality, and they initially rejected Scottish theatre-makers and even a Bridie-authored play.[42] The blocking manoeuvres, in which Bridie was implicated, to prevent Glasgow Unity from participating in the Festival on the grounds of low artistic standards, inadvertently led to the first Edinburgh Fringe.[43]

The Gorbals' location of the adopted permanent home of the Glasgow Citizens' Theatre in 1945 was emblematic of complex social, political and artistic relationships. The Royal Princess's Theatre, built at the height of mass immigration into the city to share in Glasgow's Victorian prosperity, was by then a pantomime and variety house serving an explosively heterogeneous and declining population crowded into squalid tenements.[44] The renamed theatre's board of businessmen and eminent professionals led by Bridie were 'citizens' as Alfred Wareing defined the term. A donation of £10,000 from a leading local industrialist secured the purchase of the ten-year lease, and there was the cushioning effect of Arts Council guarantees.[45] It was vital that Glasgow's intelligentsia should be lured south across the Clyde. Bridie certainly did all he could to foreground and develop Scottish plays, some of which were new, and plays programmed to appeal to the Irish in the local community, but the core was the English repertoire.[46] The original building was to be inscribed with a new set of ideological and aesthetic principles, creating a disjunction between the idealised interior and the material reality outside.

In 1950, tours of Robert McLeish's dramatisation of the poverty and religious and ethnic divisions within the Gorbals community was virtually all that was left to Glasgow Unity's 'full-time' professional venture.[47] *The Gorbals Story* had been invited to London in 1948, with performances at the Garrick Theatre and the Embassy Theatre, Swiss Cottage attracting the attention of metropolitan audiences and critics to a vicarious experience of Gorbalin adversity and resilience.[48] Linda Mackenney's account of Unity's final collapse in 1951 argues that the London appearances and English touring, which was one of the reasons given for the withdrawal of the Scottish Committee's guarantees, cut the company off from their grass-roots Glasgow constituency and exacerbated their financial woes.[49]

As an insider within the Anglo-Scottish nexus, the Citizens' surviving in the Gorbals could claim to be Scotland's leading producing theatre. In 1950, the year before his death, Bridie brought both locals and 'tourists' to see his co-written Scottish pantomime *The Tintock Cup* for a four-month run, which briefly returned the theatre to its popular roots.[50]

BRICKS AND MORTAR

Along with approval of the Citizens' enterprise, Keynes's legacy also included two other buildings. The first, the Cambridge Arts Theatre, founded and endowed by Keynes and one of the relatively small number of new 'legitimate' theatres built in the interwar period, was opened in 1936 at almost exactly the same time as he published his seminal work, the *General Theory of Employment, Interest and Money*.[51] In 1942, following an appeal from a group of local citizens, he secured the future of Britain's oldest working theatre, the Theatre Royal in Bristol. Built in 1766, the Theatre Royal had survived the bombing in 1940, which had destroyed the Prince's Theatre, and stood isolated in yet another slum area and under threat from property developers. The twenty-one years' lease taken out by CEMA together with a £5,000 bank loan, which on repayment from the first £5,000 profits would mean the trustees would own the building, was precisely the kind of optimistic interventionist strategy which characterised Keynesian economics in its most basic mode. The result was a beautifully refurbished eighteenth-century playhouse. Directly managed by the Arts Council with Charles Landstone, the assistant drama director of CEMA, appointed as general manager, and the London Old Vic supplying the productions, the Bristol Theatre Royal became the first state-supported theatre in the country.[52] 1950 saw it renamed as the Bristol Old Vic. With management shared among Bristol Corporation, the Arts Council and the Old Vic, the theatre functioned as a regional producing theatre with its own resident company and a direct link to London, which permitted a two-way traffic of actors and directors.[53]

Keynes's BBC Home Service talk, introducing the fledgling Arts Council to the nation, which was broadcast on 12 July 1945 just before the General Election, has been much analysed by critics determined to interrogate the ideological anomalies at the heart of the institution. Keynes's vision of the artist 'individual and free, undisciplined, unregimented', walking 'where the breath of the spirit blows him' is unashamedly romantic, apparently brushing aside the economic engine of the free spirit.[54] It was also, as Landstone was to discover in his tussle with Keynes over the provenance of the artistic product to be delivered in Bristol, disingenuous about the kind of freedom represented by economic interests. Local preferences and financial imperatives could not be served by Lord Keynes's favoured toured-in metropolitan product bolstered simply by a guarantee against loss.[55]

Speaking only a few weeks after the end of the war in Europe, Keynes was also careful to emphasise reconstruction priorities: 'Houses for householders have to come first.' But again, and characteristically, he puts in a plea for 'a few crumbs of mortar' to permit places of 'congregation and enjoyment'. The biggest problem as he saw it was the

shortage – in most parts of Britain the complete absence – of adequate or suitable buildings. There never were many theatres in this country or any concert-halls or galleries worth counting. Of the few we once had, first the cinema took a toll and then the blitz; and anyway the really suitable building for a largish audience which the modern engineer can construct had never been there. The greater number even of large towns, let alone the smaller centres, are absolutely bare of the necessary bricks and mortar.'[56]

The assertion that 'There never were many theatres' is of course manifestly untrue. Although the impact of cinema and war had been considerable, the numbers, quality and capacity of theatre buildings in the post-war period was a good deal more complicated. Keynes was dead less than a year after his broadcast, but the preoccupation with what later came to be known as 'housing the arts' remained a constant in Arts Council policy.

COMPETING PATTERNS

As in 1900, the topography of theatre in 1950 requires more than one map to reveal the competing sets of spatial patterns. That Churchillian image of the intersection of over-lapping circles had relevance for a theatre industry poised as it was between the circle of influence maintained by a very powerful metropolitan commercial sector – the widening circle of Arts Council outreach policy, which was again essentially metropolitan in origin but did radiate out across the United Kingdom – and a far more diffuse regional theatre sector, which was very fragmented and, still, for professional practitioners predominantly commercial. The very heavy concentration of both financial and thus artistic resources was as ever still held in London and this impacted directly on how some major regional resources were managed. But the core–periphery relationship had reconfigured. The majority of the pre-war initiatives to provide independently produced theatre for audiences outside London had, on the whole, survived, albeit very precariously and lacking the capacity for artistic innovation. Theatre galleries were no longer packed with the poor – cinema was cheaper, and anyway, American films especially promised a more glamorous escape from the greyness of austerity Britain. But as Dan Rebellato has pointed out, theatre-going in the late 1940s and early 50s was 'a profoundly social activity',[57] offering, in a period of austerity, afternoons, which included matinée teas consumed in the auditorium, or a regular evening out complete with boxes of chocolates and the opportunity to meet with friends. Amateur theatre, another profoundly social activity, was firmly established, and in many areas was effectively the main source of theatre.

Tensions had begun to accumulate around the strength of the amateur sector. The Little Theatre Guild founded in 1946 was growing in membership as more groups established their own premises. One of the resolutions passed by the British Theatre Conference, held under the chairmanship of J. B. Priestley in 1948, which tackled a number of important industrial and professional concerns, was to ensure greater co-operation between amateur and professional theatre.[58] But ACGB policy had been steadily widening the gap for some time. As Ted Willis's failure to sustain a professional London Unity company had demonstrated, for some amateurs professional status was too onerous and ideologically suspect.[59] Well-established amateur groups were also capable of putting up a determined resistance to attempts to import alien professional ventures into their home territory. This may well have been a factor in 1950 when the Arts Council was compelled to admit defeat in efforts to grow a permanent repertory company at the Grand Theatre in Swansea.[60]

On the level of more direct governmental policy, the 1948 Local Government Act permitted up to 6d in the pound from the rates levied by local authorities to be spent on arts and leisure, but this was discretionary, not obligatory, and by 1950 comparatively few authorities had taken up the opportunity to assist theatres in their localities. The Arts Council's annual report for 1950–1 singles out Bristol, Nottingham, Kettering and Guildford as municipalities prepared to offer financial support, but 'these and other examples of civic aid to local theatres remain a disappointing drop in the ocean of need'.[61] At this point in time when government resources were so overstretched and the concept of state and civic-subsidised, not-for-profit theatre was only patchily recognised, the balance of power was still heavily weighted towards commercial interests.

MAPPING THE SPACE

Two mapping exercises undertaken in 1950 on behalf of the industry demonstrate findings about the distribution of theatre that are in broad agreement about numbers of dedicated buildings across the British Isles but are less clear about the criteria of provenance and function for inclusion in the specific category of 'theatre'. The primary objective of the two surveys was also quite different. The report *Theatre Ownership in Britain* commissioned by the Federation of Theatre Unions focused on who owned and thus controlled theatre-building stock.[62] Leaving aside the holes in the landscape caused by the war, the location of buildings and their fitness for purpose was largely the effect of industrial ebb and flow governed by underlying economic trends. The economics of theatre had changed because of new competing sources of entertainment, but the other factor which particularly exercised the Federation was the impact of corporate ownership, which now fifty years into the century had grown ever more monolithic.

The Federation report was confined to England, Scotland and Wales. There had been an initial intention to include Northern Ireland, but as the introduction explains the Province was omitted because 'there appear to be only two regular theatres there, both in Belfast'.[63] In fact, war-damaged Belfast with its sectarian-driven inequalities still relatively contained was something of a microcosm of interrelated strands of activity that reflected what was happening elsewhere in the UK. The British government remained tied to the fiscal policy and welfare services required to give Ulster 'special treatment', but there was still a tendency to ignore what was happening in this patch of Britain across the Irish Sea.

The Federation report was a one-off exercise digging deep into the industrial landscape to determine exactly who owned theatres as a capital asset, and where and how influential business networks and monopolies operated. One function of the listings in *The Stage Year Book*, which had only resumed publication in 1949 after an absence since 1928, was for industry professionals to assess commercial possibilities. But the scope of the survey gave a much broader picture of theatre's place in a nationswide spectrum of cultural practice. The editors blithely ignored political boundaries, so that the 'provincial' guide extended across the whole of Ireland as well as the nations officially in the British construct. It was thus possible to compare the resources on offer in Galway on the west coast of Ireland with Norwich in the east of England. Galway had no designated theatres, but did have two public halls and a 'repertory' group Taidbearc na Zaillime performing Gaelic plays. In Norwich the venerable Theatre Royal was still functioning as a No. 1 legitimate theatre; the Hippodrome offered twice-nightly variety; and Nugent Monck's amateur Norwich Players performed a 'repertory' of classical plays in the Elizabethan-styled Maddermarket playhouse.[64] Readers could assess whether the theatre ecology was mainly professional or amateur, or indeed if the lack of resources meant there was no relevant opportunity of any kind.

Overall *The Stage* guide covers 574 cities, towns and even villages outside London with populations which ranged from over a million in Birmingham (1,099,850) and Glasgow (1,075,000) to 161,000 in Swansea and 2,500 in Wem in Shropshire to communities of a few hundred. Each entry supplied information on local newspapers, halls, cinemas and theatres and, in a data requirement which indicated the shifts in theatre as cultural practice, whether there were open-air sites, local amateur clubs and societies and whether theatre classified as 'repertory' operated in the area. In Blakeney, a coastal village in Norfolk with a population of 800, there were some contradictions in the entry, which declared no cinemas, theatres or clubs, but conceded a British Legion Hall with 'stage, wings, lights, dressing rooms, stock scenery' and the 'Drama Section of Women's Institute' was 'responsible for plays'. Some five hundred miles away in Dornoch, in the Scottish Highlands with an even smaller population of 700, the village acknowledged the Dornoch Amateur Dramatic Society, which again in the absence of cinemas and theatres presumably performed in the Drill Hall, which according to the entry had a capacity of approximately 300. Relatively few towns listed had no theatre activity at all. Strathpeffer Spa in Ross-shire with no societies, cinemas and theatres listed and just one hall advertised itself as eager for development.

Attempting to disentangle frequently hidden and very complicated control networks, *Theatre Ownership in Britain* lists 425 theatres in England, Scotland and Wales outside London. The 95 Greater London theatres, treated separately and at much greater length, were categorised by location and then not simply listed but examined under ownership headings. West End theatres included buildings located 'from Victoria to Kingsway and from the Thames to the Euston Road'[65] but excluded private club and experimental ventures. The area covered by suburban theatres, here including the Old Vic, and music halls stretched from Kingston to East Ham, and from Watford to Croydon. Added together the Report gives the total number of British theatres as 520. *The Stage* guide, however, supplies a more straightforward London listing. 'Theatres', which included the Old Vic and the Lyric Hammersmith, came to 47. There

were 21 music halls listed. Other theatres which *Theatre Ownership* designated 'Outer-London' went into *The Stage* provincial guide. Both surveys
note war-damaged theatres and music halls.

The provincial landscape sketched out by *The Stage* is complex. Less
than half (about 245) of the cities or towns surveyed specifically identified 'theatres' within their localities, thus potentially putting them into
the Arts Council's category of 'theatreless'. But when local amateur dramatic societies and the availability of public halls were put into the frame,
it becomes clear that very substantial theatrical performance of varying
levels of provenance and expertise was integrated into the leisure pursuits
of the area. Thus in Northern Ireland, Newry (population *c.* 1,400) in
County Down technically had no theatres, but four amateur societies
were listed and an annual Drama Festival was held in the town hall. In
the 2000 *Theatres Trust Guide to British Theatres*, what is now known as
Newry Town Hall Theatre is described as 'a most picturesque sight standing astride a three-arched bridge over the Clanrye River in the centre
of the town'.[66] Similarly, the entry on theatres for Portadown (population 16,300) in County Armagh puts 'none'. But the town sustained three
societies, cited Portadown Arts Theatre under 'repertory' and noted a
1,000-person-capacity town hall.

The Stage guide specifies the existence of 413 designated working theatres, but comparing the two surveys it becomes immediately obvious
that there is ambiguity around the status of different types of venues.
Some Little Theatres, for example, come into the category of theatres,
others are entered as public halls. Of the other kinds of venue listed
in the *Theatre Ownership* report, town halls were not included unless
they regularly presented professional companies, and pier and prom-
enade pavilions were only counted if they were 'capable of mounting
productions more ambitious than the traditional concert party'.[67] A significant number of these, however, were listed as owned by the local
corporation. Indeed, the continuing construction of 'Pavilions', or similar
live entertainment venues in seaside resorts in the interwar period, was
a noticeable phenomenon indicative of the uneven distribution of economic distress. In English areas made affluent by the development of
new industries, in the Midlands or the South, regular holidays by the
sea became even more securely the norm for the more prosperous members of the working population. The compilers of the *Theatre Ownership*
report had to signal a conscious decision to exclude the small theatres
attached to holiday camps, by then a rapidly growing model of affordable
holiday provision.

The greatest area of ambiguity by far, however, is created by the numbers of cinemas which also functioned as theatres. Unlike *The Stage* guide, the *Theatre Ownership* Federation report is at pains to tackle problems of definition and admits from the outset that no complete list could meet with universal agreement. Even 'the hard core' [*sic*] in the commercial sector oscillated between film and live entertainment. The example of the Mansfield Palace is given: 'which is controlled by a cinema group, has been a cinema, a variety theatre and a repertory theatre, all within the last twelve months'.[68] There were literally hundreds of cinemas that had appeared on the landscape since the First World War. Out of the 574 localities surveyed in *The Stage* guide, only 4 can confidently be said to have had no cinemas within easy reach. Predictably big cities had many serving the whole urban area. Manchester with a population of 693,000 had 101 cinemas as against 5 (*Stage* guide) or 7 (*Theatre Ownership*) theatres. Birmingham had 80 cinemas trading alongside 7 (*Stage* guide) or 5 (*Theatre Ownership*) theatres. But small towns or villages could sustain at least one cinema, sometimes more. Upton-on-Severn in Worcestershire with a population of 2,000 had a cinema. Nairn in the Scottish Highlands with a population of 5,000 had two. Dundee, which still sustained its not-for-profit repertory theatre and the Palace Theatre, had 25 cinemas for a population of 175,583. By 1950 in Scotland as a whole numbers of cinemas had peaked at over 600.[69]

Although both the quality and original function of cinema premises varied, many did present a substantial amount of live entertainment and thus were 'equipped as theatres', i.e. had practicable stages, often dressing rooms and an orchestra pit. A surprising number had fly towers. Of course a substantial number dated back to the cine-variety theatres, which even Frank Matcham was building by 1912. Many theatre-boom buildings from the beginning of the century had been converted to cinema use by the Second World War. Somewhere in the region of 55 of the theatres listed in *Theatre Ownership* were owned by cinema chains, but this did not mean a block on live performance, rather increased product choice and more returns on the capital investment.

Theatre Ownership disregards Belfast and the *Stage* guide entry for the city is incomplete on numbers of theatres and halls – just the Grand Opera House and the Empire Theatre of Varieties are entered – and omits any reference to local societies. Thus there's no mention of the Ulster Group Theatre, or the importance of the Ulster Minor Hall as a performance venue. Nor is the Belfast Arts Theatre Studio, led by Hubert and Dorothy Wilmot then delivering an ambitious repertory programme in one of a series of temporary buildings in the city centre, included.[70] But the involvement of corporate cinema interests in larger-scale entertainment is instructive. George Young, the general manager of Imperial Cinema and Cinematograph Theatres, had a controlling interest in four Belfast theatres, the Imperial, the Royal, the Royal Hippodrome and, most importantly, the Grand Opera House. Despite the business priorities of cinema, live theatre especially at the Grand Opera House was sustained. Moreover, in association with CEMA Northern Ireland the Opera House was presenting, amongst the regular variety shows, high profile, toured-in drama, opera and ballet some of which was boosted by Tyrone Guthrie's active involvement. In 1950 negotiations were underway with Guthrie about the creation of an Ulster Drama Company to present three productions for the 1951 Festival.[71]

In the wider landscape what the 1950 *Theatre Ownership* report demonstrated quite clearly were the shifts in patterns of locational density, in England especially. It was most obvious in the North-East where the consequences of the depression had been so devastating. Howard & Wyndham still owned the Theatre Royal in Newcastle, but the Theatre Royal in Blyth, the Empire in Gateshead and the Empire in Chester-le-Street were owned by Sol Sheckman's expanding Essoldo cinema company. Sheckman, based in Newcastle, had developed his chain by buying up and converting music halls before the war. One of his more opulent variety-theatre ventures had been the Queen's Theatre in South Shields which was bombed in 1941.[72] But on the whole live performance was usually a substitute when the best films were unavailable. By 1950 all that was left in South Shields to warrant listing in the *Theatre Ownership* report was the Pier Pavilion. The Grand in Byker was also listed to a cinema company. Of only nine more theatres listed for the conurbation, two, the People's in Newcastle and the Little Theatre in Gateshead, were both run by limited liability companies set up by amateurs. Indeed *The Stage* guide entry for Gateshead places particular emphasis on the Little Theatre as a centre for church, school and other amateur dramatic societies. The entry for Jarrow refers to several amateur societies, but the Mechanics Institute – the only hall identified – had 'no equipment except a few loose seats'. The nearest theatre was in Newcastle; the nearest music hall was the Gateshead Empire.

OWNERSHIP AND CONTROL

In terms of the ownership of the bricks and mortar of commercially run theatres, boundaries between legitimate and illegitimate theatre were irrelevant. What was more important was the status of each venue and the extent to which audiences were admitted to the circulation of the best available metropolitan product. The pooling of theatrical business interests and acumen, which had begun in the 1920s, reached a decisive moment in 1942 when, on the death of Sir Oswald Stoll, the management shares of the Stoll Theatres Corporation were taken over by the newly registered Prince Littler Consolidated Trust Ltd., and thus accelerated the emergence of the most extraordinarily complex amalgamation of major corporate enterprises which was dubbed 'The Group'. A process that had begun as separate variety and legitimate theatre ventures with Oswald Stoll, Edward Moss and J. H. Howard and F. W. P. Wyndham in the 1890s had been extended by further property acquisition and multiple company directorships by Prince and Emile Littler, acting in alignment with A. S. Cruikshank and his son Stuart. The elder Cruikshank was dead by 1950, but the other three remained as the main drivers and beneficiaries of corporate theatre interests, which literally extended the length and breadth of 'mainland' Britain. The *Theatre Ownership* report named 76 functioning theatres in London, the English regions, Scotland and Wales that were all strategically linked together. Nine producing managements, including the Littler companies, Howard & Wyndham, Tom Arnold (a significant figure in music theatre and another major Group shareholder), C. B. Cochran and, most importantly, H. M. Tennent, were directly connected, along with 14 catering, publicity and brewery companies.[73]

The main point that the writer of the *Theatre Ownership* report wanted to hammer home was not so much the number of capital assets involved, but their acknowledged importance within the industrial economy. In London's West End the Group directly controlled 18 out of 42 functioning theatres, with interests in two others. Those theatres, however, held over 50 per cent of the available West End seats in such celebrated venues as Drury Lane, His Majesty's, the Coliseum, St James's, the Aldwych, the Apollo, the Prince of Wales, the Palladium, etc. The fact that control of buildings was coupled with creative production capacity through managements directed by the same individuals gave them enormous artistic as well as economic influence. Outside London, roughly 70 per cent of the No. 1 touring houses were associated either directly, or indirectly through satellite companies, with the Group.[74] This meant that these same productions would be presented in Group theatres, sometimes initially as pre-London tryouts in which case the original star actors might test their roles in front of regional audiences, or in post-London touring versions where audiences had to be content with a second-generation cast. Clearly the agglomeration principle, which had served metropolitan managements so well at the beginning of the century, had been exploited to the point where each regional outpost functioned as a major outlet supplying each element of the theatre-going experience through a carefully constructed mutual support system of supply and demand.

Within the overall topography, the Group sphere of influence formed the most prominent layer of the landscape focused almost exclusively on the No. 1 circuit. As *Theatre Ownership* points out there was ambiguity around the No. 1 classification, but broadly each of the major UK cities plus Dublin were industry-recognised 'No. 1 towns' with usually one main No. 1 presenting house.[75] Leading Group-owned variety theatres came into the same category. Thus in Liverpool, for example, both the Royal Court (Howard & Wyndham) and the Empire (Moss) were No. 1's. In Manchester Howard & Wyndham controlled the Opera House while Moss owned the Palace. In Cardiff the New Theatre lease was held by Stoll; the Prince of Wales was a Littler property. As *Theatre Ownership* is careful to admit, this virtual monopoly did not theoretically prevent the access of other managements to Group theatres, nor did it have the effect of pushing up rents – the symbiotic relationship between owners, lessees and producing managers provided safeguards against that.[76]

But the concentration of producing interests in variety, pantomime, musical theatre and straight drama enabled a very small number of Group directors to exert a disproportionate control over a wide range of theatre product and the theatre artists who were materially dependent on their patronage. In legitimate theatre in particular, where Binkie Beaumont as managing director of Tennent's ran the most powerful producing management, the metropolitan aesthetic was as dominant as it had been in 1900. Unlike fifty years earlier, however, when that aesthetic was toured-out by artists who directly communicated with their regional audiences, the fact that the *producer* was rarely now simultaneously the actor took some of the economic pressure off actors, and significantly reduced the need for a successful play launched with leading actors to reach the provinces with those same actors.

During the war years, more metropolitan actors had a visible regional presence. London during the Blitz was dangerous – the Old Vic Company relocated to Burnley until 1942, and maintained a resident company at the Liverpool Playhouse until 1946.[77] Encouraged by CEMA, touring in general was seen as part of the war effort, especially to the hostels attached to armaments factories moved away from vulnerable cities. By 1950, safely back in London, actors could play for comfortably lengthy, but not intolerable runs in Group-controlled West End theatres, and if the production was successful anticipate a transfer to Broadway as well. Regional No. 1 audiences could see the most potentially profitable of the plays, if not the original actors, following a calculated time-lapse from the point of origin. During that time more affluent and/or mobile playgoers may have seen the show in London anyway. The power of the Group was a matter of growing concern for industry professionals and subsequently for critical commentators and historians focused primarily on metropolitan theatre. But the regional experience was increasingly diffuse and fragmented. In general, touring patterns could no longer be seen as the primary index of what constituted popular theatre success, but represented different strands of industrial and artistic provenance and priority.

PATTERNS OF TOURING

In the wider physical landscape, basic communication networks, especially the rail network, had scarcely altered since the beginning of the century, and transport by train was still an important means of travel for the majority of the population for whom car ownership was not an option. Individual actors could still travel by train for 'special' weeks of employment in regional theatres, but the days of the stately progresses of entire actor-manager companies by train were over. Large-scale commercial shows would be moved by road. Small travelling companies were also more likely to use road transport in cars, vans and lorries and even buses unless the distances were exceptionally great. Old-style commercial fit-up companies such as Tod Slaughter's melodrama company and the Kinloch Players, who toured a stock of plays including *Rose O' Tralee* and *Auld Robin Gray* and summer pantomimes around village halls in Scotland,[78] were co-existing in the same precarious way as companies launched during the war, including the Adelphi and Compass Players, with specifically social or religious aims.[79] Theatre Workshop, as the reformed Joan Littlewood/Ewan MacColl collective was now known, spent much of 1950 touring and by the autumn had embarked on a gruelling two-year period of one-night stands, often following the theatreless trails in South Wales and the North-East of England. But with no official subsidy they were effectively an alternative commercial fit-up surviving on ticket sales for plays such as MacColl's anti-nuclear war *Uranium 235* and working-class homage *Landscape with Chimneys*. By early 1951 they were travelling in a 1938 Post Office lorry to which the top of an old furniture van had been fixed.[80]

Arts Council intervention was no guarantee of economic viability. By 1950 specifically commissioned Arts Council tours, now mostly confined to areas deemed in particular need of access to professional provision in Wales and the North-East, usually lost money – small non-theatre venues rarely had the audience capacity necessary to recoup costs.[81] Writing in 1956 about the Perth Theatre Company's record of Arts Council-encouraged tours dating back fifteen years, David Steuart produced a map of over 130 visited towns and villages all over Scotland, including Orkney and Shetland, and Northern Ireland. The cost of freightage and company travel by trains and boats over great distances far outweighed ticket revenue, although the reception appears to have been welcoming for what was very much the Anglo-centric repertoire of an ambitious British repertory company. The nearest the audiences in Orkney and Shetland and the Highlands got in 1950 to a play by a Scottish dramatist was *The Chiltern Hundreds* by the Edinburgh-born aristocrat William Douglas Home.[82]

New models of portable theatres were given Arts Council blessing. By 1950 the Caryl Jenner Mobile Theatre was in its third year of touring with the primary objective of reaching children's audiences but also playing for adults. Set up at the end of 1947 with a three-ton second-hand civil defence van travelling around isolated communities in Buckinghamshire and Hertfordshire, in 1950 there were two companies with two vans touring the UK with a self-contained compact performance unit.[83] The Arena Theatre, which grew out of the amateur Highbury Little Theatre Centre in Sutton Coldfield, in Birmingham also in 1947, was more authentically portable, carrying a steel-framed tent-like structure with its own seats. Creating spatially what resembled a classical Greek amphitheatre with the audience seated in tiered rows on three sides, it was a conscious attempt to achieve greater engagement between audience and actors. George Devine wrote of the excitement of 'being *possessive* towards the characters of the drama'.[84] What became a summer feature in Birmingham parks, could be set up in town halls and was touring more widely in 1950, it did not achieve the profile of Tyrone Guthrie's celebrated Glasgow Citizens' production of *Ane Satyre of the Thrie Estaitis*, staged with a similar spatial impact in the Church of Scotland's Assembly Hall for the Edinburgh Festivals of 1948 and 1949.[85] But in the damaged, make-do-and-mend landscape of 1950 it was a signal of new perspectives for the future.

The fact that the touring lists published in *The Stage* for October 1950 occupy fewer column inches than the comparable pages at the beginning of the century might suggest that the list was no longer an automatic choice for publicity purposes, possibly because of cost.[86] There does seem to be evidence of a significant decline. Compared with the 281 companies advertised in the same month in 1900, there were a total of 118 advertised fifty years later. Of those, 72 were in a separate category of travelling revue companies, a not insignificant proportion of which rejoiced in such show titles as *Fanny Get Your Fun*, *Fig Leaves and Apple Sauce*, *Red Hot and Saucy* and *Nude, Neat and Naughty*. At a time when the Lord Chamberlain still rigidly controlled the capacity of legitimate theatre to explore contemporary sexual mores, the variety stage at arguably the most economically desperate end of the market, calculated its survival on the extent of female flesh exposed to its audiences. Revue had been a popular theatre staple since the First World War, and fashionable West End revues provided elegant showcases for star musical and comic entertainers. In the 1950 sample week some like *Stand Easy*, *Prairie Roundup* and *Let the People Sing* were destined for genial nights out in No. 1 theatres. *Black and White* and *Harlem Comes to Town* may or may not have featured 'real' black performers. The majority of the revues went to No. 2 venues and of course the comparatively limited production requirements would have suited the more constrained resources of theatres that also functioned as cinemas.

The other 46 companies listed together were not in a separate 'legitimate' category – there were at least nine tours of well-known musicals as well as ballet and some opera, and nearly all went to No. 1 Group associated theatres. The Donald Wolfit Company, playing weeks at the Group-incorporated Sheffield Lyceum and the Leeds Grand, was the only advertised example of an independent actor-manager-led, classical play-producing company which would have been recognisable to the self-reliant doyens of the past such as Frank Benson. The Old Vic Company playing at the New Theatre in Oxford and George Devine's Young Vic children's theatre company scheduled to play at the No. 1 Dolphin Theatre in Brighton followed by the Social Centre in Slough represented the state-subsidised model of the future. At the time, however, very few would have confidently predicted that possibility.

Commercially, the most dominant presence was Irving Berlin's musical *Annie Get Your Gun*, first seen by British audiences in a production by Emile Littler at the London Coliseum in 1947, and by 1950 packaged for nations-wide distribution in three separate tours. New dynamic American musicals had taken London by storm. Rodgers and Hammerstein's *Carousel* had opened at the Theatre Royal, Drury Lane, in June replacing *Oklahoma!*, which had run for over 1,500 performances. Touring revivals of pre-war American musicals, Sigmund Romberg's *The Desert Song*,

Lilac Time and *The Student Prince*, were all on the road simultaneously. In October 1950 only the Bristol Hippodrome had the relatively new British musical *Bless the Bride* by Vivian Ellis and A. P. Herbert, originally produced by C. B. Cochran at the Adelphi Theatre in 1947.

DISTAFF PLAYS

That there had been a significant number of women playwrights whose work had been premiered on the London stage in 1948 and 1949 had provoked some commentary in *The Stage* in January 1950. As the article 'Distaff' in *The Stage* put it, singling out the work of Leslie Storm, Margery Sharp, Sylvia Regan, Charlotte Hastings and Eleanor Farjeon, 'each play is openly a woman's study of a woman's life'.[87] There had been substantial roles of some psychological complexity provided for distinguished older actresses such as Flora Robson and Sybil Thorndike. Daphne du Maurier's *September Tide*, which had been premiered in 1948 as a vehicle for Gertrude Lawrence, was one of at least three women's plays on tour in October 1950. Leslie Storm's *Black Chiffon*, touring to Torquay and Harrow, was simultaneously playing on Broadway with Robson in the central role of Alicia Christie, whose unprecedented crime of shoplifting is a symptom of family-induced distress. *Lace on Her Petticoat*, a tale of female friendship and social difference on the west coast of late-nineteenth-century Scotland by the Scottish playwright Aimée Stuart, was also destined for Broadway in 1951, but in the autumn of 1950 was on a pre-London tour to the Howard & Wyndham theatres in Glasgow and Aberdeen.

These plays, focusing largely on women's personal preoccupations and crises observed from a relatively affluent middle-class perspective, came from the generation of women playwrights who, Maggie B. Gale has argued, have 'been manoeuvred out of history' even though they achieved noteworthy commercial success.[88] Post-war audiences, especially women now compelled back into the confines of family and domesticity after their intense involvement in the war effort, could derive emotional satisfaction from a form of social realism based on recognisable human scenarios, even if played out in representations of a social milieu outside their daily existence. Plays grounded in the 'adult emotions', however restrained, described by Terence Rattigan in his analysis of audience response which included his famous creation of 'Aunt Edna', could be safely enjoyed within the neo-romantic ethos along with the night-out chocolates. As Rebellato points out, however, Rattigan understood that this audience of which Aunt Edna was but one constituent could not be underestimated; the playwright 'must maintain a certain distance, working with and pushing against the limits of her tolerance and understanding'.[89]

The play that stands out from the touring list, Tennessee Williams's *A Streetcar Named Desire*, which travelled from the Royal Court in Liverpool to the Theatre Royal in Birmingham in October 1950, had tested the limits of tolerance in more ways than one. The production was further proof of an American theatre influence which extended beyond dynamic musicals. The London premiere of Arthur Miller's *All My Sons* had been staged in 1948, to be followed a year later by *Death of a Salesman*. *Streetcar*, however, which Laurence Olivier directed at the Aldwych Theatre in 1949 with his then wife Vivien Leigh as Blanche du Bois, had a strong central woman's role, but the far less restrained preoccupation with sexuality and psychological disturbance proved not just controversial because of content, but also because of its production provenance.[90]

All the American plays and, indeed, the Gertrude Lawrence vehicle *September Tide* had been produced under the auspices of Tennent's subsidiary non-profit distributing company Tennent Productions Ltd., which under the earlier name of Tennent Plays Ltd. had been registered in 1942. Within the Keynesian ethos of deploying commercial expertise to nurture the new era of state-supported arts, Binkie Beaumont had taken advantage of the clause in the Finance Act of 1916 (confirmed in the 1946 Act) that granted exemption from Entertainments Tax to theatre companies whose productions could be described as 'partly educational'. This was a concession that had assisted the pre-war survival of not-for-profit companies such as the Old Vic, Birmingham Rep, the Shakespeare Memorial Theatre and the York Citizens' Theatre. Artistically, the Tennent subsidiary permitted the creative risk of classical and new play West End production by actor-managers such as Gielgud and Olivier. It set the precedent for a non-profit distributing company linked to a commercial concern, which was then followed by other metropolitan ventures once the war ended.

Financially the benefits were considerable as while the subsidiary company was obliged to plough back any profits into the not-for-profit company, that obligation was also used to justify the payment of a substantial management fee for services provided by the profit-making company. At the same time even though these companies claimed no direct state aid, the right to publicise their work as 'in association with the Arts

Council' appeared to legitimise the strategy. The ideological and ethical tensions that this provoked in the Arts Council plagued a succession of Drama Directors and polarised opinion within the organisation. By 1949 by which point Tennent had survived both legal and, indeed, parliamentary committee challenges, the combination of Group-owned theatres, the ability to outbid other attempts to produce important new plays and crucially the ability to withstand a degree of business failure had created a virtual monopoly in West End theatre, which was then capable of extension throughout the whole Group network. Furthermore, the Beaumont aesthetic, which ensured immaculate production values, fitted beautifully with a neo-romantic ethos and the controlled display of high emotion, which characterised the dominant acting style of the period. Beaumont protected the interests of actors and they rewarded him with their confidence. Both Gielgud and Ralph Richardson as Board members defended the legitimate principles of Tennent Productions Ltd.

With *A Streetcar Named Desire* tensions reached breaking point. Although Williams's play eventually came to be celebrated as a classic of American theatre, in 1949 arguments raged around the much disputed educational attributes of a drama of which at its most extreme alleged that 'audiences were chiefly composed of men who more usually went to the Windmill [for the nude shows] and who sat squirming and giggling waiting for the worst to happen'.[91] By the end of 1950 while *Streetcar* was gathering more profits playing to audiences in the major regional cities, it was agreed in the Arts Council that the right of Tennent Productions Ltd. – and, indeed, any other similarly constituted companies – to promote themselves as being 'in association' with the funding body was to be withdrawn. As a symbolic act, it looked as though the opposition of not-for-profit and commerce at the level of state-sponsored enablement of high culture might become a fixed principle.

Outside the environs of St James's Square,[92] theatre as a commodity was a matter of realpolitik. Tennent's continued to ride high, with Beaumont's influence as an invited member of the Shakespeare Memorial Theatre board of governors a major contributory factor to the SMT's rising profile and capacity to attract star actors.[93] Stratford-upon-Avon, hitherto regarded as a provincial backwater, became for the duration of the festival season an outpost of the metropolis – with the bureaucratic implications of Arts Council assistance politely rejected, the company, led by Anthony Quayle, balanced high-quality productions with modest surpluses on box-office receipts.[94] Furthermore, after three decades of an uneasy relationship with the National Theatre campaign, it had been more seriously mooted that the national flagship might be more appropriately located in Shakespeare's birthplace rather than London. Four weeks of rehearsal with some top-class actors for each production and a tour of Australia in the winter of 1949–50 were starting to shift the balance of national power.[95] At the same time, for all the surface gloss, the SMT was basically a seasonal, commercial repertory theatre albeit located in an internationally known town in the English regions.

REPERTORY

'Repertory', in models that ranged from industrially duplicated, twice-nightly commercial and often seasonal weekly rep to not-for-profit, also conducted on a twice-nightly or weekly basis or, as in a few elite, better-resourced cases such as Liverpool and Birmingham two- or three-weekly, was now everywhere. While companies could not compete with the metropolitan providers of the newest dramatic writing – there was an article in *The Stage Year Book* discussing the obstacles to the speedy release of performance rights to new plays and the issue of affordable royalty charges – repertory companies matching appropriate product to identifiable audience tastes could find a market.[96]

Of course there could be no comparison with cinema when 25 venues, as in Dundee for example, could between them offer somewhere in the region of 100 films a week. Live theatre presented by small companies of resident repertory actors could even at its most hectic offer only about 45 plays a year. Arts Council officers loathed weekly rep with its 'low standards', and what limited inducements they had at their disposal were designed to give companies opportunities to rehearse for longer, reduce the number of plays and achieve higher artistic quality. But a good night out watching a play on a weekly basis was still obviously valued as a category of popular theatre.

The social dimension incorporated both audience and actors who could build up a substantial fan base. Where companies were resident in traditional theatre settings, regular ticket holders for the same seats on the same nights each week could represent a broad social mix. There is anecdotal evidence of individuals objecting to fortnightly runs which kept them waiting for the next new production.[97] What 'standards' were represented differed according to different subcultural group criteria. The 'dissident' element, which Alan Sinfield in his analysis of post-war, welfare-capitalism-shaped cultural initiatives identifies within the educated middle-class,[98] can be said to characterise the Arts Council officers focused on developing a 'pattern' of regional theatre. Without exception highly experienced professionally and on the whole products of the exemplary theatre movement,[99] their objectives derived from a commitment to disseminating access to the combination of classical texts and intellectually authorised new drama which made up a high-theatre culture. While the imprimatur of the state-funding body brought status within this specific milieu, in the wider landscape these dissident patterns were still only faintly discernible.

The Stage Year Book lists without any hierarchical differentiation 124 theatres with resident/permanent repertory companies and 43 travelling or seasonal companies.[100] After comparison with the data in the provincial guide where there are some discrepancies, there were probably some 130 resident companies across the whole of the UK and Ireland. Many were single companies led by an actor-manager. There were a significant number of companies led by women – names which have faded from the historical record: Marie Dale and the Tudor Players, the Avon Players led by Joan Wray, the Pivot Players led by Clare Foden. Anne Sheppard ran a company at the John Gay in Barnstaple, Marie Hopps ran the Grand Theatre in Llandudno, while Joan E. Cowlishaw managed the company at the Garrick Theatre in Lichfield. Only, perhaps, Marjorie Dence, by 1950 firmly ensconced at Perth Theatre, achieved a lasting reputation.

In 1950 the two best-known No. 2 corporate managers, Harry Hanson, whose main office was located in London, and Frank Fortesque, who was based in Manchester, were operating some 20 companies distributed as far apart as Dunfermline Opera House (Fortescue) and the Palace Theatre in Westcliff (Hanson). Hanson's Court Players could be seen in Stockton-on-Tees at the Hippodrome, and the Loughborough Theatre Royal. Frank Fortescue's Players appeared at the Theatre Royal in Hyde and the Grand in Blackburn. Some were seasonal, others were permanent and survived for a long time. Harry Hanson's companies at the Pier Pavilion in Hastings and the Empire in Peterborough continued to trade on box-office takings only for thirty and twenty years respectively, each accumulating large stocks of scenery, props and furniture. Hanson, not unhappy to be dubbed 'the Woolworth of the Profession', consciously sold plays.[101]

There were other examples of multiple company management albeit on a smaller scale. Richard Stephenson ran his Saxon Players in New Brighton at the Tivoli Theatre, at the Theatre Royal in Leicester, His Majesty's in Barrow-in-Furness and the Empire in Dewsbury. The actress Billie Whitelaw who had a 'special week' of employment with Stephenson in Dewsbury and then her first 'proper job in rep' in New Brighton, later claimed that Stephenson also ran a laundry business which may well have serviced costume cleaning needs as well as earning extra revenue.[102] Rapid turnover of product, a familiar and trusted provider, an equally familiar consumer environment were key factors in the success of the industrial model. Famously John Osborne described Hanson's companies as 'the last funk-hole for any actor'.[103] But as numerous other actor memoirs demonstrate, a skills-based training combined with a professional code of practice with its own disciplinary rules supplied another set of standards.

Robert Stephens's early career trajectory took him from touring children's plays with Caryl Jenner to weekly rep at the Royalty Theatre in Morecambe, where 'crowd pleasers' were mixed with more ambitious fare including Sartre's *Crime Passionel* and Shakespeare's *Julius Caesar*. For Stephens the main benefit was 'the discipline of going on however miscast or unhappy you were. You learned a sense of responsibility.'[104] Aged 16, Whitelaw was employed to act with Hanson's Court Players at the Theatre Royal in Leeds and was castigated for the crime of missed entrances. Her work in New Brighton 'gave me a total understanding of the nuts and bolts of theatre. I learned to take the curtain up and down, cut up jellies for the electrics … cue the lights, find the props, sew costumes, make cushions, so anything that needed to be done to get the show on its feet.'[105]

The Arts Council pattern-makers, faced with hard economic choices, were increasingly oriented towards measured support and influence rather than direct intervention. Along with the tours, direct management of buildings had been cut back. Bristol Old Vic had become a more formally co-operative venture with (crucially) local authority goodwill. The Swansea Grand experiment was considered a failure, while during the 1950–1 financial year a decision was also made to cease direct management of the Salisbury Arts Theatre. Artistically Salisbury had been a success, but the company, housed in a building variously a chapel, a cinema and a wartime garrison theatre, had never made itself independent of Arts Council subsidy.[106]

Salisbury, the project in Swansea and the Midland Theatre Company, which all appear in the ACGB annual report for 1950–1, were the outcome of the strategic mapping undertaken at the end of the war. One experiment, the West Riding Theatre, set up in 1946 to plant three repertory companies exchanging productions between leased theatres in Huddersfield, Halifax and Wakefield, had been an expensive, embarrassing disaster largely because little research had been made to seek local advice and research potential audience response. Salisbury and the Midland Theatre Company had both created a local touring circuit, which gave productions a longer performance life and widened the sphere of influence. The Midland Company, by 1950 with a permanent base in the Technical College Theatre in Coventry, did not have to bear the running costs of the building and travelled out to audiences in a more densely populated industrial area. The agricultural communities surrounding Salisbury were inevitably more sparse, and the well-equipped, but small theatre a constant drain on resources.[107]

But efforts continued to sustain a policy of artistic colonisation duplicating product on the same lines as the commercial companies in order to increase rehearsal and performance time. The York Citizens' Theatre leased out the Opera House in Scarborough and ran two interchangeable companies. At the Perth Theatre a similar strategy was deployed with a company playing in the Adam Smith Hall in Kirkcaldy. The Savoy Theatre in Kettering had entered the frame as an outpost of the Northampton Repertory Theatre.[108] In the West of England, the Arts Council had redirected the interests and small capital of an ex-service actor John Worsley and his wife away from a proposed venture in Sussex towards setting up a touring theatre provision from a house on the seafront in Exmouth. With a series of dilapidated vehicles, the company mounted three-weekly tours round halls in Devon and Cornwall.[109]

Debates continued within ACGB about the importance of comfortable venues, with Charles Landstone maintaining that audience interest and attractive plays outweighed the disadvantage of scruffy halls and purgatorial seating. But the truth was that the established commercial theatre circuits whether independently or corporately owned were not on the whole accessible to the funding body. Short-term leasing brought additional costs and usually the loss of vital bar profits, which was a factor in the West Riding failure.[110] Those initiatives that developed out of local interest groups and received, at least, encouragement from the Arts Council were located in 'found' spaces. The Guildford Theatre was established in the Borough Hall, then used as a food store; Ipswich had been converted from club premises. In Kidderminster the amateur company, the Nonentities, purchased what had once been a theatre but by the end of the war was a Ministry of Food store.[111] In St Andrews, at the Byre Theatre, the partnership between the originating amateur society and an annual professional company produced plays in what in 1933 had originally functioned as a byre – a cow shed.[112]

Increasingly the Arts Council offered funding for building-based theatres only when matched from other sources. The ideal was local authority support but that tended to be tangential. While the days of a local elite coming together to build and invest in a major architectural statement of civic pride belonged to another century, fund-raising from affluent donors was still the main option. There is no doubt that a place in the circle of Arts Council influence was essential. Nottingham, where the Arts Council East Midlands Regional office was based with a future Drama Director N. V. Linklater as one of the officers, provided a test case. Because the Theatre Royal had revitalised as a No. 1 touring theatre, there was predictable resistance from the city council to first attempts to set up a not-for-profit company in what had once been one of the city's first cinemas. But there were still individuals who were nostalgic for Virginia Compton's repertory efforts in the 1920s and the cinema had recently functioned as a successful Little Theatre. When the Nottingham Playhouse did open in late 1948, the board of directors of the Nottingham Theatre Trust Ltd. was chaired by a local councillor who as Lord Mayor had led the fundraising campaign. The Arts Council contribution of £1,000 was made when the requisite target had been reached. The first Artistic Director, actor, director and expert on Russian theatre, André Van Gysegham, was an Arts Council nominee. The city council agreed to regular funding in the 1950–1 financial year, and in recognition of the company's second birthday in November 1950, the ACGB hailed the Playhouse as 'a model repertory theatre'.[113]

How the far the population of Nottingham was aware of its state- and civic-supported theatre was another matter. In the summer of 1950 at the end of a second season, which had seen erratic audiences for a programme which had included *Hedda Gabler*, *The Glass Menagerie*, *The Lady's Not for Burning* and a production of *Deep Are the Roots*, Van Gysegham used a topographical image to describe the conflict of artistic and business interests: 'Yet I believe that if we take the Box Office receipts as our sole guide … we should not be sailing a true course. We should be forsaking an ideal for immediate gain – hugging the coast instead of venturing out across the ocean, braving unknown dangers in a voyage of discovery.'[114]

In the context of a rising tide of political discontent, which would see the electorate respond to the greater individual freedom promised by the Conservative Party, the relationship of art and economics was as ambiguous as ever. In concluding the analysis of the Group's territorial expansion, the writer of *Theatre Ownership* commented that 'They are far better equipped to weather a period of theatrical slump than their less well integrated competitors. It is the latter who tend to own the marginal houses which in bad times furnish the greater proportion of dark theatres. It is these too which are most valuable to the advancements of the cinema industry and the BBC.'[115] The Report does not mention another built structure which had just appeared on the landscape. A new transmitter opened in Sutton Coldfield outside Birmingham in December 1949 enabled television to be received in the Midlands for the first time. Ownership of combined television and radio licenses had more than doubled from 126,567 in March 1949 to 343,882 a year later.[116] Clearly this related to a tiny proportion of a UK population of roughly 50 million. But the space of power represented by a small piece of electronic equipment in the corner of British living rooms was capable of an unimaginable advance, challenging a complete spectrum of live arts and entertainment interests.

CHAPTER 6

The business of theatre

In his introduction to the not-for-profit sector published in 2005, Helmut K. Anheier describes it as 'a set of organizations and activities *next* [my emphasis] to the institutional complexes of government, state, or public sector on the one hand, and the forprofit or business sector on the other'. The not-for-profit 'third sector' is effectively positioned in the middle and in its mode of operation encounters the reality that there are no clearly defined sectorial boundaries and that distinctions are quite blurred. 'Organisations', Anheier suggests, '"migrate" from one sector to another.'[1] In the era of public subsidy most theatre practitioners would recognise the necessity for day-to-day 'migration' as they attempt to balance state and civic funding with income derived from other business strategies. Whatever the proponents of theatre as a weapon of social betterment might have argued, the arts never found a secure niche within the public sector. In any case, after 1979, when the Conservative Party led by Margaret Thatcher embarked on eighteen years of government, the public sector itself had to adjust to the growing insistence on the role of the market even in the basic provision of health care and education.

While it is broadly accepted, however, as the economist Michael J. Oliver has confirmed, that the way the political landscape changed during this period had 'profound long-term effects on the economy and society of the UK',[2] the immediate tangible results in terms of public-sector funding were far less obviously ideologically determined than popular historical accounts of the period have claimed. As Oliver has pointed out, even within the Conservative Party, there were groups who remained 'implacably opposed' to the more extreme features of the dominant market-driven microeconomic policy.[3] Countervailing principles remained in place to disrupt and subvert at every level. Individual political affiliation within a quango,[4] such as the Arts Council of Great Britain, was not necessarily an automatic signifier of pragmatic decision-making. This in turn impacted on the extent to which state intervention and assistance could be reined back. As I have argued throughout this book, theatre as industrial practice is positioned within a very complex economic nexus. Even at its most idealised it cannot remain isolated from the way economic factors inhibit, for example, the circulation and costs of raw materials, and, indeed, other commodities *including people*. Legislative change, especially in fiscal policies and industrial relations, introduces structural change into the workplace – and in building-based theatre that can mean several different categories of professional and craft skill – and inevitably influences both directly and indirectly patterns of audience composition.

Ideological contestation from both sides of the political spectrum about the role of the state in the cultural life of the nation effectively began as soon the whole principle of state and civic funding was formally established. That the arguments became fiercer in the last two decades of the century derived from the macroeconomic context and the extremes of political polarisation which arose from the global economic turbulence of the 1970s, the collapse of the Keynesian social democratic consensus and the challenge to the principles of welfare capitalism which dominated the 1980s.[5] Also, in 1997 as Oliver again points out, when the Labour Party regained power under the leadership of Tony Blair, it 'later came to address a lot of the ethos, if not the rhetoric of Margaret Thatcher'.[6] Indeed, the new government committed itself to continuing the 1996 Conservative Party spending plans.

Historiographically, in relation to the theatre industry, care needs to be taken to ensure continuities of managerial practice, which spanned, albeit modified, successive governmental phases after 1945, are not occluded in the interests of ideologically oriented polemic. So little detailed work has been done on the economics of subsidised theatres and the particularities of local context, that more nuanced commentary on how inter-sectorial relationships were navigated has tended to be swept aside in favour of a more broad brush discourse about the commodification of art and the evils of 'Thatcherism'. Without doubt not-for-profit theatre makers in the 1980s and 90s were obliged more *overtly* and *systematically* to comply with models of third-sector engagement that placed heavy constraints on creative capacity. My emphasis is deliberate. These strategies and the concomitant pressures were an accepted aspect of day-to-day management from the earliest days of subsidy. The more significant change came with the trend to more specialist professional expertise in theatre business management. Also public funding bodies were increasingly driven by a new public service *managerialism* which emerged in the 1990s to draw upon private sector technologies to deliver public service outcomes with a greater emphasis on explicit measures of performance or targets.[7]

The business construct of the not-for-profit company provides a regulated framework within which public money can circulate and be dispersed in a way that is publically accountable. Practitioners are employed by a non-profit-distributing company, usually also a charity, limited by guarantees made by its directors who are not remunerated for their work and who have no personal financial stake in the form of shares. Profits which generate a surplus are ploughed back into the company which is an autonomous legal entity and separate from the individual interests of the personnel involved. This model of creative business practice, which was retained into the twenty-first century, applied to all theatre companies from the smallest radical ensemble to the largest building-based organisation which chose to be incorporated and thus became eligible for regular funding from the public purse.

By the early 1960s, however, the concept of the company as an ensemble of actors dedicated to long-term sustained commitment to intense creative experimentation had acquired an additional aura as an idealised construct quite detached from its primary economic base. Also, the shift in the nomenclature for the artistic leader of the theatre project – in whatever form it took – to 'director' from the earlier 'producer' blurred the public understanding of what were two distinct functions: responsibility for the overall economic and legal governance of the company, and for the shaping of its artistic vision. In the small companies which began to emerge in the late 1960s where 'directors' in the legal sense were also artistic directors and their collaborators, the two functions could in theory be combined. In larger organisations, especially those that were building-based with wider obligations, they were more often separate especially as the board of directors employed the artistic director.

As is well known, the semantic shift in nomenclature from 'producer' to 'director' also reflected a more decisive shift in artistic power from the actor as director to the non-acting director, especially those whose formative influences and training were academic rather than craft-skills-based. Companies as not-for-profit artistic entities, both in dedicated theatre buildings and the peripatetic alternative sector, were more and more led by university graduates. Oxford and Cambridge, in particular, became dominant in this respect with extra-curricular opportunities firmly established,

which bred in equal measure the radical progeny of Terence Gray, George
Devine and Tyrone Guthrie.

The far-reaching effect of this change in the artistic dynamic may be
seen most clearly in the series of manoeuvres that led by 1963 to the establishment of not one, but two state-funded, national, not-for-profit companies. While as a matter of historiographic principle I have tried in this
book to avoid focus on 'turning points' in the historical narrative, I would
argue that the creation of the Royal Shakespeare Company in 1961 by
Peter Hall, Cambridge-educated, and as Colin Chambers has recently
described him 'a curious mix of the public servant and the pirate',[8] represented a major watershed. The story of the contest between Hall and
Laurence Olivier, the director designate of the National Theatre Company
and their respective chairmen, Fordham Flower and Lord Chandos
(Oliver Lyttelton), has been told in detail by Chambers himself, John
Elsom and Nicholas Tomalin,[9] and Sally Beauman. Both companies had
their origins in the dreams of the great acting ensemble first promoted in
the nineteenth century. Hall's more immediate influences were the state-
funded Théâtre National Populaire and the Barrault/Renaud Company
in France and Brecht's Berliner Ensemble which visited London in 1956.[10]
What is relevant to the discussion here, however, is that Hall's project was
from the beginning predicated on the need for public funding at a time
when dependence on subsidy was by no means automatically accepted
by existing not-for-profit theatre boards who preferred to remain financially independent. First Fordham Flower and then the highly resistant
Shakespeare Memorial Theatre governors were persuaded to use up the
reserves in order to qualify for funding. As Chambers succinctly puts it,
'Stratford would have to become bankrupt in order to receive state aid,
but it would go bankrupt by supporting the vastly expanded work of the
new company.'[11]

The 'vast' expansion was physical in terms of buildings, and geographical in that what was technically a regional theatre company was to have
a metropolitan base for an artistic policy that would mount new drama
as well as reconceptualised productions of Shakespeare. By 1962 the RSC
held the lease (from Prince Littler) of the Aldwych Theatre and, less
securely, the Arts Theatre in the West End, as well as a training Studio in
Stratford directed by Michel Saint-Denis.[12] Described as 'the biggest single theatre venture in the world', the company employed nearly 500 actors
and support staff and presented 24 productions to some 700,000 people.
With Saint-Denis and Peter Brook as co-artistic directors, Hall gave himself the job title of managing director in control of a large-scale company,

which was both an entrepreneurial business and a highly ambitious artistic enterprise.[13] The battle subsequently fought to legitimise state funding for a second major company was both 'intricate and protracted', but as Chambers points out, 'the outcome not only determined the kind of future the RSC could enjoy but also moulded the pattern of the nation's major performing arts funding for the next four decades'.[14]

From the beginning there was both direct commercial engagement and the hunt for other forms of patronage. In 1960 Prince Littler's demand for 25 per cent of box-office income at the Aldwych as well as rent, was paid for by a deal struck with Keith Prowse Ltd., the biggest ticketing agency in the country. Hall's bold plan for three-year actor contracts was backed by a £5,000 a year grant from the Calouste Gulbenkian Foundation. In 1966 attempts to take accessible theatre to unconventional playing spaces in a mobile unit dubbed Theatregoround was enabled by an anonymous donation. The cultivation of a recognizable RSC brand included a new logo and the introduction of large-format programmes containing extensive historical and critical commentary and production photographs. The RSC Club launched in 1964 offered a range of privileges to consolidate the loyalty of a membership which numbered over 12,000.[15]

Hall dealt with the elder statesmen of the commercial theatre, Beaumont and the Littlers, but their influence was waning. Beaumont immediately recognised what the impact of this not-for-profit state-funded parvenu would have on the balance of metropolitan control.[16] While West End theatre remained financially dominant, the artistic opportunities represented by Tennent's had begun to lose their allure for leading actors. The decision by stars such as Peggy Ashcroft and Laurence Olivier to align themselves with the creative satisfaction and innovation represented by the English Stage Company and, in the case of Ashcroft, the RSC from its inception, shifted the focus of attention to a new high-profile, metropolitan-subsidised sector.[17]

Unofficially director of the long-awaited National Theatre Company from about 1960, Olivier's appointment became publically known in 1962, the year he assembled a proto-NT company, including Michael Redgrave, Sybil Thorndike, Lewis Casson and Joan Plowright, to present a season of plays at the newly built Chichester Festival Theatre.[18] Olivier, the old-style actor-manager, and Hall as the new model of director may have been individually in competition on behalf of their respective organizations; together, however, they represented a structural sea change in the organisation of British theatre as a whole. It was still perfectly possible to see a glamorous West End show, good well-made plays and, especially, musicals including *Guys and Dolls* (1953), *The Pajama Game* (1955) and *My Fair Lady* (1958), which were all produced by the Littlers, but the older generation of impresarios and proprietors were either fading from the scene altogether – Beaumont and Prince Littler both died in 1973 – or were forced to adjust to the different audience expectations nurtured in the not-for-profit sector.

That did not mean that commercial interests and, above all, metropolitan approval were not important as a way of enabling not-for-profit producing theatres to capitalise on artistic success and thus sustain and even enhance operational viability. The introduction of subsidy enabled regional repertory theatres to escape the treadmill of weekly changes of play,[19] but the opposite extreme of the long run, which was the basis of metropolitan theatre economics, was not tenable within the not-for-profit ethos. In the late 1960s and early 70s theatres such as Nottingham Playhouse, Birmingham Rep and the Sheffield Crucible did successfully maintain 'true' repertory, which meant productions could grow artistically and continue to attract audiences.[20] But that was based on adequate set-storage space, actor contracts of reasonable duration and ample technical and stage management capacity, all of which became increasingly difficult to sustain.

Commercial exploitation usually meant a transfer to a West End venue, which brought prestige to a regional production deemed worthy of metropolitan exposure, and once profits had been divided with the producing partner and, often at one remove, the London theatre proprietor, there could be a satisfying income stream to benefit the management of origin. A famous example from the early 1950s was the transfer to the Vaudeville Theatre of the Bristol Old Vic's 1954 production of the musical *Salad Days*, which in a run which lasted for five and half years went on to break the then record for the longest-running musical. The profits from that helped pay for the purchase of new premises for the Bristol Old Vic Drama School.[21]

While West End managers fought over *Salad Days* there was little commercial interest in Bristol's British premiere of Arthur Miller's *The Crucible* in 1956. In negotiation with Miller's agent, Oscar Lewenstein acquired the rights to a London production for 'a few hundred pounds ... as an advance on royalties', roughly the same amount his production company paid for the rights to produce Brecht's *The Threepenny Opera*.[22] Lewenstein, who was general manager and subsequently artistic director at the Royal Court, was a pivotal figure in the artistic and economic nexus of metropolitan theatre assisting, as Yael Zarhy-Levo has pointed out, in the 'mediation' of the work of new dramatists, which went on to form the accepted canon of plays and playwrights to emerge in the 1950s.[23] He is also interesting as an example of a left-leaning commercial manager. A pre-war member of the Young Communist League, employed at the centre for Left Book Club distribution, editor of *New Theatre Magazine*, Secretary of the National Society of Unity and General Manager of Glasgow Unity's professional company, he had impeccable socialist credentials.[24] His memoirs demonstrate very clearly the third-sector migration process, juggling limited amounts of subsidy, careful calculations (at the Royal Court especially) of how productions balanced out in terms of profit and loss, and the need to capitalise on success. *The Threepenny Opera* was presented in 1956 at the Royal Court not by the ESC, but by his own 'Polly Peachum Productions Ltd.' with his principal backer the wife of Group impresario Tom Arnold.[25] Lewenstein's relationship with Donald Albery, the son of Bronson Albery and thus director of Wyndham Theatres, led to the transfer of three of Joan Littlewood's Theatre Workshop productions to Albery theatres in 1959 under the umbrella of Lewenstein's producing partnership with playwright Wolf Mankowitz.[26]

In this way Shelagh Delaney's *A Taste of Honey*, Brendan Behan's *The Hostage* and by extension Littlewood's actors, many of whom were either Theatre Workshop founder-members or had Unity roots, were given metropolitan recognition and a taste of what career possibilities lay beyond the impoverished company ethos.[27] By the time the most enduringly popular success *Oh What a Lovely War* was presented at Wyndham's Theatre in 1963, Littlewood and her partner Gerry Raffles had formed their own producing company, Theatre Workshop (Stratford) Ltd., enabling them, in theory, to maximise available profits for the Theatre Royal. But with an ACGB subsidy of £3,000 as opposed to the £20,000 awarded to the ESC in 1963 and only £3,300 of local authority grants, third-sector migration was fundamentally unstable.[28] The commercial and not-for-profit could not maintain the desired equilibrium.

The historical anomaly that the company created by one of the most important post-war theatre directors never received the appropriate level of public subsidy to allow it to achieve a safe level of business independence has been much analysed, most notably by Nadine Holdsworth.[29] The individual personalities involved, not least of Joan Littlewood herself, gender bias, Cold War-induced suspicion of previous political affiliation and, above all, the magic circles of gentlemanly, Oxbridge-nurtured influence and patronage which gave the ESC the upper hand, all contributed to the slow death of Theatre Workshop as a national and, indeed, international influence. That the primary cause was commercial exploitation would be a simplistic over-statement. As Lewenstein's record demonstrates, artistic instincts which favoured the new and the unusual, along with the capacity for calculated and often personal financial risk, remained a vital factor in the larger theatre ecology. The impresario Peter Daubeny brought a series of inspirational international theatre companies to London, especially through the 1964–73 World Theatre Seasons presented annually at the Aldwych.[30] Younger commercial producers played an important part in nurturing a new generation of playwrights to public prominence. Michael Codron produced Harold Pinter's *The Birthday Party* at the Lyric Hammersmith in 1958 and despite its financial and initial critical failure, went on to present *The Caretaker* at the Arts Theatre in 1960 where against all the odds its success warded off Codron's bankruptcy.[31] As James Inverne has showed in his book *The Impresarios*, Codron's protégés included Joe Orton, Tom Stoppard, David Hare and Christopher Hampton.[32] Michael White, following an apprenticeship with Daubeny, produced the original production of Joe Orton's *Loot* in 1966, and in 1968 presented Rolph Hochhuth's politically inflammatory play *Soldiers* after the National Theatre board rejected it.[33]

Overall, the judicious alliances within the interlocking circles of influence brought a new dynamism to metropolitan theatre, and one, moreover, of sufficient confidence finally to overthrow the powers of suppression exercised by the monarch in the person of the Lord Chamberlain. The 1968 Theatres Act not only abolished the pre-censorship of new plays produced in the subsidised theatre, but enabled new and profitable freedoms for commercial theatre. The exuberantly naked bodies on display in the American hippie-rock musical *Hair*, which opened on 27 September 1968 at the Shaftesbury Theatre, the day after the Act come into force, were emblematic not just of the unexpurgated vigour with which dramatists now hoped to probe political and social issues, but of the capacity of youth-oriented popular culture to situate itself at the core of market-driven capitalist expansion. The Shaftesbury, formerly the Prince's Theatre owned by the Melville family, had been purchased and renamed by EMI (Electric and Musical Industries), rapidly becoming one of the world's most powerful record producers with the Beatles just one example of their contracted artists. *Hair* ran for a hugely lucrative 1997 performances until 1973 when part of the elderly theatre's roof fell in.[34]

ALTERNATIVE INDEPENDENCE

That a new generation of theatre impresarios chose to remain economically independent and, albeit with a wary eye on their profit margins, assist
in the 1960s' challenge to outmoded social mores, represented one facet
of the cultural climate out of which the 'alternative' theatre companies
emerged. As Steve Gooch in *All Together Now*, a retrospective discussion
of the radical movement published in 1984 pointed out, freedom to challenge in the first instance often meant surviving with part-time jobs or
unemployment benefit, and then effectively donating time and energy to
the collective artistic enterprise. The largely unacknowledged consequence
of this was a narrowing of the social composition of companies. 'Men
who were married with children, women who bore the responsibility for
child-care, and anyone who had an aged parent, sick lover or a mortgage could not commit their time as whole-heartedly as others.' The result
was that the 'field of work' tended to be the province of single, childless,
middle-class young men. Subsidy offered more security but inevitably
compromised radical principles and meant submitting to irksome bureaucratic demands. The playwright David Hare described the final disastrous phase of Portable Theatre which, set up in 1968, launched his career
and that of Howard Brenton and Snoo Wilson, and as a touring company
opened up a new circuit of non-conventional playing spaces. In 1973, the
year after Portable received more grant aid than any other comparable
company,[35] he and his co-founder Tony Bicât were prosecuted and found
guilty of non-payment of actors' National Insurance stamps. 'When the
company later went bankrupt, we learned that your debt to the state is
the one debt that can never be absolved.'[36]

The more serious debt was to the actors, and it could be argued that as
company directors they were little different from the incompetent managers of the early twentieth century who abandoned their employees.
Also, under tightly regulated company law it was much more difficult
to simply walk away from debt. The 'if-it' principle still mattered, and
theatre workers, especially those on the front line, i.e. actors, remained
as vulnerable as ever. It was important to recognise as Gooch emphasised
that within the 'free' market economy even theatre of 'the most virulently
anti-capitalist kind' constitutes an expensive package of complex component parts, which requires skill and practical acumen to assemble.[37] Some
of the most prominent companies undoubtedly benefited from early
relationships formed in elite institutions. David Hare and Tony Bicât
founded Portable after Cambridge University. Subsequently, Portable's

woeful financial collapse did not prove an obstacle to Hare becoming a director, in the business sense, of Joint Stock when the company was founded with Max Stafford-Clark and David Aukin in 1973.[38] Stafford-Clark (Trinity College Dublin) and Aukin had a strong track record in radical theatre management. Stafford-Clark brought the dramaturgical strategies developed at the Edinburgh Traverse where he had been artistic director.[39] Aukin, the 'King of Fringe', was ubiquitous in the early 70s as a producer simultaneously 'looking after' companies such as Freehold and the People Show and co-founding Foco Novo in 1972 with Roland Rees and the American dramatist Bernard Pomerance.[40] Aukin was not only an Oxford graduate but also a trained solicitor. Speaking about Joint Stock in 1987, Aukin recalled: 'Joint Stock was born with, if not a silver then certainly a brass spoon in its mouth; it was accepted [by the Arts Council] and encouraged almost before it began. Those were the days when the Arts Council had money to dole out to new ventures, and the initial approaches Max Stafford-Clark and I made for funding were met with instant support.'[41]

The key point here is that institutional networks, the 'magic circles', remained very important, and where the apparently disparate directorial roles meshed together most successfully to create a viable company in both senses of the word was where artistic ambition and business acumen and influence worked in tandem towards a common goal. Operating as a collective without a formally constituted hierarchy or fixed technical and administrative roles could be difficult to sustain. As Gooch pointed out, it tended to make the responsibilities and skills demanded by the whole theatre 'package' more, not less, onerous.[42] Also, as actors such as Simon Callow discovered in relation to Joint Stock's collective era, democratic accountability did not necessarily extend to directorial (in the artistic sense) imperatives.[43]

Where there was greater awareness of the dangers represented by what Gillian Hanna called 'the hidden hierarchy', a women's collective such as Monstrous Regiment, founded in 1975, did at least attempt to show 'that a company could work efficiently, and honestly' driven by the frustration of women's subordination and marginalisation as creative artists. With company members whose career experience had been both significantly broader and more community-oriented, there appears to have been greater stamina to survive the rigours of co-operative policy-making combined with extensive touring. Also, as Hanna recognised, a realistic understanding of the need for specialist skills such as play writing helped ease potential tensions over the allocation of roles and responsibilities.[44]

Even so the 'pure' collective principle did not survive beyond 1979 when an artistic crisis combined with increasing exhaustion compelled a gradual shift to more traditional management structures.[45]

BOARDS OF MANAGEMENT

For the most durable of the touring companies who went on to receive ACGB revenue funding in the 1970s and early 1980s, the board of management could consist of a group of like-minded spirits, at least until the more stringent governance demands of the later 1980s imposed a broader base of financial and legal experience.[46] Building-based theatre especially outside London was a different matter. Company directors could bring skills to the organisation as a business that might appear far removed from artistic vision. Not-for-profit theatre companies controlled by boards of directors drawn from the local elite and/or with professional expertise which lay outside the theatre were familiar, of course, from before the Second World War. Chairmen such as Charles Reilly and J. J. Shute (Liverpool Playhouse), Archibald Flower (SMT) and Seebohm Rowntree in York were powerful charismatic men in their own right. Post-war the lawyers, accountants, retailers and manufacturers who joined academics and *some* artists on not-for-profit boards were often capable of an unexpectedly high level of passion in support of *their* artistic enterprise. Oscar Lewenstein described the businessman Neville Blond, who became Chairman of the first Council of the English Stage Company, as both 'insensitive and basically unsympathetic' to the artistic policy, 'yet totally loyal to the Royal Court and on the side of its artists when they were under attack'.[47] Given the establishment credentials of the ESC Board – George Devine's main ally, Lord Harwood, was the Queen's cousin – it is not unreasonable to suggest that other kinds of tribal loyalties safeguarded the company's survival. As Irving Wardle has noted, Blond could be abominably rude to Devine while still prepared to pick up the telephone to secure large overdrafts.[48] In the case of both the RSC and the National, powerful chairmen and their ability, as Peter Hall put it, to shape events by just 'having a word' with even more powerful people was vital to company success.[49]

In the new regional producing theatres, local elites wielded local if rarely national power. Civic involvement and investment especially in the development of new buildings ensured the automatic appointment of local authority councillors with voting rights to theatre boards. Coventry City Council was hailed for its civilised generosity in paying for the new

Belgrade Theatre in 1958. But ultimately it was intended that the theatre should pay for itself. Once the Belgrade opened in 1958 the annual operating costs included a very heavy rental charge of £17,000 levied by the Council to cover capital and interest expenses on the building. Out of the fifteen nominated members of the Board, no less than ten were to be local councillors.⁵⁰ Under these and similar circumstances, the removal of the individual-profit motive did not remove a whole raft of vested interests at either local or national level. For the salaried artistic team, the aspirational, vocational dimension of their work had to be tempered by an informed understanding of the constraints imposed by the not-for-profit sector – as well as the opportunities. When financial accountability failed and the business failed, the principal victim was often the artistic director unless very firmly supported by his or her chair.

Legally board members *are* the company. They have to agree policy and they employ all the staff including the artistic director. Where conflict arose over artistic matters, as it could when theatre-makers chafed under the apparent philistinism or obduracy of their board, resignation or actual sacking could result. The most frequently quoted example of this was when a proffered resignation over inadequate Arts Council funding by the actor John Neville, as artistic director of Nottingham Playhouse, turned into a rancorous and widely publicised row about Board management which ended with Neville's departure in 1968.⁵¹ Richard Eyre, who took over the Nottingham job in 1973, acknowledged the board's reputation for strong government, but unlike Neville who was effectively an actor-manager, he was one of the new breed of director-administrators. The chairman, Cyril Forsyth was a well-known local businessman who looking like 'a cross between Eric von Stroheim and the bald member of the Crazy Gang was capricious, bullying, wilful, loyal and generous in equal measure. But he had a passion for the theatre and crucially he and his board never transgressed the line between the responsibilities of the board and those of the artistic director; the "art" was my job, and if I messed that up, then it was alright with me if he handed me my cards.'⁵²

Equally the board could also be deemed culpable. In Birmingham in 1973, faced with a request for an annual grant increase of nearly 50 per cent to help tackle a £50,000 deficit, the City Council insisted on board restructuring. Out went Sir Robert Aitken, the elderly distinguished physician who had chaired the board since the death of Sir Barry Jackson in 1961. In came Councillor Marjorie Brown, Birmingham's first woman Lord Mayor and a former welfare officer at the local engineering factory GKN.⁵³ Company directors in this sense have to be responsible for the

organisation as a going concern and this inevitably becomes more onerous when buildings are involved. But any building and its contents are
capital assets. Once the decision is made to use public money to make a
visible commitment to a designated building, the decision to withdraw
support and risk collapse is not easily made. Thus the investment made by
the state and/or civic authorities is potentially more secure.

BUILDINGS

At its best the producing theatre functions as a highly organised and
intensely collaborative manufactory which commands substantial loyalty from the work force. If the right ambience was created that loyalty
also extended to the audience. In an essay published in *Scottish Theatre
Since the Seventies*, Mark Fisher pondered the relationship and legacy
of a nation's theatre-building stock to its theatrical output, the impact
of architectural design and the cultural context out of which building
concepts emerge. 'We erect buildings to match our needs, but we can't
help getting values mixed in with the cement.'[54] Writing in 1996 when the
newly built £3.3 million Traverse Theatre in Edinburgh and the 'found'
Tramway in Glasgow were celebrated for their flexibility and multiple
playing spaces, Fisher pointed out that these theatres reflected the rapid
changes and insecurity of 1990s' theatre culture. The mix of old and new,
rescued and refurbished or defiantly contemporary exemplified the shifting aesthetic and ideological contours of postmodernity. Fisher recounted
an anecdote about a Perth Theatre subscriber who took his seat for a performance in the *fin de siècle* Victorian auditorium and only then looked to
see what play was to be presented:

> I doubt … that gentleman would ever have stopped to articulate what it was
> about the ambience of Perth Theatre – or more probably the ambience created
> by the company in that space – that kept him coming back. Even if he tried, he
> would probably have talked about his liking for the repertoire in general, long
> before he tried to explain what it was about the design of the building that made
> him feel comfortable.[55]

The Perth Theatre was an example of a building that had survived – despite a proposal in 1973 to demolish and build a new theatre – since it
first opened in 1900. Apart from its historic charm one reason why the
ambience felt comfortable was that efforts had been made to create more
intimacy by reducing the audience capacity: first in 1967 when the gallery was closed reducing seating from 800 to 600, and then again in 1981
when the seating went down to 490.[56]

The network of new theatre buildings which followed on from the Coventry Belgrade were very much the product of the needs and values of the 1950s and 60s. The focus on buildings has to be seen against an economic growth statistic that saw the UK devote about 15 per cent of gross domestic product to investment in physical capital (excluding housing). Despite the fact that UK economic performance had been overtaken first by the United States and then by other European countries, there was a trend of steady growth in the second half of the century.[57] Indeed, irrespective of the changing political complexion of government, social expenditure grew in real terms between 1960 and 1975 from just over 11 per cent to 19 per cent of the gross national product, representing an unprecedented shift in public resources.[58] Urban renewal programmes, which prioritised slum clearance and provided better standard homes on new estates, or the new high-density housing provided in tower blocks – on paper attractively landscaped – which became ubiquitous in the 1960s, were seen to be socially essential. Older theatre buildings sometimes occupied land that was needed for other development purposes. In St Andrews, the Town Council provided the largest proportion of the public funding – supplemented by the Scottish Arts Council and Fife County Council – towards the building of a new Byre Theatre in 1970. The removal of the original Byre made room for the construction of a new housing complex.[59] In Sheffield where again the council made the largest contribution to the building of the new Crucible Theatre, the old repertory playhouse was on land needed for a new road system.[60]

But the other factor was the new era of civic confidence represented in public buildings that made optimistic architectural statements of modernity and progress. In 1958 Coventry's Belgrade Theatre, so named because of a gift of timber from the city of Belgrade in Yugoslavia, was a vital part of the wholesale reconstruction of the bombed city centre, which included a new Cathedral as well as a new art gallery, and had tremendous symbolic importance.[61] Unlike the theatres of the late nineteenth century, which were integrated into the frontages of streets populated with other commercial businesses, many of the new theatres and arts centres were both more visually prominent and physically separated within landscaped open spaces.

An 'Housing the Arts' policy had been pursued by ACGB even before Britain's first minister for the arts, Jennie Lee, formalised it as a key objective of the 1965 Government White Paper, *A Policy for the Arts – The First Steps*. Prime minister Harold Wilson's Labour government elected with a tiny majority in 1964 accelerated the steady if more cautious commitment to social expenditure maintained by the Conservatives in the 1950s. Many of the new arts venues, like the new hospitals, universities and polytechnics, were already in the planning stage before the sudden injection of new cash made them concretely possible. Just as Harold Wilson celebrated the white heat of a new technologically driven era, so Lee's rhetoric rejected 'the drabness, uniformity and joylessness of much of the social furniture we have inherited from the industrial revolution'.[62] The £250,000 of additional money granted to ACGB's separate Housing the Arts Fund was to assist in making Britain 'a gayer and more cultivated country'. But as gaiety gave way to economic gloom so the structural instability of the planning behind this new stratum of buildings became more obvious.

The accumulative effect of economic growth was increased consumer confidence, a visible rise in standards of living for a significant proportion of the population – student numbers in higher education doubled for example – and totally unsustainable pressure on the national budget. As Peter Clarke points out, expectations had been pushed up to levels that were 'simultaneously difficult to satisfy and difficult to afford'.[63] In truth, the fabled 'never had it so good' period lasted a very short time until the devaluation of the pound in 1967, followed by intractable financial and industrial relations problems. The shock delivered to all advanced industrial nations of the fourfold increase in oil prices in 1973 led to considerable inflation in the cost of oil-based goods which had serious consequences for theatre resources. The Housing the Arts Fund satisfied expectations up to a point but inevitably generated aspirations for more. In the ten years up until 1973–4, grant aid from the Fund amounting to £5,835,000 and matched with donations from local authorities and private sources resulted in new or reconstructed buildings costing £34 million. By then as the Arts Council's annual report makes clear, the scheme had begun to lose momentum as 'the amounts which can be offered from the annual commitment ration of £750,000 for Great Britain as a whole, become less and less meaningful in relation to current building costs'.[64]

THE SPREAD OF BUILDINGS

Inevitably England with the largest population saw the most new buildings. By the late 1970s, twenty completely new theatres had been built in the English regions with an additional clutch of new university theatres. Geographically the locations ranged from Bolton (Octagon 1967), Sheffield and Birmingham (Crucible and the new Birmingham Rep, both 1971), Leicester (Phoenix, 1963, Haymarket, 1973) to Guildford (Yvonne

Arnaud, 1965), Ipswich (Wolsey, 1979) and Chichester. The Nuffield in Southampton, the Gulbenkian Theatres in Newcastle upon Tyne and Canterbury, the Northcott in Exeter and the Contact Theatre in Manchester were all university theatres.[65]

Theatre auditoria were also incorporated into the increasing number of cross-disciplinary arts centres which emerged at the same time. In 1976 *A Directory of Arts Centres in England, Scotland and Wales* listed 133 arts centres, 111 of which had been converted from existing buildings.[66] The rationale behind the establishment of a building-based, multi-purpose arts provider varied. Some opened in towns such as Shrewsbury or less heavily populated areas such as Alfreton in Derbyshire or Abingdon in Oxfordshire could more economically serve the local community. Others such as the Midlands Arts Centre in Birmingham opened in 1962 with a particular focus on young people. Several, including the MacRobert Arts Centre in Stirling (1971) and Theatr y Werin in Aberystwyth (1971), the Sherman Theatre in Cardiff (1973), were established on university campuses.

Theatr Ardudwy in the Coleg Harlech Arts Centre was part of the Harlech College of Adult Education in 1972. Indeed, in Wales it was suggested in 1979 that the model of the purpose-built centre based on a theatre had supplied 'a distinctive pattern for a nationwide development of arts resources'.[67] These, it was argued, had not been the product of centralised planning but were closely associated with the extension of public arts patronage through the Regional Arts Associations by then gathering strength with centralised support.

Theatr Clwyd in Mold in North Wales was originally conceived in 1969 by Flintshire County Council. Opened in 1976 and serving both Welsh and English audiences within a 40-mile radius, it was claimed to be the first local initiative of its kind in Wales. By 1981 in Cardiff, Chapter Arts Centre, which had been operating out of a converted Edwardian school since its inception a decade earlier, provided a base for six professional theatre companies including Moving Being and Cardiff Laboratory Theatre. Long-term residencies had also been undertaken by companies such as People Show, Lumiere & Son and Pip Simmons.[68]

The metropolitan apogee of these developments after years of consultation and delay was the opening in 1976 on London's South Bank of the National Theatre with three auditoria of different spatial configurations and capacities, and, in 1982, the Barbican Arts Centre in the City of London, which included two new theatre auditoria for the Royal Shakespeare Company. As an index of rising prices the difference between

the costs of the very first twentieth-century civic theatre, the Belgrade
Theatre opened in Coventry in 1958, the National and the Barbican, is
breathtaking. The Belgrade cost about £275,000 of public money. The
National cost an estimated £16.8 million; the Barbican Arts Centre,
which also included a cinema, concert hall and exhibition halls, came to
£163 million.[69] Set in the heart of London's financial district and opened
at a moment of economic slump when unemployment (mostly male and
mostly in heavy industry) was creeping towards 3 million, the Barbican
was an emblem of the economic and cultural disjunctions in Britain at
that time. As criticism mounted of the Barbican's bleak environs and a
complex of spaces which were both externally and internally difficult
to access and navigate, it was easy to forget that it was built in an area
completely devastated in the war and was intended by the Corporation
of London as 'the City's gift to the nation'.[70] The problem, as with so
many building managements that faced the economic chill and inflationary pressures of the post-oil-crisis era, was the length of time which had
elapsed between the original conception – eighteen years in the case of
the Barbican – and the final realisation sometimes decades later.[71]

THE BATTLE FOR BUILDINGS

The absence of a clear-cut economic function, let alone proven benefit,
and the reality that these resources were ultimately paid for through direct taxation and local rates ensured that the case for non-commercial,
publically dependent arts buildings had to be argued every step of the
way, usually by campaigning groups from within the 'dissident' educated
middle class. Outside the metropolitan bastions of high culture, the consciousness, despite the rise in living standards, of continuing failures in
the housing and social welfare system made graphically obvious in films
such as *Cathy Come Home*, broadcast by the BBC in 1966, placed even the
most sympathetic of local authorities in what could be an intolerable position of divided responsibilities.[72]

Although separate Arts Councils were established for Scotland and
Wales in 1967 following that for Northern Ireland in 1962, their grants
were still allocated by central government through the umbrella ACGB.
Funding policy was firmly predicated on the 1948 assumption that local
authorities would contribute their share. Arts Council annual reports
would trumpet examples of civic generosity while implicitly attempting to
shame the others. In complete contrast to the industrial insouciance that
stimulated the boom of speedily constructed theatre building at the end

of the nineteenth century, the new theatre venues, which emerged under subsidy, many of which were based on flexible, innovative designs, came about through the convergence of frequently conflicting aspirations and stakeholder agendas. The circumstances surrounding the achievement of each project had a significant impact on subsequent managerial attempts to create viable business practice.

Relatively few had an uncomplicated passage to completion and many suffered the time-lag exemplified by the Barbican project. In these economically volatile decades, delay meant not only a substantially more expensive building, but a greater challenge to long-term viability. In the 1950s and early 60s attention focused on the economics of ticket yield and the assumption that increased audience capacity and more congenial surroundings would increase revenue and thus boost the plausibility of business plans. In Birmingham, negotiations with the City Council to replace the Birmingham Rep with an architecturally ambitious building with double the seating capacity (464 to 900) began as early as 1955 when plans for major urban reconstruction were underway. After the final commitment was made, arguments between traditionalists and modernists about the external appearance of the theatre, intended as an iconic feature in a proposed new civic centre, led to a delay and thence to a complete halt when a government ban on local authority spending intervened in 1966. By the time the theatre opened in 1971, after attempts to abandon the project had contemplated renovating one of Birmingham's remaining commercial theatres, the cost had risen from £493,000 to £1,016,000, and the management were faced with a building, twice the size of the old theatre, in the context of the state of emergency caused by the strikes and power cuts which plagued Edward Heath's Conservative government.[73]

It took twenty-six years to establish the West Yorkshire Playhouse. In 1964 the group of mostly Leeds University lecturers and other local educators, who began the campaign for Leeds to have a producing theatre, were given a new build estimate of £220,000. The City Council's dogged resistance was bolstered by the animosity of the theatre critic of the *Yorkshire Post*, and the counter-claims of the by then financially troubled Grand Theatre and Opera House. The temporary Leeds Playhouse, built in a converted sports hall on a vacant university campus site, was the result of an acrimonious battle, but ultimately served as an interim measure from 1970 until 1990 by which point the ethos of local authority support had changed significantly.[74] The final cost was £13 million.

In Inverness the fierce arguments over the proposal first made in 1966 to create the largest performing arts venue to serve the Scottish

Highlands divided the community and also stumbled into restrictions on local authorities ordered by central government. Ultimately the costs were partly borne by the Scottish Arts Council and the Highlands and Islands Development Board with the remainder raised by public appeal. Controversially more donations were made from outside the town – even the Queen Mother was a donor. The building would continue to provide a base for community performances, but was also a facility that would enable audiences to access high-profile, large-scale performances by companies such as the Scottish Opera. Partly incorporating the old nineteenth-century Bishop's Palace and on a spectacular site on the River Ness, Eden Court opened in 1976.[75]

In Dundee, following a fire in 1963 which completely destroyed the repertory theatre and eighteen years in a 'temporary' home in a converted church, it was 1982 before the new 450-seat theatre opened. Work had begun in January 1979, but again inflation and rising prices, which exacerbated the city's economic recession, stopped the process. Only a public appeal, which raised £60,000 in less than six weeks and eventually reached a total of £200,000, enabled completion.[76]

BUILDING FOR TROUBLE

In Northern Ireland fraught attempts to establish a producing theatre encapsulated the economic, political, industrial and artistic challenges experienced by other British companies but in a particularly acute way. As a producing theatre company, the Belfast Arts Theatre survived a number of relocations, but defeated by a combination of deficit and sectarian violence, was forced to close its purpose-built theatre in 1971.[77] The Lyric Theatre proved more durable. Established originally in 1951 in the home of the founders Mary and Pearse O'Malley, up until 1960 when the Lyric Players Theatre Trust was formally constituted, this was a private, amateur, highly specialised 'poets' theatre' for a select audience of friends and literary and theatrical aficionados.[78] Increasing esteem which extended outside Ireland, more varied and ambitious activity and a widening audience-support base raised costs to the point that a properly resourced building-based professional company appeared unavoidable.[79] Funding from the Northern Ireland Arts Council was agreed only on the basis of an audience capacity of 300, which might give the new business some chance of survival.[80]

Mary O'Malley and her son Conor O'Malley wrote separate accounts of the protracted and tortuous route to the playhouse erected on a scenically pleasing, but very cramped site on the banks of the River Lagan. They both record the repeated last-minute, probably politically inspired, withdrawals of land available for purchase, and the lobbying and manoeuvring necessary among the Arts Council, City Council and the Stormont parliament.[81] The audience was undeniably composed of the local, predominantly middle-class intelligentsia, but the enterprise was also suspect for sectarian reasons. The celebration of the canonical Abbey playwrights, especially Yeats, amongst a classical European repertoire imparted an 'Irish' orientation. Mary O'Malley herself was regarded as problematic because of her background in Dublin theatre and her 1952–4 role as an elected Labour councillor for the deprived Catholic Smithfield district of Belfast.[82] In a Unionist- and Protestant-dominated city it was difficult to secure large donations from leading industrialists even with the assistance of professional fund-raisers.[83]

At a more basic level, even after opening, the theatre was briefly closed to enable the management to learn the business of running a company, not made any easier by the closed-shop rules of British Actors' Equity. The trade union's increasingly militant policy on restricting access to an overcrowded profession, by limiting the essential allocation of Equity cards by theatre managements, hindered the development of a professional Lyric ensemble with a strong local identity. A strategy designed to protect 'mainland' actors failed to recognise the exceptional working conditions faced in Belfast, and moreover, established mainland actors were nervous of joining a company in a city seething with rising levels of sectarian violence. Regular intransigence in Arts Council funding decisions also meant actors could not be offered the security of long-term contracts.[84]

The Lyric Theatre opened three weeks after street battles had erupted in Derry, and throughout the 1970s and early 80s it doggedly continued as Ulster's only full-time repertory theatre. Broad-based programming policy included in the 1970s the plays of John Boyd and Patrick Galvin that directly addressed the impact of the conflict on Belfast communities.[85] Company members from both religious and cultural traditions had to make agonising decisions in the face of external demands on their personal loyalties. The theatre building, despite its difficult birth, did represent a visible commitment to a cultural enterprise, but as a place of collective, creative assembly was also a target for mass killing and maximum economic disruption. Located in the leafier south side of the city, and not far from Queen's University, the Lyric endured bomb threats, a very serious near-miss in 1973, but no major damage apart from that inflicted by unstable trading conditions.[86]

Just over a mile away in the centre of Belfast and next door to the Europa Hotel – 'the most-bombed building in Europe' – the Opera House became an emblem of attempts to make theatre a focus for the cultural life of the city in defiance of the Troubles. Sold to the Rank Organisation in 1960, badly damaged and closed, Matcham's iconic building was rescued from property developers and refurbished under the auspices of the Arts Council of Northern Ireland. As artistic director from 1980 until 1994, Michael Barnes, a former history lecturer from Queen's University, juggled a mixed programme, which ignored the boundaries between high and popular art, professional and amateur, and survived two major bombings. The first in December 1991 put a stop to the highly lucrative annual pantomime. The second in May 1993 occurred in the middle of the Ulster Amateur Drama Finals. Each time the theatre closed for repairs for several months before reopening. Closure inevitably brought staff redundancies, and the loss of other trading opportunities for the Opera House as host venue and for guest companies. There was a city-wide impact on access to popular culture as well as nationally recognised opera and ballet.[87] Even so the theatre reopened and in 1994 the ACNI handed over responsibility to a board of trustees trading on the basis of a mix of public subsidy and commercial relationships.

The particular context of the Belfast Opera House's continuing survival as a high-profile mixed-use receiving and presenting house was obviously exceptional. However, the transition from a purely commercial enterprise to one that was saved by a public body and supported by a local authority was typical of what began to happen to selected numbers of the old established commercial theatres from the 1970s onwards.

COMMERCIAL ALLIANCES, CORPORATE INTERESTS AND NEW TECHNOLOGY

The commercial and not-for-profit sectors were probably at their most polarised in the mid to late 1950s and early 60s as the cultural high ground was steadily appropriated by the growing number of theatre companies deemed eligible for charitable status and public subsidy. Outside London the older corporate commercial interests were acting to shed former capital assets, which were now perceived to be loss, rather than profit-making, and shifting the focus of activity to the new technology-driven source of mass entertainment. It was worth repairing the Shaftesbury, but most of the Victorian and Edwardian theatres spread out across the UK were dilapidated, technically inadequate and with minimal resident staff apparently not worth the expenditure. Audiences were demonstrating growing indifference to pre-London commercial production try-outs which were frequently little better than dress rehearsals. Greater mobility through car ownership and the advance of the American model of the motorway system first launched in 1958 meant that more affluent patrons could go to see London productions in London.

While it is commonplace to state that the steep rise in television ownership in the late 1950s and early 60s effectively killed the commercial touring circuits and weekly rep housed in commercially owned theatres, what is probably not so well understood is that the key individuals who formulated enterprise strategies for corporate shareholders in live theatre played an active role in the engine of change. Of the four original companies granted franchises by the ITA (Independent Television Authority) to broadcast commercial television to different British regions in 1955 and 1956, two had particularly strong origins as mass entertainment providers. Granada Television emerged out of the Granada chain of cinemas and super-cinemas, first established in the 1920s by Sidney and Cecil Bernstein and incorporated as Granada Theatres Ltd. in 1934. Some live theatre had been presented in the Granada cinemas which mainly located in the south of England.[88] ITC (Independent Television Corporation), however, brought together the merged interests of the two leading casting agencies: the prestigious legitimate actors' agency London Artists, with the variety agency run by Lew Grade and his brother Bernard Delfont, and Stoll Moss, as represented by Prince Littler as Chair and Val Parnell as Managing Director. What became, following yet another merger with a franchise competitor, ATV (Associated TeleVision) was driven by Lew Grade to offer attractive viewing options such as top-class variety shows, especially 'Sunday Night at the London Palladium' produced directly from the theatre by Parnell, and a succession of romantic costume/adventure drama series starting with *The Adventures of Robin Hood*. Many of the essential ingredients of the best of live popular theatre were beamed via 'The People's Channel' into domestic sitting rooms.[89]

An important aim of the separate regional franchises was to give some local identity to what was transmitted. Up until 1968 ATV had contracts to broadcast London's weekend programmes and a weekday schedule in the English Midlands. Inevitably, the orientation of the company was towards London with a major studio centre at Elstree, and although television studios were established in Birmingham, by 1981, having lost the London weekend franchise, there was criticism that Midlands provision was too weak.[90] Granada Television was from the beginning very firmly located in the north, with Sidney Bernstein insistent on the strength of northern identity. A revolutionary purpose-built studio complex was built on bomb-clearance land in Manchester, and in 1968 a unique experiment was set up to employ actors to work in both television and theatre on the same contract. Not only did this have significant implications for the quality of drama output, but Bernstein's socialist allegiance also influenced the polemical content of documentary series and news commentary.[91]

While the collaboration of business interests through advertising was vital to the survival of the second television channel, it did not by any means imply the commodification of mediocrity. But the very substantial financial resources required to sustain the franchises meant that the buildings that had housed the popular product of the past had to pay their way. By the 1960s Granada cinemas had been largely given over to the contemporary craze for the commercialised parlour game bingo – an uncomfortable move that was made more respectable by the 1968 Gaming Act. The Victorian and Edwardian touring theatres erected quickly to capitalise on an entertainment boom, could be taken down just as quickly to make way for other kinds of capital exploitation. The Theatre Royal in Birmingham went as early as 1956.[92] Leicester lost all its theatres. Others in the Moss chain which were demolished included the Empires in Swansea, Nottingham, Sheffield, Newcastle and Leeds, allegedly due to the activities of Val Parnell and his involvement in the murkier side of property development.[93]

RESCUING THE COMMERCIAL

By the time the report of the enquiry into subsidised and unsubsidised theatre in England and Wales was published by the Arts Council in 1970,[94] the complicated construct of horizontally and vertically integrated theatre business interests once known as the Group had become the Octopus.[95] ATV and EMI were now major corporate players and through further mergers, acquisitions and speculative investment were locked into the older networks of metropolitan theatre ownership and production managements. The brothers Delfont and Grade were now as powerful as the Littlers. The committee that produced the ACGB report and whose members included Lewenstein, Bernstein, Derek Salberg (son of Leon Salberg), Michael Elliott (founder of Theatre 69 Company, the forerunner of the Manchester Royal Exchange Company) and Binkie Beaumont, professed themselves relatively unworried by evidence of continuing monopoly of London property and product. There were concerns, however, that the vertical integration of theatrical agency control might adversely impact on employment opportunities for actors. But the greatest perceived need, however, was to address the collapse of commercial theatre outside London and the consequences of the loss of old, large performance venues.[96]

Spectacular variety, star-laden pantomimes remained, as they had throughout the century, an essential feature of the annual urban entertainment calendar and needed the big stages, flying facilities, orchestra pits and ample audience capacity of the No. 1 theatres. However, it was also incumbent on the heavily subsidised national companies – Royal Opera House with the Royal Ballet, Sadler's Wells Opera and Ballet companies, the Royal Shakespeare Company and the National Theatre Company – to undertake some touring. The Dramatic and Lyric Theatres Association (DALTA) had been originally formed by Covent Garden and Sadler's Wells to co-ordinate touring schedules and negotiate manpower needs, and by 1970 was considering widening the co-operative circle.[97] But the commercial/non-profit balance of power had shifted to the extent that Arts Council guarantees against loss and ticket-yield agreements significantly favoured the subsidised companies, making it difficult for the receiving houses to recoup costs and make sufficient profit.[98] The additional fiscal burden of Selective Employment Tax, introduced in 1966, hit theatres (classified as a service and not a manufacturing industry) not protected by non-profit distributing status particularly hard.[99] Deciding at this juncture that the alternative models of financing represented by the commercial sector should be preserved, the solution offered by the 1970 enquiry committee was a Theatre Investment Fund. This was a pool of capital, part public money, part individual contribution, from which commercial managements could borrow in proportion to their own investment. As a way of enabling the production of new plays on a commercial basis which would then tour outside London, an agreed percentage of profits would feed back into the Fund before distribution to other backers.[100]

THE RETREAT FROM MODERNISM

The move away from automatic assumptions about the desirability of new buildings was partly a matter of economic expediency, partly a retreat from modernist architecture and the recognition that an important older architectural heritage was being destroyed. Theatres previously controlled by commercial interests and thus off-limits for other artistic priorities were being offered for sale, but that also involved protracted negotiations. Stoll Theatres Corporation's purchase of the Cardiff New Theatre from the Redford family in 1956 for £20,000 was a liability by 1961 when demolition was proposed in order to build offices. A campaign group which included Welsh actors, reinforced by a Preservation of Use order placed on the building, initiated a series of transactions which culminated in 1969 with Cardiff City Council buying the theatre from the new owners Mecca Ltd. for £104,000 and leasing it back to the New Theatre Trust which ran the company.[101]

For over a decade of haggling with local authorities, Howard & Wyndham tried to retain their producing and presenting profile while off-loading, or at least sharing, the burden of building ownership. In 1957, the Theatre Royal in Glasgow had been sold to the Canadian newspaper magnate Roy Thomson as a base for his ITV franchise Scottish Television, while theatre-producing activity shifted to the Alhambra.[102] In Edinburgh after the Royal Lyceum was taken over by the City Council in 1965, the need for a suitable venue for opera during the Festival was a major bargaining chip in negotiations over the future of the King's Theatre, which was eventually sold to the council. The response from Newcastle City Council to a threat to sell off the Theatre Royal was another Preservation of Use order and again the purchase of the theatre as a civic property. By 1976, the establishment of the Theatres Trust by Act of Parliament to protect theatres 'for the benefit of the nation' was followed in 1978 by the Theatres Trust (Scotland) Act. Unchallenged demolition was no longer an option with listed-building status giving added protection. The last of the Howard & Wyndham theatres, the New in Oxford, was sold to Apollo Leisure, a company founded by Paul Gregg, a former cinema manager. As Howard & Wyndham faded away,[103] Apollo Leisure began a new cycle of corporate expansion. By the time Gregg sold Apollo to the American SFX Group in 1999, the company was the UK's largest theatre owner and largest privately owned company operating in Western Europe.[104]

When, in 1994, the Northern Irish Arts Council relinquished direct management of the Grand Opera House in Belfast, the lease was transferred to a board of trustees. This brought together representatives from leading accountancy firms such as Coopers & Lybrand, the NI Tourist Board, the chairman of the Association of Business Sponsorship and the Arts, marketing professionals, former Arts Council panel members and the past chair of the Arts Council, and Eleanor Methven, one of the founder members of Charabanc, the Belfast-based women's theatre company. The business record of the chairman, the marketing specialist

George Priestley, included an appointment as managing director of the
loss-making Tyrone Crystal which he restructured and stabilised. His
statement on the enlarged board hailed it as 'a unique blend of experienced professionals, representing Commerce and Industry, the Arts and
Private and Public Sectors'.[105]

In the final years of Conservative government led by John Major, the
Opera House model of management was paradigmatic of the way commercially honed processes of economic engagement were combined with
insider knowledge of the workings of subsidy within the state system. The
appointment of Derek Nicholls, as theatre director, would have signalled
very clearly how the priorities of the two sectors were intended to braid
together. An Englishman and former teacher, founder of the Birmingham
Youth Theatre and successively Director of the Midlands Arts Centre,
Associate Director at Birmingham Rep and Director of the York Theatre
Royal,[106] he presided over what remained recognisably the legitimate/
illegitimate, professional/amateur mixed presenting programme of the
old commercial regime, but positioned within third-sector principles.

QUESTIONS OF COMMODIFICATION

The business model put in place at the Grand Opera House could be
read as a perfect example of the phenomenon described by Baz Kershaw
in an essay on British theatres and economics published in 1999. In it
he states that up until the 1980s the 'principle of cultural enfranchisement' enshrined in the first two objects of the 1945 ACGB Royal Charter
had ensured that the money thereafter distributed 'ensured that much of
British theatre was *largely protected* [my emphasis] from the subsequent
growth of the Western capitalist market and the cultural ascendance of
the consumer'. He continues, 'But the 1980s witnessed major modifica-
tions to this policy for cultural provision, and theatres became subject
to increasing marketisation and commodification. In effect, British theatres were forced to incorporate into a service-oriented economy and so to
compete with other attractions in the burgeoning media, heritage, tourist
and related industries.'[107]

That theatre was indeed competing with other attractions is undeniably true as is the fact that the UK had moved towards a 'service-oriented
economy', but theatre had always competed with other attractions, and
we have seen after the First World War that changing trends in the manufacturing base of the UK economy combined with the introduction of the
mass electronic media had left a damaging legacy of distance between

live theatre and the general population. The expertise represented by the Trustees of the Belfast Grand Opera House was selected in order that the company would be best equipped to survive within the dominant economic order, which arguably and controversially offered a stronger position more publically aligned with the other commodified cultural industries. Of course the Grand Opera House was not a producing theatre and what had happened by the 1990s was the outcome of the gradual rapprochement between commerce and not-for-profit. However, to suggest that up until the 1980s the 'principle of cultural enfranchisement' contributing to what Kershaw calls 'a delicate balance between culture and economics' had served largely to protect regional producing theatres is to ignore the locally specific records of theatres, which had faced major artistic challenges necessitated by recurrent financial crises pretty much since the late 1960s. So delicate was the balance that falling off the tightrope was a regular prospect.

SUBSIDY AND CONSUMER CULTURE

The 1970 Enquiry Report (commissioned in 1967) was forthright in its advocacy for more public funding, but it was equally clear about the need for additional sources of revenue. While the ACGB annual report for 1969–70 boasted that a total of 105 companies or theatres in England, Scotland and Wales had received support, it also pointed out that rising costs meant that artistic ambition was difficult to satisfy. Grants in many cases had been at standstill for the second or even third year in succession.[108] The recommendations made by the Enquiry committee included not only the proposed public/private Theatre Investment Fund, but also more pressure on local authorities and barbed comments on the relative lack of financial support from both the BBC and Independent Television. However, the statistical survey of costs, revenue and subsidies over the period 1966–9 supplied in the 1970 annual Report showed that rising levels of subsidy did not necessarily result in greater net-trading revenue.

In 1968–9 with a total of £84,315 in Arts Council and Local Authority grants, Bristol Old Vic's operating costs had reached £141,833 while its trading revenue was £61,287. In Bolton at the Octagon Theatre, which had opened in 1967, costs as the company became fully operational had increased by 101.3 per cent from £37,860 in its first year to £76,247 in its second. Although trading revenue had increased by 107 per cent from £16,411 to £33,953, with grants totally £27,047 again there was an unbridgeable gap. By 1971 the company had a deficit of £31,000.[109]

Within a year of the Sheffield Crucible Theatre opening it was facing deficit with operating costs for 1971–2 of £187,878 and a trading revenue of £58,286, a gap that could not be bridged with £96,135 in combined Arts Council and local authority funding together with a few hundred pounds in other industrial support.[110] A report by the City Treasurer demanded cost cutting and more popular shows to attract bigger audiences. The recognition that more importance should be attached to financial expertise was signalled in changes introduced into the management structure.[111] What in the first instance had been an equal partnership between Colin George as artistic director and ex-solicitor David Brayshaw as administrative director was supplemented in 1972 with the creation of the role of management accountant, the equivalent in later years of a finance director. In the same year the introduction of the new value added tax (VAT), which imposed a fiscal levy of 10 per cent on ancillary theatre services such as set-building and costumes, print and advertising as well as ticket revenue, imposed a another burden.[112] In 1975 the structure changed again to place the director in the person of the new artistic director Peter James at the head of the management hierarchy responsible to the board, but then brought together key aspects of the other two roles in the appointment of the management accountant Roger Heath as administrative director.[113] Throughout the sector of regional producing theatres as a whole, managerial structures and thus the balance of authority between artistic and business responsibility tended to remain fluid depending on specific economic circumstances.

Those circumstances inevitably shifted artistic policy. While Colin George, an Oxford graduate, actor and director of the old Sheffield Playhouse, launched the new Crucible with ambitious large-scale classical plays such as Ibsen's *Peer Gynt*, Dekker's *The Shoemaker's Holiday* and a production of Aeschylus' *The Persians*, by 1973 musical theatre had entered the frame in Alan Cullen's *The Stirrings in Sheffield on a Saturday Night*. What began, following a trend apparent in other theatres[114] for connecting with the industrial heritage of local communities with a home-grown musical about steel grinders, climaxed in 1975 with George's farewell production of a full-blown Hollywood musical *Calamity Jane*. His successor Peter James, who had been one of the founders of the Liverpool Everyman Theatre, embraced the popular and revenue-generating possibilities of the musical with greater gusto. He staged *Cabaret* in 1977, and in 1978 struck gold with the British premiere of *Chicago* which transferred to the West End. In 1980 the British premiere of *The Wiz*, the black version of *The Wizard of Oz*, was publicised as Sheffield's 'most lavish production ever' and ran for an unprecedented seven weeks in the early autumn.[115]

The hunt for business sponsorship along with the need for specialist advice to identify appropriate sources was under way in Sheffield by 1976, the year the Association of Business Sponsorship (ABSA) was founded. Locally based firms such as Batchelors Foods and Thorntons, billed as the 'Special Toffee People', were amongst the earliest sponsors of productions. The Crucible Theatre Shop, which also opened in 1976, sold goods associated with Sheffield including stainless steel products. Catering which provided the theatre restaurant, bars, coffee shop, etc. was franchised out. In 1977 in a move that capitalised on the wider possibilities represented by the open space of the Crucible's thrust stage, the long-running contract to give over the theatre to the World Snooker Championship was signed.[116]

The historical fact which has to be acknowledged is that in both the immediate urban context and wider national economic context regional theatres had to engage with consumer culture from very early on in the development of the subsidised sector. In Bristol where commercially advantageous transfers and tours were seen as a mixed blessing during Val May's 1961–75 tenure as artistic director, sponsorship encouraged by his successor Richard Cottrell, which came from high-profile estate agents and the wine merchants Harveys, was seen as a means of maintaining a stronger local presence.[117] Widening and diversifying sources of revenue was seen not only as a means of company survival, but also a way of sustaining the more adventurous work: educational outreach, new writing and the greater experimentation possible in smaller studio spaces.

For a substantial number of radical touring companies, especially once the sector expanded outside London, the studios attached to the big producing theatres featured prominently on their touring schedules and contributed to their exposure to wider audiences. Between 1972 and 1974 the Brum, the studio at Birmingham Rep, hosted companies including the Ken Campbell Road Show, Joint Stock, Welfare State International and the Bradford-based General Will out of which David Edgar emerged to become the Rep's resident dramatist. In all theatres, however, the bigger capacity auditorium had to be the economic driver. If that failed, the other activities had to be curtailed with further knock-on effects. In the case of Foco Novo, the loss, in 1986, of expected additional finances from a co-production with Birmingham Rep began the slide into deficit, which culminated in company liquidation when ACGB revenue funding was cut in 1988.[118]

John Pick, who established the first European academic department to train arts administrators at City University, and became one of the most vociferous critics of the Arts Council's practice of deficit funding, highlighted in 1985 the core problem facing regional managements. 'Around almost every theatre, an interlocking series of potential audiences, different groups of people who will react positively to pantomime but won't watch modern dramas, to pop concerts but not music hall, to musicals but not light comedies, and to Shakespeare but not Shaw.'[119] What the Arts Council planners who had envisaged one not-for-profit theatre as part of their ideal menu of arts provision in regional towns and cities had failed to recognise was the plural nature of urban audiences. Sinfield's dissident middle class had achieved their civic playhouses and then were dismayed when the artistic product appeared overly populist and main season programmes based on predictable formulas targeted identifiable schools and family audiences and, indeed, the tax-paying citizens who enjoyed the skilful depiction of their own domestic milieu reflected back to them in the prolific writing of Alan Ayckbourn.[120]

Pick did, however, produce a systematic analysis of the Glasgow Citizens' Theatre in 1984, which under the three-man directorate of Giles Havergal, Philip Prowse and Robert David MacDonald had by and large since 1972 managed to keep the theatre out of deficit by charging a very low all-seat ticket price, and operating an artistic policy based on their defiantly idiosyncratic and flamboyant personal tastes.[121] Production costs were strictly controlled, there was a short season of popular visiting companies, sixty performances of the Christmas show each year had to fill the theatre to capacity – a teachers' strike in 1985 which kept school children out of the theatre caused a serious loss – and box-office policy was considered as creatively as what was put onstage.[122] It operated on a very skillfully honed knife edge, however, with books balanced on the basis that the theatre earned roughly half as much again as it was given in subsidy. While it was a rigorously honourable approach to the principle of subsidy, the few thousand pounds surplus each year would not easily withstand a drop in public largesse or a loss-provoking miscalculation.

ACTORS AND THEIR PROSPECTS

The mainly young Citizens' actors were all paid the same salary in an employment culture where as front-line workers they were, as ever, vulnerable to business failure. That said, the career choices made by actors in their own self interests was a major contributory factor to the way theatres and their products, especially in the regions, were perceived and thus how successful they were. Ironically, providing the company continued to trade, the subsidised producing theatres could provide a reasonably secure long-term working environment but not for actors and indeed other key free-lance artists such as playwrights, designers and musicians. The permanent staff, sometimes for decades, were technicians, stage managers, costume and wig makers, set painters, etc., as well as the growing numbers employed in administration, marketing and front-of-house.

The extent to which a resident ensemble of actors could be retained within building-based theatre became more and more difficult during the 1970s. Inflationary pressures drove up salaries and actors' professional lives became increasingly fragmented. As early as 1961 when Peter Hall attempted to create his RSC ensemble with what were proclaimed as revolutionary three-year actor contracts, it was soon found that well-known actors succumbed to film offers, and the contracts proved too inflexible, difficult to administer and expensive to sustain.[123] Even in the beginning, as Chambers points out, contracts could only be issued on a yearly basis and then renewed. A decade on industrial relations more generally between managers and theatre artists and workers became more strained. Union membership in theatre companies became more common especially amongst technical and other backstage staff. Staff associations with powers of negotiation with managers began to replace the old informal 'family' relations of the past.[124] What had been necessary for fairness and good working conditions turned into channels for the industrial militancy, which at its most extreme in the case of the National Theatre delayed its opening in 1976, and in 1979 led to two strikes that Peter Hall, by then the artistic director, defied by running productions without stage crew.[125]

In his autobiography published in 2001, the actor and director Timothy West, the son of an actor (Lockwood West), the husband of an actor (Prunella Scales) and the father of an actor (Samuel West) commented that:

the high level of unemployment in our profession is so well known as to have become a cliché, but what is not so generally understood is the number of existing jobs that people actually cannot afford to do. Much of the work in the subsidized theatre is so poorly paid that actors who have dependants, mortgages or other financial commitments are actually better off waitressing or driving mini-cabs. This creates huge problems for the producers concerned.

The very substantial rates of pay offered by the domestically available mass media, in particular television after 1955, created increasingly wide pay differentials. West tells of how in the late 1970s while director of the cash-strapped Old Vic Company (formerly the touring Prospect Theatre Company), he was paid the equivalent of his entire year's salary as artistic director for four hours' work on a television advertisement for sherry.[126] Remuneration for selling products in commercials or voice-overs meant that individual artists rapidly learnt to cross sectoral boundaries. Commercial engagement cushioned the financial consequences of opting for more creative satisfaction in live theatre.

Surveys conducted in Scotland and England in the 1990s produced statistical evidence to reinforce personal anecdotes about unemployment and low pay. Equity and TMA records identified an overall long-term decline in actor weeks (i.e. the number of weeks of employment available for actors) of 20.9 per cent in the decade 1983–93. *A Socio-Economic Study of Artists in Scotland*, commissioned by the Scottish Arts Council in 1994, reported that the average annual earnings for all artists interviewed were £8,700 at a time when, in general, British manual workers earned in the region of £13,500 and equivalent professional salaries hovered around £23,700. Actors, it appeared, accepted the low pay, irregularity of income and regular periods of unemployment as 'givens'. When employed the average working week could be as long as sixty hours. But 67 per cent had experienced unemployment in the previous twelve months and 79 per cent in the previous five years; 16 per cent had earned no more than £5,000. The highest paid amongst the Scottish sample appeared in popular television series which, in confirmation of Timothy West's experience, could enable much lower paid work in the theatre, but also 'highly lucrative ancillary activities – long term advertising contracts, training films, newspaper columns, personal appearances, after-dinner engagements etc. which provided up to 50% of the highest earners total incomes'. [127]

As the decade grew to a close, an ACE-commissioned consultation that focused exclusively on English regional producing theatres (ERPTs) found a nearly 30 per cent drop in actor weeks between 1983 and 1999. A survey of 42 ERPTs in 1983–4 had provided a statistic of 26,547 actor weeks. By 1998–9, the data supplied by 47 theatres showed a drop to 19,483 actor weeks in 'main houses', i.e. the largest capacity auditorium in the theatre.[128] Legitimate sources of actor employment towards the end of the century had become increasingly diverse, and a statistical concentration on ERPT main houses was not necessarily a reliable indicator of the actor experience across the board. But it was indicative of economic pressures in subsidised building-based theatres and of the way in which the choices

made by actors continued to exacerbate the continuing metropolitan/
regional imbalance in the core–periphery relationship.

The drop in actor weeks identified in 1998 could be attributed to a
number of reasons, not least that it was too expensive to mount large-cast
productions, and that gaps in programming could be more pragmatically
filled with toured-in work. But there was another underlying factor in the
reluctance of actors to leave London where the most theatrical agents were
still based and where networking opportunities were the most plentiful.
Agents would often encourage their clients to go for better-paid television
work which included advertising rather than journey out to the regions.
Also the metropolitan phenomenon of small experimental venues, where
dilapidated resources imparted a kind of perverse glamour and where crucially highly sophisticated audiences and critics would attend, could be
more professionally advantageous despite the lack of remuneration.[129]

In 1980 writing as a former ACGB drama director, N. V. Linklater
described the changing pattern in regional employment.[130] It had become
very difficult, if not impossible, for regional managements to engage well-
known theatre actors who would attract enthusiastic audiences. Thus a
vicious circle was set up. Sometimes employing a popular television actor
would bring audiences in. Often it did not. Regional work was seen as
less dynamic or even substandard, in part because rehearsal periods were
relatively short compared with the national companies. Audiences dwin-
dled, deficit loomed, jobs became less likely. At Birmingham Rep in 1997,
a 'stabilisation' award of £5,773,000 was intended to relieve the company
of a huge capital debt. But it was also designed to improve production
values and entice prestigious actors with higher salaries. Even when specifically invited, targeted actors declined to come.[131]

STABILITY AND THE REGIONS

The 'Stabilisation' programme which was announced by the Arts Council
of England in August 1996 represented a kind of *terminus ad quem* of all
that had been attempted over the best part of twenty-five years to rec-
oncile business and artistic imperatives in arts management. The fact
that it was designed to use National Lottery money 'to enable an arts
organization faced with imminent insolvency to develop recovery plans'
was a tacit admission that the exclusive concentration on capital building projects, which had been the primary benefit offered to the arts by
the Lottery launched in 1994, had failed to buttress improved physical
resources with the means to maintain them. The very high grants made

in the first flush of National Lottery largesse, in particular the award of £78 million to the Royal Opera House, had served to reinforce still further the inequality in the relationship between the metropolis and the regions. There had been attempts since the publication in 1984 of the ACGB strategy paper *The Glory of the Garden* to redress the balance of support in favour of the regions, but the controversy created by proposals to weed and/or prune out selected companies in order to nurture others inflamed an already simmering climate of resentment. The narrative of ideologically motivated persecution of not-for-profit theatre companies, which began with the notorious 'Christmas cuts' of 1980 and gathered momentum throughout the decade worsening with every company collapse, was typically articulated by D. Keith Peacock in *Thatcher's Theatre: British Theatre and Drama in the Eighties* published in 1999. In 2008 Olivia Turnbull's *Bringing Down the House* illustrated her thesis of turn-of-the-century crisis in regional theatres with detailed case studies of the particular circumstances that caused closure or change of use in selected producing theatres.[132]

The problem with what can only be described as a tunnel-vision version of history is that it fails to see the complexity of the wider landscape. Indeed, the topographical survey for 2000 will reveal that the steady growth of more regional small enterprises based on an alternative business model, boosted by the greater devolved powers granted to regional arts associations, was adding yet more layers to the landscape of community activity. There is no doubting, as Ros Merkin's recent examination of frequently haphazard and contested attempts at regional devolution has demonstrated, the succession of funding crises which hit regional building-based theatres through into the 1990s.[133] But the triangular relationships between the Arts Council, local authorities and what became known as Regional Arts Boards were very much locally specific, and where the dynamic was supportive, producing theatres survived albeit within constantly changing trading circumstances.

In a series of essays published between 1996 and 2010, former ACGB drama director (1986–94) Ian Brown, together initially with Rob Brannen, presented a much more nuanced account of funding history, grounded in the first instance on direct experience of the process behind the publication of the 1986 *Theatre IS for All* inquiry chaired by Sir Kenneth Cork, and of the governmental pressures and individual personalities which shaped it.[134] As Brown admits in his explication of the Platonic 'noble lie': that is, that the guardian elite can prove to be 'self-serving and self-justifying' while confident that they act in the best interests of those they serve, conflicts of sincerely held values are nevertheless 'unavoidable in a pluralist democracy'.[135] But what also comes across is that the greatest tension fundamental to the principle of subsidy lies in estimations of artistic quality and 'deservedness', and the recognition that companies both as artistic and business constructs come to the end of their useful life giving way to new initiatives.[136] The deeper-rooted problems lay with the failure to keep pace with rising costs, much more complex organisational demands and decaying building fabric. Stabilisation, which was also introduced in Scotland, where among the beneficiaries were the deficit-troubled Edinburgh Royal Lyceum and, for different reasons, the Glasgow Citizens' Company,[137] was designed to give companies a fresh start by clearing major debts, but it also demanded that a rigorous process of business 'change' should be contemplated.

Claimants with an annual turnover of at least £250,000 and annual audiences in excess of 25,000 had to compete with each other. The Bristol Old Vic was turned down. West Yorkshire Playhouse still plagued with outstanding new building debts was awarded £2 million.[138] Birmingham Rep's award cleared a development debt burden of £1.5 million. This had hung over the joint management of artistic director Bill Alexander and executive producer John Stalker since an ill-advised 1991 building extension, encouraged by the City Council, had both failed to raise the additional funds to pay for it and failed to bring in the anticipated additional revenue in set-building contracts and conference facilities. I have described in considerable detail elsewhere the intensive process in which the company was encouraged with the 'technical assistance' of externally provided theatre management consultants to scrutinise every aspect of its business operation and the extent to which this too failed.[139] In late 2000 when Alexander felt compelled to resign, his vision of an exemplary regional producing theatre of equivalent status to the national metropolitan companies had been defeated. The deep fault-line in the core–periphery relationship appeared intractable. The business model adopted did not offer a panacea, and perhaps most significantly the 'purity' in the regional context of the producing theatre ethos had to be modified to accommodate the plurality of the communities which it served. Yet again third-sector migration had to be held in reasonable equilibrium in order to succeed.

In 1999 the consultants Peter Boyden Associates were commissioned by ACE to undertake a review of 'The Roles and Functions of the English Regional Producing Theatres'. The report published in 2000 emphasised the wealth of creative product that each company brought to its specific environment. It also concluded that '20 years of strategic confusion and funding attrition' had brought many theatres to an alarming 'deficit-stable' position.[140] The immediate prospect at that time was a government commitment of £25 million of grant-aid to enable companies to put their creative and financial strategies on a securer footing. But it was also clear that public funding was never going to be unconditional. The business of theatre had to continue to adapt to whatever the macroeconomic conditions brought in the future.

CHAPTER 7

The changing demographic of performance

Demographic change manifests itself in the way the conditions of life in communities change over time. It is experienced both physically and psychologically in movement across particular kinds of community boundaries, be it the imagined communities of specific ethnicities or communities created by socio-economic or political categories and structures. In her discussion of social formations of identity and the power relations which control them, the geographer Cindi Katz has stated that 'all societies are relational in that they are produced through uneven social relations that create and maintain particular identifications and formations of difference'. 'Under contemporary conditions,' she claims, 'the most formidable sources of power remain capitalist production, patriarchy and racism.'[1] All three impacted on the way the British theatre community divided and subdivided into different spatial locations and categories of cultural practice throughout the century. Where uneven social relations were renegotiated success or failure often depended on the actions of the 'knowledge elite', who both exercise and broker power extending far beyond the actual physical boundaries of where they are located.

In the case of social formations of class which I want to address in the first part of this chapter, I would wish to argue that the social mobility, which produced the phenomenon of the 'new' actor, was primarily enabled by opening up access to local spaces of metropolitan power during the 1950s and 60s. It was limited and it was gendered. Women did not achieve the same degree of mobility during this period. Where greater fluidity of access was subsequently achieved was through the medium of television. The spatial effects of this new medium of mass communication could more readily cross social categories. Although spatially controlled within the domestic space, it nevertheless permitted the visual representation of hitherto marginalised 'other' communities on a previously unimaginable scale.

Television far more than radio also offered windows to selected communities within the other nations of the UK, in particular to Scotland in the 1960s where the widely disseminated success of popular drama series starring Scottish actors began to make native voices and settings professionally advantageous. Theatre produced in Scotland in the 1960s and 70s began to reflect a renewed confidence in Scottish national aspirations. The discovery of rich oil fields off the north coast of Scotland and the resultant debate about which 'nation' should benefit began to increase pressure on the Scottish-British Union. At the same time the flow of capital interests in the wake of the flow of oil was more international than national, reconfiguring migratory patterns and raising questions about economic alignment yet again.[2] What became clear was that it was possible to imagine more dynamic theatre communities within Scotland made stronger by a multiplicity of agents of change.

The most profound demographic change, however, literally altered the face of the nation and disrupted any monolithic concept of British identity and, indeed, challenged the legitimacy of imagined cultural distinctiveness in all the component nations of the UK. If Katz is correct and racism remains one of the most formidable sources of power, then it was clearly still exercising a malign influence at the end of the century. Indeed, in 2001, the first year of the new century, there was an explosion of anger about what had become known as 'institutional racism' as experienced by theatre artists from migrant communities.[3] Nevertheless, compared with the conditions of life experienced by British migrants from the former colonies half a century earlier, there had been a considerable widening of opportunity. What had not significantly changed, however, were the structural power relations which remained profoundly unequal.

EDUCATION, TRAINING AND 'NEW' ACTORS

As the previous chapter has charted, pressures on theatre institutions were imposed through fluctuating government policy and the associated economic climate. However, to take the historical long view, over a half century, is to see how the national *mentalité* formed and reformed in awareness of social divisions and the implications for greater equality. Also, it is important not to forget that the structural changes that increased the velocity of social mobility had their roots in the social and educational initiatives of the 1920s and 30s. The availability of free places in maintained grammar schools, which had offered selected numbers of bright working-class children academically ambitious educational opportunity not predicated on the ability to pay, had been gathering momentum since 1907. As described in chapter 4, purposeful leisure-time activity was also deployed to stimulate potential in children who proved less receptive to the formal curriculum.

While the 1944 Education Act did indeed represent a watershed in social engineering designed to benefit the children born after the early 1930s, the subsequent exposure of the flawed thinking based on unexamined hierarchical attitudes, which meant that education could continue to reinforce structural inequality, especially for girls, served to ensure that education would continue to be an ideological battleground for the rest of the century.[4] The opportunities that opened up post-war for a relatively small proportion of the 1930s and 40s' generation destined by birth to low socio-economic status arose primarily through admission to elite educational institutions: long-established traditional grammar schools (and their Scottish equivalents), universities, especially Cambridge and Oxford, and, for a significant proportion of the actors who achieved national recognition, through subsidised places at the most prestigious of the metropolitan drama schools.

That 'a new type of actor', as Michael Sanderson puts it, began to emerge in the 1950s within the context of more state-assisted social mobility is undeniably true. The phenomenon of the working-class 'scholarship boy' vaulting, via the educational system, over sometimes multiple social boundaries was an important component in the growing climate of cultural challenge. Moreover, it contributed an extra dimension of individual social dislocation and class anxiety to the literary and theatrical 'angry young man' and 'kitchen-sink' constructs of popular parlance. But as my discussion of the class basis of the amateur movement in the interwar years makes clear, the category of 'worker' is very complex with innumerable gradations of social function and status. Sanderson states simply that 'the post-war profession was taking its entrants from a somewhat different social spectrum than had the previous generations'.[5] The spectrum was not only quite broad, but opportunity came by a variety of means, which included old, if rapidly contracting, industrial practice, and it tended to favour men more than women. The perceived authenticity of social difference was also an issue, with the sheer serendipity of place of birth a contributory factor in fitting the new model. The combination of new dramatic writing for screen as well as stage and the challenges presented by the directorial ambitions leading the new national companies – and I include the English Stage Company in that category – made significantly greater artistic and intellectual demands on actors.

In her autobiography *Private Faces*, the Welsh actress Siân Phillips describes her perplexity in 1956 at the Royal Court cult of working-class anger which seemed to her 'as a *foreigner* [my emphasis] it all seemed to be part of the bottomless English preoccupation with class'. The Welsh-speaking extended family of farmers, miners, and teachers Phillips was born into in 1934 near the Black Mountain range in South-East Wales, was emblematic of what for her was 'a truly classless society', grounded as her recollections make abundantly clear in physically hard work. In mid-50s' London:

> There was a rush to portray people who didn't belong. I didn't 'belong' but it didn't bother me much and I didn't recognize myself in any of the plays I saw or read. I was asked to go to the Royal Court for a chat and spent a depressing hour with a group of middle-class people in working-class disguise who told me a lot of things about the importance of the working-class point of view. The concept of the daring, strong, powerful, articulate working-class woman, familiar to me from childhood, was not, I felt, one that would fit in any framework devised in SW1 and to mention such a creature would be tactless.[6]

Bilingual since childhood, and by the age of thirteen manoeuvring between regular broadcasting for BBC Radio Wales in Cardiff and grammar school education in Pontardawe, the valorisation of 'characters speaking with regional accents or 'lower class' accents as somehow more 'real' and genuine than characters who spoke with standard English accents was another source of skepticism.[7] For all that 1950s' 'New Wave' drama has been historically foregrounded in scholarly analysis, the reality as evidenced in pragmatic theatre programming policies, especially outside London, was that roles that required theatre actors to exploit the vocal distinctiveness of their class and regional origins were comparatively rare and, ultimately, professionally limiting. For most actors the ability to speak standard English was an essential prerequisite for career flexibility.

Robert Stephens, born in Bristol in 1931 the son of a violent shipyard labourer, had unimpeachable bottom-rung credentials to qualify as a new actor. He went to 'an ordinary secondary school' but won prizes for verse speaking, and through the National Association of Boys Clubs was introduced to acting. Courtesy of a Bristol local authority scholarship in 1949, he was sent to train in Esmé Church's acting school in Bradford in what was to become subsequently the Northern heartland of regional vocal authenticity. Scathing in later life of what he called 'this slack-jawed, regional, lazy nonsense' as applied to classical acting, he was clear at the outset that he needed to lose his Somerset accent. 'When I was training,

I knew that I wouldn't get on unless I did something about my voice. If I was going to talk like a country bumpkin then that was all I could expect to be playing. And I didn't want that.'[8]

The acting school based at the Bradford Civic Playhouse was set up by Esmé Church in the immediate post-war period consciously to challenge metropolitan hegemony.[9] Historically, geographically and artistically she operated on the cusp of change. As an actress and former assistant to Tyrone Guthrie – she directed Edith Evans and Michael Redgrave in the 1937 Old Vic *As You Like It* – Church trained students including Stephens, Bernard Hepton, Tom Bell and Edward Petherbridge in the disciplines of classical acting. But she also engaged Rudolf Laban, who ran his Art of Movement Studio in Manchester between 1948 and 1955, to work on movement training. While Stephens states that most of his fellow students were middle class, Church's attempts to identify and develop acting talent in young people created some significant individual convergences. As early as 1943, Billie Whitelaw, whose father before his early death in wartime Bradford was a foreman electrician,[10] and William Gaskill, the son of a local grammar-school master, were both members of Church's Saturday morning children's class. Gaskill later wrote that 'it was there that I first learned about directing and her very simple explanations of the texts of *Twelfth Night* and *The Tempest* have stayed with me ever since'. Tony Richardson, two years older, the son of a pharmacist and a close neighbour of Gaskill's, was less impressed and formed his own Young Theatre before both he and Gaskill went up to Oxford in 1948. Richardson, in an early prophetic gesture as 'part of a generation elbowing its way into the Establishment by glorying in its provincial vitality … proudly kept his Yorkshire accent',[11] while entering the Oxbridge magic circle which now exerted even more power than in the pre-war era.

Stephens, who like Whitelaw became a member of Laurence Olivier's National Theatre Company at the Old Vic in the early 1960s, was something of an exception in his generation of high-flying theatre artists in not attending a grammar school. Before the 1944 Act Whitelaw had passed an examination to qualify her for secondary education at Thornton Grammar School just outside Bradford.[12] At the same time she was also broadcasting semi-professionally on a regular basis from Manchester for BBC North Region's *Children's Hour*. She and Siân Phillips were amongst a growing number of young people providing much needed radio voices. But what also comes across in auto/biographical accounts is the effect of drama and performance taught both academically, and as an extra-curricular activity, often by charismatic teachers committed to widening access to the benefits of a traditional grammar-school ethos.

Famously, Richard Burton, born Richard Jenkins in 1925, in Pontrhydyfen, South Wales, the son of a miner, took his teacher's name, a part of the process of remaking himself.[13] Clifford Williams, who by the 1960s was directing in Peter Hall's Royal Shakespeare Company, was born in Cardiff in 1926, the son of a plumber, but was educated in London at Highbury County Grammar School, a newly established 1920s' grammar school in a working-class catchment area.[14] Hall himself, as is well known, was born in 1930 the son of a railway clerk.[15] After winning a place at the Perse School in Cambridge paid for by the local authority, the path to St Catherine's College, Cambridge, was leavened by a series of influential school masters.[16] In the case of Albert Finney, who became one of the first of the vocally distinctive new actors, the fact that he was younger, born in 1936, the son of a Salford bookmaker, was an added advantage. Bright, but not academic, at Salford Grammar School he was encouraged to act and then steered towards an application to RADA in 1953 where his classmates were Alan Bates (Belper Grammar School, Derby) and Peter O'Toole (Catholic school educated in Leeds).[17]

The ultimate influential school master was Michael Croft, whose productions of Shakespeare at Alleyn's school in Dulwich, in South London, between 1950 and 1955 laid the foundation for the boys' theatre group which eventually evolved into the National Youth Theatre of Great Britain. While not conceived as a drama school as such, annual production activity (exclusively classical until 1966) provided a space for individual growth and creativity for boys up to the age of 21. Girls were not admitted until 1960. Indeed, Helen Mirren, who played Cleopatra for the company at the age of 18 in the mid-1960s, described being 'psychologically tortured as a girl'.[18]

As an offshoot of Alleyn's, the public school element within the membership was another potential early barrier, but Derek Jacobi, an East London grammar-school boy whose parents ran a sweet shop and tobacconist, acted with the group in 1957 before going up (another scholarship boy) to St John's College, Cambridge, in 1958.[19] Oxbridge remained an important launch pad. Ian McKellen, brought up in Wigan the son of a civil engineer, went to St Catherine's College in 1959, while his near contemporary Trevor Nunn, whose father was an Ipswich cabinetmaker, was at Downing. The next step for all three, as it was for Albert Finney, Alan Bates and Peter O'Toole, was regional repertory theatre. Finney, and subsequently Jacobi, joined the Birmingham Rep company. O'Toole went to the Bristol Old Vic. Alan Bates joined the Midland Theatre Company before creating the role of Cliff in *Look Back in Anger* at the Royal Court in 1956. McKellen went to the Coventry Belgrade in 1961, followed by Nunn who was awarded an ABC director traineeship in 1962.[20]

To be sure the spectrum of regional and social origin widened, and structural change within the educational system, including crucially the provision of local authority grant-aid, brought actors and directors into the theatre capable of representing areas of submerged societal experience with a hitherto unprecedented degree of authenticity. But the actors who benefited from new admission policies, operated by most notably John Fernald, who became principal of RADA in 1954,[21] were highly trained in the standard British theatre repertoire. Arguably innovation lay not so much in new *actors* but in new *acting* and the calibre of performer capable of responding to new influences. By the time Finney gave his chilling 1960 performance as the cocksure Nottingham cycle factory worker, Arthur Seaton, in *Saturday Night and Sunday Morning*, the most celebrated of the Woodfall film adaptations of the new social realist novels,[22] he had played substantial Shakespearean roles in the final season of the Shakespeare Memorial Theatre[23] as well as Birmingham Rep.[24] Tom Courtney, who took over the stage role of Billy Fisher in *Billy Liar* from Finney in 1961, followed immediately by the Borstal boy Colin Smith in Richardson's film of *The Loneliness of the Long Distance Runner*, came from a family of workers in Hull's fish docks. There was the same pattern of grammar-school drama but in Courtney's case this led to three years at University College London before RADA in 1958. His professional debut was in Chekhov at the Old Vic.[25] With the exception of Derek Jacobi whose career trajectory took him straight from Birmingham Rep to Olivier's proto-National Theatre Company in Chichester, a common factor was Northern England origins. The North was no longer the hub of Britain's industrial wealth, but a cultural capital had begun to accumulate round the trope of 'gritty northern realism' which was to prove artistically, and by extension professionally and economically, very rewarding.

At a time when the availability of grammar-school places for girls[26] was capped, and there was continuing pressure for young women to fulfil traditional domestic roles rather than careers, the women graduating from the best-known drama schools who then went on to establish themselves successfully in the theatre (Julie Christie, Frances de la Tour, Judi Dench, Susan Fleetwood, Sara Kestelman) tended to come from firmly middle-class/professional backgrounds. Glenda Jackson, who went to RADA in 1957, was an exception in that she was a Birkenhead bricklayer's daughter but she was also educated at West Kirby County Grammar School.[27] Frances Cuka, who created the role of Jo in Joan Littlewood's produc- tion of *A Taste of Honey*, had trained at the Guildhall School of Speech and Drama and as a schoolgirl in Hove had broadcast regularly for the BBC. Rita Tushingham, whom Tony Richardson cast as Jo in his film of *A Taste of Honey*, was a Liverpudlian who began her professional career as an ASM at the Liverpool Playhouse when she was 16. But she had been educated at the very well-resourced La Sagesse Covent School and was enrolled at the College for Dance and Drama, which the dance specialist Shelagh Elliot-Clarke established in Liverpool in 1925.

As the original author of both the play and film scripts of *A Taste of Honey*, Shelagh Delaney (an 11 plus failure) stood out as a rare female voice amongst the New Wave writers whose stories of frustrated hopes and blighted lives reached the stage and screen in the mid to late 1950s and early 60s. The female characters, either youthful objects of desirable social status and freedom, or older and victimised by the aspiring and/or embittered male-authored, working-class male protagonists of *Look Back in Anger*, *Room at the Top*, *Billy Liar*, *This Sporting Life*, *A Kind of Loving*, *Saturday Night*, were played by actresses from middle-class backgrounds (Mary Ure, Helena Hughes, Claire Bloom, Heather Sears, June Ritchie, Julie Christie).[28] Rachel Roberts, who played opposite Albert Finney in *Saturday Night* and then Richard Harris in *This Sporting Life*, gave award-winning perform- ances as older, sexually unawakened working-class northern women, but she was Welsh 'gentility', the daughter of a Baptist minister, graduate of the University of Wales at Aberystwyth and then RADA.[29] What was import- ant was not so much actual class origin, but the ability to play convincingly a broader range of experience.

In what is thought of chronologically as the first of the New Wave films *Room at the Top* (1958), the archetypal working-class, upwardly mobile Joe Lampton was played by Lithuanian-born, South African-educated Laurence Harvey (another RADA graduate). For the pivotal role of the older, unhappily married woman Lampton falls in love with, the film producers introduced an element of European erotic appeal by casting the French actress Simone Signoret, a strategy which was also designed to be a box-office draw.[30] A similar commercially driven decision cast Richard Burton as Jimmy Porter in the film of *Look Back in Anger*, rather than Kenneth Haigh who created the role at the Royal Court.[31] The other strong contender for the role of Alice in *Room at the Top* was Pat Phoenix with absolutely authentic credentials: working class, born in Manchester and with ten years professional experience as an actress, but without the allure of continental otherness which Signoret possessed. Two years later Phoenix's class and regional origins were put to more credible use for what became the iconic, tempestuous working-class woman, Elsie Tanner, in Granada Television's new soap opera *Coronation Street*.[32]

TELEVISION AND THE POPULAR ACTOR

The importance of television as a means of transmitting broader perspectives on the heterogeneity of British society to a mass audience cannot be overestimated. Indeed, I would argue that this had a much profounder effect on the demographic changes experienced by both artists and audiences than the wider perspectives presented in the theatre. Richard Hoggart, whose own roots as a cultural critic lay in the Leeds urban working class, was deeply suspicious of the commercial degradation he associated with the 'all-smelling, all-touching, all-tasting TV'.[33] Robert Hewison points to the irony that Hoggart's lament in *The Uses of Literacy* for the solidarity of pre-war working-class life centred on 'groups of known streets, on their complex and active group life' was published only three years before the 'mythopoeic' soap opera *Coronation Street* was launched in 1960.[34] By the end of the century there was a whole sector of actors whose training and employment were focused almost exclusively on television. But the *Street* actors and, indeed, all the others in the 1950s and 60s who became household names in soap operas, comedy series and played leading roles in the one-off serious television drama were essentially theatre actors. The fact that drama of all genres was transmitted live in the early years meant that the skills of fast line-learning based on limited rehearsal time, sure footedness (literally) in and around the studio performance spaces and rapid response to unexpected crises, all of which had been acquired through the rigours of weekly and fortnightly rep opened up a new and infinitely more lucrative phase of employment opportunity.

At the point when Pat Phoenix was cast as Elsie Tanner, her stage career, along with many others of her generation who had entered regional repertory in the late 40s and early 50s, was effectively over, reduced to little more than film extra work. The much-loved *Coronation Street* cast, who included Violet Carson, Margot Bryant, Lynne Carol, Doris Speed, Arthur Lowe and Jack Howarth, were mostly veterans of the northern repertory and variety circuits and worked together as a true ensemble.[35] These actors, through the characters they played, the dominant naturalism and the accents and speech patterns which were deployed, brought recognisable 'ordinariness' into the nations' living rooms. Whatever the antipathy of the spokesmen of what Sinfield called 'left-culturalism',[36] the franchise holders of commercial television instantly tapped into popular sensibility, forcing BBC managers to recognise that even their success-ful soap opera *The Grove Family* was too genteel and too southern, as it mixed suburban, lower-middle-class domesticity with public service information.[37]

A stroke of programming genius that saw the 'original, live and *popu-lar*' Armchair Theatre series scheduled after *Sunday Night at the London Palladium* effected a coup which brought the top-rated variety show together with new plays by writers like Alun Owen, Alan Plater, Ted Willis, Robert Muller and Harold Pinter as a complete Sunday evening entertainment package.[38] The outcome of the remit given to the Canadian producer Sydney Newman by ABC Television in 1958 was to 'shake loose the metropolitan, theatrical and patrician codes which had defined the role of television drama in a public service era'.[39]

Although the production process accommodated actors' other profes-sional commitment – plays were presented on Sundays as theatres were closed and rehearsals tended to take place in London – transmission was from ABC's studio in a converted cinema in Didsbury, Manchester, so the physical site of production had shifted. Newman's interest in 'agi-tational contemporaneity'[40] created formal and thematic synergies with the strand of social realism in theatre, which was evident in the work of John Osborne and Arnold Wesker, for example, and which immediately required the naturalistic acting skills which had emerged through the educational and training opportunities discussed earlier. Thus actors such as Billie Whitelaw, Colin Blakely, Jack Hedley, Tom Bell, Alfred Lynch and Peter McEnery were cast in plays that included Alun Owen's *No Trams to Lime Street* (1959) *Lena, O My Lena* (1960) and *After the Funeral*. Ted Willis, whose *Women in a Dressing Gown* with Yvonne Mitchell as the central character was transmitted in June 1956, and arguably, pre-empted some of the gendered preoccupations of *Look Back in Anger*, sub-sequently focused on rising racial tensions.[41] His stage play *Hot Summer Night*, first seen at London's St Martin's Theatre, featured the Jamaican actor Lloyd Reckford as a black factory worker whose relationship with the daughter of a white trade union official exposes unacknowledged racial prejudice. The play opened in November 1958 just a few months after race riots took place in Notting Hill. The Armchair Theatre broad-cast the following February would have brought the issues to a much wider audience.[42]

It has been suggested that Harold Pinter's first television play *A Night Out*, shown a few days before *The Caretaker* opened at the Arts Theatre in London in April 1960, was watched by 6.4 million viewers.[43] If *The Caretaker* was the play that really turned the tide of critical opinion in Pinter's favour, it was Armchair Theatre that disseminated his name and style to a majority audience. There were also later attempts to create more linkage between television and theatre in the short-lived Stables Theatre venture led by former Granada production trainee and artistic director of the Edinburgh Traverse Theatre, Gordon McDougall. Launched in 1969, with a theatre converted from a stable in the builders' yard on Liverpool Station road in Manchester, actors such as Richard Wilson, Maureen Lipman, John Shrapnel and Zöe Wanamaker moved among as many as 13 theatre shows, 12 television shows and 'countless late-night and lunch-time pieces' in a single year. Despite the important new writers, including Trevor Griffiths, whose work was staged, and the critical excitement which this generated, what McDougall later described as a 'Frankenstein's monster' was deemed economically unviable and shut down in 1971.[44]

Independent Television's early success 'scared the BBC', as John Caughie puts it, into a recognition that artistic product had to become more relevant to viewers' lives.[45] Under Hugh Carleton Greene as director general, Sydney Newman was poached from ABC, and introduced the 'Wednesday Play' (1964–70), which was to bring on another generation of writers. The other important innovation was the police drama *Z Cars* (1962–78), created by Troy Kennedy Martin and set in a fictional Northern overspill town of Newtown and the neighbouring Seaport. From a popular culture perspective, the series was the first of the tough cop/detective genre which was to become so dominant into the twenty-first century. From a socio-political perspective, especially in the hands of the first writers John McGrath, John Hopkins and Allan Prior, the police narrative was a structural device to enable the 'finding out about people's lives' not, as McGrath later stated, because of interest in policemen as such.[46] The topographical allusion to Liverpool as an intra- and inter-national melting pot enabled a range of characters and thus actors who were much less solidly identified with one homogeneous identity. The creation of a 'new town' so typical of 1960s' urban regeneration strategies offered insights into the problems of communities in flux. The actors reflected this. The setting was northern working class but the actors' voices evidenced migratory patterns: Joseph Brady, Glaswegian working class, trained at the Royal Scottish Academy of Music and Drama; James Ellis, Queen's University, Belfast, and the Bristol Old Vic School; Jeremy

Kemp born in Chesterfield, trained at Central; Brian Blessed, a miner's son born near Doncaster, trained in Bristol; John Woodvine, from South Shields and RADA-trained. Terence Rigby and John Thaw were contemporaries of Tom Courtenay at RADA.

BORDER CROSSINGS

The televisual transmission of individuals whose voices evoked other regional and national interests broadened the scope of demographic representation and as a by-product added an extra dimension to the national feeling, which grew steadily in the 1960s and 70s, especially in Scotland. But the individual and corporate tensions around the core–periphery relationship remained. The sheer expense of producing television drama meant that UK network priorities had to take precedence over more nuanced local narratives and identities to be found in the population of the smaller nations.[47] *Dr Finlay's Casebook*, a hugely popular BBC networked series (1962–71) which brought together veteran Scottish-born, but primarily English stage-oriented, actor Andrew Cruickshank with former Scottish radio announcer Bill Simpson to play senior and junior doctors in a small-town medical practice in interwar Scotland, capitalised on Kailyard-style rural nostalgia.[48] Conversely, the other stereotype of the macho, urban Scottish 'hard man' underpinned the trend for crime dramas which in series such as London Weekend Television's *Budgie* made Iain Cuthbertson playing Glaswegian gangster Charlie Endell one of the most recognisable actors on 1970s' TV. *The View from Daniel Pike* (BBC2 1971–3) saw ex-Unity and Glasgow Citizens' actor Roddy McMillan cast as the eponymous tough private investigator and debt-collector Pike.[49]

Even if reinforcing national stereotypes, the raised popular profile of distinguished Scottish theatre actors including McMillan and Cuthbertson did mean that the Scottish voice could be a professional asset and thus be retained in a creative equilibrium with the English dimension of the British construct. The Glasgow College of Dramatic Art, established in 1950 as part of the Royal Scottish Academy of Music, began to produce new generations of Scottish actors, albeit trained to be effectively bilingual – 'naturally' speaking with an English accent, but capable of assuming different Scottish voices. Edinburgh-born Ian Richardson graduated from the College with the James Bridie Gold Medal in 1957, but went straight to Birmingham Rep and then to the new RSC with all traces of his native accent obliterated.[50] By the late 1960s young graduates of what had matured into the Royal Scottish Academy of Music and Drama had more immediately available, if not necessarily entirely secure, local sources of professional employment. Ambitious theatre artists such as Ian McDiarmid, Tom Conti and Brian Cox still took the classic migrant route south, but there was more flexible movement and creative cross-border exchange as home-grown opportunities began to grow.

Iain Cuthbertson and his near contemporary Tom Fleming represented an older generation of Scottish actors who achieved recognition within the English metropolitan system but remained actively committed to Scottish institutional innovation. Fleming developed a lucrative and lengthy parallel career as the silky-voiced BBC commentator on royal and other state events. In 1953 he provided a commentary on Queen Elizabeth's coronation in London, but in the same year was a co-founder with the dramatist Robert Kemp and the actress Lennox Milne of the Edinburgh Gateway Theatre Company, which aimed to prioritise Scottish dramatic writing played by Scottish actors.[51] Subsequently, three seasons of leading roles with Peter Hall's RSC were followed in 1965 by an invitation to lead the new Royal Lyceum Theatre Company which, by mutual consent, superseded the Gateway. Fleming's inaugural production of *The Servant O' Twa Maisters*, Victor Carin's Scots language version of the Goldoni original, was played by a cast which included Cox and Conti working with veterans such as Russell Hunter, Una McLean and Eileen McCallum.[52]

Fleming's ambitious attempt to forge a policy that was both firmly Scottish in its allegiance and artistically outward looking was mirrored by Cuthbertson's even more ambitious venture in Perth two years later. Both were forced to admit defeat after only a few months largely because of nervousness generated by box office shortfalls. Cuthbertson had worked at the Gateway, but his most prominent experience had been as an actor and then, 1962–5, director of productions at the Glasgow Citizens'. His response to calls for a more international repertoire saw Albert Finney playing the title role in Pirandello's *Henry IV* and Cuthbertson's own powerful performance as the sixteenth-century Scottish feudal chief in the premiere of John Arden's *Armstrong's Last Goodnight*. As associate director at the Royal Court in 1965, he continued his relationship with Arden, creating the role of Musgrave in *Sergeant Musgrave's Dance*.[53] The aim in Perth was a dynamic all-singing, all-dancing troupe of Scottish performers simultaneously resident at the theatre and on tour as 'The Gangaboots', exuberantly challenging the expectations of traditionalists and targeting young audiences.[54] Following his departure and in a sense picking up from where the company's much-loved founder Marjorie

Dence had left off, the appointment of the English director Joan Knight was intended to create 'a Theatre that belongs'. What was required at this point was local reassurance and stability.[55]

AGENTS OF CHANGE

It may not be unreasonable to suggest that the dilemmas and contradictions facing the Scottish theatre community in the 1970s were emblematic of the cultural complexity that resulted in the failure of the 1979 Scottish Devolution Bill. For Donald Smith attempting to tease out the different strands in Scottish theatre practice in this period, the 'uneasy combination of loyalties' which derived from dual Scottish/British identity did not necessarily signal continuing English dominance, but rather the importance of making theatre 'a legitimate expression of international cultural citizenship'.[56] That meant balancing initiatives to grow new native voices rooted in a distinctively Scottish culture, while avoiding narrow parochialism. The key agents of indigenous change and growth, along with the consolidation of the institutional and organisational strength of Scottish theatre, were both native and non-native crossing and re-crossing the national borders in response to a gathering sense that Scottishness, as Randall Stevenson puts it, was 'an asset' rather than a liability.

The policies of the two most radical venues that put theatre produced *in* Scotland on the international map: the Traverse in Edinburgh, producing new or cutting-edge drama from within the safe haven of club theatre status, and the Glasgow Citizens', focusing after 1969 on a revisioned European and British classical repertoire, refused any artistically compromised concessions to an indigenous Scottish tradition. Both theatres were inspirational albeit in very different ways. Of the series of artistic directors who followed on from the American Jim Haynes at the Traverse in the 1970s, none was Scottish but Gordon Smith singles out Chris Parr, director from 1975 to 1981, whose commitment to new Scottish writing 'caught the national mood ... as the political debate on nationalism gathered pace'.[57] The new writers, including Tom Gallacher, Tom McGrath, Hector Macmillan, John Byrne, Jimmy Boyle and C. P. Taylor, were showcased in the tiny 100-seater space created from a former sailmaker's loft. Seamlessly aligned with the metropolitan networks created by the Edinburgh International Festival, the Traverse was growing a reputation which would make it the only equivalent outside London of the dynamic small spaces in the British capital.

Inevitably, a tiny theatre with a small, if dedicated audience was not going to provide copious opportunities for actors. Also, in the predominantly male-authored, male-community-oriented plays of the 1970s, women were more marginalised as artists, audiences and protagonists.[58] In Glasgow the Citizen's Theatre with its prevailing camp ethos was a source of theatrical excitement to young Scottish actors in training, although as Michael Coveney has pointed out, comparatively few were recruited into the company.[59] Bill Paterson, trained at RSAMD and a qualified teacher, joined the Citizens Theatre for Youth group at a time which coincided with the beginning of Giles Havergal's controversial regime – 'the Citizens at its most outrageous and us going round schools trying to explain to head teachers why we were doing *Antony and Cleopatra* as Watusi warriors with leather thongs on'[60] – was an exception. So was David Hayman who played Hamlet in the scandal-provoking 1970 production and stayed for ten years. Ian McDiarmid, a 1968 Bridie Gold Medal winner, spent eighteen months with the company, but together with his future collaborator Jonathan Kent, went south in 1973 as part of a splinter group led by the director Keith Hack who wanted the validation of London success. Other, mostly English or English-trained company members, including young actresses such as Paola Dionisotti, Sian Thomas, Cheryl Campbell and Di Trevis, imbibed the rich stylistic nourishment provided by the repertoire and then took themselves off to consolidate their careers in England.[61]

A KIND OF FLOWERING

In 1970, the chairman of Scottish Equity, Alex McCrindle, declared that seventeen years after the actors' union had been set up in Scotland the lack of opportunity for young actors caused by the demise of Howard & Wyndham and the arrival of 'Oxbridge directors' bringing their own actors with them had created a 'catastrophic situation' forcing actors to go to London.[62] Certainly at a time when McCrindle was part of an attempt to sustain the short-lived Scottish Actors Company, the Traverse appeared to facilitate what was effectively an Oxbridge–Edinburgh axis. McCrindle's other primary targets would have been the Edinburgh-born, but Oxford-educated Havergal and Clive Perry, an Englishman and Cambridge graduate, who took over the directorship of the Royal Lyceum in 1966 following Fleming's resignation. He brought another Cambridge graduate, Richard Eyre, to assist him. By 1970 Eyre was director of productions at the Lyceum, directing a wide range of modern classic drama and new work.[63] Perry, meanwhile, enlarged his responsibilities to Edinburgh Corporation by combining the management of the King's and Church Hill theatres with the Lyceum to create what was hailed as a unique municipal group of touring, repertory and amateur theatre. None of these 'alien' directors was a novice in the business of running theatres and in each case there was a strong economic pragmatism despite, in the case of Havergal and Perry especially, radically different artistic temperaments.[64] Arguably what was gradually happening was that the metropolitan knowledge elite was creating a new kind of structural stability, which would provide the necessary conditions for more durable local initiatives.

Out of this emerged two other key individuals whose radical interventions in the early 1970s proved transformative for Scottish artists and audiences. Bill Bryden and John McGrath both straddled television and theatre across national boundaries and brought a dynamic local knowledge and political alignment. Greenock-born Bryden, who was appointed Associate Director to Clive Perry at the Lyceum in 1971, had started his career as a documentary scriptwriter for Scottish television. Subsequently a beneficiary of the ATV directors training scheme, he then worked as associate director at the Coventry Belgrade and the Royal Court.[65] McGrath, from a Liverpudlian Irish Catholic family, schooled in Wales, and at Oxford at the same time as Havergal, honed his writing skills at the Liverpool Everyman as well as with *Z Cars*, before setting up 7.84 Theatre Company in 1971 with his Scottish wife Elizabeth McLennan.[66]

As John Bett, a 7.84 (Scotland) founder member, later recalled, Bill Bryden's work with Scots language plays at the Lyceum started to generate 'an excitement, a kind of flowering of theatrical and cultural enterprise'.[67] Working with a company of Scottish actors of the calibre of Rikki Fulton, Fulton Mackay and Eileen McCallum, Bryden staged a series of groundbreaking productions beginning with Stewart Conn's non-naturalistic Scots-language *The Burning* in 1971, and then in 1972 drawing on his own family memories in *Willie Rough* about the fire-brand Greenock shipyard worker and strike leader. Roddy Macmillan's 1973 *The Bevellers* was set in a Glasgow glassworks, while Bryden's 1974 *Benny Lynch: Scenes from a Short Life* was based on the blighted life of the Scottish world flyweight boxing champion. As Stevenson puts it, 'the dramatic power of Scots speech in creating solidarities and immediacies of communication between stage and audience … helped to make the theatre a unique public space at the time'.[68]

Viewed as an event arising from a convergence of propitious circumstances, the establishment of 7.84 (Scotland) in 1973 can be seen as building on this new-found confidence. McGrath's hybrid heritage augmented by McLennan's Highland family roots imparted, as Ian Brown has recently suggested, a particular sensitivity to the historical and political complexity of the landscape the company encountered.[69] The Highlands were not virgin territory theatrically, given the touring legacy of companies such as the Scottish National Players and the Perth Theatre. But McGrath was able to recruit strongly versatile Scottish actors and musicians who quite literally embodied plural cultural traditions. Dolina MacLennan was a Gaelic singer from the Outer Hebrides. The musician Allan Ross whose ancesters had suffered in the Highland Clearances was a virtuosic, popular fiddle player. Bill Paterson, Alex Norton and John Bett were all 'discovered' by McGrath performing in *The Great Northern Welly Boot Show*, produced in Glasgow in 1972 and starring ex-shipyard worker and comedian Billy Connolly.[70]

Despite reservations expressed by Elizabeth McLennan about the show's unashamed sexism,[71] this exuberant satirical romp inspired by a Clydeside workers' strike was grounded in the popular vigour of Scottish variety theatre, which then became one of the essential ingredients of 7.84's *The Cheviot, the Stag and the Black, Black Oil*. Urban and rural Scotland converged in Paterson's and Norton's Glaswegian origins and Bett's Isle of Skye-influenced childhood. Indeed, Bett had already written and performed a play about the Highland clearances in Dundee.[72] The social 'event' of *The Cheviot*, rounded off by the traditional ceilidh which brought actors and audiences physically in touch in the same community-owned spaces, was subsequently more permanently memorialised in the 1974 BBC1 *Play for Today* version filmed live in Dornie village hall.[73]

Exposure to an unexpectedly large UK-wide domestic audience was not only a politically disruptive 'foray'[74] into an ideologically constrained mass media, but the surviving documentation has served the function of reifying the ephemeral performance moment, assisting in the transformation of a collection of memories about a small radical touring company into a historical event of iconic importance in Scottish theatre history. *The Cheviot* along with the subsequent work of 7.84 (Scotland) in the 1970s was just one strand of the strengthening Scottish theatre culture. It paved the way for other companies such as the breakaway Wildcat, Borderline and the longer-surviving Communicado.[75] However, 1979 brought what the Scottish political commentator Lindsay Paterson called 'the debacle of the referendum', when one-third of the Scottish population voted against devolution and one-third did not bother to vote at all. At the same time, however, he felt in Scottish theatre 'where – as throughout

Scottish culture at that time – there was a growing sense of Scottishness tied to a vague internationalism and a millenarian socialism'. Writing in 1994, only three years before the referendum which did bring devolution, he described an increasing acceptance of 'the immense complexity of politics and society', and in a scenario, which might well have applied to the cross-border relations of his native theatre as well as the evolving power balance of political relations, contemplated what might emerge from 'a conflict between the safety of managed autonomy and the risky but exciting prospects of participation'.[76]

BREAKING DOWN DOORS

Class, cultural identity, nationalism, constructs of race and ethnicity and, arguably, the most destabilising challenge to 'Britishness' as a unified concept, all converge in the history of attempts by non-white theatre artists of British migrant heritage to achieve employment and recognition in the theatre during the second half of the twentieth century. Historiographically, the narrative has been further complicated by the fragmented and inadequate published record, itself a product of marginalisation within the academy. Only in the first decade of the twenty-first century were more systematically researched extended histories published.[77] Furthermore, there are ongoing ideological tensions associated with constantly shifting nomenclature: from the initially emollient 'coloured', ultimately seen as insulting, to the universal 'Black' as an all-embracing political category, to the more culturally specific, albeit still portmanteau terms, Black British, British Asian, African-heritage, Asian-heritage, all indicative of classification anxiety grounded in racialist understanding of cultural difference.

Even the term 'Asian', as Jatinder Verma, the director of Tara Arts, the first fully professional Asian theatre company, has suggested, has its origins in a bureaucratic category invented in colonial Kenya in 1948 for the migrants or descendents of migrants from the Indian subcontinent.[78] Bureaucracy and the need to create statistical categories for census purposes were also responsible for the British Minority Ethnic (BME) classification. This, as the Parekh Report into multi-ethnic Britain published in 2000 points out, has the effect of marginalising and subordinating and, moreover, ignores the multiple ethnic complexity of the white population.[79] Despite the fact that Naseem Khan's 1976 report *The Arts Britain Ignores*[80] was in many ways ground-breaking in its mapping of the arts practised in different migrant communities, one of the principle objections raised against it was, in Kwesi Owusu's words, that it 'ushered in the period of

'Ethnic Minority Arts' policies'.[81] Faced with this marginalising tendency, the choice forced on struggling artists was whether to go down the route of accommodation and integration within the white 'mainstream', or to prioritise separate and, indeed, oppositional development.

In truth, it was never possible to separate black and Asian theatre from the politics of race and ethnicity, based, notwithstanding the UK's long history of migrant settlements, in anxieties around skin colour. As John Solomos has emphasised in his account of immigration legislation after 1945 and, in particular, the nine successive Acts placed on the statute books between 1962 and 1999, 'the question of immigration *per se* has become inextricably linked to black immigration, that is the arrival of migrants from the New Commonwealth and Pakistan'.[82] At the same time as both Conservative and Labour governments reacted to popular fears of alien invasion with increasing restrictions on rights of immigration, parallel legislation on race relations amounting to seven acts between 1965 and 2000,[83] all targeted at eliminating discrimination in housing, employment, education, etc. on racial grounds, signalled ambiguous and contradictory agendas. In the theatre there was no doubting visible evidence of increased opportunity in the last two decades of the century, but progress was slow and tended, as the experience of individual artists shows, to come in fits and starts. In an interview published in 1992, the British Guiana-born actor and singer Thomas Baptiste, who had been a founder member of the Actors Equity Advisory Committee on the employment of black actors, reflected on the extent of progress since his arrival in England in 1950:

There are now many more black people in this country, and many more black drama students at colleges, but they aren't getting the work. So it's funny when I'm asked whether there has been progress, because my whole career seems to have been about breaking down doors. Of course my experience is not a yardstick, but I would say that young actors today are having even more difficulty in getting their careers started than I did.[84]

The attempt to break down doors was, as I have shown, already underway by 1950, and from very early on it brought together British migrants who were far from homogeneous in their geographical, social and cultural origins. Because of the complex history of colonisation, slavery and settlement, the British-colonised Caribbean islands incorporated a range of ethnicities and linguistic heritage, all superimposed with an educational system which foregrounded British history and culture. Many of those who arrived to become aspiring actors and playwrights were ambitious, well-schooled in English literary and theatrical texts especially Shakespeare, and, often born into professional families, eager to extend their education. Carmen Munroe, after taking the Cambridge School Certificate in Guiana, came for that purpose in 1951 and initially worked in a South London library where her skin colour was an object of curiosity for local children. 'Blackness', however, is a physical palimpsest of multiple heritage. Yvonne Brewster, who arrived in 1956 from Jamaica to train at the Rose Bruford College of Speech and Drama, could trace a line of descent from grandparents who were a mixture of Polish Jew, Indian, Cuban and Scottish.[85] Mona Hammond, who was a co-founder of Talawa Theatre Company with Brewster and Munroe in 1986, emigrated from Jamaica in 1959 and was half Chinese and half black Jamaican.[86]

'Asian' identity was even more complex after each successive wave of migration between 1947 and the 1970s. The list published in the Parekh Report ranges amongst 'Bangladeshis, Gujaratis, Pakistanis and Punjabis; between South Asians, East Asians and Chinese; and between Hindus, Muslims and Sikhs'.[87] Jamila Massey, possibly the longest-serving professional actress in the British context, came from India in 1946. The director and film-maker Pervaiz Khan was born a Pakistani Moslem in Azad Kashmir and educated in Birmingham.[88] Jatinder Verma was born in Tanzania, educated in Kenya and defines himself as an East African Hindu Punjabi.[89] Each became part of the spectrum of British Asianness.

As the biography of Pauline Henriques showed, there were opportunities for high-level theatre training even before the Second World War. Zia Mohyeddin, who was born in Lahore before the creation of Pakistan, trained at RADA in 1953.[90] Jamaican-born Lloyd Reckford studied at Bristol Old Vic.[91] Mona Hammond won a scholarship to RADA in 1959.[92] In the early 60s, several South Asians including Alaknanda Samarth, Madhav Sharma, Roshan Seth and Renu Setna went to RADA.[93] But as Yvonne Brewster was told at the outset by Rose Bruford herself *because* she was Jamaican there would be no prospect of work.[94] However, 1956 was not just the fabled *annus mirabilis* in the development of new British drama, it was also (albeit not historically much noted) the year the Edric Connor Agency was established to promote, represent and protect the professional interests of Black, Afro-Asian, South and East Asian theatre, film and television artists.[95]

Both Trinidadians, Edric and Pearl Connor's commitment to emerging Caribbean and African national and political consciousness ensured that in London, they were part of the nexus surrounding leading black politicians and activists not just from the West Indies but also Africa and

America.[96] As a singer, actor, film-maker and champion of Trinidad's cultural identity, Edric Connor was well known in liberal progressive arts circles, frequently acting as an informal advisor and broker on artistic projects of non-European interest. Like the Guyanese Cy Grant who had served as an RAF navigator during the war and had qualified as a barrister in London before turning to the theatre and calypso singing,[97] Connor promoted traditional Caribbean music, especially folk and spirituals. Pearl Connor's training for a law degree at King's College ensured much of the legal backbone for what became the Afro-Asian Caribbean Agency, providing representation for black artists across all art forms. Faced with the near impossibility of artists achieving the necessary forty weeks of West End work required for an Equity card, the agency, run initially from the Connor home, created its own 'Spotlight' with photographs and individual artist details. Pearl Connor later claimed some 90 per cent of artists of colour were represented as well as a few 'Israelis and Anglo Saxons'. 'They felt at ease with us because we had a similar background ... we had all been ruled by other people and we were now becoming ourselves.'[98] Even so it was hard to combat the subaltern position imposed – albeit unacknowledged – by their white counterparts. Speaking in 1997, Pearl Connor recalled that:

the theatre establishment had no room for us ... we had a hidden colonial history, quite unknown to the producers and directors. There was no level of recognition. We belonged to the colonial past as second class citizens, nevertheless we knew more about their playwrights like Shakespeare, Dickens and Sheridan than they knew about us.

The signs in 1958 that black theatre artists were achieving greater recognition on white stages collided with more alarming evidence of growing social tension about rising levels of immigration. Edric Connor, cast as a calypso-singing Gower in Tony Richardson's production of *Pericles*, became the first black actor to appear at the Shakespeare Memorial Theatre.[99] The first professional productions of two plays by Black British writers, *Flesh to a Tiger* by Barry Reckford and *Moon on a Rainbow Shawl* by Errol John, were mounted at the Royal Court. Reckford's play staged in May was directed by Tony Richardson with an almost entirely Black cast which included the jazz singer Cleo Laine, Lloyd Reckford and Johnny Sekka.[100] Almost simultaneously the African American musical *Simply Heavenly* was given its London premiere, while in the same month Joan Littlewood's production of *A Taste of Honey* featured Jimmie Moore as the black sailor who leaves Jo pregnant.[101]

In late August, however, the first of the serious post-war race riots exploded in the St Ann's district of Nottingham,[102] followed only days later by Notting Hill. While poor living conditions and anger about growing unemployment were the root cause of each disturbance, what appears to have sparked the violence was resentment about relationships between black men and white women. As noted earlier in the chapter, Ted Willis's play *Hot Summer Night* with Lloyd Reckford, produced in November, was a clear response to the racism exposed by this comparatively unfamiliar phenomenon in British society. *Moon on a Rainbow Shawl* like *Flesh to a Tiger*, set respectively in Trinidad and Jamaica, were attempts to reflect on the lives left behind, the dreams and tensions derived from colonialism. What was groundbreaking about *Moon on a Rainbow Shawl* was its use of 'Nation Language': language that eschewed standard English in favour of the distinctive forms which had developed in the Caribbean.[103]

It is worth, however, being precise about the chronology surrounding the production of Errol John's play and the circumstances surrounding its Royal Court staging which impacted on its reception. As the winner in 1957 of the *Observer* play competition, it was optioned by Binkie Beaumont, deemed uncommercial, handed over to the not-for-profit Tennent Productions and directed by Frith Banbury, the doyen of the classic West End production. Not only was John persuaded to rewrite the play substantially, but the three leading characters were played by imported African American actors with Black British actors cast in secondary roles. The assumption that American actors performed to a higher standard died hard. After a poorly supported pre-London tour to Manchester, Leeds and Brighton, the production was offered to the Royal Court for opening in December 1958 – and thus after the riots – because it was considered too financially risky for the West End.[104]

Institutional racism grounded in unexamined prejudices and assumptions about artistic quality produced, as Deirdre Osborne has pointed out, 'a dynamic of paternalism and discrimination against black arts organizations and artists which was as inhibiting of creative endeavour as the limits imposed by racialising immigration legislation'.[105] There were attempts to set up autonomous black-led companies such as the New Negro Theatre Company and New Day Theatre Company, which mounted productions at the Theatre Royal Stratford East and at the Royal Court. Pearl Connor went on record as stating that George Devine and Oscar Lewenstein 'were the greatest friends black artistes ever had',[106] and certainly in 1960 the Royal Court produced further work by Barry

Reckford and presented Lloyd Reckford's double bill production of Derek Walcott's *Six in the Rain* and *The Sea at Dauphin*. In 1961 Lewenstein presented Roger Blin's English-language production of Genet's *The Blacks* with an all-black cast, as part of a season of French plays. Even so in 1963 Barry Reckford's play *Skivvers* was performed by blacked-up white actors at the Royal Court because it was claimed no suitable Black actors could be found. This was in the year Errol John played Othello at the Old Vic, the first recorded performance in the role by a professional Black British actor. Subject to white institutional hegemony, black artists were chronically positioned as subaltern.[107]

IMAGINED REALITIES

In her critical survey of how Black Britain has been represented on television, 'the primary site where the nation is imagined and imagines itself',[108] Sarita Malik argues that drama 'more unequivocally' represents rather than reflects society. 'There is no pre-given reality to reproduce in dramatic form, only a set of choices about *whom, how* and *what* to represent.'[109] Black and Asian actors anxious for work and recognition had to accept the implications of the imagined realities they were called on to represent and were not, as Colin Prescod explained in 1996, 'too critical of the hands held out to them by liberal Whites who wanted to do Black stuff'.[110] Television could in theory disseminate knowledge and fresh perspectives on a rapidly changing human landscape to a mass audience. What it did not, arguably would not, do was normalise the results of that change. Black and Asian migrant difference, their separateness as a demographic category, was emphasised from the beginning and was inevitably subject to stereotyping in dramatic roles. Despite fitful employment opportunities, however, television paid better and, indeed, as a result sometimes contributed to the instability of theatre companies which could not command unswerving commitment.

The two major complaints made by black actors were about, first, why in an increasingly hybridised society everyday roles normally played by white actors could not just as easily be played by black. Secondly, in a society where the workforce now included so many 'new' British employed in basic but vital roles such as nurses, bus conductors, machinists, postmen, etc., there appeared to be a complete disjunction between the way a monochrome white society was depicted on television and the multicoloured reality. In both theatre and television actors grew weary of being offered stereotypes. In Lloyd Reckford's case it was a succession of young black men in love with white girls. Carmen Munroe vowed to resist the kind of maid roles she played in her stage debut.[111]

Naturally, the agenda of white liberal producers and writers varied, sometimes, as in the examples of John Elliot and John Hopkins, markedly so. Elliot's 1956 drama documentary *A Man from the Sun* created from research in Brixton focused on relations between black and white in London's West Indian communities. What one later commentary describes as an 'instructional manual' that 'pulls many punches' about the West Indian experience emphasised the potential rewards of community cohesion.[112] The cast including Earl Cameron, Errol John, Cy Grant, Gloria Simpson and Nadia Cattouse, plus a large number of supporting actors found by the Connor agency, brought a relaxed Caribbean inflection to the live dialogue.[113] By 1967 when Elliot wrote, produced and directed the six-part BBC drama series *Rainbow City*, the landscape had changed considerably. Racial tensions had increased and the first wave of East African Asians had come to Britain from Kenya. Working, however, with the Trinidadian Horace James as co-writer and actor, and with music by the Guyanese actor and singer Ram John Holder, this short-lived project was more genuinely collaborative. The eponymous city was Birmingham; the central protagonists, a black lawyer and his white wife played by Errol John and Gemma Jones, were depicted in a middle-class environment, attempting professionally and personally to build bridges between the communities.[114]

Actors called on to represent John Hopkins's most uncompromising dramatic statements on racism were certainly given psychologically challenging roles to play. The Senegalese actor Johnny Sekka and the Indian actress Alaknanda Samarth were cast as a mixed Black African/Indian married couple in a 1964 *Z Cars* episode, 'A Place of Safety', faced with the collapse of their lives when the husband driven to despair attacks a white bailiff with an axe.[115] In the 1965 Wednesday Play *Fable*, which achieved notoriety when the BBC delayed transmission allegedly because of the tensions created by the Leyton by-election fought on immigration issues, Hopkins imagined a nation where apartheid had been reversed putting power over the white population into black hands.[116] In a mixed cast which included black actors such as Rudolph Walker and Frank Singuineau, Thomas Baptiste played a liberal black writer under house arrest in a totalitarian society, while Eileen Atkins and Ronald Lacey played a white couple suffering displacement, rape, castration and murder. Carmen Munroe later recalled, 'It was actually a very frightening piece to be in, because suddenly you were being asked to perform the sort of acts that were performed against you in real life.'[117] However, what Munroe saw as opening up new possibilities for black actors backfired with some audiences who read it as a warning against potentially barbaric black monsters.

Soap operas upped the ante on the who, how and what choices made by dramatic writers. From 1959 onwards when the Jamaican Joan Hooley was cast as an African doctor in the hospital soap opera *Emergency-Ward 10*, experienced first-generation black actors were given some limited story lines.[118] Typically, as Sarita Malik has emphasised, the 'slice of life' local realism was represented as white with token or underdeveloped black characters often functioning as 'narrative donors',[119] or as Carmen Munroe complained little more than set dressing. Not only as Equity's Coloured Artists Committee pointed out in 1974 was there a conspicuous paucity of the black presence in soap operas, but the increasingly diverse demographic of the viewing audience was also being ignored.[120] The rationale for the prevailing whiteness, given by an early *Coronation Street* writer, was that the long-term inclusion of black residents of 'the Street' would mean that 'unhelpful comments' put into the mouths of very familiar fictional characters might be dangerous, was a tacit admission that another kind of reality would have to address 'authentic' racism.[121] *Crossroads*, however, the Midlands-made and set soap opera, which tended to be derided for poor production values, was genuinely pioneering in integrated casting. The English-born, Trinidadian-heritage Cleo Sylvestre created a long-running character, while Renu Setna and Jamilla Massey played Asian shopkeepers.[122]

The emergence of the Guyanese playwright Michael Abbensetts, whose 1973 play *Sweet Talk* was staged at the Royal Court in the same week as his first television play *The Museum Attendant*, directed by Stephen Frears, was shown on BBC2, contributed to a fertile period of drama produced from BBC Pebble Mill in Birmingham.[123] In 1977, Abbensetts's play *Black Christmas*, also directed by Frears, was set in a Birmingham home on a disastrous Christmas Day. A family celebration turned into a family battle of frustration, lost hopes and longing for 'home' fought out by Norman Beaton, Shope Shodeinde, Stefan Kalipha and Janet Bartley and presided over by the appalled family matriarch played by Carmen Munroe. What was described as one of the best television dramas of the 1970s ended with the painful recognition that England is now home.[124]

Abbensetts's symbolically named drama series *Empire Road*, produced the following year for BBC2 and set in Handsworth in Birmingham, built on that recognition and extended the drama to a whole mixed

community. Norman Beaton, who played Everton Bennett, the leading community 'godfather' figure, and Rudolph Walker, who played the
competing landlord, Sebastian Moses, had both become well-known
black comic celebrities through the ITV sitcoms *Love Thy Neighbour* and
The Fosters, but *Empire Road* allowed the representation of a localised
reality which avoided stereotypes and allowed pain as well as humour.[125]
The fully integrated casting included Thomas Baptiste, Corinne Skinner-
Carter, Trevor Butler, Joseph Marcell with Asian actors Jamila Massey,
Tahir Mahmood and Nalini Moonasar. Birmingham Rep actress and director Sheila Kelley and locally born Julie Walters were among the white
actors. *Empire Road* was withdrawn in 1979 after the second series, which
had seen three episodes directed by the Trinidadian film-maker Horace
Ové who brought some unsettling West Indian brio into the recording
studio.[126] Internal institutional politics, economic and scheduling priorities, the fact that the 'highbrow' BBC2 channel was not natural viewing
for the target audience, all contributed to the loss of an important creative
project.

MAKING A HISTORY

Two edited collections of transcribed interviews with black actors and
writers were published in 1992 beginning the process of documenting
and thus effectively, making a history. In the case of *Black and White in
Colour, Black People in British Television Since 1936*, edited by the African
American film scholar Jim Pines, evidence goes back to before the Second
World War and has supplied much of the detail contained in the previous section. *Fringe First, Pioneers of Fringe Theatre on Record*, edited by
Roland Rees, ranges very widely over the record of 'New Theatre' in general from the 1960s through a series of conversations held almost entirely
with theatre-makers he had worked with. The recollections of black artists
including Norman Beaton, Stefan Kalipha, Oscar James and Mustapha
Matura, who migrated from the Caribbean as adults, and Claire Benedict
and Tunde Ikoli, who were brought up in England, not only describe the
enabling networks and alliances formed through the alternative movement in the late 1960s, but also generational differences.[127]

Benedict compares younger black actors asked to play roles set in the
Caribbean with Mona Hammond 'the island of her birth is within
her … it's her heritage, her culture. But young black Britons find it much
more difficult. They are concerned with what confronts them as someone
born here.'[128] Ikoli, born in London, the son of a Cornish mother and a

Nigerian father, described being unable to read the 'nation language' of Matura's dialogue at a Royal Court audition.[129] Ikoli, who went on to write the semi-autobiographical *Scrape off the Black*, was saved from the consequences of institutional ignorance by further opportunities offered by Oscar Lewenstein, but increasingly producers and directors had to become accustomed to black voices that were British, not Caribbean. Yvonne Brewster wrote of *Scrape off the Black* 'that arguably you could not get more English than this play'.[130] Cleo Sylvestre – born in England, white mother, black father – was given roles by Ken Loach in *Cathy Come Home* and *Up the Junction* in part because she spoke with a cockney accent.[131]

In *Fringe First*, Roland Rees himself and Foco Novo are foregrounded as pivotal in the development of the next phase of Black writing.[132] Rees directed the first short plays of Mustapha Matura, as an 'indigenous' counterpart to the new American black writers, staged at Ed Berman's InterAction, and then subsequently directed plays by Alfred Fagon as well as the later work of Tunde Ikoli.[133] What Matura describes as 'the whole kind of West Hampstead life' sums up another small navigable society of black migrants coming together to benefit from the alternative theatre scene of the late 1960s and early 70s. Rees' conversation,[134] however, took place in 1991 at the National Theatre where rehearsals for Matura's play *The Coup* were progressing, in itself indicative of how far the theatre establishment had been penetrated.[135]

Nevertheless, the interviews recorded in *Black and White in Colour* still convey a strong sense of disappointment that white contemporaries had experienced a smoother career trajectory. Despite a career which had revived and was far from over in 1991, Carmen Munroe describes the despair felt in the mid-1970s when there was 'not much point in even living'.[136] Judith Jacob, second generation and born in London, entered television in the late 1970s through the Anna Scher School (an increasingly influential training ground for young working-class actors) and worked with the Black Theatre Cooperative, commented on the lack of continuity in Black programming and the impossibility of Black British actors like Norman Beaton, Carmen Munroe and Rudolph Walker achieving the same star status as their American counterparts.[137]

RUBBING OUT THE COLOUR

Institutional racism was exacerbated by the historiographic failure to record and thus mediate to a wider public understanding the moments

when theatre artists were offered major opportunities in the British mainstream. Blatant inconsistencies in managerial policy continued in both
theatre and television with extraordinary lapses in time from potentially
one important casting decision to another. Milestones like Errol John's
performance as Othello were wiped from the historical record and further
obliterated by Laurence Olivier's much-lauded negroid impersonation in
1964. Cy Grant played Othello at the Phoenix Theatre in Leicester in
1965, a modest regional intervention which went largely unnoticed.[138] As
early as 1960 Zia Mohyeddin achieved a brief flurry of fame when he was
invited to play the role of Dr Aziz in an Oxford Playhouse adaptation of
Forster's *A Passage to India*, which was then taken up by Tennents and
transferred to the Comedy Theatre in the West End.[139] Five years later
he was invited to Birmingham Rep to play Shylock in Peter Dews's production of *The Merchant of Venice*, only a few months after Dews had
directed Michael Gambon as a blacked-up Othello.[140] Seven years after
that Akaknanda Samarth became the first Indian-heritage woman to
play with the National Theatre Company in John Dexter's British Raj-
set production of *Phaedra Britannica*. She was asked to darken her skin
to match the make-up of browned-up actresses.[141] In 1981 the impact of
Michael Rudman's bold experiment with an all-black cast for *Measure
for Measure* at the National Theatre, which included Beaton, Singuineau,
Kalipha, Bertice Reading and Yvette Harris, was undermined by the row
that erupted over the BBC's Television Shakespeare production of *Othello*.
Again there were allegedly no suitable Black British actors. But Equity's
refusal to allow Jonathan Miller to import the African American James
Earl Jones resulted in Anthony Hopkins playing a browned-up Moorish
Othello.[142]

Progress at the RSC was painfully slow although so-called 'colour-
blind' casting, i.e casting black actors in traditionally white roles, began
tentatively as far back as the 1960s. In an article published in *Marxism
Today* in 1984, which also attacked the company for structural conservatism and sexism, Paul Allen pointed to the failure to nurture good
black actors. He gave the example of Alton Kumalo cast in the 1960s in
roles 'at a level one or two steps up from spear-carrying' but no further,
and listed the supporting roles played by the 'intelligent, graceful and
thoughtful' Josette Simon up until that time.[143] There were signs of more
decisive action. In 1981, the St Lucian actor Joseph Marcell was cast as
Puck in *A Midsummer Night's Dream*, while in 1983 the director Trevor
Nunn faced down the opposition of some company members in offering
the plum role of Hotspur in *Henry IV Part One* to the Ghanaian-born

Hugh Quarshie.[144] Allen also refers to the 1984 RSC premiere of Louise Page's *Golden Girls*, which saw Simon playing alongside Kathy Tyson and Alphonsia Emmanuel as three black women athletes. The problem at this point in time was the way in which black artists were vulnerable to the instabilities of white managerial policy.

STAKING A CLAIM

The reasons why a small number of more durable autonomous black and Asian-led companies began to emerge in the 1970s and 80s vary from the racially motivated attack on a Sikh boy in South London in 1976, which led to the formation of Tara Arts, to the determination to produce theatre on their own terms, which stimulated a group of black actresses to set up Talawa Theatre Company in 1985. That more substantial records of these and other companies such as Temba (1972), Black Theatre Co-operative (1979), which evolved into Nitro in 1999, Tamasha (1989) and Kali (1990) are now available, is in part due to the desire of the founding artists to memorialise and bring into public consciousness their work, and to the recent writing of scholars such as Dimple Godiwala, Dominic Hingorani, Victor Ukaegbu and Graham Ley.[145] Jatinder Verma and Yvonne Brewster have been particularly influential in exploring their own experiences of migration and British hybridity in the context of their artistic practice. Brewster also mourned the companies which did not survive within the complexity of subsidy criteria into the 1990s. As I noted in relation to the death of other leading small companies in the 1980s, there were question marks around assessments of artistic quality. Temba, which premiered such important plays as Athol Fugard's *Sizwe Bansi is Dead*, was set up by Alton Kumalo in 1972 and had a turbulent relationship with the Arts Council. It survived under the artistic direction of Alby James after *The Glory of the Garden* had proposed withdrawing its grant. Finally, it was cut in 1992.[146]

In terms of formally constituted organisations this was a metropolitan phenomenon. To use statistical terminology, the BME population of London was much higher than anywhere else in the UK.[147] Many artists were already Londoners or gravitated there in search of like-minded collaborators. This fact combined with the importance of influential artistic networks meant that companies could benefit from a greater critical mass of enabling structures. Alda Terracciano has described in some detail the impact of Black Theatre Forum, which began in 1983 with the first Black Theatre Season supported by the Greater London

Council (GLC) and acted as an umbrella organisation for seventeen London-based African, Caribbean and Asian companies. The succession of Black Theatre Seasons mounted annually until 1990 survived the abolition of the GLC in 1985, and then sustained by the Greater London Arts Association aimed to demarginalise black artists by presenting productions in more high-profile theatres, away from the perceived ghettos of fringe and community venues.[148] What the Forum failed to do, however, despite expansion into additional training and development initiatives, was to establish a permanent-building base.[149] The need to shift from organisational legitimacy to a more assured recognition conferred by building ownership or control would continue to trouble ambitious artists for the remainder of the 1990s and beyond. Always subject to, and dependent on, white institutional gatekeepers of public subsidy, and further divided by the homogenising implications of *one* all-purpose black venue, attempts were dogged by controversy and disappointment.

Institutional support both in the metropolis and the regions took on greater urgency in the wake of the inter-communal violence which broke out in 1985 in Brixton and Peckham in London, Toxteth in Liverpool and Handsworth in Birmingham. The Arts and Ethnic Minorities Action Plan launched by the Arts Council in February 1986 referred to 'grave social and cultural problems' that arts organisations in their exemplary capacity were directed to address. Regional Arts Associations, especially those whose purview included the urban areas with a high density of migrant communities, were required to formulate strategies which would encourage more creative opportunity and widen access. Demographic change was now as much about audiences as it was about artists.[150]

Naseem Khan's investigation in the 1970s identified culturally specific amateur activity in various urban community settings but very little evidence of professional companies. In 1986 in Birmingham where West Midlands Arts was based, there was an initiative in collaboration with the West Midlands Probationary Service to launch a new professional black company led by Don Kinch, the Barbadian-born director of the London company Staunch Poets and Players. For a short time the fledgling company, Third Dimension, achieved some local success with a play about the overcrowded housing conditions experienced by new migrants in the post-war period but the lack of a secure local infrastructure doomed it to failure.[151] What was required was a much slower organic growth. Kinch himself turned to community work in Handsworth, especially with young people.[152]

For the most part professional opportunity lay in the policy objectives of the white-led theatres and arts centres. There were two strands to this. First, the extent to which black actors were cast in white-produced work, and secondly, the capacity to host touring metropolitan companies. Tara toured widely. Temba regularly toured until it was forced into liquidation. As early as 1978 at the Sheffield Crucible David Halliwell wrote and directed Temba actors in his controversial play *Prejudice*. The play was then revived at the Liverpool Everyman in 1979 with a new cast.[153] In 1985 the Everyman produced Trevor Rhone's 1982 comedy *Two Can Play*, focused on the dilemmas faced by a husband and wife who leave conflict-torn Jamaica for America.[154] Foco Novo's touring circuit permitted greater dissemination of the work of Tunde Ikoli in particular. Arguably one of the most flamboyantly successful co-productions was Talawa's all-black production of *The Importance of Being Earnest*, launched on the big stage of the Newcastle Opera House in 1989 – Yvonne Brewster defiantly laying claim to a white classic with Mona Hammond playing Lady Bracknell.[155]

At Birmingham Rep under the artistic director John Adams, colour-blind casting was equally defiant and at times very controversial. Plays, which ranged through the white western canon from the sixteenth century onwards such as *A Midsummer Night's Dream*, *Women Beware Women*, *The Relapse*, *School for Scandal*, *When We Are Married*, *Hobson's Choice*, *Noises Off*, etc., all had black actors in white roles. Even Yvonne Brewster worried about casting 'that makes nonsense of life' when white and black actors played brothers in *The Relapse*. Local critics waxed apoplectic when Vivienne Rochester was cast as the black daughter of the white Henry Hobson and was matched with a black suitor played by Haydn Forde.[156]

An important relationship forged in Birmingham with Tamasha began in 1994 with a production of Abhijat Joshi's *A Shaft of Sunlight*. Thereafter co-productions included the premiere of Ayub Khan Din's *East is East* (1996), an all-singing, all-dancing Bollywood spoof *Fourteen Songs, Two Weddings and a Funeral* (1998) and, in 1999, *Balti Kings*, which saw the whole studio space transformed into one of Birmingham's famous balti kitchens. At a time when attempts to showcase black actors was not translating into significant audience attendance, an autonomous British Asian women-led company was able to colonise a regional studio space with its own work, and through vigorous audience development strategies in the local community established a strong regular presence.[157]

What was missing was institutional power at a higher level. In the 2000 topography I will refer to the difficulty of establishing black-led arts centres in Manchester and Birmingham. Integration was practised at the subaltern level, but not at the level of executive authority. One initiative signalled a change, however. In Nottingham in 1997, Nairobi-born British Asian Venu Dhupa was appointed Executive Director of Nottingham Playhouse, succeeding another highly effective woman senior manager Ruth Mackenzie.[158] At a time when the Playhouse along with Leicester Haymarket was tasked within ACE's Black Regional Initiative in Theatre (BRIT) with formulating strategies which reached out to all their local communities, Dhupa was the first non-white woman to hold such a senior post in regional theatre. Under her the Playhouse hosted the 2001 Eclipse Conference, which both in terms of official statistics and copious oral testimony demonstrated the extent of structural racism in theatre. Instrumental in both purging past pain and eliciting at least some commitment to change from the power brokers, it did represent, albeit tentatively, a kind of turning point.[159]

As the sociologist Geoff Payne writing about uneven social relations has stated, 'the idea of social division entails both extensive differences and a continuity of existence over time, which stems from its integration in the social order through values, institutions and day-by-day interactions … it is not easy to challenge and change the boundaries'.[160] Clearly, as this chapter has sought to show, socially constructed boundaries in theatre were challenged and did change. Spatial relations changed physically in terms of access and spaces of shared engagement. How far social and national formations would continue to change or what new boundaries might be erected were important questions for the new century.

CHAPTER 8

The topography of theatre in 2000

This attempt to construct a topography of theatre in 2000 takes as its starting point the thoughts on space expressed by the geographer Nigel Thrift:

As with terms like 'society' and 'nature', space is not a commonsense external background to human and social action. Rather, it is the outcome of a series of highly problematic temporary settlements that divide and connect things up into different kinds of collectives which are slowly provided with the means which render them durable and sustainable.[1]

Coming after the socio-political theatrical experiments that were associated with the 1970s, the term 'collective' has a very particular resonance for theatre scholars, and, indeed, one aspect of the spatial-temporal outcomes discernible in 2000 is the means by which old-style collectives had evolved into something more sustainable. However, to delineate the features of the landscape as whole in 2000 it is now necessary to think of collectivity and connectivity in much broader terms.

For 1950 I used the image of the intersection of over lapping circles to show the spatial relationships formed by commercial, metropolitan theatre, theatre strategically promoted through the emerging state funding body, and a diffuse and mainly commercial regional theatre sector. For 2000 the most appropriate image might be theatre as an organism formed from interlocking cells or clusters of activity, each corresponding to a different embodied constituency of interest whether composed of audiences or participants. I would argue that this is certainly the best way to think about regional theatre, although the way in which power was exercised spatially, both materially and in the abstract from the metropolis, showed that the geo-economic model of the core–periphery relationship was still highly relevant. But there was no doubt despite the complexity of economic relationships across sectors, that public funding for the arts had physically transformed the

239

built landscape, and moreover, enabled other models of theatre 'settle-ment' which were strategically connected.

After one hundred years, more control of absolute space, as delineated by the physical features of the landscape, had been literally engineered by more advanced road construction, especially the system of motorways which had brought even more flexible spatial-temporal proximity than that provided by the rail network in 1900. All kinds of touring theatre, especially small-scale, non-building-specific companies, benefited from this. But equally what took theatre *to* an audience could just as easily take audiences *away* from a local provider to more attractive sources of theatre product, especially in London. Of UK households 73 per cent had access to at least one car or van which in enabling fast independ-ent travel increased the capacity for consumer choice.[2] More connectiv-ity had at least been partially achieved through the (partial) upgrading of major roads like the A9, which went up the east coast of Scotland to Thurso, and the A470 in Wales, which (albeit with some difficulty through the central mountainous region) ran from Cardiff to Llandudno in the north.

More important, however, was the electronic dominance of space and the rapidly emerging control of the virtual environment. In 2000 the national spaces of communication and recreation had been transformed by what Raymond Williams called 'the dramatised society'. Multiple forms and genres of drama could be accessed in the home at any time of the day 'beyond', as Williams put it, 'occasion or season'.[3] Even com-mercially produced television advertisements could be transmitted as micro-dramas analogous to variety theatre sketches with actors playing named characters with identifiable personalities sometimes over several years. An explosive event in a soap opera like *Coronation Street* watched by millions of viewers could be a topic of conversation in hundreds of workplace and domestic environments the following day. Crucially, this was a technology that could be accessed by anyone irrespective of income levels. In 2000 examples of extreme poverty could still be found in Great Britain, but even the poorest could, if they wished, catch sight of a television set. Access to the World Wide Web was more dependent on individual socio-economic circumstances but, nevertheless, was rapidly developing enhanced opportunities for global communication and know-ledge exchange. Given the dominance of the electronic media then, the experience of live performance in a designated site of performance was noteworthy as something consciously *chosen* whether as an active agent or as spectator. What was chosen depended on the circumstances which had formed a particular constituency of interest and how by 2000 that had been developed and maintained.

BUILDINGS AGAIN

The end-of-century material basis of theatre as a live medium was most clearly laid out in a comparatively new annual publication, the *British Performing Arts Yearbook*, which by 2000/2001 had reached its thirteenth edition. Institutional and organisational structures were comprehensively listed and described in what was declared by the three women editors to be 'the complete guide to venues, performers, festivals, arts courses, support organisations and services for the arts professional'.[4] As with *The Era* and *The Stage* earlier in the century, such claims need to be treated with caution by the historian. The lists were not complete and the extent to which comprehensive coverage could be achieved was dependent on the efforts and capacity of individual artists and organisations to promote themselves through this medium. In the case of small companies, membership of the Independent Theatre Council (ITC), which had risen to 450 by 2000,[5] was sufficient to signal artistic and ideological affiliation and alignments. Nevertheless, the *Yearbook* is an excellent starting point for the mapping process, especially of buildings.

'British' was an umbrella term for the official political construct – the Republic of Ireland was now a significant absence. But at a time when devolved, if circumscribed, national legislative powers had been given to Scotland and Wales by means of the Scottish Parliament and the Welsh Assembly, and a fragile Northern Irish Assembly based on an equally fragile cross-party peace process had been created following the 1998 Belfast Agreement,[6] the *Yearbook* respected devolved sensitivities. Nowhere was described as provincial and even the performance resources of the small islands of the archipelago, including the Channel Islands, the Isle of Wight, the Isle of Man, Orkney, Shetland, etc., were covered. Also, while the *Yearbook* was clearly intended to facilitate the dissemination of professional opportunities, amateur building-based producing theatres either as self-financing or funded venues were listed alongside their professional counterparts. In the additional data provided with each entry, it was made clear where amateur and community engagement was a strategic priority.

Metropolitan venues, however, were in a separate category subdivided into Inner and Outer London. Within Inner London, there were approximately 150 buildings that were listed as offering spaces for theatre performance of some kind. Old-style commercial theatres now categorised as 'bricks and mortar' with reference to their status as capital assets were still a dominant presence with 42 venues listed. Indeed, the core of the West End as established at the beginning of the twentieth century was recognisable with venerable theatres like the Criterion, Wyndham's, the Garrick, the Savoy, Her Majesty's, etc. still trading. In all 38 of these 'self-financed' theatres, i.e. under commercial management, had been built by 1930. The demolition of the St James's Theatre despite vociferous protests in 1957 had marked the beginning of campaigns to safeguard others of similar age.[7] The Lyceum Theatre, threatened with demolition as early as 1939, leased to Mecca as a ballroom and then with the freehold acquired by the Theatres Trust and leased to Triumph Apollo, had reopened in 1996 as a venue for major musicals.[8] A more visible corporate control, however, was exercised by the music theatre composer Andrew Lloyd Webber whose company Really Useful Theatres bought Stoll Moss' Theatres including Her Majesty's Theatre and the London Palladium in 2000. At the same time the Ambassador Theatre Group, a relatively new power in theatre ownership led by the producers Howard Panter and Rosemary Squire, was steadily adding to a portfolio of venues which had begun in the mid-1990s with the purchase of the 1892 Duke of York's Theatre and the 1913 Ambassadors Theatre.[9]

The mixed public/private economy was much in evidence with some elements of London's theatrical heritage preserved through state subsidy. Unlike the Royal Court and the London Coliseum, which had found new roles within the subsidised sector and were thus preserved through public funding, the Old Vic had been supplanted by the architectural monolith of the National Theatre. Bought and refurbished by the Canadian businessman 'honest' Ed Mirvish in 1982, it was saved on resale in 1998 from conversion to a themed pub or lap-dancing club by the setting up of the Old Vic Theatre Trust 2000 by the producer Sally Greene.[10] With no subsidy in 2000 it was facing an uncertain future and does not appear in the *Yearbook* except in an advertisement for rehearsal rooms. The most unlikely brand-new playhouse, which was also positioned outside the subsidised sector, was the replica of Shakespeare's Globe Theatre installed within the International Shakespeare Globe Arts Centre on the banks of the Thames in 1998. It traded independently on the allure of a popular tourist attraction, but against all the odds was proving a dynamic artistic success.

In general, there was very little completely new build. Venues like the prefabricated Hampstead Theatre, the Cochrane Theatre, the Bloomsbury, the Peacock and the Cockpit were all over thirty years old.

Stratford Circus proclaimed as East London's first ever purpose-built arts centre and bolstered by a large National Lottery grant was due to open in December 2000, perhaps the nearest the locality was ever going to get to Joan Littlewood's dream of a people's fun palace. Virtually all the other small-scale producing theatres, pub theatres and studio theatres had been inserted or squashed into old 'found' spaces: Victorian schools and libraries, hospitable public houses, etc. Everything was packed into an inner London area of roughly eight square miles.

Even the over 30 Outer London venues listed were contained within a direct radius of little more than twelve miles. These ranged from the Tricycle Theatre located in Kilburn in the north-west to the Churchill Theatre in Bromley in the east. The Theatre Royal Stratford East was oddly designated outer London despite its physical proximity to the Stratford Circus. The Warehouse Theatre in Croydon was some thirteen miles due south. There was the Orange Tree in Richmond, as well as the Richmond Theatre itself in the south-west. Further west in the London borough of Hounslow there was the Paul Robeson multi-purpose centre: so named because Robeson had filmed *Sanders of the River* in the nearby Isleworth Studios. The Watermans Arts Centre in Brentford, which promoted a strong black arts policy, was situated on the north bank of the Thames overlooking Kew Gardens. North-east of central London, the Questor's Theatre in Ealing was an amateur, self-financed theatre, which had also benefited from a capital Lottery grant and claimed to be the largest 'community' theatre in Europe.[11] All in all what was delineated, which also included music venues such as the Royal Opera House, Festival Hall and the Royal Albert Hall, may (even in comparison with New York) have represented the most densely packed concentration of performing arts-dedicated buildings in the world.

THE REGIONAL LANDSCAPE

There was nothing on this scale comparable in any British city outside London. If one of the key differentials in 1900 had been London's capacity to create original theatre product from within a building-based manufactory, that functional imbalance was still apparent in 2000, albeit within a substantially reconfigured pattern of distribution. While the Boyden Report had exposed the financial constraints facing regional producing theatres in England, there was a network of 38 autonomous building-based professional companies which could only have been dreamt of a century earlier. The regional economic imbalances which had evolved during the twentieth century had reversed the north-favouring divide discernible in the late nineteenth century, but the historical legacy of conurbation ensured a preponderance 'upwards' from the Midlands to the North of England. Less urbanised, and thus less heavily populated areas in the South-West and East presented other challenges.

Thus, there were producing theatres in Bristol, Plymouth, Exeter, Salisbury, Canterbury and Southampton, but travelling north through the Midlands there were more, for example, in Birmingham, Nottingham, Leicester, Newcastle-under-Lyme, Chester, Leeds, York, Liverpool, Bolton, Scarborough, Lancaster and Newcastle upon Tyne, etc. What is important to stress, however, is that in the majority of cases, just one producing theatre served an entire city. There were some exceptions. Manchester, which in terms of civic kudos had probably emerged stronger following the 1996 IRA bomb blast which wrecked its commercial heart, maintained a more substantial critical mass of producing capacity. The Royal Exchange, billed as the largest theatre in the round in Britain, had acquired a studio theatre along with its post-bomb repair.[12] The Library Theatre Company had two homes: the Library Theatre itself, incorporated into the 1933 Central Library, and the Forum Theatre, located some eight miles from the city centre in Wythenshaw. The Contact Theatre, which had been a purpose-built university initiative in 1965, had reopened in late 1999 as a radically redesigned 'eco-friendly' building which targeted young people.

But, as was the case with other cities that promoted the dynamism of their commitment to the arts, there were major disjunctions in the capacity to access these resources. Manchester was a regional centre city located within the combined conurbations of Greater Manchester and Merseyside which, overall, were suffering high levels of unemployment. The creative industries model of the 'cultural quarter', which as we shall see had become an increasingly widespread strategy for physically rehabilitating decayed areas of old abandoned central districts, carried with it exclusionary social risks as well as some undoubted economic benefits.[13] In Manchester, the Northern Quarter, an area of fifty-six acres to the north of the city centre which had once been the centre of market activity, especially for the textile trade, became in the 1990s a quirky complex of streets designed to attract artists and their clients.[14] To the south side of the city in Hulme, however, regeneration efforts, reliant on a mix of public and private funding to remedy the dire social effects of poor 1960s' housing, allegedly led to the tensions which contributed to the collapse of the Nia Centre. Proclaimed on opening in 1991 to be the

UK's first professional African and Caribbean Cultural Centre, the Nia (a Ki-Swahili word meaning purpose) was established in the refurbished 1902 Hulme Playhouse and funded by the Moss Side and Hulme Business Association as well as North West Arts and the local authority. By 2000 the venue was dark, yet another failed attempt to establish black-led, building-based autonomy.[15]

SCOTLAND: AN INDEPENDENT PROVISION

In Scotland there were now twelve designated producing theatres with several of the more recent following the amateur-beginnings-to-professional-venture trajectory which began before the Second World War. The 1970 Brunton Theatre in Musselburgh, just six miles from Edinburgh, was built following a community initiative. The Cumbernauld Theatre, in the 1960s' new town outside Glasgow, had been originally converted by amateurs from a set of seventeenth-century farm cottages. The Mull Little Theatre, on the Isle of Mull off the west coast, was a stone-built coach house converted in 1966, and like the Pitlochry Festival Theatre in a new building since 1981, capitalised on the influx of spring and summer visitors.[16] Relative to the size of the population, which was recorded in the 2001 census as just over 5 million,[17] Scotland was well-stocked with built theatre spaces, especially in the geographical, urbanised 'trapezoid' of the Central Belt[18] served by a network of fast roads. Even further north and separated from the Central Belt by Britain's highest mountain range, Eden Court continued to bring theatre to the 'mini-metropolis' of Inverness.

Edinburgh and Glasgow, linked by the M8 motorway, no longer formed a shared theatre space in corporate-managed commercial terms, but their producing capacity, sheltering under the umbrella of Scottish Arts Council subsidy and boosted by the festival culture of both cities, had achieved significant international representational power. In Edinburgh, the Traverse, having relocated twice from its former homes in a Lawnmarket brothel and a Grassmarket sailmaker's loft, was now part of a high-profile arts enclave in a new glossy 1992 building situated behind the Royal Lyceum and the Usher Hall. In Glasgow, the Tron and the Tramway were both established in found spaces on either side of the River Clyde and not far from the Citizens' Theatre. In 2000, the Tramway, which had transmogrified into an internationally known performance venue for Peter Brook's celebrated production of *The Mahabharata* in 1988, had just reopened after a SAC Lottery grant had enabled more exploitation of the original tram-shed's vast spaces.[19] With yet more generous capital funding to refurbish and extend the former church building of the Tron and its historical environs, what in the early twentieth century had been known as 'the dark side of Glasgow' had been regenerated to serve the cultural industries.[20]

WALES AND NORTHERN IRELAND:
DIFFERENT LANDSCAPES, DIFFERENT NEEDS

In Wales and Northern Ireland not only were the numbers of designated producing theatres much smaller, but exact status and functionality had become more slippery, raising other questions about how theatre provision was to be defined. In Wales there were five listed but scattered widely apart. Theatr Colwyn, in Colwyn Bay, appeared to function more as a mixed-use presenting house appropriate for a seaside resort on the popular north coast, while Theatr Fach in Llangefni in Anglesey was a member of the Little Theatre Guild of Great Britain and technically amateur. There were only two publicised as producing theatres in the south of the country, and both were products of the changing educational and industrial climate of the 1970s. The Sherman Theatre in Cardiff had been built on the campus of the University College in 1973, and in 2000, like the Contact in Manchester, prioritised theatre for young people. Milford Haven, where the small Torch Theatre had opened in 1977, had become a major oil refinery port on the south-west coast.[21] The other factor which drove the work of the Torch seasonal repertory company in 2000 was the importance of local tourism in Pembrokeshire.

The theatre which had achieved an unexpected status in the Welsh theatre ecology, however, had become more prominent since 1998 under the English director Terry Hands as Clwyd Theatr Cmyru based in the arts centre complex in Mold in Flintshire. Despite its unlikely small North Walian town setting, its proximity to the border with England within relatively easy reach – again by good roads – for targeted income-generating audiences from Merseyside and Cheshire, for example, and its wider Welsh and English touring policy, led by a former artistic director of the Royal Shakespeare Company, had secured it a strong position in the subsidy hierarchy of the Welsh Arts Council. The anger expressed by Welsh critics such as Ruth Shade about CTC's high level of funding was further inflamed by its designation as '*the* English-language Welsh *National* Performing Arts Company'. Added to the historic tensions between North and South Wales, English speakers and Welsh speakers, was the issue that there was virtually no tradition of professional, building-based producing theatre in Wales. In 2000, at a time when CTC also had an £800,000 deficit, controversy had only just subsided after a decision to cut back eight Theatre for Young People companies to five.[22]

In Northern Ireland, the absence of 'theatres' from the landscape was even more noteworthy. The Lyric in Belfast was flagged as Ulster's only professional producing theatre, while the Bardic Theatre located on the outskirts of Dungannon claimed producing status for its amateur productions programmed with professional touring shows. As this last example shows determining exactly what kind of enterprise qualified as a producing theatre is not a simple exercise. Also the question had to be asked about what kind, if any, of built resource best suited the particular political, social and economic circumstances that had shaped the Welsh and Ulster landscapes in the course of the century. At the beginning and indeed the middle of the century, the autonomous purpose-built or refurbished producing theatre appeared the ideal. By the end of the century there were other options.

A WORLD CITY

But what was absolutely clear, however, from a survey of the whole British landscape, was the numerical disparity between London and the rest of the UK. In 2000 there were approximately 55 dedicated professional producing theatres trading outside London. In London itself, and its immediate environs, there were roughly 36. Thus nearly 40 per cent of all UK producing theatres were located in London. In the capital city the agglomeration principle was vigorously maintained, *metropolising* the most publically recognised creative opportunity and innovation.

As the urban geographer Phil Hubbard has pointed out, London is classified as a 'world city', that is, in common with cities like New York and Tokyo, London is a global 'control and command centre', where in a knowledge-rich environment, knowledge-rich personnel cluster together, benefiting even in the era of globalisation and virtual communication with opportunities for face-to-face networking.[23] Extrapolating from that in relation to theatre clearly shows that the dense concentration of artistic expertise and cultural capital represented by metropolitan theatre-makers as a 'knowledge elite' ensured, as it had throughout the century, access to sources of influence and patronage.

AN EMBEDDED THEATRE

What had developed regionally and nationally outside London, however, was a very complex theatre environment serving a multiplicity of interests and needs. What in 1900 I described as a bustling optimistic industry was in 2000 embedded in the fabric of the built landscape as broad-based cultural practice. Theatre as public service appeared to function in equilibrium with theatre as industrial commodity. In the commercial sector, despite the demolitions and redevelopment which had seen so many of the early-twentieth-century buildings vanish, a good number of the old receiving houses survived to function in a not dissimilar way to a hundred years earlier. As described in chapter 6 some of the most architecturally important buildings had been rescued by local authority intervention and refurbishment, and then offered as home bases to high-profile performing arts companies as a means of boosting civic cultural prestige. The Leeds Grand now housed Opera North; the New Theatre in Cardiff, Welsh National Opera; while Birmingham City Council had enticed the Sadlers Wells' Royal Ballet to relocate to the Birmingham Hippodrome as Birmingham Royal Ballet. A similar BCC five-year plan in 1990 to subsidise the D'Oyly Carte Opera Company at the former Salberg-family-owned Alexandra Theatre ultimately failed to secure the company's long-term future.[24]

In 2000 Apollo Leisure controlled the Alex along with 28 other theatres, some more glamorous than others. Their most dominant presence apart from five London venues was in Manchester where the company managed the major touring product, especially musical theatre, which went to the No. 1 Opera House and Palace Theatre, as well as Labatt's Apollo Theatre, originally a cinema and now used mostly for rock concerts. There was also the former Empire Theatre in Ashton-under-Lyne, by 2000 known as Tameside Hippodrome. The combination of a relatively strong subsidised producing sector contributing to a climate of live performance-going with high-quality commercial product would have offered potentially good returns on capital investment. Outside the Apollo chain, many smaller venues often in local authority hands, such as the Pomegranate Theatre in Chesterfield or the Palace Theatre in Redditch, offered mixed programmes to local audiences of variety acts, stand-up comedians, concerts and the ubiquitous tribute bands, often with home-grown or off-the-shelf pantomimes and amateur shows. The artistes' advertisement pages of *The Stage* were no longer as closely packed as in 1900, but the photographs and promotional material offered glimpses of another stratum of live performance surviving in the marketplace and with popular appeal. In October 2000 acts such as Ward Allen and Roger the Dog, 'The Sensational' Heather Williams, the Fabulous Antons, and Jimmy Carlo and Crystal appearing with the Ken Dodd Happiness Show were all on tour. Some were appearing in pubs and theme bars, hotels, holiday centres and, indeed, cruise ships, which were also a regular source of employment.[25]

ARTS CENTRES

The biggest change, however, signalled by buildings which contributed to the perception of embeddedness and represented a major cultural shift from the landscape of 1900, were the numbers of arts centres where theatre functioned in synergy with other art forms. The majority of the 223 three arts centres formally listed in the *British Performing Arts Yearbook* were funded by local authorities. If civic centres and community venues, which operated similar mixed art-form, combined professional and amateur, participatory or audience-driven policies, are added in the number comes to well over 300. At the grass-roots level, a model of theatre was functioning that could adapt more readily to a greater range of environmental circumstances. Some centres were major professional artist receiving/hosting venues incorporating theatre auditoria into complexes which also accommodated art galleries, cinemas and concert halls. The Warwick Arts Centre, part of Warwick University, with a 573-seater main theatre together with a 150-seater Studio, came into this category. The newly built (1998) Courtyard in Hereford boasted two flexible auditoria (main house 400, studio 150), cinemas, galleries and rehearsal rooms. The Arnolfini in Bristol, which focused on new work in all art forms including non-narrative theatre and live art, had occupied a converted nineteenth-century tea warehouse on the city waterfront since 1976. The Lemon Tree in Aberdeen had originally been a 1930s' YMCA, but, an arts centre since 1992, it presented a wide range of music, dance, physical theatre and small-scale touring drama. The Café Theatre seated 500 with table and chairs; raked the Studio held 150 or 350 standing. Like Warwick in relation to the Coventry Belgrade, and the Arnolfini, which offered alternative programmes to the Bristol Old Vic, the Lemon Tree could potentially both complement and offset the more traditional product on offer at His Majesty's Theatre. In Hereford, in the centre of one of the most thinly populated rural English counties where throughout the century there had been short-lived attempts to utilise existing buildings as theatres, the Courtyard represented a major triumph of modern, well-resourced arts provision.[26]

Many, especially the smaller centres, had been converted successfully from older buildings and balanced a professional receiving programme with an amateur performance and/or educational activity. In Wales, the historic combination of deeply entrenched community engagement with participatory arts and a landscape where buildings bore witness to the lives and priorities of a collapsed industrial past, arts centres as new or revitalised places of congregation had a particular resonance. Chapter Arts Centre in Cardiff remained an important base for national and international companies. Outside Cardiff some arts centres were relatively new builds: Theatr Mwldan in Cardigan, Wyeside Arts Centre in Builth Wells, Theatr Gwynedd in Bangor. Others mediated between past and present. The Blackwood Miners' Institute in Gwent, in the valleys where community arts were 'extremely prominent', had been originally built with miners' contributions and then refurbished and reopened in 1992 funded by the Welsh Office and the local borough council. Further west in Blaengarw in Mid Glamorgan, the Workmen's Hall built in 1894 became an Arts Centre in 1992, financed by Bridgend Borough Council. In Machynlleth in Powys, Y Tabernacl had been, as its name suggests, converted from a Methodist chapel.

In Northern Ireland *the* dominant built-provision hosting theatre was the arts/leisure/civic centre with some 30 listed out of a total number of 51 venues which advertised details. In 1995 in *To the Millennium: A Strategy for the Arts in Northern Ireland*, the Arts Council of Northern Ireland had announced the objective of ensuring that within six years there would be a dedicated arts facility within a twenty-mile radius of every member of the population.[27] In this 'region' of Great Britain where physical fabric in the shape of buildings, vehicles and human bodies had been regularly destroyed, the modern, appropriately resourced venue where people could safely come together to enjoy the arts had a symbolic function beyond utility or capital asset. Even after the Belfast Agreement was signed in 1998, Omagh in County Tyrone, where an Arts Committee and an arts officer worked to promote a modest number of events each year in the multi-purpose leisure centre, became notorious because of a car bomb which killed 29 people, mostly women and children.[28] But the fact is, however, that the towns identified in the 1995 strategy document (including Newry, Antrim, Craigavon and Newtownards) had centres dated like Omagh's from the 1980s. All like Omagh had well-documented histories of sectarian violence, but their arts centres signalled the resilience of other community priorities.

Indeed, as early as 1993 *Playing the Wild Card*, a report produced by David Grant following a survey of community drama and smaller-scale theatre from a community relations perspective, had clearly shown the richness of grass-roots activity in amateur/community initiatives, youth theatre and educational projects. These along with a growing cluster of small emerging professional companies could act as a catalyst for the development of a more dynamic theatre ecology *and* improve community relations.[29] Grant himself had been instrumental in the late 1980s in the creation of an arts centre in the nearly derelict Old Museum in Belfast. By 2000 it was a well-established public performance venue for Belfast-based companies such as Tinderbox and Ridiculusmus, and supplied office space for others such as Kabosh and the TIE company Replay Productions.[30]

However, in the 1995 ACNI map of publicly funded arts venues, the clustering of state-funded buildings in the industrialised east, in and around Belfast, and towards the south-east had been very obvious. In the west Omagh was not marked and indeed County Tyrone was literally a blank space. The Arts Council argued that limited resources had to be concentrated in the more heavily populated areas, while admitting to the comparative paucity of venue subsidy in the rural west.[31] In County Fermanagh, the long border with the Republic and a predominantly Catholic population meant that the distance from Belfast was political and cultural as well as geographical. Enniskillen, Fermanagh's principal town however, boasted Ardhowen, the Theatre by the Lakes, a modern award-winning building, designated and funded as a national touring house, and attached to one of the Edwardian great houses which were emblematic of the town's colonial past.[32] Only a year after the theatre opened in 1986, Enniskillen became notorious when an IRA bomb killed 11 and injured a further 60 at a Remembrance Day ceremony. The resulting widespread outrage provoked a turning point in the long road towards a negotiated settlement. By 2000 in the town of Castlederg in north Tyrone – which had the dubious honour of being dubbed the most bombed small town in Northern Ireland – the advertised partnership between the local arts advisory committee and ACNI was committed to making the leisure centre a focal point for arts in the community. In Cookstown, to the east of the county, the new Burnavon Arts Centre opened on the site of the town hall in 1999 was just a year old.[33] In Armagh, the Market Place Theatre and Arts Centre, built where a bomb had destroyed the local cinema, was also winning awards for its graceful architecture.

Without a doubt the built landscape flourishes best in a secure social and economic context. Northern Ireland's first arts centre, the Flowerfield Arts Centre, opened in 1980 in Portstewart in County Londonderry, was established in an elegant Victorian house which had been rescued from dereliction by Coleraine Borough Council in 1973.[34] It was almost certainly no accident that Big Telly, the longest-established regional (i.e. outside Belfast) professional theatre company founded in 1987, had its home base there.[35] Portstewart, and indeed the house, had its origins in the settlement of the Scottish colonial 'planters' who came to Ulster in the eighteenth century, and subsequently the town on the spectacularly beautiful northern coast had developed into a quietly prosperous seaside resort. By 2000 the area was becoming the most affluent in Northern Ireland, with its ambience and reputation as a town where Catholics and the majority Protestant population appeared well-integrated, significantly boosted by the proximity of the Coleraine Campus of the University of Ulster. The pre-Troubles decision to site the New University of Ulster, opened in Coleraine in 1968, on territory more safely associated with Unionist control, rather than in the more obvious, but politically riven second city of Derry, was not only highly controversial but also brought more economic development and expansion to Coleraine itself.[36] The Riverside Theatre, established on the campus in 1976 and promoted in the 2000 *Yearbook* as a national touring house, had the advantage of a purpose-built, flexible 358-seater auditorium which threw into sharp relief when it opened, the complete lack of dedicated professional performance spaces in Derry.

As Christopher Morash has pointed out in his vivid account of the premiere of Brian Friel's play *Translations* in Derry's Guildhall in September 1980, when the newly formed Field Day Theatre Company sat down for a read-through in the Victorian neo-Gothic civic building, it was the first time in two centuries that a professional theatre company had rehearsed in the city.[37] Twenty years on, the imagined 'Fifth Province', created by the founders of Field Day as a public sphere for rational debate about nationalism, cultural essentialism and the influence of history, continued to be powerfully resonant even though the theatre company had effectively ceased to function.[38] In the Guildhall in 2000, the traces of the Field Day performances, as evidenced by preserved posters, could be seen alongside the triumphalist iconography of imperial power – stained glass images of London mercantile success, royal busts, gilded shields – served as a reminder of the momentary symbolic confluence of *Translations*, which had been enabled by transnational, cross-border and cross-party co-operation despite the immediately dire political and economic context in 1980. In 2000 the efforts to neutralise and even domesticate the imperial spaces of the Guildhall through performance could be seen in the offers to host not just drama and music, but boxing tournaments, photography exhibitions, lectures, youth theatres, etc.

In the venues which had appeared most recently, attention had shifted to Derry's other even more dominant bulwark against unwelcome forces, the city walls which enclose the historic central area. The Playhouse multi-media arts centre with a 200-seater auditorium and a smaller dance studio had been created in 1992 from the conversion of two convent schools in Artillery Street where the remains of the façade of the first 1795 Derry theatre had survived close to the walls. In 2000 the brand-new Derry Theatre with over 1,000 seats in its main auditorium, which was nearing completion as part of the multi-million pound Millennium Forum, was in the design and stone-clad fabric of its architecture effectively an annexe to the walls.[39] The history of the fortifications which made Derry one of best-preserved walled cities in Europe included of course the much-memorialised Protestant barricading of the city against the besieging armies of the Catholic James II in 1688–9. One of the topographical consequences of the dominant power structures which emerged from that victory could be seen from the northern side of the walls across the River Foyle to 'Free Derry' and the Catholic Bogside and Creggan estates, where the perpetual iteration of unresolved histories of past political and military injustices, especially the Bloody Sunday killing by British soldiers of 14 local people in 1972, formed a narrative counterpoint to the parallel history of community theatre efforts, such as Derry Frontline in the 1980s and early 1990s, to use the arts to help unemployed young people engage with more deep-seated psychological barriers to social healing.[40] As the walls of the city itself were subsequently made more fully accessible by the removal of the barbed wire and steel-plated barriers erected by the security forces, and Derry prepared to move forward economically by exploiting the tourism potential of its built heritage, there were still questions about the physical resources required to enable communities to come together. The Derry Theatre was specifically intended for both professional and amateur community use.

THE POST-INDUSTRIAL SOCIETY AND ITS EFFECTS

The remodelling of Great Britain as a post-industrial society, where heavy industry, the extraction and/or exploitation of natural resources and related manufacturing was no longer seen as the principal driver of the economy, had significantly reconfigured the population. Over the course of the century the population had risen by nearly 60 per cent to close on 59 million, but the downward trend in areas of former industrial prosperity observed in 1950 had continued. Much of the English northern regions where heavy industry had collapsed had suffered due to population drift towards the Midlands and the South. Both Scotland and Wales had grown relatively slowly with Scotland demonstrating an actual decline in population at the 1991 census – a situation which had only just stabilised by 2000.[41] In the 2001 census the combined populations of London and the South-East of England, recorded as 15,872,586, numbered more than the populations of Scotland, Wales and Northern Ireland put together by very nearly 40 per cent – a statistic which in itself might seem to account for the numerical disparity in the provision of theatre as a physical resource.

Where the rate of growth was faster, however, was in Northern Ireland where the population rose to 1,685,267 by 2001 largely through 'natural increase' (more births than deaths). The average age of the population was younger than in the rest of the UK.[42] In a paper given at the Cultural Traditions Group Conference at Queen's University in Belfast in 1997, John Darby asked his audience to imagine the events of the previous two decades in a series of freeze-frame photographs where careful study would show that the background had been subtly changing. Northern Ireland, he claimed, was now a more fair society 'and this change had been achieved gradually, almost imperceptibly'.[43] Certainly, the concrete evidence provided by the visible presence of more built provision for arts practice, however modest, had been steadily increasing since the 1980s. By 2000 high-profile buildings such as the Derry Millennium Forum were the product of significant externally derived economic investment aimed at promoting the cultural industries in the interests of tourism. The material relics of the histories that had torn local communities apart in the past were now in the process of being uncoupled from their origins in colonial power and sectarian difference to assume a new identity as artefacts incorporated into the heritage industry.

EUROPE AND STRUCTURAL CHANGE

That radical British theatre had been influenced by the European avant-garde throughout the twentieth century is well known and not quite as heavily repressed in the historical record as Jen Harvie has recently suggested.[44] However, by the end of the century social and economic structural intervention from Europe had begun to influence the landscape of theatre in different ways. In the third edition of their *Regional Economics and Policy* published in 2000, the economists Harvey Armstrong and Jim Taylor highlighted 'the immense changes' brought about by radical new policies introduced by the European Union. In 1985, they argued, when the first edition was published, regional policy in Britain was under considerable threat.[45] Altered strategies in the 1990s, in part brought about by the ratification of UK membership of the European Union under the terms of the 1993 Maastricht Treaty, 'resulted in a transformation of attitudes towards regional issues at all levels of government, from the local level to the supranational level'.[46]

Between 1994 and 1999 Northern Ireland along with Merseyside and the Scottish Highlands and Islands were identified as 'lagging regions' in need of development and structural adjustment, and thus were designated Objective 1 areas in need of assistance from the financial instruments – including the European Regional Development Fund (ERDF) and the European Social Fund (ESF) – which made up the EU Structural Funds.[47] The potential benefits of this were flagged up by the 1995 ACNI strategy document which presented a simple economic equation: 'the average earnings in our workforce are lower than across the water and therefore less money is likely to be available for arts spending by audiences.'[48] More disposable income for the general population meant more income for the livelihood of arts workers. Furthermore, major investment in the built presence of the arts, it was argued, could have knock-on effects for employment in associated industries.

In relation to the arts, the most visible outcome of European strategic promotion of stakeholder economic partnerships, produced in response to substantial local authority commitment, were the large-scale, flagship, multi-purpose arts and conference venues. The Millennium Forum in Derry, at an eventual cost of over £13 million pounds, was the second most ambitious building project after the £32 million Waterfront Hall, which opened in Belfast in 1997. The main auditorium capacity of the Waterfront was a lavish 2,235, with a studio theatre which held 500. The exhibition space, bars, restaurants and retail outlets which extended up four levels were there to entice not just audiences for a range of performances, but also conference delegates who, it was hoped, would flock to use the facilities. The high glass frontages offered spectacular views over the River Lagan, while the copper coating of the domed roof was designed to turn green to echo the copper lantern crowns of the towers of Belfast's 1906 City Hall and other Victorian buildings. The visual rhetoric of the elegant, spacious Waterfront was intended to promote the image of an economically regenerated city while referring back to former icons of power.[49] The cost to Belfast City Council was £21.5 million, supplemented by £6.5 from the Government's Urban Development Group, and £4 million in European funding.

If in the nineteenth century arts buildings such as the 1878 Leeds Grand Theatre, erected as triumphant architectural statements, were a final flourish of confidence in economic success, by the end of the twentieth century such buildings were expensively speculative, aiming to create the impression of confidence in order to attract the investment needed for long-term prosperity. Urban development strategists in the last two decades of the twentieth century were confronted with large tracts of derelict land and disused buildings which no longer provided employment, but where the insouciance which had seen Victorian civic leaders unashamedly juxtapose recreation, culture and commerce was increasingly constrained by anxieties about what or who was to be represented by the re-inscription of the landscape.

The Laganside Corporation, established in 1989, took on Belfast's polluted, foul-smelling river attempting to reconceptualise the regeneration models already controversially in place in London's Docklands and on Merseyside, especially in relations with local communities. By 2000 the Corporation acquisition of inner-city land had been extended into the old mercantile centre round the Protestant St Anne's Cathedral, where vacant sites and under-used buildings had already been colonised by artists in search of short leases and low rents. The offices of the Community Arts Forum, founded in 1993, were there and thus access to community consultation opened up more readily. This new Cathedral Cultural Quarter, constructed from the buildings from where the shipbuilding industry and the linen trade had once been financed and administered, was classified as a 'culture-led' approach to urban regeneration, which offered hopes that the more problematic 'objectivated cultural capital' associated with the Waterfront Hall could be mediated to enable the use of historical associations to link public art with local identity.[50]

In 2000 Northern Ireland, however, was about to embark on a second round of Objective 1 status, unsurprisingly given the volatile state of political consensus which saw devolved powers suspended for four months. Deep-seated problems were not easy to resolve. The other two UK beneficiaries of Objective 1 status, Merseyside and the Scottish Highlands and Islands, could not have been more different topographically from each other, although each for quite different reasons exemplified the consequences of Great Britain's colonial past. The history of theatre in each was thus quite different. In some respects the comparative emptiness of the formally built landscape of theatre in Northern Ireland and the north of Scotland offered more opportunity for intervention. Merseyside's complex industrial history had left a landscape littered with the detritus of previous activity.

Harold Ackroyd's *The Liverpool Stage* describes the demolition of seven theatres either through wartime bombing or, in more cases and more recently, as the final outcome of failed attempts to bring customers to buildings variously converted to use as cinemas, dance and bingo halls. Indeed, bingo, long after the 1960s' boom in its popularity had abated was still ensuring the survival of the 1915 Garston Empire theatre and the Pavilion Theatre, once a popular variety house. Commercial theatre, like the city itself, struggled to find a secure basis for prosperity. The 1905 Frank Matcham-designed Olympia, described architecturally in the *Guide to British Theatres* as a 'sleeping beauty of national significance', was closed. Grade II listing of the former Robert Arthur/Howard & Wyndham Royal Court had provided some protection in 1992, but there had been a chequered history of ownership, and the Arts Council, forced to choose, was only prepared to recognise the Apollo Leisure-owned Empire Theatre in its strategic planning. Both theatres offering mixed programmes were self-financed in 2000, and the Royal Court management had carved out a particular niche as a venue for rock concerts and popular music theatre. In the not-for-profit sector, the two nationally celebrated producing theatres, the Liverpool Playhouse and the Everyman, had been brought together under one management. Separately neither had been able to trade successfully. The Neptune Theatre, unusually located on the second floor of what had been the largest music store in the North, had originally served amateur groups and in 2000 hosted both amateur and professional. Unity Theatre was installed in Hope Place near the Everyman in a former Victorian synagogue recently refurbished through a Lottery grant.[51] As a survivor of the Unity movement, Merseyside Unity as an acting company had finally disbanded in the mid-1980s, but the theatre itself was managed and developed under the auspices of the Hope Place Community Association. By 2000 the two small Unity spaces hosted a range of professional touring and community-based product.

Since the 1981 Toxteth riots had drawn attention to social deprivation and economic decline in Merseyside, Liverpool city and the wider region had been targeted by national government for economic recovery schemes. The policies adopted by the Merseyside Development Corporation saw prestige projects like Liverpool's 1984 International Garden Festival, based on the reclamation of acres of derelict land, and most famously, the £200 million poured into regenerating the Albert Dock as a major tourist attraction. While 3.5 million visitors had enjoyed the combination of enterprise and heritage, many residents of Liverpool were leaving the city. In the decade between 1981 and 1991, 50,000 jobs disappeared. By 2000 the population had dropped by more than 4 per cent from a 1991 census statistic of 480,700 to 457,000.[52] Despite five years' effort and some £1.6 billion of funding generated by Objective 1 status and spent on nearly 5,000 projects, it was shown that Merseyside still had, at 8.5 per cent, an unemployment statistic double the UK average of 4.2 per cent. In addition the region had the fourth highest economic inactivity rate in the UK.[53]

It is difficult not to link this intractable economic malaise with the turbulent record of the two Liverpudlian producing theatres. In 1998 the Playhouse, the longest surviving of the early-twentieth-century repertory theatres, went dark. During the early 1980s the popular local dramatists Alan Bleasdale, Willy Russell and Christopher Bond were part of a directorial group who tried to rejuvenate the Playhouse with a commitment to new writing, but gave up when the pressures became too great. An attempt between 1991 and 1996 by the locally born, metropolitan impresario Bill Kenwright to rescue the theatre by using it to produce and receive his large-scale touring productions failed, as had a final last-ditch return to the repertory ethos.[54] The Everyman, launched in 1964 when Liverpool was at the height of its fame as a centre of popular culture and creativity, traded on a rough-edged, youthful image that by the 1990s was not enough to save it from chronic financial crisis. There was a three-month closure in 1996 when both the artistic director and administrative director resigned.[55] The historians of the Liverpool Playhouse, Pelham McMahon and Pam Brooks, refused to attribute the cause to competition between the two theatres, and traced the problems back to the fragmentation in regional funding which resulted from the abolition of the Merseyside County Council in 1986. The Playhouse, the Everyman and the Royal Liverpool Philharmonic Society struggled with inconsistent support from five local authorities. Decisions by central government had the effect of reducing regional autonomy.[56]

In his critical appraisal of the lessons to be learnt in 2000 from the management of the first cycle of Objective 1 status in Merseyside, the urban planning expert Philip Boland emphasised the importance of involving local stakeholders in social as well as economic development.[57] The process of 'governance', that is, the power to govern at regional level, is, he claimed, 'played out at many spatial resolutions, from the heights of the macro international stage down to the micro community level'. At the micro level in Merseyside where 31.2 per cent of the working population were not participating in the formal labour market, there needed to be more 'genuine inclusivity and a more equitable and effective allocation of resources' as the 'city-region' embarked on a second six-year round of Objective 1 status.[58] For the two beleagured Liverpool theatres, partnership in the acquisition and deployment of limited resources appeared to be the best way forward.

The merger in 2000 of the two theatre companies as the Liverpool and Merseyside Theatres Trust, with a single management programming both buildings, was intended to elide generational differences and break down barriers to flexible practice created by worries on either side about relinquishing their autonomous producing theatre ethos. As third-sector business strategists in a wider urban economy in urgent need of rehabilitation by a diverse range of social partners and agencies, more public funding could only be generated by the prospect of stable management. In the event grant-aid rose to £900,000 and £2.6 million was dedicated to the repair and refurbishment of the Victorian Playhouse building.[59] The Everyman's proximity to Unity Theatre a short distance away with its community-related managerial framework, and the prospect of renewed attempts at urban regeneration in Merseyside focused more directly on addressing social exclusion through what in EU parlance was known as CED (Community Economic Development),[60] offered further opportunities on the Belfast model for exploiting 'a cultural quarter' in the future.

SHIFTING THE FOCUS

European-led initiatives to ameliorate the social and economic consequences of regional stagnation and decline in the UK added other strategic maps of deprivation to competing spatial patterns which challenged metropolitan complacency, and turned the eyes of grateful recipients away from the insularity of the British Union. This in turn had implications for the politics of national devolution. In relation to what he termed 'the old Scottish preference for an assimilationist nationalism', Lindsay Paterson argued in 1994 that new opportunities for careers and development were shifting the focus towards Europe. 'In the new Scottish culture of the 1980s and 1990s, to be European has been equated to being progressive and democratic, in almost the same way as being British was in the eighteenth and nineteenth centuries; and to be British has been tantamount to being anachronistic.'[61] For the new leaders of Scottish institutions, the ambition to be progressive and in democratic control was an inevitable consequence of this perception. Despite a numerical decline in the population largely because of the loss of mass employment opportunities in the old staple industries, over one-third by the end of the century was categorised as belonging to the professional and managerial classes.[62] The growth of an educated elite, 'careerists and professionals ... with diverse origins in the upward mobility of the post-war years',[63] was an important contributory factor in the push towards national autonomy.

Jonathan Hearn, in his critical reappraisal of the concept of nationalism published in 2006, traced the way changing economic trends were altering the cross-border relationship with England. Scottish capital was increasingly being invested abroad and inward investment into light industries such as electronics and chemicals came from outside the country. Even the exploitation of North Sea oil which had been a focal point for nationalist campaigns in the 1970s, was dependent on external technical and economic expertise. In other words the Union no longer brought automatic economic advantage, and throughout the 1980s and 90s as ailing industries were steadily deprived of state assistance, the momentum in favour of a devolved parliament to protect Scottish national interests became irresistible.[64] While a desire to ameliorate prevailing social conditions was a powerful reason for seeking control, another resided with what Hearn identifies as the way 'motives and interests of smaller groups are generalised' and 'geared up into a broader movement ... a process of instrumental, self-interested manipulation by elites'.[65] It could be argued, extrapolating from this, that as an autonomous urban Scottish theatre grew steadily more dynamic from the 1980s onwards, so this instrumentalism framed in nationalist terms contributed to the 'self interests' of Scottish theatremakers and promoters as they shaped the industry in 2000.

A DEFINED SPACE TO MAP IDENTITY

As I have shown in previous chapters, the Scottish Highlands had been a magnet for theatrical 'missionaries' throughout the twentieth century. By 2000 more decisive structural interventions had been created on the back of the general economic development strategies enabled by Objective 1 status and the Highlands and Islands Enterprise agency. The region was still spectacularly empty. A report produced in 2000 for the Scottish Executive stated that the population of 370,376 represented about 7 per cent of the entire Scottish population spread over 50 per cent of the land mass. There was a population density of only 9.5 people per square kilometre compared with 241 people per square kilometre in the UK as a whole.[66] In the summer, however, the romantic emptiness attracted some 4 million visitors. As a result, employment in what was termed in the report as 'distribution' and hotels and restaurants was exceeded only by public administration, education and health as the principal provider of paid work. That said, a 45 per cent increase in the environmentally related industries of agriculture, fishing and forestry by 1997 was characteristic of EU-supported projects; 25 per cent of the economically active were classified as self-employed.[67]

It was within this context that the Highlands and Islands Theatre Network was set up, following a decision made in 1994 by a range of funding agencies not to establish a Highland Theatre Company but to nurture a more organic growth of professional theatre in the region. In 2000 12 regionally based touring companies gave 279 performances in some 40 different venues.[68] Grey Coast Theatre Company, founded in 1992 by the Caithness-born poet and playwright George Gunn, with Inverness-born Matthew Zajac, was based furthest north in Thurso, serving the counties of Caithness and Sutherland with their 250 miles of grey coastline.[69] Another company, initially known as The Collectors, was launched in Inverness in 1998 with a one-man comedy *Redcoats, Turncoats & Petticoats* presented by the company's founder Hamish MacDonald in a town-centre pub. By 2000 the company had embarked on a second Highlands' tour of *The Captain's Collection*, a musical play about Captain Simon Fraser of Stratherrick, an officer in the government army who collected hundreds of Gaelic tunes forbidden after the 1745 Jacobite Rebellion.[70] On the Isle of Skye, Gaelic-language theatre produced by Tosg had been promoted by Simon Mackenzie, former 7.84 (Scotland) actor and well known to viewers of the Gaelic soap opera *Machair*.[71]

George Gunn, attempting to classify Highland Theatre, described it as 'a defined space where identities are mapped, where memory and experience are presented – all of these drawing on traditions with an eye on the future. All of these identities come from the ground and with which we struggle, through action and story, to make articulate.' Between 1998 and 1999 his company had produced *Egil, Son of the Night Wolf*, which had used professional and community actors to create six versions of the same play based on a ninth-century Icelandic saga, and *Camster*, a collection of ten short plays which depicted modern life in the Highlands and Islands. *Atomic City*, which launched its tour at the Eden Court Theatre in 1999, tackled the dilemma posed by the proximity of the Dounreay nuclear reactors just nine miles from Thurso. The former cattle town, named Bunillish in the play, had grown in response to the job opportunities offered by the complex. Even though the reactors had been shut down in 1994, many of the local population were still employed in what promised to be a lengthy operation to clean the site.[72] As Gunn later emphasised, the story of the Highlands is not a happy one in human terms, and *Atomic City*, which was presented in Aberdeen, Glasgow and Edinburgh, as well as extensively in the north, drew attention to the way geographical remoteness had been used to generate spaces of power in more than one sense of the term, by external interests.

SMALL AND MEDIUM ENTERPRISES

Neither Grey Coast, nor The Collectors, nor the Highlands and Islands Theatre Network as a support organisation, appears in the *British Performing Arts Yearbook*, thus compounding the impression of absence from the wider landscape. Overall, however, listings of companies under the headings of Drama and Community run to 240. Some were the legally constituted, not-for-profit companies registered to manage the large building-based producing theatres. The majority were small businesses, many of which functioned within the not-for-profit subsidised sector and with charitable status. In business terms, however, what is interesting is the extent to which these reflected changing patterns of employment related to levels of industrial concentration.

Armstrong and Taylor draw attention to the unprecedented growth in small and medium enterprises (SMEs) across the UK as a whole in the last two decades of the century. Through to the late 1960s industrial concentration in large firms, with government actively encouraging takeovers and mergers in the manufacturing sector, had been the prevailing trend. The result with recurring economic crisis had been increased employee vulnerability to large-scale industrial collapse and the regional economic imbalances which had devastated whole communities. Paradoxically, while on the super-macro level the global corporate economy burgeoned, the revival of the SME sector had led by 1998 to a situation where out of 3.7 million UK businesses, 99.2 per cent contained fewer than 50 employees.

The very smallest – those with under 5 employees – comprised 89.2 per cent of all businesses and contained among them 5 million jobs.[73] In theatre a high proportion of building-based producing companies could be classified as SMEs with the core staff hovering around 50 or fewer. But what was particularly significant was that the small theatre companies, which either toured nationally – in some cases internationally – or mainly served clusters of audiences/clients in specific regions, were typically very small with perhaps only two or three permanent staff. A company such as Out of Joint, founded by Max Stafford-Clark in 1993 after he stepped down as artistic director of the Royal Court, could with a small core staff of five, actors on fixed-term contracts and the judicious use of strategic producing partnerships, exert an extensive artistic influence, touring to middle-scale theatres and arts centres across the UK from an administrative base in London.

While commercially promoted productions of West End successes with ad hoc casts continued to tour the larger theatres – and these were not necessarily confined to commercial receiving houses, but could also be presented as part of a mixed-economy producing theatre season – a particular ecology had developed around the dissemination of the work of the best known of the small, independent, avant-garde producing companies. Those based in London such as Shared Experience or Theatre de Complicite could command audiences outside the capital of between 400 and 600 a performance, typically of those who attended the larger arts centres or sympathetic producing theatre spaces. There was thus a strong, if discrete, network of regional following derived from local intelligentsia and theatre aficionados, especially those who were part of the academic community.

The extent of European influence in performance aesthetic was an important factor in their success, both for creative innovation in its own right and in terms of European showcase opportunities. Thus, while EU social and economic policies were instrumental in effecting some infrastructural change in British society, the cross-fertilisation of theatre practitioners interacting through performance encounters in European cities and international arts festivals served to enhance the international reputation, and by extension domestic durability, of well-established British theatre companies. London offered the most diverse and concentrated experience of the avant-garde; however, the touring system ensured that there were selected regional clusters of audiences open to the dissemination of radical influences.

There were some well-known English companies that chose to locate themselves in a regional home while cultivating national and international networks. In 2000, the base in Sheffield of Forced Entertainment, which had survived as a company with six founder members since 1984, had its origins in the collapse of the city's traditional industrial strength in cutlery, steel and coal. The Cultural Industries Quarter, which had been one of the first examples of this 'cultural' model of urban regeneration, had been a Sheffield City Council initiative in 1988, established in a run-down but accessible three-quarters of a square mile on the edge of the city centre between the railway station, the town hall, the main shopping street and the ring road. Within reach of these key resources and Sheffield Hallam University, it was designed to stimulate the growth of a new sector in music, art, performance and film which in turn would nurture new audiences. The Workstation, where Forced Entertainment was based, was a large five-floor 1930s' building which since 1993 had been taking in SME tenants from a range of creative industries.[74] Indeed, the fact that the company's decision to diversify its performance practice into film, video, CD-Rom, etc. was one of the reasons for its durability and was clearly advantaged by the agglomeration effects of its location.

In general, the cross-over among theatre, film, installation and live art characteristic of Forced Entertainment's work was representative of a widening category of experimental activity, which in consciously eschewing traditional performance spaces created an alternative topography where any natural or human-made site could be invested with meaning. In the case of Forced Entertainment, making performance about the experience of contemporary life at the end of the twentieth century, which, as the director Tim Etchells put it, could be understood by someone 'who was brought up in a house where the TV was always on', was in part enabled by acting as 'voyeurs, watching people' in their host city.[75] However, as Liz Tomlin pointed out in a critique published in 1999 of *Nights in the City*, a 1995 mobile site-specific piece which took actors and audience on a guided coach tour round Sheffield to disrupt and re-imagine the 'facts' of historical memory, Sheffield was presented as a 'a virtual city that exists everywhere and nowhere'.[76] Compelled at one point as a tourist-spectator to gaze at the residents of the Manor, one of the city's most deprived housing estates, she was uncomfortably aware both of the objectification of non-consenting but '"performing"/subjects' but also of the distance in every sense between the resources enjoyed by the company in the Workstation and the everyday circumstances of the people on the housing estate.

The applicable anywhere non-site-specificity of the model of performance intervention created was re-emphasised when the piece was reworked for a similar exercise in Rotterdam in 1997. By 2000 the map of the company's work continued to extend from the local to the global. *And on the Thousandth Night* was made in September for the Festival Ayloul in Beirut. *Scar Stories*, 'an experiment in exploring a single subject across several art forms', was commissioned by the Kunstenfestivaldesarts in Brussels. In *Hotel Binary*, a four-channel video installation, company members listed the things that frightened them while seated in the sort of anonymous non-domestic locations, such as hotel lobbies and airport departure lounges, which had become familiar within the globalised economy. *Disco Relax*, which toured to venues such as Chapter Arts Centre in Cardiff, Dartington Hall in Devon and the Phoenix Arts Centre in Leicester, combined drunken and disjointed live dialogue and performance with fragments of film, video and television.[77] Although a million miles away aesthetically from Yeats and his friends in the impoverished Dublin of 1900, and for all Forced Entertainment's commitment to the postmodern apprehension of the anxieties and dislocations of end-of-century human existence, both projects were linked by their dependence on a coterie audience whose embodied habitus – economic, social and educational – ensured the maximum receptiveness to avant-garde ideas. It was no accident that the map of Forced Entertainment's touring was dominated in the UK by university or university-associated venues.

Tomlin's critique was stimulated as co-director with Steve Jackson of Open Performance Centre Limited (OPC) by experience of a considerably more grass-roots engagement with Sheffield communities especially the young. Point Blank, a small professional touring company, legally constituted in 1998, was formed at OPC while at the same time training courses, work placements, schools projects and participatory productions with local people were offered. In 1999 the first OPC trainees were launched on professional careers, while Sheffield's Library Theatre (next to the Lyceum Theatre) was the venue for a millennium community project, 'Now Then Sheffield'. In 2000 'Goldstar', an ambitious multi-schools project, was presented on the Crucible's main stage, while the 'Steel City Youth Project' was performed in Birmingham and at an International Youth Festival in Bussang in north-eastern France.[78]

Companies like OPC, which multi-tasked working across generations and constituencies of specific interests and social needs, moving between amateur and professional, quotidian and avant-garde, and generally sustained by a mixed portfolio of public funding sources, could be found throughout the UK. New companies were constantly forming, but within each region there were groups which had survived the economic challenges of the past two decades and evolved into small but settled units creating another spatially distributed but connected topography. Within a geographical area overseen by one Regional Arts Board such as Yorkshire Arts, it was possible to see in microcosm how theatre companies functioning as not-for-profit SMEs were achieving durability through a range of working methods and target audiences. In Leeds, the veteran Red Ladder had gone through several incarnations: from 1968 agit prop to a company policy in 2000 focused on young people, interculturalism and disability. Also in Leeds, the Theatre Company Blah Blah Blah, founded in 1985, worked with children and young people, using participative theatre programmes as a way of developing touring product. Interplay, established in 1990, also worked with young people experiencing economic, social and sensory exclusion. Yorkshire Women Theatre, again based in Leeds, dated from 1983 and toured devised theatre-in-health and social education work. Mind the Gap, set up in 1988 and based in Bradford, was a professional theatre company for learning-disabled actors. By 2000 the company had started to diversify from purely devised work to creating adaptations of classic texts.[79] Blaize in Ilkley on the edge of the Yorkshire moors concentrated on rural touring. Mikron, founded in 1963 and based in Huddersfield, toured in the summer months by narrow boat, playing in non-theatre venues and promoting the national inland waterways – the bulk carrier of the early industrial revolution – as a twenty-first-century source of recreation and commerce.[80]

FAMILIAR STRANGERS

In 1900 what bound the nations of Great Britain together, provoked migratory patterns and ensured that national boundaries were infinitely permeable was mutual interest in the industrial and economic success of the imperial project. In 2000 the visible demographic legacy of empire seen in the complex heritage represented by now two, three or even four generations of migrant families challenged any attempt to imagine a homogeneous national identity. At the end of the century the estimated size of the 'minority ethnic' population of Great Britain was 4 million – a little more than 7 per cent of the whole; 50 per cent had been born in the UK and the majority were young. Between 1992 and 1999 this 'new' British population had grown by 15 per cent, compared with an increase of 1 per cent of the 'white' population.[81] Soon statistical calculations would begin to suggest that by the end of the first decade of the twenty-first century at least one of the major English cities – the possibilities were Manchester, Leicester and Birmingham – would have a majority minority ethnic population.[82]

That said, by the time of the 2001 census, 45 per cent of the total non-white British population lived in London. As noted in chapter 7, this in part explains why there were so few Black British and British Asian-*led* companies based outside London. The same global city factors, in particular the networking opportunities and likelihood of more sympathetic audiences which concentrated so much of the theatre industry in the metropolis, inevitably drew in artists from the migrant communities. In 2000, Tara, Tamasha, Kali, Nitro, Yellow Earth, Talawa all had London addresses. Slough, where Rifco Arts, founded in 1997 by a consortium of British Asian directors and actors, was based, was within striking distance of London.

Regionally, the isolated examples of professional companies which identified with a non-white heritage sheltered within a wider theatre-friendly environment and, moreover, drew consciously on the multiple cultural traditions which reflected the complexity of the migrant experience. The name of one of the newest, Rasa, set up in Manchester in 1998 by Malaysian-born Rani Moorthy, signalled the shifts in meaning within three different Asian languages for the rapture generated between actor and audience.[83] In Huddersfield the intercultural Chol Theatre established by the poet Adam Strickland in 1989 took its name from the Bangladeshi word for 'come on let's get going'.[84] Peshkar Productions, named after a tabla music form, had been launched in Oldham in 1991 with community arts workshops, and by 2000 was developing a profile for South Asian theatre in the North-West with a strong, youth-oriented participatory policy.[85] Indeed, work within the community and especially with young people, the majority of whom were born in Britain, was seen as vital in the forging of new hybrid identities firmly integrated within British society, but aware of the creative possibilities of their other cultural heritage. In Leeds, Red Ladder's intercultural, cross-community projects dated back to the mid-1980s. The distinctive Asian strand of their work, which included in 2000 a play *Picture Me* by Noel Greig, set in Mumbai and England exploring the impact of HIV/Aids on British Asian teenagers, was part of the trajectory that would culminate in 2002 with the setting up of the British Asian-led Asian Theatre School.[86]

Despite the goodwill generated by these developments, as highlighted in chapter 7, the consciousness of institutional racism amongst all non-white theatre artists would find its fullest expression in the Eclipse Conference held at the Nottingham Playhouse in 2001. But in 2000, in the context of the widespread acceptance of integrated casting in regional producing theatres and the regular employment of individual Black and

Asian actors in small-scale theatre companies, the greatest attention was directed towards growing audiences from within the Black and Asian communities, who thus far had displayed a marked reluctance to engage with artistic product designed to attract them in more than relatively modest numbers.[87]

In the West and East Midlands there were substantial urban settlements. But despite the efforts promoted by BRIT at Nottingham Playhouse with the African-heritage community and at Leicester Haymarket with the Asian-heritage community, as well as Birmingham Rep's record of artistic integration over more than a decade, each theatre for regional audiences remained largely what a Sikh practitioner later called 'a white man's space'.[88] In general, multi-disciplinary cultural and arts centres, which could enable participation in a range of culturally specific art forms as well as professional practice, could appear more inclusive. In Bristol the African Caribbean resource centre Kuumba, located in the St Paul's area with its links back to the city's slave-trading past, had been launched in 1974 to offer the large black migrant community experience of the arts.[89] In Liverpool, where again the slave trade had brought both wealth and early non-white communities, the Blackie Arts Centre, opened in 1968, built its policy around its proximity to what was claimed to be Britain's oldest African Caribbean community and Europe's first China Town.[90]

To return to Nigel Thrift in relation to this final topographical pattern, quite obviously the early post-war migrant dispersal across the UK could be described as 'highly problematic temporary settlements' – indeed, for many from the Caribbean or South and East Asia the longing for 'home' included the hopes for eventual return. The process of dividing and connecting up into different kinds of collectives had brought together groups of people into the major, usually urban, centres of employment, who for all their superficial 'racial' similarity, in fact, came from widely dissimilar geographical, linguistic and religious backgrounds. That the ensuing collectives had found the means to be sustainable and durable was often the result of looking inwards in search of communal solidarity and familiar cultural traditions very different from the dominant Western model on offer from mainstream British arts institutions. While unemployment, poverty, poor health and educational achievement could be found in many migrant communities and certainly contributed to sporadic urban unrest, it was also the case that groups could travel long distances and pay high prices to see and hear invited artists from the home country.

This was one of the findings of the report *Arts – What's in a Word? Ethnic Minorities and the Arts*, commissioned by Arts Council England

and published in 2000.[91] Another competing if effectively invisible alternative theatre was supplied for South Asian audiences in the form of
the home-language dramas performed by amateur groups ranging from
Bangladeshi and Bengali or Punjabi-Hindi speaking, or, indeed, professional troupes from Pakistan. What a practitioner such as the Indian-born
Vayu Naidu, contracted as associate producer at the Leicester Haymarket
in 1999 as part of BRIT, discovered was the need to be aware of the particular cultural sensibilities of the largely Hindu, East Africa-originating
population.[92] In Birmingham over half the South Asian population came
from Pakistan and were Muslim with different traditions. In Nottingham
while the non-white population was a smaller proportion of the whole,
the Black and Asian communities were more evenly balanced. But given
the multiple routes whereby slaves captured in Africa were brought and
then dispersed amongst the different Caribbean islands, the classification
'African Caribbean' again covered a multiplicity of different identities.

In Birmingham the Drum Arts Centre, which publicised itself as
the only promoting venue of its kind in Europe, had opened in 1998 to
develop and celebrate African, Asian and Caribbean arts. Built at a cost
of £5.1 million on land once occupied by the 1908 Aston Hippodrome in
the Newtown area bordering on Handsworth in the north-east of the
city, the layers of human intervention in the site and its environs might
serve as a local emblem of the century. From manufacturing prosperity which had once sustained the old variety house and the magnificent
Victorian public house close by; to the factories which drew the first
post-war black migrants to live in the big old houses which formed one
of the black ghettos created by Birmingham's housing policy; to the disastrous alienating 1960s' construction of *New*town (my emphasis), and
the arrival of the first South Asian migrants; and to the intercommunal
violence seen in the 1981 Handsworth Rebellion which jolted the city
council into reviewing its race relations, the Drum staggered under the
weight of responsibility and the difficulty of attracting audiences from
an area which suffered some of the worst levels of social deprivation in
the country.[93]

In 2000 as the Drum faced an uncertain future, the Report commissioned by the Runnymede Trust on the future of multi-ethnic Britain was
published. Chaired by the Indian political philosopher Bhikhu Parekh, the
commission took the broadest possible view of the ethnic groupings which
made up the British population, including the far from homogeneous white
ethnic majority. In attempting to imagine a multi-cultural *post*-nation, it
was stated that not only was 'Britishness … less unified, more diverse and

pluralistic, than is normally imagined', but the same applied to migrant communities. While differences now mattered profoundly, 'differences are not necessarily either/or – many people are learning to live "in between"'.[94] Throughout this book I have sought to show the 'in betweenness' which I believe characterised theatre as economic activity and socially important cultural practice across the four nations in the twentieth century. As the new century began, each component part of the UK to a greater or lesser degree was coming to terms with the now indigenous 'familiar strangers' who had literally changed the faces of Great Britain. From lives lived in between traditions, generations, class and gender formations, new theatres would emerge.

Conclusion

Looking back over the one-hundred-year segment of the twentieth century, what conclusions can be reached about continuity and change in British theatre? I suspect that in 1900 relatively few could have confidently predicted the colossal changes in mass creative communication soon to be wrought by the electronic media. It is thus in the arena of technological innovation that the new continuity was forged. Throughout the book I have examined the impact this had on the making of live theatre: on the diversifying of opportunity for actors and the evidence that regional and national differences could be more readily recognised and disseminated. At the same time the economics of cinema and, then, as a more durable presence, television, not only meant that live theatre was no longer *the* dominant form of popular entertainment, but the major disparities in revenue-generation capacity linked to the concentration of centres of production in or near London also contributed to the contraction of the human and financial resources available for more ambitious theatre projects across the UK. By 2000 the digital revolution was well under way in transforming the means by which performance could be virtually manipulated and transmitted. Artists who remained committed to the live interaction of actor and audience in the same physically shared spaces were squaring up to the threat of another major technological change. And yet theatre-makers were proving adept, as always, in absorbing and working with change.

At my own university in Worcester, the resident C&T Theatre Company, which as the small theatre-in-education company Collar and Tie had faced liquidation within a bleak educational and local authority environment, had transformed itself by using new technology to enhance the participatory experience of young people in schools. Funded by Arts Council England and the West Midlands Regional Arts Board, which had designated it a Key Regional Organisation, C&T also received European funding through the European Social Fund Objective 5B targeted at work in isolated rural areas. In 2000 further boosted by a capital Lottery grant of £83,000, the company was travelling around Herefordshire and Worcestershire with two Touring Digital Media Units. Both a successful SME *and* a small-scale example of the exemplary theatre operating at the grass-roots of the community, C&T was clearly in the vanguard of change, but with artistic and pedagogic principles which would have been very familiar to the rural touring initiatives of the 1920s.

C&T flourished where other companies had collapsed by manoeuvring adroitly within the third-sector mixed economy, which appeared to be firmly entrenched in 2000. As the statistics which I cite in chapter 6 demonstrate, however, the lives of the majority of theatre workers remained insecure and peripatetic despite the greater regulation of employment conditions and the wider opportunities for education and training. In *Theatre in a Cool Climate*, a collection of practitioner-written essays commissioned by Vera Gottlieb and Colin Chambers to give a snapshot of theatre at the end of the century, Venu Dhupa described her early-career struggle to achieve a reasonable standard of living even when fully employed within the subsidised sector.[1] As the Executive Director of Nottingham Playhouse, and thus at the head of the management hierarchy of a major regional producing theatre, she commented that: 'at Nottingham we often feel we are training people only for them to leave our profession which in turn, reduces the number of possible inspirational role models'.[2]

That she herself, given her gender and cultural heritage, was clearly an inspirational role model was an index of the distance travelled since 1900, as was the fact that Nottingham, a small city in the East Midlands of England, had its own not-for-profit producing theatre sustained by state and civic funding, and overseen by a board of volunteer directors who by law could not seek pecuniary advantage for their efforts. That Dhupa's declared role was to 'maintain a balance between the business and the art',[3] however, was an overt statement of end-of-century priorities which would have been instantly endorsed a hundred years earlier. That her carefully cultivated trainee theatre professionals despaired of better prospects also hinted at other lingering inequalities which went beyond sectoral instability.

For a whole raft of reasons ranging from the major political changes brought about by national devolutionary initiatives, and the slow-burning effects of equal opportunities legislation, to the impact of the media referred to above, professional theatre artists were far more broadly representative of social, ethnic and national differences. I would hesitate to state firmly that British audiences had access to more live theatre at the end of the century than they had in 1900, but I would argue that theatre in 2000 was multifaceted beyond anything dreamt of at the beginning of the century. Many of the large theatres so eagerly erected at the end of the nineteenth century in anticipation of big profits from mass audiences had either disappeared or were vestiges of their former glory. But if in 2000 it were possible to calculate the number of people who attended the venues I counted in my end of century topography, and then add in the attendance capacity of the schools, colleges, community and rehabilitation centres, prisons and church halls, etc. where theatre continued to happen, then it might be proved that more of the population than ever before had access to some sort of live-theatre experience.

There was much greater opportunity even on the most modest scale for independent production projects, and theatre's social exemplary function embedded in local communities was far more widely distributed. Of course as the Eclipse Conference was graphically to illustrate in the case of the 'new' British just eighteen months into the new century, unexamined if not overtly discriminatory practices could still be found to exclude and marginalise. In the highly competitive environment of theatre where so much can depend – not least economically – on entrenched concepts of artistic charisma and equally entrenched assumptions about audience taste and preference, the reasons to block access are not hard to find.

My attempt to present a more integrated narrative of the plurality of British theatre during the twentieth century is inevitably partial and awaits expansion and, doubtless, correction by other scholars. In asking the reader to stand, as it were, in different places to survey the landscape I wanted to re-orientate the gaze away from the dominant metropolitan narrative to account through a greater understanding of the structural basis of theatre for the differences, separate trajectories and inequalities. In my discussion of amateur theatre in the first half of the century, for example, I set out to explain not only why in circumstances of economic constraint or stress established models of professional theatre were not viable, but also why the various models of non-professional participatory practice were nevertheless unequivocally still *theatre*, delivering substantial affective properties for community actors and audiences. Amateur 'playing' can have profound aesthetic effects in terms of human sensibility and communal values and beliefs. The practice of art can float free of the economic sphere even as the lives of participants continue to be constrained in other ways.

My focus on the amateur was one component in the over-arching strategy of bringing together the three key terms 'industry, art and empire' which make up the subtitle to the book. Unfettered by quotidian concerns, art can inhabit a liminal space that can take it in the direction of radical and disruptive innovation or serve as a tool for the preservation of collective certainties. As productive, economic activity, however, theatre is an industry employing a range of craft, trade and other professional skills. Its success is dependent on the complex economic relations that derive from more broad-based industrial stability. Each of my topographies has provided evidence of the way in which the visible concentration of theatre, as manifested in its buildings and other means of production and circulation, was dependent on changing industrial patterns which in turn depended on wider national and international economic trends.

By the end of the century, and not uncontroversially at a time of increasing dependency on service industries, theatre had been designated as one of the *cultural* industries not only because of efforts to prove statistically that commercially successful theatre products were net contributors to the national purse through tourism, etc., but because of theatre's envisaged role in the sphere of community animation. As the relics of the old industrial heritage were revalorised and refashioned to repair dereliction in deprived and/or troubled areas, so the restorative possibilities of a whole spectrum of creative activity including theatre were incorporated into renewal programmes. In these cases, European economic intervention brought welcome resources for grand capital projects and small artistic enterprises alike, but also reinforced the growing perception that the boundaries of the unitary nation state could be renegotiated both internally and externally. While the legacy of empire was everywhere apparent, especially demographically, it was no longer the means of marshalling the collective allegiance and energies of the UK population.

Metropolitan power as originally exercised from the heart of empire, however, had transformed and reinvigorated itself as part of the process of globalisation. As a world city London was a global control and command centre largely because of the economic attributes which Phil Hubbard lists: 'number of corporate headquarters, stock exchange activity, presence of international banks', etc.[4] The presence of 'knowledge-rich individuals' and the face-to-face networks created through close physical proximity vastly increased the cultural capital of the city. By the end of the century the critical mass of theatre located in London was almost certainly greater and more various, drawing strengths from both the commercial and subsidised sectors. In terms of how fruitful creative exchange was engineered across the UK, the relationship between the core and the periphery was certainly more complex and more dynamic. But there was no doubting that the greatest kudos and cultural prestige lay with the exercise and exploitation of artistic attributes analogous to the other economic and political resources clustered together in the metropolis.

In 2003 a Catalyst Paper authored by three cultural geographers attempted to diagnose the causes of the intractable problems of regional inequality: 'a structure has been allowed continually to re-assert its will to centralisation, repeating over and over again what might be called a "courtly" structure. Social differentiations have tended to ossify around this geographical structure, providing spatial refrains that echo down the ages.'[5] To extrapolate from this in relation to theatre and recall the historic monarchical/state strategies I referred to in my introduction is to find the term 'courtly structure' particularly resonant. In 2000 within the 'cool climate' for theatre identified by Vera Gottlieb and Colin Chambers, there was a general feeling of qualified optimism which extended across the whole landscape, but there was no denying the artistic, economic and social differentiation which derived from the centuries' old spatial inequalities.

That said the one fundamental continuity which the interwoven stories of twentieth-century theatre demonstrates is how resilient the instinct for live performance and collective story-telling is. In my introduction I asked what difference it would make to the historical record if the experience of the greater majority of the theatre-going or theatre-making population were examined. I think it has thrown into much sharper relief the extent to which it mattered and continued to matter that different communities of interest develop and strive to retain their preferred models of theatre. What I have tried to show is how dominant priorities were contested from both ends of the economic and ideological spectrum and how attempts were made to reach an accommodation with varying degrees of success. While the reasons for long-term structural inequalities have been made more visible, so too have the means by which these were confronted or ameliorated. At the local level it is possible to see more clearly the multiple factors of enablement which need to coalesce to make theatre happen and these depend on the stability of 'the ordinary business of life'. The key question at the end of the one-hundred-year segment of twentieth-century history is what new factors might emerge to disrupt that stability.

Notes

INTRODUCTION

1 Dewey Ganzel, 'Patent wrongs and patent theatres', *PMLA*, 76 (1961), 384–96.
2 Michael Booth, Clifford Leech, T. W. Craik et al., *The Revels History of Drama in English, Vol. 6, 1750–1880* (London: Methuen, 1975); Simon Trussler, *The Cambridge Illustrated History of British Theatre* (Cambridge University Press, 1994); Simon Shepherd and Peter Womack, *English Drama: A Cultural History* (Oxford: Blackwell, 1996), p. x.
3 George Rowell and Anthony Jackson, *The Repertory Movement: A History of Regional Theatre in Britain* (Cambridge University Press, 1984).
4 Kate Dorney and Ros Merkin (eds.), *The Glory of the Garden: English Regional Theatre and the Arts Council 1984–2009* (Newcastle upon Tyne: Cambridge Scholars Publishing, 2010).
5 Arts Council of Great Britain, *The Glory of the Garden: The development of the Arts in England – A Strategy for a Decade* (London: Arts Council of Great Britain, 1984).
6 Benedict Anderson, *Imagined Communities: Reflections on the Origin and Spread of Nationalism*, rev. edn (London: Verso, 1991), p. xiii.
7 Kenneth O. Morgan, 'Editor's foreword', in Kenneth O. Morgan (ed.), *The Oxford Illustrated History of Britain* (Oxford University Press, 1984), pp. v–ix, p. vi.
8 Since the mid-1990s a number of separate national theatre histories have been published. These include Randall Stevenson and Gavin Wallace (eds.), *Scottish Theatre Since the Seventies* (Edinburgh University Press, 1996); Bill Findlay (ed.), *A History of Scottish Theatre* (Edinburgh: Polygon, 1998); David Adams, *Stage Welsh: Nation, Nationalism and Theatre: The Search for Cultural Identity* (Llandysul: Gomer, 1996); Anna-Marie Taylor (ed.), *Staging Wales: Welsh Theatre 1979–1997* (Cardiff: University of Wales Press, 1997); Ruth Shade, *Communication Breakdowns: Theatre, Performance, Rock Music and Some Other Welsh Assemblies* (Cardiff: University of Wales Press, 2004); Christopher Morash, *A History of Irish Theatre 1601–2000* (Cambridge University Press, 2002).
9 These include Jan McDonald, 'Towards national identities: theatre in Scotland'; Adrienne Scullion, 'Theatre in Scotland in the 1990s and beyond'; Ioan Williams, 'Towards national identities: Welsh theatres'; Roger Owen, 'Theatre in Wales in the 1990s and beyond', all in Baz Kershaw (ed.), *The*

Cambridge History of British Theatre, Vol. 3, Since 1895 (Cambridge University Press, 2005), pp. 195–227; 470–84; 242–72; 485–97.

10 Irish historians from both sides of the border are addressing the vacuum. These include Morash, *A History of Irish Theatre*, and Ophelia Byrne, *The Stage in Ulster from the Eighteenth Century* (Belfast: Linen Hall Library, 1997); Imelda Foley, *Girls in the Big Picture* (Belfast: Blackstaff Press, 2003); Tom Maguire, *Making Theatre in Northern Ireland: Through and Beyond the Troubles* (Exeter University Press, 2006). What I am trying to do within my imperial framework is to view this history alongside that of other British theatres to offer a partial, but relational, exegesis.

11 Jen Harvie, *Staging the UK* (Manchester University Press, 2005), pp. 59–67.

12 Ibid., p. 2.

13 Robert Winder, *Bloody Foreigners: The Story of Immigration to Britain* (London: Little, Brown, 2004), p. 257.

14 James Mitchell, 'Scotland in the Union, 1945–1995', in T. M. Devine and R. J. Finlay (eds.), *Scotland in the Twentieth Century* (Edinburgh University Press, 1996), pp. 85–101, p. 97; J. G. Kellas, *The Politics of Nationalism and Ethnicity* (Basingstoke: Macmillan Education, 1991), pp. 66–7.

15 Edward W. Said, *Culture and Imperialism* (London: Vintage, 1994), p. 59.

16 Claire Cochrane, '"The contaminated audience": researching amateur theatre in Wales before 1939', *New Theatre Quarterly*, 74 (2003), 169–76.

17 This is explained in chapter 2. See Harley Granville-Barker, *The Exemplary Theatre* (London: Chatto and Windus, 1922).

18 Tracy C. Davis, *The Economics of the British Stage 1800–1914* (Cambridge University Press, 2000), p. 2.

19 Ibid., p. 4.

20 As identified in Thomas G. Rawski, 'Economics and the historian', in Thomas G. Rawski (ed.), *Economics and the Historian* (Berkeley: University of California Press, 1996), p. 1.

21 Quoted in Everett Johnson Burtt, Jr, *Social Perspectives in the History of Economic Theory* (New York: St Martin's Press, 1972), p. 201.

22 Jim McGuigan, *Modernity and Postmodern Culture* (Buckingham: Open University Press, 1999), p. 1.

23 Rawski, 'Economics and the historian', p. 5.

24 Richard Schechner, *Performance Theory*, 2nd edn (New York and London: Routledge, 1988), pp. 120–4.

25 I have explored historiographic issues surrounding scholarly preference and judgements of taste drawing on Pierre Bourdieu in Claire Cochrane, 'The pervasiveness of the commonplace: the historian and amateur theatre', *Theatre Research International*, 26 (2001), 233–42; Pierre Bourdieu, *Distinction: A Social Critique of the Judgement of Taste*, trans. Richard Nice (London: Routledge & Kegan Paul, 1984).

26 For a discussion of the concept of cultural 'needs', see Stephen Mennell, 'Theoretical considerations on the study of cultural "needs"', *Sociology*, 13 (1979), 235–57.

27 For example, Robert Hutchison, *The Politics of the Arts Council* (London: Sinclair Browne, 1982).

28 John Pick, *The Theatre Industry Subsidy, Profit & the Search for New Audiences* (London: Comedia, 1985), p. 12.

29 David Grant, *Playing the Wild Card, A Survey of Community Drama and Smaller Scale Theatres from a Community Relations Perspective* (Belfast: Community Relations Council, 1993); Greg Giesekam, *Luvvies and Rude Mechanicals? Amateur and Community Theatre in Scotland* (Glasgow: Scottish Arts Council, 2000); Shade, *Communication Breakdowns*.

30 Simon Shepherd, *The Cambridge Introduction to Modern British Theatre* (Cambridge University Press, 2009), p. xiii.

31 See Wolfgang Reinhard, 'The Idea of Early Modern History', in Michael Bentley (ed.), *Companion to Historiography* (London: Routledge, 1997), pp. 281–90, p. 281.

32 Thomas Postlewait, *The Cambridge Introduction to Theatre Historiography* (Cambridge University Press, 2009), p. 161.

33 W. A. Green, 'Periodisation in European and world history', *Journal of World History*, 3 (1992), 14.

34 Edward W. Soja, *Postmodern Geographies: The Reassertion of Space in Critical Social Theory* (London: Verso, 1989), p. 1, quoted in Claire Cochrane, 'Theatre and urban space: the case of Birmingham rep', *New Theatre Quarterly*, 26 (2000), 137–47.

35 Alan Townsend, *Uneven Regional Change in Britain* (Cambridge University Press, 1993), p. 17.

36 For an explanation of the core–periphery relationship, see John Langton and R. J. Morris (eds.), *Atlas of Industrialising Britain 1780–1914* (London: Methuen, 1986), p. xxvii.

37 Henri Lefebvre, *The Production of Space*, trans. Donald Nicholson-Smith (Oxford: Blackwell, 1991), p. 49.

38 Barney Warf, 'Nigel Thrift', in Phil Hubbard, R. Kitchen and G. Valentine, *Key Thinkers on Space and Place* (London: Sage, 2004), pp. 294–300, p. 296.

1 THE TOPOGRAPHY OF THEATRE IN 1900

1 Lefebvre, *The Production of Space*, p. 49.

2 As discussed in Mennel, 'Theoretical considerations on the study of cultural "needs"', pp. 235–7.

3 Ganzel, 'Patent wrongs and patent theatres'.

4 Davis, *The Economics of the British Stage*, pp. 17–41.

5 Allardyce Nicoll, *English Drama 1900–1930: The Beginnings of the Modern Period* (London: Cambridge University Press, 1973), pp. 139–41.

6 Langton and Morris, *Atlas of Industrialising Britain*, p. xxvii.

7 Frederick Ledger (ed.), *The Era Almanack 1894* (London: 1894), pp. 58–62; Frederick Ledger (ed.), *The Era Almanack 1900* (London: 1900), pp. 88–92.

8 John Earl and Michael Sell, *The Theatres Trust Guide to British Theatres 1750–1950: A Gazetter* (London: A & C Black, 2000).

9 Frederick Ledger (ed.), *The Era Annual 1907* (London: 1907), pp. 83–7.

10 Mervyn Heard, '"Come in please, come out pleased": the development of British fairground Bioscope presentation and performance', in Linda Fitzsimmons and Sarah Street (eds.), *Moving Performance: British Stage and Screen, 1890s–1920s* (Wiltshire: Flick Books, 2000), pp. 101–11.

11 Ledger, *The Era Almanack 1900*, pp. 73–7.

12 See alphabetical listings in Nicoll, *English Drama*.

13 Michael Holroyd, *Bernard Shaw, Volume 2, 1898–1918, The Pursuit of Power* (Harmondsworth: Penguin, 1991), pp. 23 and 177.

14 Morash, *A History of Irish Theatre*, p. 118.

15 Rosalind Mitchison, *A History of Scotland*, 2nd edn (London: Routledge, 1982), pp. 303–17.

16 Langton and Morris, *Atlas of Industrialising Britain*, p. xxvii.

17 John Davies, *A History of Wales* (Harmondsworth: Penguin Books, 1994), p. 439.

18 For detailed accounts of the topography and industrial context of individual cities, see George Gordon (ed.), *Regional Cities in the UK 1890–1980* (London: Harper & Row, 1986), especially Frederick Boal and Stephen Royle, 'Belfast: boom, blitz and bureaucracy', pp. 191–215, 191.

19 R. S. Sayers, *A History of Economic Change in England 1880–1939* (Oxford University Press, 1967), p. 13.

20 Patrick Geddes, *Cities in Evolution* (London: 1915), cited in T. W. Freeman (ed.), *The Conurbations of Great Britain* (Manchester University Press, 1966), p. 1. Data on conurbation populations is taken from chapters dealing with each area.

21 Earl and Sell, *Theatres Trust*, p. 260. All data on numbers of theatres are taken from relevant listing for each town or city.

22 These included George Stephenson, 'The father of the railways', and his son Robert, inventors of 'The Rocket'; Charles Mark Palmer, inventor of the steam-propelled iron ship; Charles Parsons, inventor of the steam turbine; Robert Armstrong, inventor of the hydro-electric generator and hydraulic crane and then the Armstrong breach loading gun which laid the foundations for an armaments' firm which rivalled Krupps of Essen. C.M.Fraser and K. Emsley, *Tyneside* (Newton Abbot: David & Charles, 1973).

23 Harold Oswald, *The Theatre Royal in Newcastle upon Tyne: Desultory Notes Relating to the Drama and Its Homes in That Place* (Newcastle upon Tyne: Northumberland Press, 1936).

24 Davis, *The Economics of the British Stage*, p. 56.

25 Theatrical Management Association, *The First Hundred Years 1894–1994* (London: Theatrical Management Association, 1994), no pagination.

26 Davis, *The Economics of the British Stage*, pp. 384–5.

27 Suzanne Grahame, 'The Theatres', 'The Grand Theatre', 'Discovering Leeds', www.leodis.net/discovery/discovery.asp?page=2003218_251720608&topic=2003219_253704250&subsection=2003625_136486233.

28 Marvin Carlson, *Places of Performance: The Semiotics of Theatre Architecture* (Ithaca and London: Cornell University Press, 1989), p. 105.

29 Grahame, 'The Theatres', 'Discovering Leeds'; also description in Earl and Sell, *Theatres Trust*, p. 87.

30 Richard Rodger, 'Urbanisation in twentieth-century Scotland', Devine and Finlay, *Scotland in the Century*, pp. 122–52, 124–5.

31 Adrienne Scullion, 'The eighteenth century', in Findlay, *A History of Scottish Theatre*, pp. 80–136, 112.

32 Paul Iles, 'Issues in theatrical management: Howard and Wyndham and the evolution of the British touring circuit', unpublished MPhil thesis, Glasgow University (1997), pp. 37–8.

33 Ibid., p. 124. As explained by Iles, gradings for theatres dependent on size, location and reputation. Theatre Royal in Edinburgh would be a No. 1 Theatre; theatres in smaller towns or seaside resorts were No. 2; No. 3 denoted a small theatre in a market town or suburb.

34 Townsend, *Uneven Regional Change in Britain*, p. 13.

35 Ibid.

36 Ibid., p. 16.

37 Michael Freeman, 'Transport', in Langton and Morris, *Atlas of Industrialising Britain*, pp. 80–93, 90.

38 Lionel Carson (ed.), *The Stage Year Book 1910 with which is included The Stage Provincial Guide 1910* (London: The Stage, 1910), p. 299.

39 Ewen A. Cameron, 'The Scottish Highlands from congested district to objective one', in Devine and Finlay, *Scotland in the Twentieth Century*, pp. 153–69, 158.

40 Hugh Trevor-Roper, 'The invention of tradition: the Highland tradition of Scotland', in Eric Hobsbawm and Terence Ranger (eds.), *The Invention of Tradition* (Cambridge University Press, 1983), pp. 15–41.

41 Barbara Bell, 'The nineteenth century', in Findlay, *A History of Scottish Theatre*, pp. 137–206, 186–7.

42 Kenneth O. Morgan, *Rebirth of a Nation: A History of Modern Wales* (Oxford University Press, University of Wales Press, 1982), p. 92.

43 Ibid.

44 Ibid., p. 364.

45 Cecil Price, *The Professional Theatre in Wales* (Swansea: University College of Swansea, 1984), p. 13.

46 Cecil Price, 'Portable theatres in Wales, 1843–1914', *National Library of Wales Journal*, 9 (1955) 66.

47 Ibid.

48 Ibid., pp. 85–8.

49 Ibid., p. 87.

50 D. Densil Morgan, '"The essence of Welshness"?: some aspects of Christian faith and national identity in Wales, c. 1900–2000', in Robert Pope (ed.), *Religion and National Identity: Wales and Scotland c. 1700–2000* (Cardiff: University of Wales Press, 2001), pp. 139–62, 140.

51 Ibid.

52 Price, *The Professional Theatre in Wales*, pp. 20, 33.

53 Cochrane, '"The contaminated audience"', pp. 172–3.

54 Morgan, *Rebirth of a Nation*, p. 14.

55 Morash, *A History of Irish Theatre*, pp. 104–6.

56 Ibid., p. 106.

57 Ibid., p. 68.

58 R .F. Foster, *Modern Ireland 1600–1972* (Harmondsworth: Penguin, 1989), pp. 373–99.

59 Ibid., pp. 388–9.

60 Ibid., p. 424.

61 Morash, *A History of Irish Theatre*, p. 115.

62 Lionel Pilkington, *Theatre and the State in Twentieth-Century Ireland* (London: Routledge, 2001), p. 2.

63 Ibid., p. 10.

64 Ibid., pp. 6–7.

65 Morash, *A History of Irish Theatre*, p. 117.

66 Foster, *Modern Ireland*, pp. 436–7.

67 Morash, *A History of Irish Theatre*, pp. 109–10.

68 Denis Judd, *Empire: The British Imperial Experience from 1765 to the Present Day* (London: Harper Collins, 1996).

69 Winder, *Bloody Foreigners*, pp. 149–64.

70 Ibid., pp. 174–91.

71 David Mazower, *Yiddish Theatre in London*, 2nd edn (London: Jewish Museum, 1996).

72 John Solomos, *Race and Racism in Britain*, 3rd edn (Basingstoke: Palgrave Macmillan, 2003), pp. 35–47.

73 'Immigration and Emigration, South East Wales, Somali Community', www.bbc.co.uk/legacies/immig_emig/wales/w_se/article_1.shtml.

74 Richard I. Lawless, *From Ta'izz to Tyneside: An Arab Community in the North-East of England During the Twentieth Century* (Exeter University Press, 1995).

75 Ibid., pp. 207–9.

76 Michael Pickering, 'Mock blacks and racial mockery', in J. S. Bratton et al., *Acts of Supremacy: The British Empire and the Stage 1790–1930* (Manchester University Press, 1991), pp. 179–236.

77 Ibid., pp. 180–1.

78 Victor Glasstone, 'Charles John Phipps, FSA, FRIBA (1835–1897)', in Earl and Sell, *Theatres Trust*, pp. 280–1.

79 Victor Glasstone, 'Frank Matcham (1854–1920)', in Earl and Sell, *Theatres Trust*, pp. 276–8.

80 Carlson, *Places of Performance*, p. 152.

81 For detailed accounts of individual theatres, see Brian Walker (ed.), *Frank Matcham – Theatre Architect* (Belfast: Blackstaff Press, 1980).

82 'Belfast, Grand Opera House', in Earl and Sell, *Theatres Trust*, pp. 11–12.

83 Rex Pogson, *Miss Horniman and the Gaiety Theatre Manchester* (London: Rockcliff, 1952), p. 51.
84 H. C. G. Matthew, 'The Liberal Age (1851–1914)', in K. O. Morgan, *Oxford Illustrated History of Britain*, pp. 463–522, 507–10.
85 J. F. C. Harrison, *Late Victorian Britain 1875–1901* (London: Fontana, 1990), p. 59.
86 'Daily Mail', www.spartacus.schoolnet.co.uk/Jmail.htm.
87 '"The Absent Minded Beggar" – An Introduction', www.sfowler.force9.co.uk/page_10.htm.
88 Matthew, 'The Liberal Age', in K. O. Morgan, *Oxford Illustrated History of Britain*, p. 509.
89 Harrison, *Late Victorian Britain*, pp. 68–75.
90 Ibid., p. 69.
91 Angela Hewins (ed.), *The Dillen: Memoirs of a Man of Stratford-Upon-Avon* (London: Elm Tree Books, 1981), pp. 56–58.
92 Violet Godfrey Carr, *From Portable Days by Violet Godfrey Carr: A Personal Account of Life in the Theatre as Told to Neil McNicholas* (Stocksfield: Spredden Press, 1991), pp. 5, 10–11.
93 Dr Andrew Smith, Theatre Scrapbooks, 1900–1950, held in Tyne and Wear Archives, Newcastle upon Tyne, DX 972.
94 Harrison, *Late Victorian Britain*, pp. 54 and 72.
95 Matthew, 'The Liberal Age', in K. O. Morgan, *Oxford Illustrated History of Britain*, p. 512.
96 Eric Hobsbawm with Chris Wrigley, *Industry and Empire*, 2nd edn (Harmondsworth: Penguin, 1999), p. 132.
97 Harrison, *Late Victorian Britain*, pp.119–203, 84.
98 Ibid., pp. 142–3.
99 Ibid., pp. 144–9.
100 Ibid., pp. 22–5.
101 A. St John Adcock, in George R. Sims (ed.), *Living London*, 3 vols (1901), quoted in Russell Jackson, *Victorian Theatre* (London: A & C Black, 1989), pp. 72–6, 73.
102 Hobsbawm with Wrigley, *Industry and Empire*, pp. 150–1.
103 Townsend, *Uneven Regional Change in Britain*, pp. 20–1.
104 Clive Lee, 'Services', in Langton and Morris, *Atlas of Industrialising Britain*, pp. 140–3, 140.

2 STRUCTURES OF MANAGEMENT

1 M. F. K. Fraser, *Alexandra Theatre, The Story of a Popular Playhouse* (Birmingham: Cornish Brothers Ltd., 1948), p. 8.
2 Granville-Barker, *The Exemplary Theatre*, pp. 34–5.
3 Dennis Kennedy, *Granville Barker and the Dream of Theatre* (Cambridge University Press, 1985).
4 William Archer, 'A plea for an endowed theatre', *Fortnightly Review*, 45, ns (1 January–1 June 1889), 610–26.

5 Alan Hughes, 'The Lyceum staff: a Victorian theatrical organization', *Theatre Notebook*, 28 (1974), 11–17.

6 Davis, *The Economics of the British Stage*, pp. 224–5.

7 Leslie Hannah, *The Rise of the Corporate Economy*, 2nd edn (London: Methuen, 1983), p. 18.

8 H. C. G. Matthew, 'The liberal age (1851–1914)', in K.O. Morgan, *Oxford Illustrated History of Britain*, p. 513.

9 Tracy C. Davis, *George Bernard Shaw and the Socialist Theatre* (Westport, Conn./London: Greenwood Press, 1994), p. 64.

10 Barry Jackson, 'Introduction', in Bache Matthews, *A History of the Birmingham Repertory Theatre* (London: Chatto & Windus, 1924), pp. xi–xv, xv.

11 Ben Iden Payne, *A Life in a Wooden O* (New Haven and London: Yale University Press, 1977), p. 63.

12 Winifred F. E. C. Isaac, *Ben Greet and the Old Vic, A Biography of Sir Philip Ben Greet* (London: Miss Winifred F. E. C. Isaac, 1964), p. 20.

13 Ibid., p. xviii.

14 Charlotte Canning, 'What was Chautauqua?', University of Iowa Libraries, http://sdrc.lib.uiowa.edu/traveling-culture/essay.htm.

15 William Greet's career is difficult to track. He is listed as an original member of the TMA as the manager of the Avenue Theatre (TMA, *The First Hundred Years*). His various managerial tenures can be established by reference to individual theatre and production advertisements that appear in successive editions of *The Era Almanack, Era Annual* and *The Stage Year Book*.

16 Isaac, *Ben Greet and the Old Vic*, p. 10.

17 J. C. Trewin, *Benson and the Bensonians* (London: Barrie and Rockliff, 1960), p. 129.

18 Sally Beauman, *The Royal Shakespeare Company: A History of Ten Decades* (Oxford: Oxford University Press, 1982), pp. 55–6.

19 Davis, *The Economics of the British Stage*, pp. 164–7.

20 Diana Howard, *London Theatres and Music Halls 1850–1950* (London: Library Association Publishing Ltd., 1970), p. xi.

21 Barry Duncan, *The St. James's Theatre, Its Strange & Complete History 1835–1957* (London: Barrie and Rockliff, 1964), p. 215.

22 Hesketh Pearson, *Beerbohm Tree* (London: Methuen, 1956), p. 101. A debenture is a sealed bond issued by a corporation or company in respect of a long-term loan.

23 Wendy Trewin, *All on Stage: Charles Wyndham and the Alberys* (London: Harrap, 1980), p. 142.

24 Howard, *London Theatres and Music Halls*, p. 111.

25 *Theatre Ownership in Britain: A Report Prepared for the Federation of Theatre Unions* (London: Federation of Theatre Unions, 1953), pp. 12–14. Explores the growth of Associated Theatre Properties (London), Ltd.

26 Charles B. Cochran and A. P. Herbert, *I Had Almost Forgotten …* (London: Hutchinson & Co., 1932).

27 For brief notes on the introduction of Entertainments Tax and wartime restrictions, see selected entries by year in TMA, *The First Hundred Years*; also Bernard Weller, 'The War-Time Stage', in Lionel Carson (ed.), *The Stage Year Book 1919* (London: The Stage, 1919), pp. 23–30.

28 *TMA Journal* (August 1925), p. 8.

29 Phyllis Philip Rodway and Lois Rodway Slingsby, *Philip Rodway and a Tale of Two Theatres* (Birmingham: Cornish Brothers, 1934), pp. 205–6.

30 See W. Trewin, *All on Stage*, pp. 199–214, for an account of Bronson Albery's career and personality.

31 Useful accounts of the business dealings of Granville Barker, Shaw, McCarthy, Vedrenne and Frohman are to be found in Davis, *George Bernard Shaw and the Socialist Theatre*; Kennedy, *Granville Barker and the Dream of Theatre*; Holroyd, *Bernard Shaw, Volume 2*.

32 Gertrude Kingston, *Curtsey While You're Thinking* (London: Williams and Norgate, 1937), p. 45.

33 Savoy Theatre lessee details in Howard, *London Theatres and Music Halls*, pp. 214–15.

34 Lena Ashwell, *Myself a Player* (London: Michael Joseph, 1936), pp. 131–57.

35 Ibid., pp. 156–7.

36 Holroyd, *Bernard Shaw, Volume 2*, p. 282.

37 Building and lessee details in Howard, *London Theatres and Music Halls*, pp. 137–8.

38 Lillah McCarthy, *Myself and My Friends* (London: T. Butterworth Ltd., 1933), pp. 134–8.

39 Michael Maclagan, 'Ellis, Thomas Evelyn Scott-, eighth Baron Howard de Walden (1880–1946)', *Oxford Dictionary of National Biography*, www.oxforddnb.com.

40 Harley Granville Barker, 'Preface', in William Archer and Harley Granville Barker, *A National Theatre: Schemes and Estimates* (London: Duckworth, 1907), pp. xix, 112–13.

41 *Parliamentary Debates*, Commons, Vol. 52, cols.454–94, 23 April 1913; on the donors, see John Elsom and Nicholas Tomalin, *The History of the National Theatre* (London: Cape, 1978), pp. 28–9.

42 George Rowell, *The Old Vic Theatre: A History* (Cambridge University Press, 1993), p. 77.

43 Ibid., pp. 86–7.

44 Ibid., p. 85.

45 Ibid., p. 92.

46 Suz Winspear, *Worcester's Lost Theatre: The Story of the Worcester Theatre Royal* (Hallow, Worcester: Packbarn, 1996), pp. 93–102. Theatre listings in *The Era Almanack* supply more detail on Carlton's lesseeships.

47 'A Chat with Milton Bode', *The Era*, 2 February 1901.

48 For outline biographical details of Bode, Compton and Courtneidge, see entries in John Parker (ed.), *Who's Who in the Theatre: A Biographical Record*, 3rd edn (London: T. S. Clark, 1916), pp. 63, 130, 140; Lou Warwick provides

information on the family and business relationships of all three including theatre purchase in Lou Warwick, *The Mackenzies Called Compton: The Story of the Compton Comedy Company Incorporated in the History of Northampton Theatre Royal and Opera House 1884–1927* (Northampton: the Author, 1977).

49 Donald Campbell, *A Brighter Sunshine: A Hundred Years of the Edinburgh Royal Lyceum Theatre* (Edinburgh: Polygon, 1983), pp. 64–5.

50 Ibid., pp. 54–5.

51 'Kennington Theatre, Kennington Park Road, Kennington Formerly The Princess of Wales' Theatre', www.arthurlloyd.co.uk/KenningtonTheatre.htm.

52 *Theatre Ownership in Britain*, p. 20.

53 Harold Ackroyd, *The Liverpool Stage* (Erdington, West Midlands: Amber Valley Print Centre, 1996), pp. 30–2.

54 Grace Wyndham Goldie, *The Liverpool Repertory Theatre 1911–1934* (London: Liverpool University Press and Hodder and Stoughton, 1935), pp. 38–42.

55 '1915', in TMA, *The First Hundred Years*.

56 Iles, 'Issues in theatrical management', p. 24.

57 Byrne, *The Stage in Ulster*, pp. 25–8.

58 Iles, 'Issues in theatrical management', pp. 24–6.

59 Kathleen Barker, *Bristol at Play: Five Centuries of Live Entertainment* (Bradford-on-Avon: Moonraker Press, 1976), pp. 34–8.

60 Ibid., p. 49.

61 Fraser, *Alexandra Theatre*, pp. 32–4, 38.

62 Rodway and Slingsby, *Philip Rodway*, p. 177.

63 Ibid., pp. 244–5.

64 Ibid., pp. 503–5.

65 Davis, *The Economics of the British Stage*, p. 181.

66 Ibid., pp. 176–7, for a full explanation of the mergers of Oswald Stoll, Edward Moss and Richard Thornton.

67 Ibid., pp. 66–7.

68 Barker, *Bristol at Play*, pp. 46–7.

69 Granville-Barker, *The Exemplary Theatre*, p. 28.

70 Helmut K. Anheier, *Nonprofit Organisations: Theory, Management, Policy* (London: Routledge, 2005), pp. 174–5.

71 W. B. Yeats quoted in Hugh Hunt, *The Abbey: Ireland's National Theatre 1904–1978* (Dublin: Gill and Macmillan, 1979), p. 19.

72 Archer, 'A plea for an endowed theatre', p. 617.

73 Hunt, *The Abbey*, pp. 57–60.

74 Winifred F. E. C. Isaac, *Alfred Wareing: A Biography* (London: Greenbank Press, [1951]), p. 35.

75 Payne, *A Life in a Wooden O*, p. 79.

76 Isaac, *Alfred Wareing*, pp. 34–5.

77 Claire Cochrane, *Shakespeare and the Birmingham Repertory Theatre 1913–1929* (London: Society for Theatre Research, 1993), pp. 44–7.

78 McDonald, 'Towards national identities: theatre in Scotland', in Kershaw, *The Cambridge History of British Theatre*, pp. 198–9.

79 Donald Campbell, *Playing for Scotland: A History of the Scottish Stage 1715–1965* (Edinburgh: Mercat Press, 1996), pp. 93–7.

80 Goldie, *The Liverpool Repertory Theatre*, pp. 95–111.

81 Pogson, *Miss Horniman and the Gaiety Theatre Manchester*, pp. 22–3.

82 Ibid., pp. 173–5.

83 J. C. Trewin, *The Birmingham Repertory Theatre 1913–1963* (London: Barrie and Rockliff, 1963), pp. 78–9.

84 Pogson, *Miss Horniman and the Gaiety Theatre*, pp. 181–96.

85 Trewin, *The Birmingham Repertory Theatre*, p. 66.

86 Jackson, 'Introduction', in Matthews, *A History of the Birmingham Repertory Theatre*, p.xiv.

87 For a full account of Jackson's London productions, see George W. Bishop, *Barry Jackson and the London Theatre* (London: Arthur Barker, 1933).

88 Jon Lawrence, 'The First World War and its aftermath', in Paul Johnson (ed.), *20th Century Britain: Economic, Social and Cultural Change* (Harlow: Longman, 1994), pp. 151–68, 163.

89 Dudley Baines, 'The onset of depression', in Johnson, *20th Century Britain*, pp. 168–87, 177.

90 Lawrence, 'The First World War and its aftermath', in Johnson, *20th Century Britain*, p. 166.

91 Baines, 'The onset of depression', in Johnson, *20th Century Britain*, p. 175.

92 Lionel Carson (ed.), 'Theatre and Music Hall Companies', *The Stage Year Book 1917* (London: The Stage, 1917), pp. 65–73.

93 *Theatre Ownership in Britain*, pp. 19–21.

94 Richard Huggett, *Binkie Beaumont: Eminence Grise of the West End Theatre 1933–1973* (London: Hodder & Stoughton, 1989), pp. 84–183.

95 Cochran, *I Had Almost Forgotten ...*, pp. 108–9.

96 For an account of the development of 'The Group', see *Theatre Ownership in Britain*, pp. 7–28.

97 Ibid., pp.10–11 24. See also Derek Salberg, *Once upon a Pantomime* (Luton: Cortney Publications Ltd., 1981), pp. 61–7.

98 Sybil Rosenfeld, *The York Theatre* (London: Society for Theatre Research, 2001), p. 323.

99 Fraser, *Alexandra Theatre*, p. 43.

100 Rosenfeld, *The York Theatre*, pp. 324–6.

101 Warwick, *The Mackenzies called Compton*, pp. 206–14.

102 For an account of the founding of the Bristol Little Theatre, see *A Short History of Bristol's Little Theatre: First & Second Seasons 1923–24–25* (Bristol: Partridge & Love, 1925).

103 Richard Foulkes, *Repertory at The Royal: Sixty-Five Years of Theatre in Northampton 1927–92* (Northampton: Northampton Repertory Players, 1992), pp. 9–14.

104 Goldie, *The Liverpool Repertory Theatre*, pp. 213–15.

105 Foulkes, *Repertory at The Royal*, p. 14.

106 Rosenfeld, *The York Theatre*, pp. 330–1.

107 *The Era* lists 23 non-resident companies for 1933. Viv Gardner, 'Provincial stages, 1900–1934', in Kershaw, *The Cambridge History of British Theatre*, pp. 60–85, 84.

108 Cecil Chisholm, *Repertory: An Outline of the Modern Theatre Movement* (London: Peter Davies, 1934), pp. 245–7.

109 David Hutchison, '1900–1950', in Findlay, *A History of Scottish Theatre*, pp. 218–19.

110 *Perth Theatre Company 21st Anniversary September 1935–September 1956* (Perth: Perth Theatre, 1956), pp. 4–9.

111 Jonathan Bardon and David Burnett, *Belfast: A Pocket History* (Belfast: Blackstaff Press, 1996), pp. 100–1.

112 These were the The Little Theatre, Belfast, and The Playhouse, Belfast. See Byrne, *The Stage in Ulster*, pp. 42–4.

113 Gardner, 'Provincial stages, 1900–1934', in Kershaw, *The Cambridge History of British Theatre*, p. 85.

114 For a full contemporary account of these theatres, see Norman Marshall, *The Other Theatre* (London: John Lehmann, 1947).

3 THE PROFESSION OF ACTING

1 Harold Perkin, *The Rise of Professional Society: England Since 1880* (London: Routledge, 1989), pp. 18–21.

2 Michael Sanderson, *From Irving to Olivier: A Social History of the Acting Profession 1880–1983* (London: Athlone Press, 1984), p. 231.

3 For a detailed account of the debate amongst the profession on 'The making of Equity', see Joseph Macleod, *The Actor's Right to Act* (London: Lawrence and Wishart for the Friends of Equity, 1981), pp. 169–88.

4 Sanderson, *From Irving to Olivier*, p. 234.

5 Macleod, *The Actor's Right to Act*, pp. 58–64.

6 Ibid., pp. 69–74.

7 Carr, *From Portable Days*, p. 5.

8 Hewins, *The Dillen*, pp. 123–6. In 1983 the Royal Shakespeare Theatre in a production by Barry Kyle staged Ron Hutchinson's dramatisation of *The Dillen*, which took the audience on a journey around Stratford-upon-Avon.

9 See both Macleod and Sanderson for detailed accounts of these developments.

10 Macleod, *The Actor's Right to Act*, p. 93.

11 Sanderson, *From Irving to Olivier*, p. 111.

12 Ibid., pp. 241–2.

13 Maud Gill, *See the Players* (London: Hutchinson & Co., 1938).

14 Ibid., pp. 36–8.

15 Ibid., p. 69.

16 Ibid., p. 105.

17 Ibid., p. 47.

18 Garry O'Connor, *Ralph Richardson, An Actor's Life* (London: Hodder and Stoughton, 1982), p. 32.

19 See Sanderson, *From Irving to Olivier*, pp. 18–23, on the changing class base of the profession.
20 Ibid., pp. 39–45.
21 Isaac, *Ben Greet and the Old Vic*, p. xviii; also Russell Thorndike, *Sybil Thorndike* (London: T. Butterworth, 1929), pp. 114–20.
22 Sanderson, *From Irving to Olivier*, pp. 36–8.
23 Basil Dean, quoted in Robert Speaight, *William Poel and the Elizabethan Revival* (London: William Heinemann, 1954), p. 96.
24 Charlton F. Fry, *Charles Fry, His Life and Work* (London: printed by J. M. Baxter, *c.* 1932); also Diana Devlin, *A Speaking Part: Lewis Casson and the Theatre of His Time* (London: Hodder and Stoughton, 1982), pp. 18–24.
25 Constance Benson, *Mainly Players* (London: Thornton Butterworth, 1926), p. 249.
26 Scottish National Players, *The Scottish National Theatre Venture (The Scottish National Players), Its Birth, History, Work and Influence 1921–1948* (Glasgow: Scottish National Players, 1953), p. 21.
27 Franklin J. Hildy, *Shakespeare at the Maddermarket: Nugent Monck and the Norwich Players* (Ann Arbor, Mich.: UMI Research Press, *c.* 1986), pp. 18–32.
28 Frank Fay, quoted in Speaight, *William Poel*, p. 139.
29 Speaight, *William Poel*, p. 139.
30 Hunt, *The Abbey*, p. 35.
31 Whitford Kane, *Are We All Met by Whitford Kane* (London: E. Mathews & Marlot, 1931), pp. 31–2.
32 Ibid., p. 59.
33 Ibid., p. 33.
34 Cathleen Nesbitt, *A Little Love and Good Company* (London: Faber & Faber, 1975), pp. 43–66.
35 Kane, *Are We All Met*, pp. 70–3.
36 Ibid., pp. 78–90.
37 'Cambridge', in Phyllis Hartnoll (ed.), *The Oxford Companion to the Theatre*, 4th edn (Oxford University Press, 1983), pp. 126–7.
38 Trewin, *Benson and the Bensonians*, p. 7.
39 Ibid., pp. 110–1.
40 Robert Speaight, *The Property Basket: Recollections of a Divided Life* (London: Collins and Harvell Press, 1970), p. 65.
41 Emlyn Williams, *George; An Early Autobiography* (London: Reprint Society, 1962), pp. 276–331.
42 Speaight, *The Property Basket*, pp. 85–7.
43 Irving Wardle, *The Theatres of George Devine* (London: Jonathan Cape, 1978), pp. 14–25.
44 Beauman, *The Royal Shakespeare Company*, pp. 82–9.
45 Fraser, *Alexandra Theatre*, p. 43.
46 Kate Dunn, *Exit Through the Fireplace: The Great Days of Rep* (London: John Murray, 1998), pp. 123–4.

47 Fraser, *Alexandra Theatre*, p. 45.
48 Richard Jerrams, *Weekly Rep – A Theatrical Phenomenon* (Droitwich: Peter Andrew Publishing, 1991), p. 37.
49 Fraser, *Alexandra Theatre*, p. 44.
50 Ibid., p. 46.
51 Foulkes, *Repertory at the Royal*, pp. 21–53.
52 Ibid.
53 For details of the early careers of Richardson and Olivier with Birmingham Rep together with lists of roles played, see O'Connor, *Ralph Richardson*, and Terry Coleman, *Olivier* (London: Bloomsbury, 2005).
54 See John Gielgud, *Early Stages*, pp. 48–53; Bryan Forbes, *Ned's Girl: The Authorised Biography of Dame Edith Evans* (London: Elm Tree Books, 1977), pp. 68–73; Michael Billington, *Peggy Ashcroft* (London: John Murray, 1988), pp. 21–3.
55 Billington, *Peggy Ashcroft*, p. 57.
56 Rachael Low, *The History of the British Film 1918–1929* (London: George Allen & Unwin, 1971), pp. 220–1.
57 Ibid., pp. 260–2.
58 Sanderson, *From Irving to Olivier*, pp. 210–11.
59 Ibid., pp. 145–6.
60 Ibid., p. 216.
61 Ibid., p. 214.
62 Tyrone Guthrie, *A Life in the Theatre* (London: Hamish Hamilton, 1961), pp. 105–15.
63 Roy Armes, *A Critical History of the British Cinema* (London: Secker & Warburg, 1979), pp. 113–14.
64 Michael Balcon, *Michael Balcon Presents … A Lifetime of Film* (London: Hutchinson, 1969), p. 37, quoted in Armes, *A Critical History*, p. 81.
65 Adrienne Scullion, 'Media Culture for a Modern Nation?: Theatre, Cinema and Radio in Early Twentieth-century Scotland', unpublished PhD thesis, University of Glasgow (1992), p. 245.
66 Davies, *A History of Wales*, pp. 564–5, 590.
67 Paddy Scannell, *A Social History of British Broadcasting, Volume 1, 1922–1939: Serving the Nation* (Oxford: Blackwell, 1991), pp. 304–5.
68 Adrienne Scullion, 'Scottish theatre and the impact of radio', *Theatre Research International*, 17 (1992), 118.
69 Ibid., pp. 121–5.
70 Ibid., p. 118.
71 Asa Briggs, *The History of Broadcasting in the United Kingdom, Volume 1, The Birth of Broadcasting* (Oxford University Press, 1961), pp. 280–1.
72 Devlin, *A Speaking Part*, p. 154.
73 Ian Rodger, *Radio Drama* (London: Macmillan, 1982), p. 12.
74 Briggs, *The History of Broadcasting*, p. 282.
75 Rodger, *Radio Drama*, pp. 12–13.
76 Scannell, *A Social History of British Broadcasting*, pp. 338–47.

77 See Joan Littlewood, *Joan's Book: Joan Littlewood's Peculiar History as She Tells It* (London: Methuen, 1994); Ewan MacColl, *Journeyman: An Autobiography* (London: Sidgwick and Jackson, 1990); Howard Goorney, *The Theatre Workshop Story* (London: Eyre Methuen, 1981).

78 Goorney, *The Theatre Workshop Story*, p. 19.

79 Derek Paget, 'Theatre Workshop, Moussinac, and the European connection', *New Theatre Quarterly*, 11 (1995), 211–24.

80 Billington, *Peggy Ashcroft*, pp. 19–20.

81 John Gielgud, *Early Stages* (London: Sceptre, 1990), pp. 63–8.

82 Cochrane, '"The contaminated audience"', p. 172.

83 Beauman, *The Royal Shakespeare Company*, pp. 125–49.

84 Wardle, *The Theatres of George Devine*, p. 26.

85 Ibid., pp. 45–83.

86 Campbell, *Playing for Scotland*, pp. 126–31.

87 Ibid., pp. 131–2.

88 Deirdre Osborne, 'Writing Black back: an overview of Black theatre and performance in Britain', in Dimple Godiwala (ed.), *Alternatives Within the Mainstream: British Black and Asian Theatres* (Newcastle upon Tyne: Cambridge Scholars Press, 2006), pp. 68–9.

89 'Wilson Frank from Encyclopedia of the Harlem Renaissance: K–Y Index Volume 2', www.bookrags.com/tandf/wilson-frank-tf/.

90 Anonymous press reviews, *Morning Post* and *Daily Herald*, 18 June 1929.

91 Billington, *Peggy Ashcroft*, pp. 37–42.

92 Steve Nicholson, *The Censorship of British Drama 1900–1968, Volume 1 1900–1932* (Exeter University Press, 2003), pp. 268–91.

93 Osborne, 'Writing Black back', in Godiwala, *Alternatives Within the Mainstream*, p. 70.

94 Colin Chambers, *The Story of Unity Theatre* (London: Lawrence & Wishart, 1989), pp. 151–9. Ironically the 40-year-old Robeson was playing a character originally envisaged as a white teenager.

4   THE AMATEUR PHENOMENON

1 Elan Closs Stephens, 'Drama', in Meic Stephens (ed.), *The Arts in Wales 1950–1975* (Cardiff: Welsh Arts Council, 1979), pp. 236–96, 237.

2 Raphael Samuel, 'Introduction: theatre and politics', in Raphael Samuel, Ewan MacColl and Stuart Cosgrove, *Theatres of the Left, 1880–1935: Workers' Theatre Movements in Britain and America* (London: Routledge & Kegan Paul, 1985), pp. xiii–xx, xi.

3 See also Chambers, *The Story of Unity Theatre*; Richard Stourac and Kathleen McCreery, *Theatre as a Weapon: Workers' Theatre in the Soviet Union, Germany and Britain, 1917–1934* (London: Routledge & Kegan Paul, 1986); Linda Mackenney, *The Activities of Popular Dramatists and Drama Groups in Scotland 1900–1952* (Lewiston: Edwin Mellen Press, 2000).

4 Geoffrey Whitworth, *The Making of a National Theatre* (London: Faber and Faber, 1951), p. 149.

5 Ibid.

6 *Drama, The Quarterly Theatre Review*, ns 2, 13 (December 1921).

7 *25 Years of the British Drama League* (London: British Drama League, 1945).

8 Katharine Cockin, *Edith Craig 1869–1947, Dramatic Lives* (London: Cassell, 1998), pp. 162–4.

9 Sam Hanna Bell, *The Theatre in Ulster* (Dublin: Gill and Macmillan, 1972), p. 57.

10 Mackenny, *The Activities of Popular Dramatists and Drama Groups in Scotland*, p. 72.

11 See my discussion of amateur theatre and the avant-garde in Cochrane, 'The pervasiveness of the commonplace', pp. 233–42.

12 W. G. Fay and Catherine Carswell, *The Fays of the Abbey Theatre: An Autobiographical Record* (Dublin: Rich & Cowan Ltd., 1935), pp. 25–176.

13 Cochrane, *Shakespeare and the Birmingham Repertory Theatre*, pp. 24–31.

14 David Kennedy, 'The drama in Ulster', in Sam Hanna Bell, Nesca A. Robb, John Hewitt (eds.), *The Arts in Ulster, A Symposium* (London: Harrap, 1951), pp. 47–68, 57.

15 For a full account of the ULT, see Bell, *The Theatre in Ulster*, pp. 1–51.

16 Hagal Mengel, 'A lost heritage: Ulster drama and the work of Sam Thompson', *Theatre Ireland*, 1 (September/December 1982), 19.

17 Bell, *The Theatre in Ulster*, pp. 126–7.

18 Ibid., pp. 56–8.

19 Cockin, *Edith Craig*, pp. 162–4.

20 Fay and Carswell, *The Fays of the Abbey Theatre*, p. 178.

21 Scottish National Players, *The Scottish National Theatre Venture*, pp. 22–4.

22 David Hutchison, *The Modern Scottish Theatre* (Glasgow: Molendinar Press, 1977), p. 46.

23 Ibid., p. 45.

24 J. Ellis Williams, 'Welsh drama to-day', *Welsh Review* (March 1939), 346.

25 Cochrane,'"The contaminated audience"', p. 170.

26 Marshall, *The Other Theatre*, p. 86.

27 Katherine Newey, 'Home plays for ladies: women's work in home theatricals', *Nineteenth Century*, 26 (1998), 97.

28 Ibid., pp. 109–10.

29 For a comprehensive account, see Thomas Kelly, *A History of Adult Education in Great Britain from the Middle Ages to the Twentieth Century* (Liverpool University Press, 1962), especially pp. 217–65; also J. F. C. Harrison, *Learning and Living 1790–1960, A Study in the History of the Adult Education Movement* (Aldershot: Greg Revivals, 1994).

30 Harrison, *Learning and Living*, p. 260.

31 Basil Dean, *Seven Ages, Volume 1, An Autobiography 1888–1927* (London: Hutchison, 1970), p. 55.

32 Ibid.

33 Raphael Samuel, 'Theatre and socialism in Britain, (1880–1935)', in Samuel, MacColl and Casgrove, *Theatres of the Left*, pp. 3–73, 17.

34 MacColl, *Journeyman*, p. 206.

35 Harrison, *Learning and Living*, pp. 261–74.

36 E. Martin Browne with Henzie Browne, *Two in One [by] E. Martin Browne with Henzie Browne* (Cambridge University Press, 1981), pp. 11–12; Harrison, *Learning and Living*, p. 311.

37 J. B. Priestley, *English Journey* (London: Heinemann, 1934), pp. 304–6, 324–6.

38 'The drama in the countryside', in Great Britain Board of Education, Adult Education Committee, *The Drama in Adult Education* (London: HMSO, 1926), pp. 129–50, 146.

39 Steve Nicholson, 'A critical year in perspective: 1926', in Kershaw, *The Cambridge History of British Theatre*, pp. 127–142, 128–9.

40 'The drama and the churches', in G B Board of Education, *The Drama in Adult Education*, pp. 121–8, 123–4.

41 Nicholson, 'A critical year in perspective', p. 134.

42 Martin Pugh, *The Making of Modern British Politics 1867–1939*, 2nd edn (Oxford: Blackwell, 1993), p. 255.

43 Ibid.

44 K. O. Morgan, *Rebirth of a Nation*, p. 210.

45 Cochrane, '"The contaminated audience"', pp. 170–1.

46 K. O. Morgan, *Rebirth of a Nation*, pp. 20–1.

47 Accounts of specific plays and the production context may be found in over 150 scrapbooks of clippings and articles preserved in the D. R. Davies Collection, National Library of Wales; Drama Scrapbooks, 26/1–3, Censorship in Wales 1926–53, No. 2.

48 J. Ellis Williams, 'The drama in Wales', *Welsh Review* (February 1939), 34.

49 *Hwyl* was highly emotional, extemporary preaching. See the entry in Meic Stephens (ed.), *The New Companion to the Literature of Wales* (Cardiff: Welsh Arts Council, 1979), pp. 172–3.

50 David Egan, *Coal Society: A History of the South Wales Mining Valleys, 1840–1980* (Llandysul: Gomer Press, 1987), p. 75.

51 Richard Hughes, *Bookman* (November 1934), 97–8, 97.

52 Tim Williams, 'Language, religion, culture', in Trevor Herbert and Gareth Elwyn Jones (eds.), *Wales 1880–1914* (Cardiff: University of Wales Press, 1988), pp. 73–87, 81.

53 Undated press clipping, D. R. Davies Collection, Four Scrapbooks: Welsh Drama, Drama in Wales 1922–1972, 2/3.

54 Olive Ely Hart, *The Drama in Modern Wales: A Brief History of Welsh Playwriting from 1900 to the Present Day* (University of Philadelphia Press, 1928), pp. 9–43.

55 Hughes, p. 97.

56 Carol Trosset, *Welshness Performed: Welsh Concepts of Person and Society* (Tucson: University of Arizona Press, 1993), pp. 66–7.

57 Prys Morgan, 'From a death to a view: the hunt for the Welsh past in the romantic period', in Hobsbawm and Ranger, *The Invention of Tradition*, pp. 43–100.

58 Cecil Price, 'Towards a National Theatre for Wales', *Anglo-Welsh Review*, 12, no. 29 (1962), 18.

59 Ioan Williams, 'Towards national identities', in Kershaw, *The Cambridge History of British Theatre*, pp. 242–72, 249.

60 J. Ellis Williams, *Inc yn Ngwaed* [Ink in My Blood] (Llanybie: Llyfrau'r Dryw, 1963), p. 54. Translation from the Welsh by Marisa O'Hara.

61 Ibid., p. 22.

62 Ibid., pp. 34–6.

63 *Western Mail*, 8 February 1935; I. Williams, 'Towards national identities', pp. 254–5.

64 Williams, 'Welsh drama to-day', p. 33.

65 K. O. Morgan, *Rebirth of a Nation*, p. 215.

66 Ibid., pp. 272–3.

67 Samuel, 'Theatre and socialism in Britain', p. 27.

68 Bernard Harris, 'Unemployment and the dole in interwar Britain', in Johnson, *20th Century Britain*, pp. 203–20, 204–6.

69 Ewan MacColl, 'Theatre of action, Manchester', in Samuel, MacColl and Cosgrove, *Theatres of the Left*, pp. 206–55, 213.

70 Dudley Baines, 'Recovery from depression', in Johnson, *20th Century Britain*, pp. 188–202, 188–90.

71 Sue Bowden, 'The new consumerism', in ibid., pp. 242–62, 246–9.

72 'Communist Party of Great Britain, History Section', www.marxists.org/history/international/cointern/sections/britain/history.htm.

73 Samuel, 'Theatre and socialism in Britain', pp. 52, 11–33.

74 MacKenney, *The Activities in Scotland*, pp. 28–56.

75 Linda Hornzee-Jones, 'Performing Suburbia: A Qualitative Examination of Late Twentieth Century Amateur Drama in South-east England', unpublished PhD thesis, University of Brighton (2001).

76 Denys and Marion Wells, 'Theatre in a Barn: From Brickwell to Handside', www.barntheatre.co.uk/archives/barn_history/earlytheatre.htm.

77 'Charles Purdom', http://en.wikipedia.org/wiki/Charles_Purdom.

78 K. O. Morgan, *Rebirth of a Nation*, p. 218.

79 T. G. H. Davies, 'The Swansea Little Theatre, the First Thirty Years, 1924–55', unpublished dissertation, University College, Swansea (1993).

80 Ibid., p. 42.

81 On-line histories of the Halifax Thespians, Bolton Little Theatre, Stockport Garrick Theatre and the Peoples' Theatre, Newcastle, together with other Little Theatres founded in the 1920s and 30s, may be found on the websites of each organisation. These can be accessed via links from the Little Theatre Guild of Great Britain website: www.littletheatreguild.org.

82 Priestley, *English Journey*, pp. 197–200.

83 Glyn Watkins, 'An Inspector Calls: A history of Bradford's Playhouse', www.mypriestley.org.uk/note.php?id=inspect3+1+3.

84 'Garrick Story', Stockport Garrick Theatre, www.stockportgarrick.co.uk/about.html.
85 Ibid.
86 Norman Veitch, *The Peoples: Being a History of the Peoples' Theatre, Newcastle upon Tyne* (Gateshead on Tyne: Northumberland Press, 1950), pp. 48–51.
87 Ibid., pp. 63–4.
88 Priestley, *English Journey*, p. 199.
89 Samuel, 'Theatre and socialism in Britain', pp. 11–33.
90 Ibid., p. 27.
91 Mackenney, *The Activities of Popular Dramatists and Drama Groups in Scotland*, p. 35.
92 Tom Thomas, 'A propertyless theatre for the propertyless class', in Samuel, MacColl and Cosgrove, *Theatres of the Left*, pp. 77–98, 83.
93 Samuel, 'Theatre and socialism in Britain', pp. 59–60.
94 Samuel, 'Introduction: theatre and politics', pp. xiii–xx, xix–xx.
95 Thomas, 'A propertyless theatre', pp. 92–3; Stourac and McCreery, *Theatre as a Weapon*, pp. 227–8. The 1932 tour to South Wales was markedly less successful.
96 Stourac and McCreery, *Theatre as a Weapon*, pp. 251–6.
97 Mackenney, *The Activities of Popular Dramatists and Drama Groups in Scotland*, pp. 132–3.
98 Ibid., p. 140.
99 Ibid., p. 152.
100 Ibid., p. 181.
101 Ibid., p. 165.
102 Ibid., p. 168.
103 For a discussion of the shift in state funding policy from CEMA to the Arts Council of Great Britain, see Hutchison, *The Politics of the Arts Council*.
104 Mackenney, *The Activities of Popular Dramatists and Drama Groups in Scotland*, pp. 221–37.
105 Bell, *The Theatre in Ulster*, pp. 60–76.
106 W. E. Williams, 'The First Ten Years', in Arts Council of Great Britain, *11th Annual Report 1955–1956* (London: Arts Council of Great Britain, 1956), pp. 5–32, 13.

5   THE TOPOGRAPHY OF THEATRE IN 1950

1 Hobsbawm with Wrigley, *Industry and Empire*, p. 234.
2 J. Davies, *A History of Wales*, p. 601.
3 Ibid., p. 579.
4 Winder, *Bloody Foreigners*, p. 262.
5 Foster, *Modern Ireland*, p. 578.
6 For data on individual city theatres, see 'Appendix 1. Demolitions', in Earl and Sell, *The Theatres Trust Guide to British Theatres*, pp. 237–58.
7 Rowell, *The Old Vic Theatre*, p. 153.

8 Peter Clarke, *Hope and Glory, Britain 1900–1990* (Harmondsworth: Penguin Books, 1997), pp. 237–8.
9 Ibid., pp. 232–3.
10 Shompa Lahiri, 'South Asians in post-imperial Britain: decolonisation and imperial legacy', in Stuart Ward (ed.), *British Culture at the End of Empire* (New York: Manchester University Press, 2001), pp. 200–16, 203.
11 Winder, *Bloody Foreigners*, p. 257.
12 Winston James, 'Black experience in Twentieth-Century Britain', in Philip D. Morgan and Sean Hawkins (eds.), *Black Experience and the Empire* (Oxford University Press, 2004), p. 349.
13 Matthew Mead, '*Empire Windrush*, cultural memory and archival disturbance', *Moveable Type*, 3 (2007), 112–27, 118.
14 Ibid., p. 120.
15 Robert Adams, 'Problems of the Negro in the theatre', *New Theatre* 4, 5 (November 1947), 11.
16 Chambers, *The Story of Unity Theatre*, pp. 270–1.
17 R. Adams, 'Problems of the Negro in the theatre', p. 11.
18 Pauline Henriques, 'Pauline Henriques', in Jim Pines (ed.), *Black and White in Colour, Black People in British Television Since 1936* (London: BFI Publishing, 1992), pp. 25–32, 28.
19 Arnaud D'Usseau, '"There is no place for neutrality in the theatre"', *New Theatre*, 4, 2 (August 1947), 12–15.
20 R. Adams, 'Problems of the Negro in the theatre', 11.
21 Henriques, 'Pauline Henriques', pp. 26–8.
22 Ibid., p. 30.
23 Clarke, *Hope and Glory*, p. 241.
24 Alan Sinfield, *Literature, Politics and Culture in Postwar Britain*, 2nd edn (London: Continuum, 2004), p. 17.
25 Robert Hewison, *Culture & Consensus, England, Art and Politics Since 1940* (London: Methuen, 1995), p. 58.
26 Ibid., p. 59.
27 Richard Findlater, 'The winding road to King's Reach', in Simon Callow (ed.), *The National: The Theatre, Its Work 1963–1997 and a Chronology of Productions 1963–1997* (London: Royal National Theatre [Great Britain], 1997), pp. 79–83.
28 Rowell, *The Old Vic Theatre*, p. 141.
29 J. C. Trewin, *The Theatre Since 1900* (London: Andrew Dakers Ltd., 1951), p. 299.
30 Hewison, *Culture & Consensus*, p. 59.
31 Ibid., p. 60.
32 J. Davies, *A History of Wales*, p. 622.
33 Richard J. Finlay, 'Continuity and change: Scottish politics 1900–45', in Devine and Finlay, *Scotland in the Twentieth Century*, pp. 64–84, 81.
34 Charles Landstone, *Off-stage: A Personal Record of the First Twelve Years of State-Sponsored Drama in Great Britain* (London: Elek, 1953), p. 144.

35 For an account of the establishment of CEMA Northern Ireland, see Gillian McIntosh, 'CEMA and the national anthem: the arts and the state in post-war Northern Ireland', *New Hibernia Review*, 5 (2001).

36 J. M. Keynes, 'The Arts Council: its policy and hopes', *Listener*, 34, 361 (12 July 1945), reprinted in Arts Council of Great Britain, *1st Annual Report 1945/6* (London: Arts Council of Great Britain, 1946), pp. 20–3, 23.

37 Arts Council of Great Britain, *6th Annual Report 1950/1* (London: Arts Council of Great Britain, 1951), pp. 32–3.

38 Ibid.

39 Andrew Sinclair, *Arts and Cultures, The History of the 50 Years of the Arts Council of Great Britain* (London: Sinclair-Stevenson, 1995), pp. 29–31.

40 Landstone, *Off-stage*, p. 108.

41 Winifred Bannister, *James Bridie and His Theatre* (London: Rockcliff, 1955), p. 251.

42 Ibid., p. 235.

43 Mackenney, *The Activities of Popular Dramatists and Drama Groups in Scotland*, pp. 223–6; 'fringe' groups who appeared at the inaugural festival included: Glasgow Unity, Christine Orr Players, Edinburgh Peoples' Theatre, Edinburgh District Community Drama Association, Pilgrim Players, Edinburgh College of Art Theatre Group, 'The Fringe', 'A History of the Edinburgh Festivals', www.edinburghfestivalpunter.co.uk/HistoryOfFestivals.html.

44 Michael Coveney, *The Citz: 21 Years of the Glasgow Citizens' Theatre* (London: Nick Hern Books, 1990), p. 9.

45 Bannister, *James Bridie and his Theatre*, p. 215.

46 Ibid.

47 See 'Appendix 10', production listings for Glasgow Unity, in Mackenney, *The Activities of in Scotland*, pp. 279–85.

48 Coveney, *The Citz*, pp. 11–12.

49 Mackenney, *The Activities of Popular Dramatists*, pp. 221–37.

50 Bannister, *James Bridie and his Theatre*, p. 243.

51 Robert Skidelsky, *John Maynard Keynes: The Economist as Saviour 1920–1937* (London: Macmillan, 1992), p. 527.

52 Audrey Williamson and Charles Landstone, *The Bristol Old Vic, The First Ten Years* (London: J. Garnet Miller, 1957), pp. 16–23.

53 Arts Council of Great Britain, *5th Annual Report 1949/50* (London: Arts Council of Great Britain, 1950), p. 19.

54 Keynes, 'The Arts Council', p. 21.

55 Williamson and Landstone, *The Bristol Old Vic*, pp. 26–9.

56 Keynes, 'The Arts Council', p. 22.

57 Dan Rebellato, *1956 and All That, The Making of Modern British Drama* (London: Routledge, 1999), p. 104.

58 A full discussion of the aims of the Conference from a range of perspectives was published in *New Theatre*, 4, 8 (February 1948); a full report on proceedings in *New Theatre*, 4, 9 (March 1948).

59 Chambers, *The Story of Unity Theatre*, pp. 265–80.

60 Landstone, *Off-stage*, pp. 183, 189–90.

61 ACGB, *6th Annual Report 1950/51*, p. 25.

62 *Theatre Ownership in Britain*, p. 1. The report was written anonymously by Malcolm Dunbar, 'an intellectual communist with a superb mind and a delightful sense of humour' who became an Equity staff member: Hugh Jenkins, *The Culture Gap: An Experience of Government and the Arts* (London: Boyars, 1979), p. 68.

63 *Theatre Ownership in Britain*, p. 2.

64 All details of individual cities, towns and villages appear in alphabetical order in 'The Provincial Guide' in Theatrical Management Association, *'The Stage' Year Book Incorporating 'The Stage Guide' 1951* (London: The Stage, 1951), pp. 199–286.

65 *Theatre Ownership in Britain*, p. 46.

66 Earl and Sell, *The Theatres Trust Guide to British Theatres, 1750–1950*, p. 169.

67 *Theatre Ownership in Britain*, p. 2.

68 Ibid., p. 1.

69 Hutchison, *The Modern Scottish Theatre*, p. 110.

70 Bell, *The Theatre in Ulster*, pp. 108–9.

71 Lyn Gallagher, *The Grand Opera House Belfast* (Belfast: Blackstaff Press, 1995), pp. 63–76.

72 'The Queen's Theatre South Shields', www.miketodd.net/tree/archives/queens/index.htm.

73 *Theatre Ownership in Britain*, pp. 58–82.

74 Ibid., p. 27.

75 Ibid., pp. 150–1.

76 Ibid., pp. 27–8.

77 Landstone, *Off-stage*, pp. 22–3.

78 'Tod Slaughter (1885–1956)', 'Star Archive', www.britishpictures.com/stars/Slaught.htm; on the Kinloch Players, see Jerrams, *Weekly Rep*, pp. 143–9.

79 See Cecil Davies and Peter Billingham, *The Adelphi Players, The Theatre of Persons* (London: Routledge Harwood, 2002); Peter Billingham, *Theatres of Conscience 1939–1953: A Study of Four Touring British Community Theatres* (London: Routledge Harwood, 2002).

80 Goorney, *The Theatre Workshop Story*, pp. 78–9.

81 For an overview of touring policy, see 'The first ten years', in ACGB, *11th Annual Report 1955–1956*, pp. 25–6, 46.

82 David Steuart, 'Perth Theatre Company on tour'; 'The passing years 1935–1956', *Perth Theatre Company*, pp. 14–5, 24.

83 ACGB, *6th Annual Report 1950/51*, p. 26; early history of Mobile Theatre outlined at Unicorn Theatre website www.unicorntheatre.com/page.php?id=112.

84 George Devine, 'The Arena Theatre – an important experiment', *New Theatre* 5.11 (May 1949), 22.

85 Bannister, *James Bridie and His Theatre*, pp. 235–8.

86 List of touring productions for weeks beginning 9 and 16 October 1950 taken from *The Stage*, 12 October 1950.

87 'Distaff', *The Stage*, 19 January 1950.

88 Maggie B. Gale, *West End Women, Women and the London Stage 1918–1962* (London: Routledge, 1996), p. 17.

89 Rebellato, *1956 and All That*, pp. 107–8.

90 See the detailed account in Landstone, *Off-stage*, pp. 89–102.

91 Coleman, *Olivier*, p. 232.

92 The post-war Arts Council headquarters.

93 Anthony Quayle, *A Time to Speak* (London: Barrie & Jenkins, 1990), p. 325.

94 Beauman, *The Royal Shakespeare Company*, p. 202.

95 Ibid., p. 201.

96 Geoffrey Robinson, 'The Repertory Movement', *'The Stage' Year Book*, pp. 44–6.

97 Jerrams, *Weekly Rep*, pp. 162–6.

98 Sinfield, *Literature, Politics and Culture in Postwar Britain*, p. 46.

99 See the chapter titles in Landstone, *Off-stage*, 'The Pattern', 'The Spokes, The Hub and Llewellyn', pp. 103–45. Drama directors were Lewis Casson; Michael MacOwan, artistic director for the Army Bureau of Current Affairs; Llewellyn Rees, General Secretary of British Actors' Equity; John Moody, actor, singer, director.

100 TMA, *'The Stage' Year Book* pp. 47–9.

101 Jerrams, *Weekly Rep*, pp. 152–8.

102 Billie Whitelaw, *Billie Whitelaw … Who He?* (London: Hodder and Stoughton, 1995), p. 57.

103 John Osborne, *A Better Class of Person, An Autobiography 1929–1956* (London: Faber & Faber, 1982), p. 246.

104 Robert Stephens and Michael Coveney, *Knight Errant, Memoirs of a Vagabond Actor* (London: Hodder and Stoughton, 1996), p. 14.

105 Whitelaw, *Billie Whitelaw*, p. 57.

106 ACGB, *6th Annual Report 1950/1*, p. 25.

107 Rowell and Jackson, *The Repertory Movement*, p. 81.

108 *Perth Theatre Company*, pp. 10–11; Foulkes, *Repertory at The Royal*, pp. 90–5; Rosenfeld, *The York Theatre*, pp. 336–7.

109 Landstone, *Off-stage*, pp. 111–13.

110 Half the early profits of the Bristol Old Vic came from bar takings, ibid., p. 126.

111 Ibid., pp. 111–19.

112 A.B. Patterson, *History of the Byre Theatre* (St Andrews: The Theatre, 1983).

113 See the account of the origins of the Playhouse in John Bailey, *A Theatre for All Seasons, Nottingham Playhouse, The First Thirty Years 1948–1978* (Stroud: Alan Sutton Publishing & Nottingham Playhouse, 1994), pp. 1–8.

114 Ibid., pp. 25–8.

115 *Theatre Ownership in Britain*, p. 28.

116 Lez Cooke, *British Television Drama: A History* (London: British Film Institute, 2003), p. 17.

6 THE BUSINESS OF THEATRE

1 Anheier, *Nonprofit Organisations*, p. 4.
2 Michael J. Oliver, 'The retreat of the state in the 1980s and 1990s', in Francesca Carnelvali and Julie-Marie Strange (eds.), *20th Century Britain: Economic, Cultural and Social Change*, 2nd edn (Harlow: Pearson Longman, 2007), p. 262.
3 Ibid., p. 264.
4 The acronym quango short for 'quasi-autonomous national government organisation' is a semi-public administrative body financed by government which also appoints its senior members.
5 In the 1980s these included: Peter Dormer, 'Bloodied but not bold: the Arts Council of Great Britain', *Political Quarterly*, 52 (1981), 416–25; Hutchison, *The Politics of the Arts Council*; John Pick, *The Theatre Industry Subsidy*.
6 Oliver, 'The retreat of the state', Carnelvali and Strange, *20th Century Britain*, p. 262.
7 Neil Wooding, 'Engaged leadership – the new public service managerialism', *Journal of Finance and Management in Public Services*, 7, 1 (2007), 41.
8 Chambers, *Inside the Royal Shakespeare Company*, p. 10.
9 Elsom and Tomalin, *The History of the National Theatre*.
10 Chambers, *Inside the Royal Shakespeare Company*, p. 12.
11 Ibid., pp. 9–10.
12 Ibid., pp. 17–20.
13 Ibid., p. 20.
14 Ibid., p. 23.
15 Ibid., pp. 17–18, 40–1.
16 Peter Hall, *Making An Exhibition of Myself* (London: Sinclair-Stevenson, 1993), pp. 152–3.
17 Ibid., pp. 150–1; Coleman, *Olivier*, pp. 292–3.
18 Coleman, *Olivier*, pp. 336–42.
19 Rowell and Jackson, *The Repertory Movement*, p. 111.
20 Ibid., p. 133.
21 Williamson and Landstone, *The Bristol Old Vic*, pp. 125, 137.
22 Oscar Lewenstein, *Kicking Against the Pricks: A Theatre Producer Looks Back: The Memoirs of Oscar Lewenstein* (London: Nick Hern Books, 1994), pp. 15, 20.
23 On the topic of 'mediation' and Lewenstein's role in the founding of the ESC, see Yael Zarhy-Levo, *The Making of Theatrical Reputations: Studies from the Modern London Theatre* (Iowa City: Iowa University Press, 2008), pp. 17, 21–2, 210–11.
24 Lewenstein, *Kicking Against the Pricks*, pp. 41–84.
25 Ibid., pp. 20–1.

26 Ibid., pp. 90–1.

27 Goorney, *The Theatre Workshop Story*, pp. 108–24. In Littlewood's auto-biography she describes how she 'heard her heart crack' when told by actors Harry Corbett and George Cooper that they were leaving the company in order to earn more money: Littlewood, *Joan's Book*, p. 465.

28 Goorney, *The Theatre Workshop Story*, p. 215.

29 Nadine Holdsworth, '"They'd have pissed on my grave": the case of Theatre Workshop and the Arts Council', *New Theatre Quarterly*, 53 (1999).

30 'Daubeny Peter (1921–75)', in Dennis Kennedy (ed.), *The Oxford Encyclopedia of Theatre & Performance*, volume 1 (Oxford University Press, 2003), p. 352.

31 Ronald Hayman, *Harold Pinter* (London: Heinemann, 1980), p. 126; also Zarhy-Levo, *The Making of Theatrical Reputations*, pp. 166–7.

32 James Inverne, *The Impresarios* (London: Oberon Books, 2000), pp. 134–43, 158–65.

33 For a full account of the controversy surrounding *Soldiers*, see Helen Freshwater, *Theatre Censorship in Britain: Silencing, Censure and Suppression* (Basingstoke: Palgrave Macmillan, 2009), pp. 66–83.

34 'History of the Shaftesbury Theatre', www.shaftesbury-theatre.co.uk/theatre-history.htm.

35 Portable was awarded £9,470. The next highest grant was £8,000 to The Combination: Arts Council of Great Britain, *27th Annual Report 1971–1972* (London: Arts Council of Great Britain, 1972), p. 59.

36 'David Hare (writer)', in Rob Ritchie (ed.), *The Joint Stock Book: The Making of a Theatre Collective* (London: Methuen, 1987), pp. 105–10, 106.

37 Steve Gooch, *All Together Now, An Alternative View of Theatre and the Community* (London: Methuen, 1984), p. 21.

38 'David Hare (writer)', in Ritchie, *The Joint Stock Book*, p. 106.

39 Joyce McMillan, *The Traverse Theatre Story 1963–1988 by Joyce McMillan with a Chronology of Productions Mounted by the Traverse During Its First 25 Years Compiled by John Carnegie* (London: Methuen, 1988), pp. 44–54.

40 Roland Rees (ed.), *Fringe First, Pioneers of Fringe Theatre on Record* (London: Oberon Books, 1992), pp. 47–9.

41 'David Aukin (producer)', in Ritchie, *The Joint Stock Book*, pp. 100–1.

42 Gooch, *All Together Now*, p. 39.

43 Simon Callow, *Being an Actor* (London: Methuen, 1984), pp. 81–7.

44 Gillian Hanna (ed.), 'Introduction', in *Monstrous Regiment, Four Plays and a Collective Celebration* (London: Nick Hern Books, 1991), pp. xiii–xlix.

45 Ibid., pp. xlix–lxxviii.

46 This was a particular issue for 7.84 (Scotland). John McGrath resigned from the company he had created in protest at the Board changes proposed by the Scottish Arts Council. See Elizabeth MacLennan, *The Moon Belongs to Everyone, Making Theatre with 7:84* (London: Methuen, 1990), pp. 171–3.

47 Lewenstein, *Kicking Against the Pricks*, p. 28.

48 Wardle, *The Theatres of George Devine*, p. 168.

49 Hall, *Making An Exhibition of Myself*, p. 197.

50 Arts Council of Great Britain, *13th Annual Report 1957–1958* (London: Arts Council of Great Britain, 1958), p. 39; on the rental charge, see Arts Council of Great Britain, *15th Annual Report, 1959–1960* (London: Arts Council of Great Britain, 1960), p. 22.

51 Bailey, *A Theatre for All Seasons*, pp. 119–24.

52 Richard Eyre, 'A Memoir Nottingham Revisited', in Bailey, *A Theatre for All Seasons*, pp. 179–82, 181.

53 Cochrane, *Birmingham Rep*, p. 70.

54 Mark Fisher, 'From traverse to tramway: Scottish theatres old and new', in Stevenson and Wallace (eds.), *Scottish Theatre Since the Seventies*, pp. 49–56, 49–50.

55 Ibid., p. 50.

56 Perth Theatre history, www.horsecross.co.uk/about/perth-theatre/history/.

57 Nicholas Crafts, 'The British economy', in Carnelvali and Strange, *20th Century Britain*, pp. 7–25, 9.

58 Clarke, *Hope and Glory*, p. 304.

59 Patterson, *History of the Byre Theatre*, p. 14.

60 N. V. Linklater, 'The achievement in drama', in John Pick (ed.), *The State and the Arts* (Eastbourne: John Offord, 1980), pp. 77–98, 86–7.

61 Rowell and Jackson, *The Repertory Movement*, p. 89.

62 Great Britain, Department of Education and Science, *A Policy for the Arts – The First Steps* (London: H.M.S.O, 1965), par. 100.

63 Clarke, *Hope and Glory*, pp. 302–7.

64 Arts Council of Great Britain, *29th Annual Report 1973–1974* (London: Arts Council of Great Britain, 1974), p. 13.

65 Rowell and Jackson, *The Repertory Movement*, p. 194.

66 For accounts of Arts Centres organised by country and in alphabetical order, see Sheena Barbour and Kate Manton (eds.), *Directory of Arts Centres 2* (Eastbourne: John Offord Publications in association with the Arts Council of Great Britain, 1981).

67 Bill Dufton, 'Housing the arts' in Stephens, *The Arts in Wales*, pp. 309–31.

68 'Chapter', in Barbour and Manton, *Directory of Arts Centre 2*.

69 'Belgrade Theatre, Coventry', 'The Olivier', 'Barbican Theatre', in Ronnie Mulryne and Margaret Shewring (eds.), *Making Space for Theatre British Architecture and Theatre Since 1958* (Stratford-upon-Avon: Mulryne and Shewring Ltd., 1995), pp. 119–23.

70 'Presenter Interview: Louise Jeffreys (Barbican Centre) Performing Arts Network Japan', 16. 3. 05, www.performingarts.jp/E/pre_interview/0503/1.html.

71 Chambers, *Inside the Royal Shakespeare Company*, pp. 76–81.

72 *Cathy Come Home* by Jeremy Sandford, produced by Tony Garnett and directed by Ken Loach, was shown on BBC1 on 16 November 1966 as part of the 'Wednesday Play' series. In the case of Theatre Workshop the reluctance of the local authorities, struggling to balance other, more pressing priorities in London's East End, to give more than limited financial support to the Theatre Royal, was officially another factor in attempts to

get matched funding from the Arts Council. See Goorney, *The Theatre Workshop Story*, p. 215.

73 Cochrane, *The Birmingham Rep*, pp. 45–57.

74 For a full account of the campaign to build the West Yorkshire Playhouse, see Doreen Newlyn, *Theatre Connections, A Very Personal Story* (Leeds: Walter Newlyn, 1995).

75 James Miller, *The Magic Curtain, The Story of Theatre in Inverness* (Inverness: Friends of Eden Court, 1986), pp. 48–59.

76 'Phase 3', in 'History', Dundee Rep website, www.dundeereptheatre.co.uk/p73.html.

77 Byrne, *The Stage in Ulster from the Eighteenth Century*, pp. 50–4. The Arts Theatre building reopened for live performance until 1998, when it closed permanently.

78 Conor O'Malley, *A Poets' Theatre* (Dublin: Elo Press, 1988), pp. 22–5.

79 Ibid., p. 25.

80 Ibid., pp. 27–8.

81 Ibid., p. 26.

82 Mary O'Malley, *Never Shake Hands with the Devil* (Dublin: Elo Press, 1990), pp. 60–84.

83 C. O'Malley, *A Poets' Theatre*, pp. 25–30.

84 Ibid., pp. 33–5.

85 See a full discussion of the plays of both John Boyd and Patrick Galvin in Roy Connolly, *The Evolution of the Lyric Players' Theatre Belfast: Fighting the Waves* (New York/Lampeter: Edwin Mellen Press, c. 2000), pp. 167–99.

86 C. O'Malley, *A Poets' Theatre*, pp. 83–4; M. O'Malley, *Never Shake Hands with the Devil*, p. 275.

87 Gallagher, *The Grand Opera House Belfast*, pp. 89–124.

88 Julia Hallam, 'Introduction: the development of commercial TV in Britain', in John Finch et al. (eds.), *Granada Television, The First Generation* (Manchester University Press, 2003), pp. 1–24, 12–21.

89 Jonathan Bignell, 'And the rest is history: Lew Grade, creation narratives and television historiography', in Catherine Johnson and Rob Turnock (eds.), *ITV Cultures Independent Television over Fifty Years* (Maidenhead: Open University Press, 2005), pp. 57–70.

90 'The ITV Story A Teletronic Television History Article', www.teletronic.co.uk/itvstory1.htm; Catherine Johnson and Rob Turnock, 'From start-up to consolidation: institutions, regions and regulation over the history of ITV', in Johnson and Turnock, *ITV Cultures*, pp. 19–21.

91 Hallam, 'Introduction', in Finch, *Granada Television*, pp. 15–19.

92 Derek Salberg, *Ring Down the Curtain* (Luton: Cortney Publications, 1980), p. 98.

93 As an impresario who brought the greatest international variety stars to London and managing director of ATV, Parnell was immensely successful in nurturing theatre-grown talent for television, but when it was discovered that London theatres including the Palladium, the Victoria Palace and the

Theatre Royal Drury Lane were threatened, Prince Littler organised a rescue bid and Parnell was forced into resignation. 'Parnell, Val (1892–1972)', Screenonline, www.screenonline.org.uk/people/id/1146747/index.html.

94 Arts Council of Great Britain, *The Theatre Today in England and Wales, The Report of the Arts Council Theatre Enquiry 1970* (London: Arts Council of Great Britain, 1970), p. 7.

95 Ibid., pp. 52–3.

96 Ibid., pp. 52–6.

97 Ibid., pp. 15–16.

98 John Elsom, *Post War British Theatre* (London: Routledge, 1976), p. 139.

99 ACGB, *The Theatre Today in England and Wales*, p. 62.

100 Ibid., pp. 20–6.

101 'History of the New Theatre', www.newtheatrecardiff.co.uk/english/history.asp.

102 Russell Galbraith, 'Happy birthday STV – 50 years of entertaining', *Scotsman*, 30 August 2007.

103 For an account of the decline of Howard & Wyndham, see Paul Iles, 'Issues in Theatrical Management', pp. 89–102.

104 Rachel Bridge, 'Boy's cinema job led to lifelong love affair with theatres', *Sunday Times*, 10 April 2005, http://business.timesonline.co.uk/tol/business/entrepreneur/article379248.ece.

105 Gallagher, *The Grand Opera House Belfast*, p. 122.

106 Ibid., pp. 123–4.

107 Baz Kershaw, 'Discouraging democracy: British theatres and economics, 1979–1999', *Theatre Journal*, 51 (October 1999), 269.

108 Arts Council of Great Britain, *25th Annual Report 1969–1970* (London: Arts Council of Great Britain, 1970), p. 19.

109 *Wigan Observer*, 27 August 1971, 'Our History 1967–1977', www.octagonbolton.co.uk/page/3014/1967+-+1977.

110 Arts Council of Great Britain, *28th Annual Report 1972–1973* (London: Arts Council of Great Britain, 1973), p. 36.

111 Kevan Scholes, 'The Crucible Theatre, Sheffield', in Gerry Johnson and Kevan Scholes (eds.), *Exploring Corporate Strategy*, 3rd edn (New York/London: Prentice-Hall International, 1993), pp. 526–57, 537.

112 'Parliament rejects pleas for VAT concession Sheffield Crucible case highlighted', *The Stage*, 20 July 1972.

113 Scholes, 'The Crucible Theatre, Sheffield', p. 528.

114 [Crucible Theatre], *Some Basic Facts* (c. 1977), anonymous publication held in Crucible Theatre File, Victoria and Albert Theatre Collections, no pagination.

115 'Sheffield Crucible stage "Wiz" premiere', *The Stage*, 17 July 1980.

116 [Crucible Theatre], *Some Basic Facts*.

117 Shirley Brown, 'The Bristol Theatre Royal – the continuing story 1966–93', in Richard Foulkes (ed.), *Scenes from Provincial Stages, Essays in Honour of Kathleen Barker* (London: Society for Theatre Research, 1994), pp. 180–94, 180–88.

118 Rees, *Fringe First*, pp. 269–70.
119 John Pick, *The Theatre Industry Subsidy*, p. 45.
120 For a discussion of the dominant mainstream dramatists after 1979, see John Bull, *Stage Right, Crisis and Recovery in British Contemporary Mainstream Theatre* (Basingstoke: Macmillan, 1994).
121 Ibid., pp. 40–4.
122 Coveney, *The Citz*, pp. 223–49.
123 Beauman, *The Royal Shakespeare Company*, p. 240.
124 An example of this could be seen at Birmingham Rep in the early 1970s: Cochrane, *The Birmingham Rep*, p. 71.
125 Hall, *Making an Exhibition of Myself*, pp. 293–97.
126 Timothy West, *A Moment Towards the End of the Play, An Autobiography* (London: Nick Hern Books, 2001), p. 154.
127 Scottish Arts Council, *A Socio-Economic Study of Artists in Scotland* (Edinburgh: Scottish Arts Council, 1995), pp. 36–9.
128 Peter Boyden Associates, *Roles & Functions of the English Regional Producing Theatres* (London: Arts Council England, 2000), p. 20.
129 Venues included the Bush Theatre, Gate Theatre, Finborough Theatre, White Bear Theatre Club and King's Head Theatre.
130 N. V. Linklater, 'The achievement in drama', in John Pick (ed.), *The State and the Arts* (Eastbourne: John Offord, 1980), pp. 77–98, 83.
131 Cochrane, *The Birmingham Rep*, p. 194.
132 D. Keith Peacock, *Thatcher's Theatre: British Theatre and Drama in the Eighties* (Westport, Conn./London: Greenwood Press, 1999); Turnbull's case studies include the Salisbury Playhouse, the 'Surrey Triangle' of the Thorndike Theatre, Leatherhead, Redgrave Theatre Farnham and Yvonne Arnaud Theatre, Guildford, and the Merseyside Everyman Theatre and Liverpool Playhouse: Olivia Turnbull, *Bringing Down the House, The Crisis in Britain's Regional Theatres* (Bristol: Intellect, 2008).
133 Ros Merkin, 'Devolve and/or die: the vexed relationship between the centre and the regions: 1980–2006', in Dorney and Merkin, *The Glory of the Garden*, pp. 69–102.
134 Ian Brown and Rob Brannen, 'When theatre was for all, the Cork Report, after ten years', *New Theatre Quarterly*, 12 (1996); Ian Brown, 'The road through Woodstock: Counter-Thatcherite strategies in ACGB's drama development between 1984 and 1994', *Contemporary Theatre Review*, 17 (2007), 218–29; Ian Brown, Rob Brannen and Douglas Brown, 'The English franchise system and political theatre', *New Theatre Quarterly*, 16 (2000), 379–87; Ian Brown, '"Guarding against the guardians": cultural democracy and ACGB/RAA relations in the *Glory* years, 1984–94', in Dorney and Merkin, *The Glory of the Garden*, pp. 29–53.
135 Brown, '"Guarding against the Guardians"', pp. 29–30.
136 The removal of funding to 7.84 (England) which precipitated the company's collapse in 1985 was one of the most controversial of ACE's decisions. For a detailed and careful discussion of the issues surrounding company

management and artistic quality and reception in both the Scottish and the English companies during this period, see Maria DiCenzo, *The Politics of Alternative Theatre in Britain, 1968–1990, The Case of 7.84 (Scotland)* (Cambridge University Press, 1996), pp. 116–28.

137 See Arts Council England, *Recovery Programme Guidelines for Applicants* (London: 1998), booklet. The Royal Lyceum received £500,000 from SAC's Advancement fund. The Citizens' Theatre was awarded £195,000 towards developing new fund-raising strategies to enable the company to increase the number of productions: 'SAC's £1.4m stabilisation awards', *The Stage*, 9 July 1998, p. 2.

138 For WYP's response to the award, see Phil Gibby, 'Community drive', *The Stage*, 3 July 1997.

139 Cochrane, *The Birmingham Rep*, pp. 176–201.

140 Boyden Associates, *Roles & Functions*, pp. 19, 29–34.

7 THE CHANGING DEMOGRAPHIC OF PERFORMANCE

1 Cindi Katz, 'Social formations: thinking about society, identity, power and resistance', in S. L. Holloway, S. P. Price and G. Valentine (eds.), *Key Concepts in Geography* (London: Sage, 2003), pp. 249–62, 249, 262.

2 Thomas M. Devine, 'Introduction', in Devine and Finlay, *Scotland in the Twentieth Century*, p. 4.

3 The term 'institutional racism' gained general currency in the aftermath of *The Stephen Lawrence Enquiry*. The background is summarised in Lynette Goddard, *Staging Black Feminisms: Identity, Politics, Performance* (Basingstoke: Palgrave Macmillan, 2007), pp. 34–5. In relation to theatre this was discussed at the Eclipse Conference held at Nottingham Playhouse in 2001. Arts Council England, *Eclipse, Developing Strategies to Combat Racism in the Theatre* (London: ACE, 2002).

4 Katherine Watson, 'Education and opportunity', in Carnevali and Strange, *20th Century Britain*, pp. 355–72.

5 Sanderson, *From Irving to Olivier*, p. 293.

6 Siân Phillips, *Private Faces, The Autobiography* (London: Hodder and Stoughton, 1999), pp. 270–1.

7 Ibid., pp. 268–9.

8 Stephens and Coveney, *Knight Errant*, p. 12.

9 Ibid., pp. 10–12.

10 Whitelaw, *Billie Whitelaw*, pp. 3, 38–9.

11 William Gaskill, *A Sense of Direction, Life at The Royal Court* (London: Faber and Faber, 1988), pp. 2–4.

12 Whitelaw, *Billie Whitelaw*, pp. 29–30.

13 'Burton [Jenkins], Richard Walter (1925–)', in *The Oxford Companion to the Theatre* (Oxford University Press, 1983), pp. 119–20.

14 Alan Strachan, 'Clifford Williams, obituary', *Independent*, 23 August 2005.

15 Hall, *Making an Exhibition of Myself*, pp. 6–7.

16 Ibid., pp. 36–55.
17 Quentin Falk, *Albert Finney in Character* (London: Robson Books, 1992), pp. 14–24.
18 Heather Neill, 'New thespians start here', *The Times*, 10 September 1998; Hilary Whitney, 'It's a stage they've all been through', *Telegraph.co.uk*, 17 July 2006, www.telegraph.co.uk/culture/theatre/drama/3653888/Its-a-stage-theyve-all-been-through.html.
19 Ibid.; ibid.
20 'Ian McKellen Stage', Sir Ian McKellen website, www.mckellen.com/stage/index.htm. For Trevor Nunn, see Beauman, *The Royal Shakespeare Company*, pp. 288–9.
21 Falk, *Albert Finney in Character*, pp. 22–3.
22 Armes, *A Critical History of British Cinema*, pp. 268–72.
23 Beauman, *The Royal Shakespeare Company*, p. 232.
24 Falk, *Albert Finney in Character*, pp. 40–1.
25 Tom Courtney, *Dear Tom, Letters from Home* (London: Black Swan Books, 2001), pp. 90–308.
26 Jenni Murray, '20th Century Britain: The Woman's Hour', BBC-History in depth: '20th Century Britain: The Woman's Hour', 5.11.2005 www.bbc.co.uk/history/british/modern/jmurray_01.shtml.
27 Christopher Bryant, *Glenda Jackson: The Biography* (London: HarperCollins, 1999).
28 'Shelagh Delaney', The Queen's Theatre Hornchurch, www.queens-theatre.co.uk/biographies/shelaghdelaney.htm; Jeanette Winterson, 'My hero: Shelagh Delaney by Jeanette Winterson', *Guardian*, 18 September 2010; Hannah Gumbrill, 'Interview with Frances Cuka', Theatre Archive Project, www.bl.uk/projects/theatrearchive/cuka.html; 'Tushingham, Rita (1942)', Screenonline, www.screenonline.org.uk/people/id/465090/; biographical files on other actors may be accessed in the Victoria and Albert Theatre Collections.
29 Rachel Roberts and Alexander Walker, *No Bells on Sunday: The Journals of Rachel Roberts* (London: Pavilion, 1984).
30 Christine Geraghty, *British Cinema in the Fifties, Gender, Genre and the 'New Look'* (London: Routledge, 2000), pp. 110–11.
31 Tyrone Stevenson, *Richard Burton: A Bio-bibliography* (New York/London: Greenwood Press, 1992).
32 Pat Phoenix, *All My Burning Bridges* (London: Arlington Books, 1974), p. 94. Phoenix gives a detailed account of her early career in touring and resident commercial theatre.
33 Richard Hoggart, *The Uses of Literacy* (Harmondsworth: Penguin, 1990), p. 190, quoted in Hewison, *Culture & Consensus*, p. 101.
34 Ibid.
35 Richard Dyer et al., *Coronation Street* (London: B.F.I. Publishing, 1981).
36 Sinfield, *Literature, Politics and Culture in Postwar Britain*, p. 282.
37 Cooke, *British Television Drama*, p. 33.

38 John Caughie, *Television Drama: Realism, Modernism, and British Culture* (Oxford: Oxford University Press, 2000), p. 51.

39 Ibid., p. 74.

40 Ibid., p. 33.

41 Cooke, *British Television Drama*, p. 37.

42 Ibid., p. 42; 'Hot summer night (1959)', Lloyd Reckford, www.screenonline. org.uk/tv/id/1134115/.

43 Cooke, *British Television Drama*, p. 42.

44 Gordon McDougall, 'En route to the stables', in Finch, *Granada Television*, pp. 78–83.

45 Caughie, *Television Drama*, p. 74.

46 Cooke, *British Television Drama*, p. 57.

47 John R. Cook, 'Three ring circus: television drama about, by and for Scotland', in Neil Blain and David Hutchison (eds.), *The Media in Scotland* (Edinburgh University Press, 2008), pp. 107–22, 108.

48 Ibid., p. 109.

49 Ibid., p. 111.

50 Aga Sikora, 'Interview with Ian Richardson', Theatre Archive Project, www. bl.uk/projects/theatrearchive/richardson.html.

51 For an account of the Gateway Theatre Company, see Donald Smith, 'The Gateway Theatre Company', in Ian Brown (ed.), *Journey's Beginning, The Gateway Theatre Building and Company 1884–1965* (Bristol: Intellect Books, 2004), pp. 53–63.

52 Michael Coveney, 'Tom Fleming, obituary', *Guardian*, 20 April 2010.

53 Anthony Hayward, 'Iain Cuthbertson: actor who played the procurator fiscal in "Sutherland's Law" and Charlie Endell in "Budgie"', *Independent*, 11 September 2009.

54 Roy Boutcher and William G. Kemp, *The Theatre in Perth: Published to Mark the Fortieth Anniversary of Perth Theatre Company* (Perth: Perth Theatre Company, 1975), pp. 38–42.

55 http://news.scotsman.com/obituaries/Stephen-MacDonald-theatre-director-and.5600056.jp.

56 Donald Smith, '1950 to 1995', in Findlay, *A History of Scottish Theatre*, pp. 253–308, 255.

57 Ibid., p. 275.

58 As late as 1986 Anne Downie complained that Scottish actresses were threatened with 'indifference and neglect': Annie Downie, 'The Actress's Lot', *Chapman 43–4 Scottish Theatre*, vols. 8 & 9 (1986), pp. 118–20, 119.

59 Coveney, *The Citz*, p. 4.

60 Catherine Deveney, 'Actor Bill Paterson recalls a Glasgow childhood that includes Hiroshima, a Scottish World Cup and the exotic old Mr Baird', *Scotland on Sunday*, 17 August 2008.

61 Coveney, *The Citz*, pp. 73–6, 251–78.

62 Alex McCrindle, (letter), *Scotsman*, 3 March 1970.

63 Richard Eyre, *Utopia & Other Places* (London: Vintage, 1994), pp. 146–52.

64 *Scotsman*, 23 June 1969; see also 'Lyceum Theatre: Inside the Lyceum History Artistic Director Clive Perry 1966–75', www.lyceum.org.uk/webpages/inside_history_directors_cliveperry.php.

65 Ian Rose, 'From Greenock to a wider stage', *Glasgow Herald*, 6 April 1974; Ian Brown, 'Plugged into history: the sense of the past in Scottish theatre', in Stevenson and Wallace, *Scottish Theatre Since the Seventies*, pp. 84–99, 88–9.

66 Michael Billington, 'John McGrath', 'Obituary', *Guardian*, 24 January 2002.

67 John Bett and Susanna Capon, 'John Bett', in David Bradby and Susanna Capon (eds.), *Freedom's Pioneer, John Mcgrath's Work in Theatre, Film and Television* (University of Exeter Press, 2005), pp. 196–205, 198.

68 Randall Stevenson, 'Border warranty John McGrath and Scotland', in ibid., pp. 73–85, 75.

69 Ian Brown, 'Celtic centres, the fringes and John McGrath', in ibid., pp. 86–99, 87–9.

70 DiCenzo, *The Politics of Alternative Theatre in Britain*, pp. 89–91.

71 MacLennan, *The Moon Belongs to Everyone*, p. 43.

72 Bett and Capon, 'John Bett', p. 198.

73 Robin Nelson, 'The television adaptation of *The Cheviot, the Stag and the Black, Black Oil*', in Bradby and Capon, *Freedom's Pioneer*, pp. 115–29.

74 McGrath used the expression 'forays and skirmishes' to describe the occasional opportunity for political intervention on television; quoted in Robert Dawson Scott, 'A good night in the Long Roads', in ibid., pp. 144–55, 147.

75 DiCenzo, *The Politics of Alternative Theatre in Britain*, pp. 223–4.

76 Lindsay Paterson, *The Autonomy of Modern Scotland* (Edinburgh University Press, 1994), pp. 7–9.

77 See, in particular, Godiwala, *Alternatives Within the Mainstream*; also Geoffrey V. Davis and Anne Fuchs (eds.), *Staging New Britain, Aspects of Black and South Asian British Theatre Practice* (Brussels: P.I.E.–Peter Lang, 2006).

78 Jatinder Verma and Maria Shevtsova, 'The generations of the diaspora and multiculturalism in Britain', *New Theatre Quarterly*, 25 (2009), p. 205.

79 Parekh, *The Future of Multi-Ethnic Britain*, p. xxiii.

80 Naseem Khan, *The Arts Britain Ignores: The Arts of Ethnic Minorities in Britain* (London: Commission for Racial Equality, 1978).

81 Kwesi Owusu, *The Struggle for Black Arts in Britain, What Can We Consider Better than Freedom?* (London: Comedia, 1986), p. 47.

82 Solomos, *Race and Racism in Britain*, pp. 48–9.

83 Ibid., p. 79.

84 Thomas Baptiste, in Pines, *Black and White in Colour*, pp. 65–9, 69.

85 Yvonne Brewster, *The Undertaker's Daughter, The Colourful Life of a Theatre Director* (London: Black Amber Books, 2004), p. x.

86 Ann Ogidi, 'Hammond, Mona', screenonline.org.uk.

87 Parekh, *The Future of Multi-Ethnic Britain*, pp. 30–1.

88 'Archer's Actor – Jamila Massey', BBC-Mid Wales, Llanidloes-Jamila Massey, www.bbc.co.uk/wales/mid/sites/llanidloes/pages/jamila_massey.shtml; for

Pervaiz Khan, see Claire Cochrane, '"A local habitation and a name": the development of Black and Asian Theatre in Birmingham since the 1970s', in Godiwala, *Alternatives Within the Mainstream*, pp. 151–73, 159.

89 Jatinder Verma, 'Cultural Transformations', in Theodore Shank (ed.), *Contemporary British Theatre* (Basingstoke: Macmillan, 1993), pp. 55–61, 57.

90 Zia Mohyeddin, in Pines, *Black and White in Colour*, pp. 70–1.

91 Lloyd Reckord, in ibid., p. 51.

92 Ogidi, 'Hammond, Mona'.

93 Sarah Dadswell, 'From Asian to British Asian: the early history of British South Asian theatre', unpublished essay, 2009, p. 31.

94 Brewster, *The Undertaker's Daughter*, p. 45.

95 Pearl Connor, in Pines, *Black and White in Colour*, pp. 33–42.

96 Pearl Connor, in Linton Kwesi Johnson et al., *Changing Britannia: Life Experience with Britain* (London: New Beacon, 1999), pp. 1–18, 7.

97 Cy Grant, in Pines, *Black and White in Colour*, pp. 43–50.

98 Pearl Connor, in Johnson, *Changing Britannia*, p. 10.

99 Stephen Bourne, *Black in the British Frame, Black People in British Film and Television 1896–1996* (London: Cassell, 1998), p. 99.

100 Deidre Osborne, 'Writing Black back: an overview of Black theatre and performance in Britain', in Godiwala, *Alternatives Within the Mainstream*, pp. 73–4.

101 A chronology of productions naming plays, actors, playwrights and venues may be found in Susan Croft with Stephen Bourne and Alda Terracciano, *Black and Asian Performance at the Theatre Museum, A User's Guide* (London: Theatre Museum, 2002).

102 Claire Cochrane, 'Opening up the garden: a comparison of strategies for developing intercultural access to theatre in Birmingham and Nottingham', in Dorney and Merkin, *The Glory of the Garden*, pp. 125–38, 128–9.

103 Osborne, 'Writing Black back', p. 73.

104 Charles Duff, *The Lost Summer, The Heyday of the West End Theatre* (London: Nick Hern, 1995), pp. 217–21.

105 Osborne, 'Writing Black back', p. 73.

106 Pearl Connor, in Pines, *Black and White in Colour*, p. 37.

107 The performance was not a critical success however. John was considered too lightweight for the role. See Bourne, *Black in the British Frame*, p. 218.

108 Sarita Malik, *Representing Black Britain: A History of Black and Asian Images on British Television* (London: SAGE, 2002), p. 2.

109 Ibid., p. 135.

110 Ibid., p. 136.

111 Lloyd Reckord, Carmen Munroe, in Pines, *Black and White in Colour*, pp. 51–69.

112 Carl Daniels, BFI Screenonline: Man from the Sun, A (1956), www.screenonline.org.uk/tv/id/475546/.

113 John Elliot, in Pines, *Black and White in Colour*, pp. 85–91, 87.

114 Ibid., pp. 89–90.

115 John Hopkins, in ibid., pp. 92–7, 92–4.
116 Ibid., pp. 94–7.
117 Ibid.
118 Joan Hooley, in ibid., pp. 98–101.
119 Malik, *Representing Black Britain*, p. 148.
120 Thomas Baptiste, in Pines, pp. 67–8.
121 Bourne, *Black in the British Frame*, p. 192.
122 Cleo Sylvestre, in Pines, *Black and White in Colour*, pp. 102–7.
123 Sarita Malik, BFI Screenonline: Abbensetts, Michael (1938–), www.screenonline.org.uk/people/id/535662/.
124 Michael Abbensetts, in Pines, *Black and White in Colour*, pp. 133–4.
125 Ibid., pp. 134–5.
126 Ibid.
127 'Black Theatre 1', in Rees, *Fringe First*, pp. 98–106.
128 Claire Benedict and Roland Rees, p. 139.
129 Tunde Ikoli, in ibid., pp. 118–9.
130 Yvonne Brewster, 'Introduction', in Yvonne Brewster (ed.), *Black Plays 3* (London: Methuen, 1995), pp. vii–viii, viii.
131 Cleo Sylvestre, in Pines, *Black and White in Colour*, pp. 102–3.
132 Rees, 'Black Theatre', in Rees, *Fringe First*, pp. 96–116.
133 Ibid., p. 102.
134 Mustapha Matura, in 'Black Theatre I', in Rees, *Fringe First*, p. 98.
135 Ibid., p. 96.
136 Carmen Munroe, in Pines, *Black and White in Colour*, pp. 56–64, 62.
137 Judith Jacob, in ibid., pp. 193–9, 199.
138 Cy Grant, in ibid., p. 43.
139 Don Chapman, *Oxford Playhouse, High and Low Drama in a University City* (Hatfield: University of Hertfordshire Press, 2008), pp. 171–2.
140 Cochrane, *Birmingham Rep*, p. 40.
141 Alaknanda Samarth interviewed by David Johnson, *Blackgrounds Interviews with Black Theatre Professionals: Produced by Talawa and the Theatre Museum. Series 1 the actor, the agent, the writer.* Interview conducted 19 May 1997.
142 Rudolph Walker, in Pines, *Black and White in Colour*, pp. 76–84, 80–1.
143 Paul Allen, 'The Royal Shakespeare Company', *Marxism Today*, July 1984, pp. 36–7, 37.
144 Hugh Quarshie, 'Black kings are old hat', *Guardian*, 20 September 2000.
145 Essays on these companies are to be found in Godiwala, *Alternatives Within the Mainstream*; Davis and Fuchs, *Staging New Britain*. Also see Dominic Hingorani, *British Asian Theatre, Dramaturgy, Process and Performance* (Basingstoke: Palgrave Macmillan, 2010); Graham Ley and Sarah Dadswell, *Critical Essay in British South Asian Theatre* (Exeter University Press, 2012).
146 www.vam.ac.uk/vastatic/theatre/archives/thm-77f.html.
147 In 2002, the Office for National Statistics stated that nearly half, 48 per cent, of the British Minority Ethnic Population lived in London, www.statistics.gov.uk/pdfdir/meg1202.pdf.

148 Alda Terracciano, 'Mainstreaming African, Asian and Caribbean theatre: the experiments of the Black Theatre Forum', in Godiwala, *Alternatives Within the Mainstream*, pp. 22–60, 23.

149 Ibid., pp. 34–5, 47–9.

150 Cochrane, '"A local habitation and a name"', in Godiwala, *Alternatives Within the Mainstream*, pp. 162–4.

151 Ibid., pp. 164–5.

152 Ibid., p. 170.

153 Ros Merkin (ed.), *Liverpool's Third Cathedral, The Liverpool Everyman Theatre in the Words of Those Who Were, and Are, There* (Liverpool: Liverpool and Merseyside Theatres Trust, 2004), p. 140.

154 Ibid., pp. 189–91.

155 Brewster, *The Undertaker's Daughter*, pp. 125–6.

156 Cochrane, *Birmingham Rep*, p. 141.

157 Ibid., pp. 170–90; see also 'Engaging the audience: a comparative analysis of development strategies in Birmingham and Leicester since the 1990s', in Ley and Dadswell, *British South Asian Theatre*.

158 Cochrane, 'Opening up the garden', p. 132.

159 For more contextual information and the aftermath of the conference, see Cochrane, 'Opening up the garden', pp. 132–4; see also Arts Council England, *Eclipse*; also 'Appendix I. The Eclipse Report', in Davis and Fuchs, *Staging New Britain*, pp. 323–5. Lynette Goddard has also reflected on the after effects in 'Black British women and theatre: an overview,' in *Staging Black Feminisms*, pp. 17–38, 35–6.

160 Geoff Payne, 'Social divisions as a sociological perspective', in Geoff Payne (ed.), *Social Divisions*, 2nd edn (Basingstoke: Palgrave Macmillan, 2006), pp. 347–59, 349.

8 THE TOPOGRAPHY OF THEATRE IN 2000

1 Nigel Thrift, 'Space: the fundamental stuff of geography', Holloway, Rice and Valentine, *Key Concepts in Geography*, pp. 95–108, 95.

2 National Statistics, 'Living in Britain – 2000', www.statistics.gov.uk/lib2000/index.html.

3 Raymond Williams, 'Drama in a dramatised society', in Raymond Williams, *Writing in Society* (London: Verso, 1991), pp. 11–21, 11–12.

4 Louise Head, Liz Cleverley and Nikki Santilli (eds.), *British Performing Arts Yearbook 2000/2001*, 13th edn (London: Rhinegold Publishing, 2001). Except where separately referenced all venue details are taken from the *Yearbook*.

5 Colin Chambers, 'The profession of theatre, 1946–2000', in Kershaw, *The Cambridge History of British Theatre*, pp. 377–396, 394.

6 A concise account of the terms of devolution in Scotland and Wales and the background to the creation of the Northern Ireland Assembly may be found in John Kingdom, *Government and Politics in Britain, An Introduction*, 3rd edn (Oxford: Polity, 2003), pp. 148–63. The Belfast Agreement, signed on

Good Friday, 10 April 1998, is also popularly known as the Good Friday Agreement.

7 Duncan, *The St. James's Theatre*, pp. 353–4.

8 Earl and Sell, *The Theatres Trust Guide to British Theatres*, pp. 123–4.

9 'The Really Useful Group', www.reallyuseful.com/theatres; Louise Jury, 'Howard Panter and Rosemary Squire – Mr & Mrs West End Theatre', *London Evening Standard*, 6 November 2009.

10 'About the Old Vic', www.oldvictheatre.com/atov.php; Sally Greene and her millionaire property-developer husband, Robert Bourne, had bought the Criterion Theatre in 1989: Simon Hattenstone, 'The queen of flirts', *Guardian* 3 March 2003, www.guardian.co.uk/stage/2003/mar/03/theatre.artsfeatures.

11 See details in *Yearbook*, p. 283.

12 Adrian Dawson, 'Anxious wait over Exchange future', *The Stage*, 20 June 1996; Phil Gibby, 'Lottery £3.2m helps Manchester Exchange', *The Stage*, 3 October 1996.

13 Townsend, *Uneven Regional Change in Britain*, pp. 90–1.

14 John McCarthy, 'Regeneration of cultural quarters: public art for place image or place identity', *Journal of Urban Design*, 11 (2006).

15 For a brief account of the NIA Centre in Hulme, see 'Acts of Achievement: Hulme Black History Trail', www.actsofachievement.org.uk/blackhistorytrail/hulme.php. Also Natalie Anglesey, 'Now here's an Afro-Caribbean centre with purpose', *The Stage*, 25 April 1991.

16 Details of specific Scottish venues in the Scotland section of the *Yearbook*, pp. 488–526; Mark Fisher, 'From Traverse to Tramway: Scottish Theatres Old and New', in Stevenson and Wallis, *Scottish Theatre Since the Seventies*, pp. 49–56.

17 www.gro-scotland.gov.uk/press/news2002/02prpoprep.html.

18 www.culcreuch-castle-hotel.com/The-Area/Central-Scotland/central-scotland.html.

19 www.tramway.org/history/.

20 For an account of the Tron area in Glasgow and the creation of the Tron as a theatre space, see: www.tron.co.uk/about/history/; also www.tron.co.uk/docs/file/History%20of%20the%20Tron%20final.pdf.

21 On the impact of the oil industry on Milford Haven, see K. O. Morgan, *Rebirth of a Nation*, pp. 315–16.

22 Alexa Baracaia, 'Welsh arts boss expected to go', *The Stage*, 21 September 2000.

23 Phil Hubbard, *City* (London: Routledge, 2006), pp. 173–5.

24 *The Stage*, 17 May 1990; Jan Smaczny, 'Operetta The Mikado/La Vie Parisienne Alexandra Theatre Birmingham', *Independent*, 26 September 1995.

25 See 'Showcall', *The Stage*, 19 October 2000.

26 Earl and Sell, *The Theatres Trust Guide to British Theatres*, pp. 78, 245.

27 Donnell Deeny (ed.), *To the Millennium, A Strategy for the Arts in Northern Ireland* (Belfast: Arts Council of Northern Ireland, 1995), pp. 112–13.

28 'Conflict and Politics in Northern Ireland (1968 to the Present', CAIN Web Service (Conflict Archives on the Internet), http://cain.ulst.ac.uk/.

29 Grant, *Playing the Wild Card*.

30 David Grant, 'Belfast's Old Museum Arts Centre. A Quarter of a Century of Lived Space', unpublished paper, IFTR 2010 World Congress, July 2010.

31 Denny, *To the Millennium*, p. 112.

32 'Ardhowen Theatre', www.nitatheatre.org/members/ardhowen.html. For Enniskillen bombing, see Thomas Hennessey, *A History of Northern Ireland 1920–1996* (Basingstoke: Macmillan, 1997), pp. 276–7.

33 'Burnavon Arts and Cultural Centre, Cookstown', in Arts Council of Northern Ireland, *Building for the Arts, Celebrating 10 years of Lottery Funding* (Belfast: Arts Council of Northern Ireland, 2005), pp. 13–15; Glenn Howells Architects Practice, Approach, Projects, 'The Market Place, Armagh', www.glennhowells.co.uk/content/public/116.

34 Flowerfield Arts Centre, 'Flowerfield through the years', www.flowerfield.org/show.php?id=1 'Portstewart', http://en.wikipedia.org/wiki/Portstewart; www.nisranew.nisra.gov.uk/census/pdf/ks_sett_tables.pdf.

35 Maguire, *Making Theatre in Northern Ireland*, pp. 86–91.

36 BBC-h2g2-Coleraine, County Londonderry, Northern Ireland, www.bbc.co.uk/dna/h2g2/A37316964; Morash, *A History of Irish Theatre*, p. 234.

37 Morash, *A History of Irish Theatre*, pp. 233–41, 233.

38 Ibid., p. 256.

39 'Millennium Forum (Theatre & Conference Centre)', www.theatrestrust.org.uk/.

40 For an account of the work of Derry Frontline, see Bill McDonnell, *Theatre of the Troubles, Theatre, Resistance and Liberation in Ireland* (University of Exeter Press, 2008), pp. 117–42.

41 House of Commons, 'A century of change: trends in UK statistics since 1900', Research Papers 99/111, 21 December 1999.

42 Northern Ireland Census of Population, www.nisranew.nisra.gov.uk/census/start.html.

43 John Darby, 'Approaches to cultural diversity in Northern Ireland', in Maurna Crozier and Richard Froggatt (eds.), *Cultural Traditions in Northern Ireland, Cultural Diversity in Contemporary Europe* (Belfast: Institute of Irish Studies, 1998), pp. 3–12.

44 Harvie, *Staging the UK*, p. 114.

45 Harvey Armstrong and Jim Taylor, *Regional Economics and Policy*, 3rd edn (Oxford: Blackwell, 2000), p. ix.

46 Ibid.

47 Ibid., pp. 326–8.

48 Denny, *To the Millennium*, p. 95.

49 For breakdown of costs of Waterfront Hall, see http://cmis.coventry.gov.uk/CMISWebPublic/Binary.ashx?Document=1119.

50 McCarthy, 'Regeneration of cultural quarters', p. 246.

51 See Ackroyd, *The Liverpool Stage*, for details of individual theatres.

52 www.statistics.gov.uk/downloads/theme_population/LAStudy_Liverpool. pdf.

53 Philip Boland, 'Urban governance and economic development, a Critique of Merseyside and Objective 1 status', *European and Urban Regional Studies*, 7 (2000), 211–22.

54 Pelham McMahon and Pam Brooks, *An Actor's Place, The Liverpool Repertory Company at Liverpool Playhouse* (Liverpool: Bluecoat Press, 2000), pp. 26, 73–4.

55 Merkin, *Liverpool's Third Cathedral*, p. 271.

56 McMahon and Brooks, *An Actor's Place*, p. 152.

57 Boland, 'Urban governance and economic development', p. 212.

58 Ibid., p. 219.

59 Merkin, *Liverpool's Third Cathedral*, pp. 273–7.

60 Boland, 'Urban governance and economic development', p. 215.

61 Paterson, *The Autonomy of Modern Scotland*, pp. 175–6.

62 Ibid.

63 Ibid., p. 170.

64 Jonathan Hearn, *Rethinking Nationalism, A Critical Introduction* (Basingstoke: Palgrave Macmillan, 2006), pp. 112–3.

65 Ibid., p. 143; see also Randall Stevenson, 'Introduction snakes and ladders, snakes and owls: charting Scottish theatre', in Stevenson and Wallis, *Scottish Theatre Since the Seventies*, pp. 1–20, 2–4.

66 Stuart Black, 'Economic trends in the Highlands and Islands during the 1990s', *Scottish Economic Report* (Scottish Executive Publications, July 2000), pp. 1–4, www.scotland.gov.uk/library3/economics/ser-21.asp, accessed 2.4.2010.

67 Ibid.

68 For the early background to this initiative, see the website www.hitn.co.uk/HITNHistory.html. The essay published in 2005 by Christine Hamilton and Adrienne Scullion as a result of a 2003–4 research project into rural arts touring gives a substantial account of developments after 2000: '"Picture it if yous will": theatre and theatregoing in rural Scotland', *New Theatre Quarterly*, 21 (2005), 61–76.

69 Grey Coast website (2001), www.greycoast.demon.co.uk December 2006; HITN Profile: Grey Coast www.hi-arts.co.uk/Features/2006/dec06-hitn-profile-grey-coast.html; www.hi-arts.co.uk/oct06_hitn_profile_tosg.html.

70 The company has now been renamed Dogstar. For an account of the development of the company, see the Dogstar website: www.dogstartheatre.co.uk/history.html.

71 Kenny Mathieson, 'October 2005 Interview with George Gunn Part 1', www.hi-arts.co.uk/oct05_interview_george_gunn.html; 'November 2005 Interview with George Gunn Part 2', www.hi-arts.co.uk/HI-Arts/Features/2005/nov05_interview_george_gunn.html.

72 See details of *Atomic City* tour dates at www.greycoast.demon.co.uk/.

73 'Showroom Workstation Sheffield Company Background', www.showroomworkstation.org.uk/aboutus/companybackground; see also Liz

Tomlin, 'Transgressing boundaries: postmodern performance and the tourist trap', *TDR*, 43 (1999).

74 Forced Entertainment Information Pack, www.forcedentertainment.com.
75 Tim Etchells, 'On performance and technology', in Tim Etchells, *Certain Fragments* (London: Routledge, 1999), pp. 94–7, 95.
76 Tomlin, 'Transgressing boundaries', p. 138.
77 www.forcedentertainment.com/page/3038/Past+Tour+Dates.
78 Data downloaded from 'OPC Historical Timeline', OPC website accessed June 2010.
79 www.blahs.co.uk/about-us/history/; www.interplayleeds.co.uk/; www.mind-the-gap.org.uk/content/story-mind-gap; www.blaize.uk.net/pages/about-us.html.
80 See the *Yearbook* entry and www.mikron.org.uk/.
81 Julie Jefferies, *The UK population: past, present and future, Focus on People and Migration 2005*, www.statistics.gov.uk/downloads/theme_compendia/fom2005/01_fopm_population.pdf, pp. 13–14.
82 Cochrane, '"A local habitation and a name"', in Godiwala, *Alternatives Within the Mainstream*, p. 158.
83 See http://rifcoarts.com/; http://rasatheatre.co.uk/; www.choltheatre.co.uk/.
84 www.statistics.gov.uk/pdfdir/ptrn0901.pdf.
85 www.peshkar.co.uk/about.html.
86 A brief overview of the history of Red Ladder Theatre Company may be found at www.redladder.co.uk; see also Swati Pal, *Look Back at Anger: Red Ladder Theatre Company from the 60s to the 90s* (Saarbrücken: VDM Verlag Dr Müller, 2008).
87 www.statistics.gov.uk/pdfdir/ptrn0901.pdf.
88 See Cochrane, '"Opening up the garden"', in Dorney and Merkin, *The Glory of the Garden*; 'Engaging the audience: a comparative analysis of developmental strategies in Birmingham and Leicester since the 1990s', in *Critical Essays in British South Asian Theatres*, ed. Ley and Dadswell.
89 'Bristol Going Out, Help Shape the Cultural Landscape', 10 May 2004, www.bbc.co.uk/bristol/content/goingout/2004/05/06/kuumba.shtml.
90 'About Us', The Black-E home page; www.theblack-e.co.uk/content/about-us/about-us.
91 Helen Jermyn and Philly Desai, *Arts – What's in a Word? Ethnic Minorities and the Arts* (London: Arts Council of England, 2000).
92 Vayu Naidu, 'Vayu Naidu Company's south, new directions in theatre storytelling', in Davis and Fuchs, *Staging New Britain*, pp. 141–5, 146–7.
93 Cochrane '"A local habitation and a name"', p. 156.
94 Parekh, *The Future of Multi-Ethnic Britain*, p. 36.

CONCLUSION

1 Venu Dhupa, 'Creative Producing', in Vera Gottlieb and Colin Chambers (eds.), *Theatre in a Cool Climate* (Oxford: Amber Lane Press, 1999) pp. 111–20, 115.

2 Ibid.
3 Ibid., p. 111.
4 Hubbard, *City*, p. 174.
5 Ash Amin, Doreen Massey and Nigel Thrift, *Decentering the Nation, A Radical Approach to Regional Inequality* (London: Catalyst, 2003), p. 2.

Select Bibliography

25 Years of the British Drama League (London: British Drama League, 1945)

A Short History of Bristol's Little Theatre: First & Second Seasons 1923–24–25 (Bristol: Partridge & Love, 1925)

Ackroyd, Harold, *The Liverpool Stage* (Erdington, West Midlands: Amber Valley Print Centre, 1996)

Adams, David, *Stage Welsh: Nation, Nationalism and Theatre: The Search for Cultural Identity* (Llandysul: Gomer, 1996)

Adams, Robert, 'Problems of the Negro in the theatre', *New Theatre*, 4, 5 (1947), 11

Amin, Ash, Doreen Massey and Nigel Thrift, *Decentering the Nation, A Radical Approach to Regional Inequality* (London: Catalyst, 2003)

Anderson, Benedict, *Imagined Communities: Reflections on the Origin and Spread of Nationalism*, rev. edn (London: Verso, 1991)

Anheier, Helmut K., *Nonprofit Organisations: Theory, Management, Policy* (London: Routledge, 2005)

Archer, William, 'A plea for an endowed theatre', *Fortnightly Review*, 45, ns (1 January–1 June 1889), 610–26

—, and Harley Granville-Barker, *A National Theatre: Schemes and Estimates* (London: Duckworth, 1907)

Armes, Roy, *A Critical History of the British Cinema* (London: Secker & Warburg, 1979)

Armstrong, Harvey and Jim Taylor, *Regional Economics and Policy*, 3rd edn (Oxford: Blackwell, 2000)

Arts Council England, *Eclipse, Developing Strategies to Combat Racism in the Theatre* (London: ACE, 2002)

Arts Council of Great Britain, *1st Annual Report 1945/6* (London: Arts Council of Great Britain, 1946)

—, *5th Annual Report 1949/50* (London: Arts Council of Great Britain, 1950)

—, *6th Annual Report 1950/1* (London: Arts Council of Great Britain, 1951)

—, *11th Annual Report 1955–1956* (London: Arts Council of Great Britain, 1956)

—, *13th Annual Report 1957–1958* (London: Arts Council of Great Britain, 1958)

—, *15th Annual Report 1959–1960* (London: Arts Council of Great Britain, 1960)

—, *25th Annual Report 1969–1970* (London: Arts Council of Great Britain, 1970)

—, *27th Annual Report 1971–1972* (London: Arts Council of Great Britain, 1972)

—, *29th Annual Report 1973–1974* (London: Arts Council of Great Britain, 1974)

—, *The Theatre Today in England and Wales, The Report of the Arts Council Theatre Enquiry 1970* (London: Arts Council of Great Britain, 1970)

—, *The Glory of the Garden: The Development of the Arts in England – A Strategy for a Decade* (London: Arts Council of Great Britain, 1984)

Arts Council of Northern Ireland, *Building for the Arts, Celebrating 10 Years of Lottery Funding* (Belfast: Arts Council of Northern Ireland, 2005)

Ashwell, Lena, *Myself a Player* (London: Michael Joseph, 1936)

Bailey, John, *A Theatre for All Seasons, Nottingham Playhouse, The First Thirty Years 1948–1978* (Stroud: Alan Sutton Publishing & Nottingham Playhouse, 1994)

Balcon, Michael, *Michael Balcon Presents … A Lifetime of Film* (London: Hutchinson, 1969)

Bannister, Winifred, *James Bridie and His Theatre* (London: Rockcliff, 1955)

Barbour, Sheena and Kate Manton (eds.), *Directory of Arts Centres 2* (Eastbourne: John Offord Publications in association with the Arts Council of Great Britain, 1981)

Bardon, Jonathan and David Burnett, *Belfast: A Pocket History* (Belfast: Blackstaff Press, 1996)

Barker, Kathleen, *Bristol at Play: Five Centuries of Live Entertainment* (Bradford-on-Avon: Moonraker Press, 1976)

Beauman, Sally, *The Royal Shakespeare Company: A History of Ten Decades* (Oxford University Press, 1982)

Bell, Sam Hanna, *The Theatre in Ulster* (Dublin: Gill and Macmillan, 1972)

—, Nesca, A., Robb, John Hewitt (eds.), *The Arts in Ulster, A Symposium* (London: Harrap, 1951)

Benson, Constance, *Mainly Players* (London: Thornton Butterworth, 1926)

Bentley, Michael (ed.), *Companion to Historiography* (London: Routledge, 1997)

Billingham, Peter, *Theatres of Conscience 1939–1953: A Study of Four Touring British Community Theatres* (London: Routledge Harwood, 2002)

Billington, Michael, *Peggy Ashcroft* (London: John Murray, 1988)

Bishop, George W., *Barry Jackson and the London Theatre* (London: Arthur Barker, 1933)

Blain, Neil, and David Hutchinson, *The Media in Scotland* (Edinburgh University Press, 2008)

Boland, Philip, 'Urban governance and economic development, a critique of Merseyside and Objective 1 status', *European and Urban Regional Studies,* 7 (2000), 211–22

Booth, Michael, Clifford Leech, T. W. Craik et al., *The Revels History of Drama in English, Vol. 6, 1750–1880* (London: Methuen, 1975)

Bourdieu, Pierre, *Distinction: A Social Critique of the Judgement of Taste*, trans. Richard Nice (London: Routledge & Kegan Paul, 1984)

Bourne, Stephen, *Black in the British Frame, Black People in British Film and Television 1896–1996* (London: Cassell, 1998)

Boutcher, Roy and William G. Kemp, W.G., *The Theatre in Perth: Published to Mark the Fortieth Anniversary of Perth Theatre Company* (Perth: Perth Theatre Company, 1975)

Boyden Associates, Peter, *Roles & Functions of the English Regional Producing Theatres* (London: Arts Council England, 2000)

Bradby, David and Susanna Capon (eds.), *Freedom's Pioneer, John Mcgrath's Work in Theatre, Film and Television* (University of Exeter Press, 2005)

Bratton, J. S., et al., *Acts of Supremacy: The British Empire and the Stage 1790–1930* (Manchester University Press, 1991)

Brewster, Yvonne (ed.), *Black Plays 3* (London: Methuen, 1995)

—, *The Undertaker's Daughter, The Colourful Life of a Theatre Director* (London: Black Amber Books, 2004)

Briggs, Asa, *The History of Broadcasting in the United Kingdom, Volume 1, The Birth of Broadcasting* (Oxford University Press, 1961)

Brown, Ian (ed.), *Journey's Beginning, The Gateway Theatre Building and Company 1884–1965* (Bristol: Intellect Books, 2004)

—, 'The road through Woodstock: Counter-Thatcherite strategies in ACGB's drama development between 1984 and 1994', *Contemporary Theatre Review*, 17 (2007), 218–29

—, and Rob Brannen, 'When theatre was for all: the Cork Report, after ten years', *New Theatre Quarterly*, 12 (1996), 367–83

—, Rob Brannen and Douglas Brown, 'The English franchise system and political theatre', *New Theatre Quarterly*, 16 (2000), 379–87

Browne, E. Martin with Henzie Browne, *Two in One [by] E. Martin Browne with Henzie Browne* (Cambridge University Press, 1981)

Bryant, Christopher, *Glenda Jackson: The Biography* (London: HarperCollins, 1999)

Bull, John, *Stage Right, Crisis and Recovery in British Contemporary Mainstream Theatre* (Basingstoke: Macmillan, 1994)

Burtt, Everett Johnson, Jr, *Social Perspectives in the History of Economic Theory* (New York: St Martin's Press, 1972)

Byrne, Ophelia, *The Stage in Ulster from the Eighteenth Century* (Belfast: Linen Hall Library, 1997)

Callow, Simon, *Being an Actor* (London: Methuen, 1984)

— (ed.), *The National: The theatre, Its Work 1963–1997 and a Chronology of Productions 1963–1997* (London: Royal National Theatre [Great Britain], 1997)

Campbell, Donald, *A Brighter Sunshine: A Hundred Years of the Edinburgh Royal Lyceum Theatre* (Edinburgh: Polygon, 1983)

—, *Playing for Scotland: A History of the Scottish Stage 1715–1965* (Edinburgh: Mercat Press, 1996)

Carlson, Marvin, *Places of Performance: The Semiotics of Theatre Architecture* (Ithaca and London: Cornell University Press, 1989)

Carnelvali, Francesca and Julie-Marie Strange (eds.), *20th Century Britain: Economic, Cultural and Social Change*, 2nd edn (Harlow: Pearson Longman, 2007)

Carr, Violet Godfrey, *From Portable Days by Violet Godfrey Carr: A Personal Account of Life in the Theatre as Told to Neil McNicholas* (Stocksfield: Spreddon Press, 1991)

Carson, Lionel (ed.), *The Stage Year Book 1910 with which is included The Stage Provincial Guide 1910* (London: The Stage, 1910)

— (ed.), *The Stage Year Book 1917* (London: The Stage, 1917)

— (ed.), *The Stage Year Book 1919* (London: The Stage, 1919)

Caughie, John, *Television Drama: Realism, Modernism, and British Culture* (Oxford University Press, 2000)

Chambers, Colin, *The Story of Unity Theatre* (London: Lawrence & Wishart, 1989)

—, *Inside the Royal Shakespeare Company* (London: Routledge, 2004)

Chapman 43–4 On Scottish Theatre, Vols. 8 & 9 (1986)

Chapman, Don, *Oxford Playhouse, High and Low Drama in a University City* (Hatfield: University of Hertfordshire Press, 2008)

Chisholm, Cecil, *Repertory: An Outline of the Modern Theatre Movement* (London: Peter Davies, 1934)

Clarke, Peter, *Hope and Glory, Britain 1900–1990* (Harmondsworth: Penguin Books, 1997)

Cochran, Charles B., and A. P. Herbert, *I Had Almost Forgotten …* (London: Hutchinson & Co., 1932)

Cochrane, Claire, *Shakespeare and the Birmingham Repertory Theatre 1913–1929* (London: Society for Theatre Research, 1993)

—, 'Theatre and urban space: the case of Birmingham rep', *New Theatre Quarterly*, 26 (2000), 137–47

—, '"It stands for more than theatre": Claire Cochrane talks to Paul Sutton about the work of C&T', *Studies in Theatre and Performance*, 20 (2000), 188–95

—, 'The pervasiveness of the commonplace: the historian and amateur theatre', *Theatre Research International*, 26 (2001), 233–42

—, '"The contaminated audience": researching amateur theatre in Wales before 1939', *New Theatre Quarterly*, 74 (2003), 169–76

—, *The Birmingham Rep: A City's Theatre 1962–2002* (Birmingham: Sir Barry Jackson Trust, 2003)

Cockin, Katherine, *Edith Craig 1869–1947, Dramatic Lives* (London: Cassell, 1998)

Coleman, Terry, *Olivier* (London: Bloomsbury, 2005)

Connolly, Roy, *The Evolution of the Lyric Players' Theatre Belfast: Fighting the Waves* (New York/Lampeter: Edwin Mellen Press, c. 2000)

Cooke, Lez, *British Television Drama: A History* (London: British Film Institute, 2003)

Cork, K. et al., *Theatre IS for All: The Report of the Inquiry into Professional Theatre in England under the Chairmanship of Sir Kenneth Cork* (London: Arts Council of Great Britain, 1986)

Courtney, Tom, *Dear Tom, Letters from Home* (London: Black Swan Books, 2001)

Coveney, Michael, *The Citz: 21 Years of the Glasgow Citizens Theatre* (London: Nick Hern Books, 1990)

Croft, Susan with Stephen Bourne and Alda Terracciano, *Black and Asian Performance at the Theatre Museum, A User's Guide* (London: Theatre Museum, 2002)

Crozier, Maurna and Richard Froggatt (eds.), *Cultural Traditions in Northern Ireland, Cultural Diversity in Contemporary Europe* (Belfast: Institute of Irish Studies, 1998)

Davies, Cecil and Peter Billingham, *The Adelphi Players, The Theatre of Persons* (London: Routledge Harwood, 2002)

Davies, John, *A History of Wales* (Harmondsworth: Penguin Books, 1994)

Davies, T. G. H., 'The Swansea Little Theatre, the First Thirty Years, 1924–55', unpublished dissertation, University College, Swansea (1993)

Davis, Godfrey V. and Anne Fuchs (eds.), *Staging New Britain, Aspects of Black and South Asian British Theatre Practice* (Brussels: P.I.E.–Peter Lang, 2006)

Davis, Tracy C., *George Bernard Shaw and the Socialist Theatre* (Westport, Conn./London: Greenwood Press, 1994)

—, *The Economics of the British Stage 1800–1914* (Cambridge University Press, 2000)

Dean, Basil, *Seven Ages, Volume 1, An Autobiography 1888–1927* (London: Hutchison, 1970)

Deeny, Donnek (ed.), *To the Millennium, A Strategy for the Arts in Northern Ireland* (Belfast: Arts Council of Northern Ireland, 1995)

Devine, George, 'The Arena Theatre – an important experiment', *New Theatre* 5, 11 (May 1949), 21–2

Devine, T. M., and R. J. Finlay (eds.), *Scotland in the Twentieth Century* (Edinburgh University Press, 1996)

Devlin, Diana, *A Speaking Part: Lewis Casson and the Theatre of His Time* (London: Hodder and Stoughton, 1982)

DiCenzo, Maria, *The Politics of Alternative Theatre in Britain, 1968–1990, The Case of 7.84 (Scotland)* (Cambridge University Press, 1996)

Dormer, Phil, 'Bloodied but not bold: the arts Council of Great Britain', *Political Quarterly*, 52 (1981), 416–25

Dorney, Kate, and Ros Merkin (eds.), *The Glory of the Garden: English Regional Theatre and the Arts Council 1984–2009* (Newcastle upon Tyne: Cambridge Scholars Publishing, 2010)

Downie, A., 'The actress's lot', *Chapman* 43–4 *Scottish Theatre*, Vols. 8 & 9 (1986), 118–20

Drama, The Quarterly Theatre Review, 2, 13, ns (December 1921)

Duff, Charles, *The Lost Summer, The Heyday of the West End Theatre* (London: Nick Hern, 1995)

Duncan, Barry, *The St. James's Theatre, Its Strange & Complete History 1835–1957* (London: Barrie and Rockcliff, 1964)

Dunn, Kate, *Exit Through the Fireplace: The Great Days of Rep* (London: John Murray, 1998)

Dyer, Richard, et al., *Coronation Street* (London: B.F.I. Publishing, 1981)

Earl, John, and Michael Sell, *The Theatres Trust Guide to British Theatres 1750–1950: A Gazetteer* (London: A & C Black, 2000)

Egan, David, *Coal Society: A History of the South Wales Mining Valleys, 1840–1980* (Llandysul: Gomer Press, 1987)

Elsom, John, *Post War British Theatre* (London: Routledge, 1976)

—, and Nicholas Tomalin, *The History of the National Theatre* (London: Cape, 1978)

Etchells, Tim, *Certain Fragments* (London: Routledge, 1999)

Eyre, Richard, *Utopia & Other Places* (London: Vintage, 1994)

Falk, Quentin, *Albert Finney in Character* (London: Robson Books, 1992)

Fay, W. G., & Catherine Carswell, *The Fays of the Abbey Theatre: An Autobiographical Record* (Dublin: Rich & Cowan Ltd., 1935)

Finch, John, et al. (eds.), *Granada Television, The First Generation* (Manchester University Press, 2003)

Findlay, Bill (ed.), *A History of Scottish Theatre* (Edinburgh: Polygon, 1998)

Fitzsimmons, Linda, and Sarah Street (eds.), *Moving Performance: British Stage and Screen, 1890s–1920s* (Wiltshire: Flick Books, 2000)

Foley, Imelda, *Girls in the Big Picture* (Belfast: Blackstaff Press, 2003)

Forbes, Bryan, *Ned's Girl: The Authorised Biography of Dame Edith Evans* (London: Elm Tree Books, 1977)

Foster, R. F., *Modern Ireland 1600–1972* (Harmondsworth: Penguin, 1989)

Foulkes, Richard, *Repertory at The Royal: Sixty-Five Years of Theatre in Northampton 1927–92* (Northampton: Northampton Repertory Players, 1992)

— (ed.), *Scenes from Provincial Stages, Essays in Honour of Kathleen Barker* (London: Society for Theatre Research, 1994)

Fraser, C. M. and K. Emsley, *Tyneside* (Newton Abbot: David & Charles, 1973)

Fraser, M. F. K., *Alexandra Theatre, The Story of a Popular Playhouse* (Birmingham: Cornish Brothers Ltd., 1948)

Freeman, T. W. (ed.), *The Conurbations of Great Britain* (Manchester University Press, 1966)

Freshwater, Helen, *Theatre Censorship in Britain: Silencing, Censure and Suppression* (Basingstoke: Palgrave Macmillan, 2009)

Fry, Charles F., *Charles Fry, His Life and Work* (London: printed by J. M. Baxter, c. 1932)

Gale, Maggie B., *West End Women, Women and the London Stage 1918–1962* (London: Routledge, 1996)

Gallagher, Lyn, *The Grand Opera House Belfast* (Belfast: Blackstaff Press, 1995)

Ganzel, Dewey, 'Patent wrongs and patent theatres', *PMLA*, 76 (1961), 384–96

Gaskill, William, *A Sense of Direction, Life at The Royal Court* (London: Faber and Faber, 1988)

Geraghty, Christine, *British Cinema in the Fifties, Gender, Genre and the 'New Look'* (London: Routledge, 2000)

Gielgud, John, *Early Stages* (London: Sceptre, 1990)

Giesekam, Greg, *Luvvies and Rude Mechanicals? Amateur and Community Theatre in Scotland* (Glasgow: Scottish Arts Council, 2000)

Gill, Mand, *See the Players* (London: Hutchinson & Co., 1938)

Goddard, Lynette, *Staging Black Feminisms: Identity, Politics and Performance* (Basingstoke: Palgrave Macmillan, 2007)

Godiwala, Dimple (ed.), *Alternatives Within the Mainstream: British Black and Asian Theatres* (Newcastle upon Tyne: Cambridge Scholars Press, 2006)

Goldie, Grace Wyndham, *The Liverpool Repertory Theatre 1911–1934* (London: Liverpool University Press and Hodder and Stoughton, 1935)

Gooch, Steve, *All Together Now, An Alternative View of Theatre and the Community* (London: Methuen, 1984)

Goorney, Howard, *The Theatre Workshop Story* (London: Eyre Methuen, 1981)

Gordon, George (ed.), *Regional Cities in the UK 1890–1980* (London: Harper & Row, 1986)

Gottlieb, Verna and Colin Chambers (eds.), *Theatre in a Cool Climate* (Oxford: Amber Lane Press, 1999)

Grant, David, *Playing the Wild Card, A Survey of Community Drama and Smaller Scale Theatres from a Community Relations Perspective* (Belfast: Community Relations Council, 1993)

Granville-Barker, Harley, *The Exemplary Theatre* (London: Chatto and Windus, 1922)

Great Britain Board of Education, Adult Education Committee, *The Drama in Adult Education* (London: HMSO, 1926)

Green, W. A., 'Periodisation in European and world history', *Journal of World History*, 3 (1992), 13–53

Guthrie, Tyrone, *A Life in the Theatre* (London: Hamish Hamilton, 1961)

Hall, Peter, *Making an Exhibition of Myself* (London: Sinclair-Stevenson, 1993)

Hamilton, Christine and Adrienne Scullion, '"Picture it if yous will": theatre and theatregoing in rural Scotland', *New Theatre Quarterly*, 21 (2005), 61–76

Hanna, Gillian (ed.), *Monstrous Regiment, Four Plays and a Collective Celebration* (London: Nick Hern Books, 1991)

Hannah, Leslie, *The Rise of the Corporate Economy*, 2nd edn (London: Methuen, 1983)

Harrison, J. F. C., *Late Victorian Britain 1875–1901* (London: Fontana, 1990)

—, *Learning and Living 1790–1960, A Study in the History of the Adult Education Movement* (Aldershot: Greg Revivals, 1994)

Hart, Olive Ely, *The Drama in Modern Wales: A Brief History of Welsh Playwriting from 1900 to the Present Day* (University of Philadelphia Press, 1928)

Harvie, Jen, *Staging the UK* (Manchester University Press, 2005)

Hayman, Ronald, *Harold Pinter* (London: Heinemann, 1980)

Head, Louise, Liz Cleverley and Nikki Santilli (eds.), *British Performing Arts Yearbook 2000/2001,* 13th edn (London: Rhinegold Publishing, 2001)

Hearn, Jonathan, *Rethinking Nationalism, A Critical Introduction* (Basingstoke: Palgrave Macmillan, 2006)

Heinrich, A., *Entertainment, Propaganda, Education Regional Theatre in Germany and Britain Between 1918 and 1945* (Hatfield: University of Hertfordshire Press, 2007)

Hennessey, Thomas, *A History of Northern Ireland 1920–1996* (Basingstoke: Macmillan, 1997)

Herbert, Trevor and Gareth Elwyn Jones (eds.), *Wales 1880–1914* (Cardiff: University of Wales Press, 1988)

Hewins, Angela (ed.), *The Dillen: Memoirs of a Man of Stratford-Upon-Avon* (London: Elm Tree Books, 1981)

Hewison, Robert, *Culture & Consensus, England, Art and Politics Since 1940* (London: Methuen, 1995)

Hildy, Franklin J., *Shakespeare at the Maddermarket: Nugent Monck and the Norwich Players* (Ann Arbor, Mich.: UMI Research Press, c. 1986)

Hingorani, Dominic, *British Asian Theatre, Dramaturgy, Process and Performance* (Basingstoke: Palgrave Macmillan, 2010)

Hobsbawm, Eric and Terence Ranger (eds.), *The Invention of Tradition* (Cambridge University Press, 1983)

—, with Chris Wrigley, *Industry and Empire*, 2nd edn (Harmondsworth: Penguin, 1999)

Hoggart, Richard, *The Uses of Literacy* (Harmondsworth: Penguin, 1990)

Holdsworth, Nadine, '"They'd have pissed on my grave": the case of Theatre Workshop and the Arts Council', *New Theatre Quarterly*, 53 (1999), 3–16

Holloway, S. L., S. P. Price and G. Valentine (eds.), *Key Concepts in Geography* (London: Sage, 2003)

Holroyd, Michael, *Bernard Shaw, Volume 2, 1898–1918, The Pursuit of Power* (Harmondsworth: Penguin, 1991)

Hornzee-Jones, Linda, 'Performing Suburbia: A Qualitative Examination of Late Twentieth Century Amateur Drama in South-east England', unpublished PhD thesis, University of Brighton (2001)

Howard, Diana, *London Theatres and Music Halls 1850–1950* (London: Library Association Publishing Ltd., 1970)

Hubbard, P., R. Kitchen and G. Valentine, *Key Thinkers on Space and Place* (London: Sage, 2004)

—, *City* (London: Routledge, 2006)

Huggett, Richard, *Binkie Beaumont: Eminence Grise of the West End Theatre 1933–1973* (London: Hodder & Stoughton, 1989)

Hughes, Alan, 'The Lyceum staff: a Victorian theatrical organisation', *Theatre Notebook*, 28 (1974), 11–17

Hughes, Richard, *Bookman* (November 1934), 97–8

Hunt, Hugh, *The Abbey, Ireland's National Theatre 1904–1979* (Dublin: Gill and Macmillan, 1979)

Hutchison, David, *The Modern Scottish Theatre* (Glasgow: Molendinar Press, 1977)

Hutchison, Robert, *The Politics of the Arts Council* (London: Sinclair Browne, 1982)

Iles, Paul, 'Issues in Theatrical Management: Howard and Wyndham and the Evolution of the British touring Circuit', unpublished MPhil thesis, Glasgow University (1997)

Inverne, James, *The Impresarios* (London: Oberon Books, 2000)

Isaac, Winifred F. E. C., *Alfred Wareing: A Biography* (London: Greenbank Press, [1951])

—, *Ben Greet and the Old Vic, A Biography of Sir Philip Ben Greet* (London: Miss Winifred F. E. C. Isaac, 1964)

Jackson, Russell, *Victorian Theatre* (London: A & C Black, 1989)

Jenkins, Hugh, *The Culture Gap: An Experience of Government and the Arts* (London: Boyars, 1979)

Jermyn, Helen and Philly Desai, *Arts – What's in a Word? Ethnic Minorities and the Arts* (London: Arts Council of England, 2000)

Jerrams, Richard, *Weekly Rep – A Theatrical Phenomenon* (Droitwich: Peter Andrew Publishing, 1991)

Johnson, Catherine, and Rob Turnock (eds.), *ITV Cultures Independent Television over Fifty Years* (Maidenhead: Open University Press, 2005)

Johnson, Gerry and Kevin Scholes (eds.), *Exploring Corporate Strategy*, 3rd edn (New York/London: Prentice-Hall International, 1993)

Johnson, Linton Kwesi et al., *Changing Britannia: Life Experience with Britain* (London: New Beacon, 1999)

Johnson, Paul (ed.), *20th Century Britain: Economic, Social and Cultural Change* (Harlow: Longman, 1994)

Judd, Denis, *Empire: The British Imperial Experience from 1765 to the Present Day* (London: Harper Collins, 1996)

Kane, Whitford, *Are We All Met by Whitford Kane* (London: E. Mathews & Marlot, 1931)

Kellas, J. G., *The Politics of Nationalism and Ethnicity* (Basingstoke: Macmillan Education, 1991)

Kelly, Thomas, *A History of Adult Education in Great Britain from the Middle Ages to the Twentieth Century* (Liverpool University Press, 1962)

Kennedy, Dennis, *Granville Barker and the Dream of Theatre* (Cambridge University Press, 1985)

Kershaw, Baz, *The Politics of Performance: Radical Theatre as Cultural Intervention* (London: Routledge, 1992)

—, 'Discouraging democracy: British theatre and economics, 1979–1999', *Theatre Journal*, 51 (1999), 267–83

—, (ed.), *The Cambridge History of British Theatre, Vol. 3, Since 1895* (Cambridge University Press, 2005)

Keynes, J. M., 'The Arts Council: its Policy and hopes', *Listener*, 34, 361 (12 July 1945), 31–2

Khan, Naseem, *The Arts Britain Ignores: The Arts of Ethnic Minorities in Britain* (London: Commission for Racial Equality, 1978)

Kingdom, John, *Government and Politics in Britain, An Introduction*, 3rd edn (Oxford: Polity, 2003)

Kingston, Gertrude, *Curtsey While You're Thinking* (London: Williams and Norgate, 1937)

Landstone, Charles, *Off-stage: A Personal Record of the First Twelve Years of State-Sponsored Drama in Great Britain* (London: Elek, 1953)

Langton, John and R. J. Morris (eds.), *Atlas of Industrialising Britain 1780–1914* (London: Methuen, 1986)

Lawless, Richard I., *From Ta'izz to Tyneside: An Arab Community in the North-East of England during the Twentieth Century* (Exeter University Press, 1995)

Ledger, Frederick (ed.), *The Era Almanack 1894* (London: 1894)

—, (ed.), *The Era Almanack 1900* (London: 1900)

—, (ed.), *The Era Annual 1907* (London: 1907)

Lefebvre, Henri, *The Production of Space*, trans. Donald Nicholson-Smith (Oxford: Blackwell, 1991)

Lewenstein, Oscar, *Kicking Against the Pricks: A Theatre Producer Looks Back: The Memoirs of Oscar Lewenstein* (London: Nick Hern Books, 1994)

Littlewood, Joan, *Joan;s Book: Joan Littlewood's Peculiar History as She Tells It* (London: Methuen, 1994)

Low, Rachael, *The History of British Film 1918–1929* (London: Allen & Unwin, 1971)

Macleod, Joseph, *The Actor's Right to Act* (London: Lawrence and Wishart for the Friends of Equity, 1981)

McCarthy, John, 'Regeneration of cultural quarters: public art for place image or place identity', *Journal of Urban Design*, 11 (2006), 243–62

McCarthy, Lillah, *Myself and My Friends* (London: T. Butterworth Ltd., 1933)

MacColl, Ewan, *Journeyman: An Autobiography* (London: Sidgwick and Jackson, 1990)

McDonnell, Bill, *Theatre of the Troubles, Theatre, Resistance and Liberation in Ireland* (University of Exeter Press, 2008)

McGuigan, Jim, *Modernity and Postmodern Culture* (Buckingham: Open University Press, 1999)

McIntosh, Gillian, 'CEMA and the national anthem: the arts and the state in Postwar Northern Ireland', *New Hibernia Review*, 5, 3 (2001), 22–31

Mackenney, Linda, *The Activities of Popular Dramatists and Drama Groups in Scotland 1900–1952* (Lewiston: Edwin Mellen Press, 2000)

MacLennan, Elizabeth, *The Moon Belongs to Everyone, Making Theatre with 7:84* (London: Methuen, 1990)

McMahon, Pelham and Pam Brooks, *An Actor's Place, The Liverpool Repertory Company at Liverpool Playhouse* (Liverpool: Bluecoat Press, 2000)

McMillan, Joyce, *The Traverse Theatre Story 1963–1988 by Joyce McMillan with a Chronology of Productions Mounted by the Traverse During its first 25 years Compiled by John Carnegie* (London: Methuen, 1988)

Maguire, Tom, *Making Theatre in Northern Ireland: Through and Beyond the Troubles* (Exeter University Press, 2006)

Malik, Sarita, *Representing Black Britain: A History of Black and Asian Images on British Television* (London: SAGE, 2002)

Marshall, Norman, *The Other Theatre* (London: John Lehmann, 1947)

Matthews, Bache, *A History of the Birmingham Repertory Theatre* (London: Chatto & Windus, 1924)

Mazower, David, *Yiddish Theatre in London,* 2nd edn (London: Jewish Museum, 1996)

Mengel, Hagal, 'A lost heritage: Ulster drama and the work of Sam Thompson', *Theatre Ireland,* 1 (September/December 1982), 18–19

Mennell, Stephen, 'Theoretical considerations on the study of cultural "needs"', *Sociology,* 13 (1979), 235–57

Merkin, Ros (ed.), *Liverpool's Third Cathedral, The Liverpool Everyman Theatre in the Words of Those Who Were, and Are, There* (Liverpool: Liverpool and Merseyside Theatres Trust, 2004)

Miller, James, *The Magic Curtain, The Story of Theatre in Inverness* (Inverness: Friends of Eden Court, 1986)

Mitchison, Rosalind, *A History of Scotland,* 2nd edn (London: Routledge, 1982)

Morash, Christopher, *A History of Irish Theatre 1601–2000* (Cambridge University Press, 2002)

Morgan, Kenneth O., *Rebirth of a Nation: A History of Modern Wales* (Oxford: Oxford University Press, University of Wales Press, 1982)

—, (ed.), *The Oxford Illustrated History of Britain* (Oxford University Press, 1984)

Morgan, Philip D., and Sean Hawkins (eds.), *Black Experience and the Empire* (Oxford University Press, 2004)

Mulryne, Ronnie, and Margaret Shewring (eds.), *Making Space for Theatre British Architecture and Theatre Since 1958* (Stratford-upon-Avon: Mulryne and Shewring Ltd., 1995)

Nesbitt, Cathleen, *A Little Love and Good Company* (London: Faber & Faber, 1975)

Newey, Katherine, 'Home plays for ladies: women's work in home theatricals', *Nineteenth Century,* 26 (1998), 93–111

Newlyn, Doreen, *Theatre Connections, A Very Personal Story* (Leeds: Walter Newlyn, 1995)

Nicholson, Steve, *The Censorship of British Drama 1900–1968, Volume 1 1900–1932* (Exeter University Press, 2003)

Nicoll, Allardyce, *English Drama 1900–1930: The Beginnings of the Modern Period* (London: Cambridge University Press, 1973)

O'Connor, Garry, *Ralph Richardson, An Actor's Life* (London: Hodder and Stoughton, 1982)

O'Malley, Conor, *A Poets' Theatre* (Dublin: Elo Press, 1988)

O'Malley, Mary, *Never Shake Hands with the Devil* (Dublin: Elo Press, 1990)

Osborne, John, *A Better Class of Person, An Autobiography 1929–1956* (London: Faber & Faber, 1982)

Oswald, Harold, *The Theatre Royal in Newcastle upon Tyne: Desultory Notes Relating to the Drama and Its Homes in That Place* (Newcastle upon Tyne: Northumberland Press, 1936)

Owusu, Kwesi, *The Struggle for Black Arts in Britain, What Can We Consider Better than Freedom?* (London: Comedia, 1986)

Paget, Derek, 'Theatre Workshop, Moussinac, and the European connection', *New Theatre Quarterly,* 11 (1995), 211–24

Pal, Swati, *Look Back at Anger: Agit Prop Theatre in Britain Red Ladder Theatre Company from the 60s to the 90s* (Saarbrücken: VDM Verlag Dr Müller, 2008)

Parekh, Bhikhu C., *The Future of Multi-Ethnic Britain: Report of the Commission on the Future of Multi-Ethnic Britain* (London: Profile Books, 2000)

Parliamentary Debates, Commons, Vol. 52, cols. 454–94, 23 April 1913

Paterson, Lindsay, *The Autonomy of Modern Scotland* (Edinburgh University Press, 1994)

Patterson, A. B., *History of the Byre Theatre* (St Andrews: The Theatre, 1983)

Payne, Ben Iden, *A Life in a Wooden O* (New Haven and London: Yale University Press, 1977)

Payne, Geoff (ed.), *Social Divisions*, 2nd edn (Basingstoke: Palgrave Macmillan, 2006)

Peacock, D. Keith, *Thatcher's Theatre: British Theatre and Drama in the Eighties* (Westport, Conn./London: Greenwood Press, 1999)

Pearson, H., *Beerbohm Tree* (London: Methuen, 1956)

Perkin, Harold, *The Rise of Professional Society: England Since 1880* (London: Routledge, 1989)

Perth Theatre Company 21st Anniversary September 1935–September 1956 (Perth: Perth Theatre, 1956)

Phillips, Siân, *Private Faces, The Autobiography* (London: Hodder and Stoughton, 1999)

Phoenix, Pat, *All My Burning Bridges* (London: Arlington Books, 1974)

Pick, John (ed.), *The State and the Arts* (Eastbourne: John Offord, 1980)

—, *The Theatre Industry Subsidy, Profit & the Search for New Audiences* (London: Comedia, 1985)

—, *Vile Jelly: The Birth, Life, and Lingering Death of the Arts Council of Great Britain* (Doncaster: Brymill, 1991)

Pilkington, Lionel, *Theatre and State in Twentieth-Century Ireland* (London: Routledge, 2001)

Pines, Jim (ed.), *Black and White in Colour, Black People in British Television Since 1936* (London: BFI Publishing, 1992)

Pogson, Rex, *Miss Horniman and the Gaiety Theatre Manchester* (London: Rockcliff, 1952)

Pope, Robert (ed.), *Religion and National Identity: Wales and Scotland c. 1700–2000* (Cardiff: University of Wales Press, 2001)

Postlewait, Thomas, *The Cambridge Introduction to Theatre Historiography* (Cambridge University Press, 2009)

Price, Cecil, 'Portable theatres in Wales, 1843–1914', *National Library of Wales Journal*, 9 (1955), 65–92

—, 'Towards a National Theatre for Wales', *Anglo-Welsh Review*, 12, no. 29 (1962), 12–25

—, *The Professional Theatre in Wales* (Swansea: University College of Swansea, 1984)

Priestley, J. B., *English Journey* (London: Heinemann, 1934)

Pugh, Martin, *The Making of Modern British Politics 1867–1939*, 2nd edn (Oxford: Blackwell, 1993)

Quayle, Anthony, *A Time to Speak* (London: Barrie & Jenkins, 1990)

Rawski, Thomas G. (ed.), *Economics and the Historian* (Berkley: University of California Press, 1996)

Rebellato, Dan, *1956 and All That, The Making of Modern British Drama* (London: Routledge, 1999)

Rees, Roland (ed.), *Fringe First, Pioneers of Fringe Theatre on Record* (London: Oberon Books, 1992)

Ritchie, Rob (ed.), *The Joint Stock Book: The Making of a Theatre Collective* (London: Methuen, 1987)

Roberts, Rachel and Alexander Walker, *No Bells on Sunday: The Journals of Rachel Roberts* (London: Pavilion, 1984)

Rodger, Ian, *Radio Drama* (London: Macmillan, 1982)

Rodway, Phyllis Philip and Lois Rodway Slingsby, *Philip Rodway and a Tale of Two Theatres* (Birmingham: Cornish Brothers, 1934)

Rosenfeld, Sybil, *The York Theatre* (London: Society for Theatre Research, 2001)

Rowell, George, *The Old Vic Theatre: A History* (Cambridge University Press, 1993)

Rowell, George, and Anthony Jackson, *The Repertory Movement: A History of Regional Theatre in Britain* (Cambridge University Press, 1984)

Said, Edward, *Culture and Imperialism* (London: Vintage, 1994)

Salberg, Derek, *Ring Down the Curtain, A Fascinating Record of Birmingham Theatre and Contemporary Life Through Three Centuries* (Luton: Cortney Publications Ltd., 1980)

—, *Once upon a Pantomime* (Luton: Cortney Publications Ltd., 1981)

Samuel, Raphael, Ewan MacColl and Stuart Cosgrove, *Theatres of the Left, 1880–1935: Workers' Theatre Movements in Britain and America* (London: Routledge & Kegan Paul, 1985)

Sanderson, Michael, *From Irving to Olivier: A Social History of the Acting Profession 1880–1983* (London: Athlone Press, 1984)

Sayers, R. S., *A History of Economic Change in England 1880–1939* (Oxford University Press, 1967)

Scannell, Paddy, *A Social History of British Broadcasting, Volume 1 1922–1939: Serving the Nation* (Oxford: Blackwell, 1991)

Schafer, E., *Lilian Baylis: A Biography* (Hatfield: Society for Theatre Research, University of Hertfordshire Press, 2006)

Schechner, Richard, *Performance Theory*, 2nd edn (New York and London: Routledge, 1988)

Scottish Arts Council, *A Socio-Economic Study of Artists in Scotland* (Edinburgh: Scottish Arts Council, 1995)

Scottish National Players, *The Scottish National Theatre Venture (The Scottish National Players), Its Birth, History, Work and Influence 1921–1948* (Glasgow: Scottish National Players, 1953)

Scullion, Adrienne, 'Scottish theatre and the impact of radio', *Theatre Research International*, 17 (1992), 117–31

Shade, Ruth, *Communication Breakdowns: Theatre, Performance, Rock Music and Some Other Welsh Assemblies* (Cardiff: University of Wales Press, 2004)

Shank, Theodore (ed.), *Contemporary British Theatre* (Basingstoke: Macmillan, 1993)

Shepherd, Simon, *The Cambridge Introduction to Modern British Theatre* (Cambridge University Press, 2009)

—, and Peter Womack, *English Drama: A Cultural History* (Oxford: Blackwell, 1996)

Sinclair, Andrew, *Arts and Cultures, The History of the 50 Years of the Arts Council of Great Britain* (London: Sinclair-Stevenson, 1995)

Sinfield, Alan, *Literature, Politics and Culture in Postwar Britain,* 2nd edn (London: Continuum, 2004)

Skidelsky, Robert, *John Maynard Keynes: The Economist as Saviour 1920–1937* (London: Macmillan, 1992)

Soja, Edward W., *Postmodern Geographies: The Reassertion of Space in Critical Social Theory* (London: Verso, 1989)

Solomos, John, *Race and Racism in Britain*, 3rd edn (Basingstoke: Palgrave Macmillan, 2003)

Speaight, Robert, *William Poel and the Elizabethan Revival* (London: William Heinemann, 1954)

—, *The Property Basket: Recollections of a Divided Life* (London: Collins and Harvell Press, 1970)

Stephens, Meic (ed.), *The Arts in Wales 1950–1975* (Cardiff: Welsh Arts Council, 1979)

Stephens, Robert and Michale Coveney, *Knight Errant, Memoirs of a Vagabond Actor* (London: Hodder and Stoughton, 1996)

Stevenson, Randall and Gavin Wallace (eds.), *Scottish Theatre Since the Seventies* (Edinburgh University Press, 1996)

Stevenson, Tyrone, *Richard Burton: A Bio-bibliography* (New York/London: Greenwood Press, 1992)

Stourac, Richard, and Kathleen McCreery, *Theatre as a Weapon: Workers' Theatre in the Soviet Union, Germany and Britain, 1917–1934* (London: Routledge & Kegan Paul, 1986)

Taylor, Anna-Marie (ed.), *Staging Wales: Welsh Theatre 1979–1997* (Cardiff: University of Wales Press, 1997)

Theatre Ownership in Britain: A Report Prepared for the Federation of Theatre Unions (London: Federation of Theatre Unions, 1953)

Theatrical Management Association, *The First Hundred Years 1894–1994* (London: Theatrical Management Association, 1994)

Thorndike, Russell, *Sybil Thorndike* (London: T. Butterworth, 1929)

Tomlin, Liz, 'Transgressing boundaries: postmodern performance and the tourist trap', *TDR*, 43 (1999), 136–49

Townsend, Alan, *Uneven Regional Change in Britain* (Cambridge University Press, 1993)

Trewin, J. C., *The Theatre Since 1900* (London: Andrew Dakers Ltd., 1951)

—, *Benson and the Bensonians* (London: Barrie and Rockliff, 1960)

—, *The Birmingham Repertory Theatre 1913–1963* (London: Barrie and Rockliff, 1963)

Trewin, Wendy, *All on Stage: Charles Wyndham and the Alberys* (London: Harrap, 1980)

Trosset, Carol, *Welshness Performed: Welsh Concepts of Person and Society* (Tucson: University of Arizona Press, 1993)

Trussler, Simon, *The Cambridge Illustrated History of British Theatre* (Cambridge University Press, 1994)

Turnbull, Olivia, *Bringing Down the House, The Crisis in Britain's Regional Theatres* (Bristol: Intellect, 2008)

Veitch, Norman, *The Peoples: Being a History of the Peoples' Theatre, Newcastle upon Tyne* (Gateshead on Tyne: Northumberland Press, 1950)

Verma, Jatinder and Maria Shevtsova, 'The generations of the diaspora and multiculturalism in Britain', *New Theatre Quarterly*, 25 (2009), 203–33

Walker, Brain (ed.), *Frank Matcham – Theatre Architect* (Belfast: Blackstaff Press, 1980)

Ward, Stuart (ed.), *British Culture at the End of Empire* (New York: Manchester University Press, 2001)

Wardle, Irving, *The Theatres of George Devine* (London: Jonathan Cape, 1978)

Warwick, Lou, *The Mackenzies Called Compton: The Story of the Compton Comedy Company Incorporated in the History of Northampton Theatre Royal and Opera House 1884–1927* (Northampton: the Author, 1977)

Wells, H., *The Maddermarket Theatre: A History of the Norwich Players* (Norwich: Eastern Press, *c.* 1992)

West, Timothy, *A Moment Towards the End of the Play, An Autobiography* (London: Nick Hern Books, 2001)

Whitelaw, Billie, *Billie Whitelaw ... Who He?* (London: Hodder and Stoughton, 1995)

Whitworth, Geoffrey, *The Making of a National Theatre* (London: Faber and Faber, 1951)

Williams, Emlyn, *George; An Early Autobiography* (London: Reprint Society, 1962)

Williams, J. Ellis, 'Welsh drama to-day', *Welsh Review* (March 1939), 32–6

—, 'The drama in Wales', *Welsh Review* (February 1939), 33–7

—, *Inc yn Ngwaed* (Llanybie: Llyfrau'r Dryw, 1963)

Williams, Raymond, *Writing in Society* (London: Verso, 1991)

Williamson, Andrey and Charles Landstone, *The Bristol Old Vic, The First Ten Years* (London: J. Garnet Miller, 1957)

Winder, Robert, *Bloody Foreigners: The Story of Immigration to Britain* (London: Little, Brown, 2004)

Winspear, Suz, *Worcester's Lost Theatre: The Story of the Worcester Theatre Royal* (Hallow, Worcester: Packbarn, 1996)

Wooding, Neil, 'Engaged leadership – the new public service managerial-
    ism', *Journal of Finance and Management in Public Services*, 7, 1 (2007),
    39–51
Zahry-Levo, Yael, *The Making of Theatrical Reputations: Studies from the Modern
    London Theatre* (Iowa City: Iowa University Press, 2008)

Index

Clements, John, 99
Clwyd Theatr Cymru, *see* Arts Centres, Theatr
 Clwyd, Mold
Cochran, C. B., 54, 73, 157, 162
Cockpit Theatre, 242
Codron, Michael, 178
Cole, Edith, 62
Collectors, The, 261
 The Captain's Collection, 261
 Redcoats, Turncoats & Petticoats, 261
Communicado, 223
Communist Party, 130, 137
 Communist International and the People's
 Front, 136
Compagnie des Quinze, 104
Companies Acts 1844–67 48
company
 as artistic ensemble, 173
 as collective, 180–1
Compass Players, 159
Compton, Edward, 60–1, 74
Compton, Viola, 74
Compton, Virginia, 169
Connolly, Billy
 The Great Northern Welly Boot Show, 223
Connor, Edric, 226, 227
Connor, Pearl, 226, 227
Cons, Emma, 58
Conservative Party, 41, 144, 171, 188, 196
 Baldwin, Stanley, 122
 Winston Churchill leadership, 144
Conti, Tom, 219
conurbations, 23–4
Cooper, Gladys, 97
Copeau, Jacques, *see* Compagnie des Quinze
Coronation Street, 215, 231, 240
corporate economy and theatre, 48
 corporate ownership, 152
 formation of the Group, 157–8
 Group becomes Octopus, 193
 Group control of creative capacity, 158
 merger and corporate expansion, 259
 monopolistic tendancy, 49
 shedding old capital assets, 191
Corrie, Joe, 106, 135
 In Time O' Strife, 131
Cottrell, Richard, 199
Council for the Encouragement of Music and
 the Arts (CEMA), 76, 137, 146, 158
 established in 1940, 146
 focus on participatory arts, 146
 regional office and national offices, 147
Countess Cathleen, The (Yeats), 87
Courtenay, Tom, 213, 218
Courtneidge, Robert, 60, 61, 64, 80

Coveney, Michael, 221
Coventry theatres, 168
 Belgrade Theatre, 182, 184, 213, 222, 249
 Technical College Theatre, 168
 Theatre Royal, 94
Cox, Brian, 219
Craig, Edith (Edy), 112, 114
Craig, Edward Gordon, 111, 114
Crawford, Andrew, 105
Crewe, 29
Croft, Michael, 212
Crossroads, 231
Cruikshank, A. S., 72, 157, *see also* Howard &
 Wyndham Ltd.
Cruikshank, Andrew, 218
Cruikshank, Stuart, 157, *see also* Howard &
 Wyndham Ltd.
Cuka, Frances, 214
cultural quarter, concept of, 244
Cumbernauld Theatre, 245
Cuthbertson, Iain, 218, 219–20

Daily Mail, 41, 42
Darby, John, 254
Daubeny, Peter, 178
Davies, James Kitchener, 128
 censorship of *Cwm Glo*, 128
Davis, Tracy C., 6–7, 12, 25, 47, 52, 65
Dean, Basil, 86, 89, 98, 111, 118
Deep are the Roots (Usseau and Gow),
 143, 169
Delaney, Shelagh, 177, 214
 A Taste of Honey, 177, 227
Delfont, Bernard, 192, 193
demographic change, 141
 challenge to British identity, 208
 colonisation in reverse, 141
 East African Asians first wave, 230
 impact of *Empire Windrush* arrival, 141–2
 settlement in industrial cities, 142
Dence, Marjorie, 76, 166, 220
Denville, Alfred, 74
Derry/Londonderry, 252
 city walls, symbolic importance of, 253
 Guildhall, 253
 Millennium Forum, 253, 254
Derry Frontline, 253
Derry Theatre, 253
Devine, George, 91, 104, 160, 174, 181, 228
Devlin, William, 92
Dews, Peter, 234
Dewsbury Empire Theatre, 166
Dexter, John, 234
Dhupa, Venu, 238, 272
Diana of Dobsons (Hamilton), 57